READ IT...LIVE IT...

Philip Yancey

Selwyn Hughes

R. T. Kendall

Tommy Tenney

Mark Buchanan

Jeff Lucas

Stormie Omartian

Sheila Walsh

Michael Apichella

Michael Green

Steve Chalke and *Alan Mann*

Vaughan Roberts

Mike Coles

Keith Warrington

Stephen Cottrell and *Steven Croft*

John Robinson with *Brenda Sloggett*

Jonathan Aitken

Elias Chacour with *David Hazard*

Steve Turner

Kurt Bruner and *Jim Ware*

Pete Greig and *Dave Roberts*

Graham Tomlin

Henri Nouwen

Peter Graystone

Erwin W. Lutzer

Ravi Zacharias

Geoffrey Hanks

Robert Harrison

Ursula Koch

J. John and *Chris Walley*

Cover Design by Philip Houghton, Carlisle
Typeset by PCS Typesetting, Shepton Mallet. 01749 344479
Print Management by Adare Carwin
Printed and bound in Denmark by Nørhaven Paperback

Contents

Contents

Foreword

There's this great scene in the film of CS Lewis' life, Shadowlands, where Lewis asks his students to return to next week's lecture with their answer to, "why do we read?" I forget the students' answers, but CS Lewis' tells his protégés, "we read to know we're not alone."

Now, I'll come clean – No, I've not read all these books featured in this sampler. My excuse? Most of them are brand new titles. But the truth is, even in a year's time, I'll not have read all these books. What is it about the important things in life that so often means they're the last to get done? I know it's great 'being in a good book', but still I don't read enough.

It's the tyranny of the URGENT over the IMPORTANT. All the trivial things get ticked off our daily "to do" lists; while our big-dream New Year's Resolutions are a joke by early Feb. And what could be more important than the theme of many of these books – living out the Christian faith; turning theory into practise; transforming theology into lifestyle – making the words count?

And by the number of top writers creating all this inspiration on how we can make the words count, surely by reading them we'll realise, along with Lewis, "we are not alone".

Rob Lacey
Author of *the street bible, street life* and *Are We Getting Through?*

'What's the point, guys, if someone spouts off about their religion but their lifestyle just doesn't add up... unless we're putting ideas into action it's a waste of space.'

James 2: 14,17 from *the street bible,* Zondervan.

Nobody's Child

John Robinson with *Brenda Sloggett*

This is the heart-rending true story of how God turned around a life which started tragically, from abusive foster homes all the way to Borstal. This is a powerful testimony of how God reached John, changed him completely and led him to work with children on the streets of Manchester.

Monarch Books
£6.99
PB / 1 8542.4623 2

£2 OFF
£4.99 with voucher

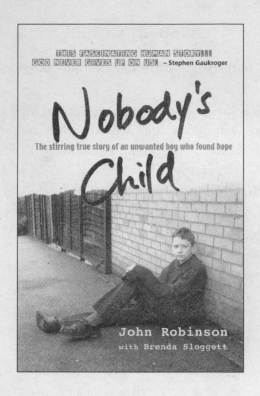

THIS FASCINATING HUMAN STORY!!!
GOD NEVER GIVES UP ON US! – Stephen Gaukroger

Nobody's

The stirring true story of an unwanted boy who found hope

Child

John Robinson

with Brenda Sloggett

Published by Monarch Books in the UK 2003
Concorde House, Grenville Place, Mill Hill, London NW7 3SA.

Destination Borstal

The staff at Barnardo's kept their word, and didn't turn me away. They let me live in a caravan in the grounds of the home. At first I thought it was great to have some independence, but the truth was that I didn't have a clue about how to live independently. I couldn't boil an egg and I didn't know how to fill in a form. I never cleaned up the caravan, and I stayed in bed a lot. Sometimes I went down the pub – I'd grown into a big lad, and I looked older than my age. I got a job hod-carrying for a local builder, but it wasn't interesting work, and it felt dull and pointless. I was fed up with everything, and I didn't have any ambition or hope for the future. I was lonely, and wished I had someone I could talk to, but I wasn't very good at relationships. Girlfriends never put up with me for long, because I expected too much of them – I always wanted them to be like a mother and sister as well. Actually, I wanted them to be like a brother, too, a mate to mess around with. Years of having nothing and no one who was special to me had made me selfish. I grabbed what I could get, on my own terms. I was fine while we were just "going out" – I liked the idea of having a girlfriend – but I felt threatened by affection or when a relationship started to get serious. As soon as anyone said "I love you", I got frightened, because I was sure that meant things were about to go wrong. I wouldn't let anyone get close to me because I was afraid of the hurt that would inevitably follow when I lost that love.

Eventually I decided I couldn't bear living alone in the caravan any longer, and I ran away to York. I don't know what I intended to do – I was probably trying to run away from myself. It was a long walk, nearly twelve miles, and when I got hungry I picked potatoes out of the fields to eat raw. When I got to York it was evening, and starting to get cold. I was hunting around in some bins – it's amazing what you can find in bins – and I came across some old clothes. I put them on to try and keep warm, even though one of them was a dress! Some people went past and saw me: I must have looked a real sight. They called the police, and just as I was settling down to try to sleep near some toilets, a police car drew up. "Come on, John," they said, "back to Barnardo's." I only wished I could go back – I always thought of it as the one warm, safe place I knew – but I didn't have a home there any longer. I was growing up, but I didn't know how to handle my independence.

I still had some old school friends in Tadcaster, though, and I started staying at their houses and sleeping on the floor. That didn't last long: no one wanted to get involved with my problems. Then someone suggested that I could get a place in a hostel. The one I found was a few miles away – not that far away really, but far enough from my friends and everything I knew. I moved there, but I was lonely, and at first I didn't find it easy make new friends. It wasn't a proper half-way house, and the residents weren't just homeless, like me. They were older lads, and tough. Most of them were on bail and waiting to go to court on charges of grievous bodily harm, assault and robbery. The staff tried to be helpful and keep an eye on me, but most of the time I felt threatened and fearful.

I tried to settle in, but all my security had gone, and I started having nightmares. I dreamt that I was back in the dark attic, but this time there was no way I would ever get out because the door was locked and the skylight had gone. I used to wake up in a cold sweat. I missed the easy friendships of my home at Barnardo's, especially my best friend Saleem. The other boys at school used to bully him a bit because he couldn't read very well, but I stood up for him. Saleem and I sometimes had mega fights, but we were really good friends, and we stuck together, a bit like my brother Kenneth and I had done. Once we went on an Outward Bound Course for three weeks. We loved it: we got up very early and went swimming in an ice-cold pool, then dressed and went rock climbing, abseiling and canoeing. We had to share the chores, cleaning the toilets and making the beds. Sometimes we made our own tea, with sandwiches made with peanut butter, jam and all sorts of weird and wonderful things. It was a fantastic experience: we had to learn to work together as a team and to look after each other. I think it made me grow up. and it helped to give me a bit more maturity and self-confidence. Unfortunately, I still didn't have enough confidence to stand up to some of the bigger lads I was mixing with at the hostel.

I was desperate for friends, and I wanted to fit in. I really wanted to be as hard as they were – I liked going to the pub with them and ordering a pint: it made me feel grown up. For them, offending was a way of life. They'd get talking and someone would say, "Let's nick that Capri from outside the fish and chip shop." And the next thing, they'd done it: someone would run into the shop, grab the car keys from behind the counter, jump in the car and drive it off. One night we had a few drinks and then broke into a factory and stole some videos to sell on. I was late getting back to the hostel and got into trouble, but that didn't stop me. I wasn't going to keep away from my mates, because I didn't have anyone else.

The hostel found me a place on a government scheme where I did a woodwork course, and that could have helped me get a job, but I didn't really want one. My friends didn't have jobs, and I wanted to hang around with them. Anyway, the scheme only paid about £25 a week, and almost all of it had to be handed over to the hostel for my keep. I couldn't see the point of working all week and still ending up with no money, just like the rest of the lads who'd been hanging out together down the town. They were all involved in crime, shoplifting and stealing cars, and I tagged along. It felt like an adventure, and it was exciting. We used to go into Dewsbury and break into places and take money – but only on commercial premises. We never broke into houses, or mugged anyone. We didn't want to hurt anyone personally, but we were all angry at "the system" and this was our way of getting our own back. I went along with it all – I was bitter, too, at a system that allowed me to be homeless and walk the streets, but was willing to spend hundreds of pounds on keeping me in a Detention Centre where I was beaten up all the time.

One evening we passed a pub where we knew the owners were on holiday, so we put a chair through the window and went in. We weren't afraid because we'd all been drinking already. We helped ourselves to bottles of whisky and even took time to empty the fruit machines. We climbed back out of the window and looked up the road, and to our horror there were masses of police cars with flashing lights coming over the hill towards us. It looked like a scene in a film! One of my mates shouted, "Run for it, or we'll be done!" We had cigarettes and bottles of whisky under our jumpers, and our pockets were filled with cash, but we still managed to run off and jump over a wall. There were bushes on the other side, and we hid there and kept quiet. My heart was pounding as I heard the police coming towards us; my foot was sticking out of the bush but I didn't dare to move. Then they went past – how the dogs didn't sniff us out I will never know! Then we heard the police talking as they boarded up the pub, and it was clear that they knew who we were. I was terrified at the thought of another conviction.

Once the police had gone we went to my mate's room and shared out the loot. Now that we'd escaped we were really pleased with ourselves. We still thought we hadn't done any harm to anyone – "The insurance'll pay" we used to say – but deep down I knew I was getting into a crazy way of life. Still, at least I belonged, and I had a gang of mates to look out for me. It wasn't what I wanted, but somehow I just accepted that this was what my life was like. These were my only friends, and if they were in trouble, and living on the wrong side of the law, so was I. There wasn't anywhere else for me to be.

In the end I left the hostel and went to live with some of my mates – they were squatting in an empty flat on a council estate. The best thing about this place was that it was warm: it had underfloor heating, which for some reason was still working. Otherwise it was horrible. The rooms were completely bare, they stank of urine and vomit, and there were old syringes and rubbish everywhere. Still, you could always get to sleep on those cosy floors. Sometimes there were quite a lot of us there, but we just used the place to hang out in: to stash stolen goods, keep a lookout for the police, and sleep – mostly the girls slept in one room and the lads in another.

We never had any money (none of us had jobs and in those days you couldn't sign on for the dole without a proper address) but there was a café up the road where we used to take the stuff we stole. They'd give us free food in exchange for stolen goods. I suppose we managed on one meal a day – and that was when we were doing well. We took the edge off our hunger with cigarettes and drink. We used to get into night clubs free, because we knew the bouncers, and we could always steal money and cigarettes there – and we'd eat people's crisps and finish their drinks when they left their tables to dance or to go to the toilet.

The people in our gang used every kind of drug: heroin, amphetamines, LSD, glue – even the stuff you could buy to get sticking plaster off your skin (you put it on a wristband and sniffed it). I tried LSD once but it gave me terrible nightmares, so I kept off it. I didn't even like cannabis much: it made me feel sick and I didn't like the feeling that I wasn't completely in control of myself I needed control, because I was always wary and on edge, and you were never sure what was going to happen next.

We always kept a lookout, afraid that the police would break the door down and raid the place for drugs or stolen goods. We always seemed to be running away from places or from the police. It was exciting and exhilarating but scary, too, with gang fights, people carrying knives and getting glassed. I carried a Bowie knife – a dagger with a blade about a foot long – and when I walked into a bar with my gang behind me I felt like something out of West Side Story. I knew I'd got a bit of a reputation to live up to. I was living a fast, hard and dangerous life, and sometimes I was sure that I would just die like this – one fight too many, picked with the wrong person, and that would be it.

Even so, deep down I knew I was always pretending to be tougher than I was. If I thought things were too dangerous, I'd back out. And sometimes I'd be in the middle of a fight and I'd start to feel sorry for the other person, if they were getting the worst of it, and hold back. I got lots of tattoos like all the other lads – it was another way of showing you belonged – but I kept choosing things that were nice designs. "You can't have that one, John," they'd say, "it's a stupid flower! You've got to have a skull!" I worked hard to cover up my soft side. It wasn't the done thing to show consideration for other people, either. I tried to join in with the dirty talk in the pub when a good-looking girl went past. If I kept quiet, they'd say "What's up with you? You gay or something?" I knew I was going against everything I'd been taught at Barnardo's. They'd given me a foundation of love and support, and taught me to respect other people – and here I was swearing and stealing and fighting and worse. But that was just how life was now. I didn't see that I had any choice.

One day I was in the flat when another gang broke in. They grabbed one of the girls and dragged her out, screaming. I was rigid with shock, but it all happened so fast, there wasn't anything I could do. Then one of our lot burst in through the door and said we were all going after them. The girl had been working as a prostitute for the other gang in Birmingham, and they'd come all the way up here to kidnap her and take her back. We all ran outside and went after them together. I wasn't afraid of a fight, and with my mates behind me I was ready for anything.

The only thing I wasn't up for was serious crime. I was sitting in a pub with a mate and he said, "We're going to do a pub tonight. We're going to hide in the toilets and open the safe when everyone's gone home – there's £25,000 there."

"Don't be daft," I said. "They won't have that much money in a pub. And anyway, what if someone hears you?"

He took a white bundle out of his pocket and showed me a gun, wrapped in a hanky.

"Hey, put that away," I said. "I don't want any guns. This is getting crazy, it's out of my league."

I backed out, but the rest of them went ahead and did the job. Of course there was only about £400 in the safe, and that wasn't enough for them to share out between them, so they started knocking on doors and threatening people with the gun and demanding money. A police armed response team were called and they were arrested and jailed for a long time.

It was a typical train of events – I was mixing with a criminal crowd, and they were all in and out of prison all the time. They were violent, too: I lost count of the number of times I was admitted to hospital with cuts that needed stitches, stab wounds or bruising. Every time I tried to leave the gang I got beaten up. Once I was pinned to the ground and stabbed in the stomach. Someone else threatened to put a knife through my tongue. Another time I had a serious slash to my leg, and a passer-by saw me bleeding and called an ambulance. When it came I said "I'm fine, don't bother," because I was really afraid for my life. In hospital, people ask questions, and I knew the gang would kill me if they thought I'd grassed on them. It was a terrible life but I couldn't see any way out: I didn't know anyone else.

Anyway, I was a useless criminal – I was always getting caught. One day two of us had stolen a television, and we were walking along a wall by the canal, carrying it between us. There was a long drop to the ground on one side, and a drop into the water on the other, and we were staggering along clumsily, like something out of a slapstick comedy, wobbling from side to side. Then my mate let go of his end, leaving me holding the whole thing, and I fell backwards into the canal with the television on top of me. As I came up, spluttering, I could see two policemen standing on the bridge, laughing, while my mate ran off.

Eventually the police caught up with me for everything else, and charged me with three burglaries in the area and 20 TICs (offences to be taken into consideration when sentencing). The magistrates wouldn't let me out on bail while I was waiting for my case to come up, because I didn't have a permanent address, so I spent five weeks in the regional Remand Centre. It was a grim place. I soon learnt some of the prison survival techniques: we used to make pieces of string from our bedding so that when we were locked in we could pass things like shampoo from window to window. There were plenty of drugs available there, and plenty of violence, too – there were regular fights in the corridors with all sorts of weapons. Then there were the suicides. You'd hear the bell go, banging on the door, panic; then hurrying feet and then silence.

One day it all got through to me, too. I was sitting in my cell and thought, "This is all there is to life: running with a gang of people I'm afraid of, or getting locked up in a prison cell. I've got no future and no hope." Nothing had any meaning any more. I had nothing except sentencing to look forward to, and I felt completely adrift with only darkness and loneliness ahead of me. One of my jobs was cleaning the staff areas – I used to collect the old fag ends and re-use the tobacco to make roll-ups. That evening as I was cleaning I picked up one of the aluminium ash trays as well. Back in my cell I worked on the metal, flexing it over and over until it was weak enough to tear into two sharp-edged pieces. Then I slashed both my wrists.

I sat and watched as the blood poured out into my lap, and I didn't feel a thing. I started to get dizzy and black buzzing clouds swam in front of my eyes, but I wasn't afraid – I just wanted to slip into the darkness and not wake up. Then the door opened and I heard screams: my room-mate had come back and seen all the blood. He called an officer and they dragged me off to the medical unit, and the doctor decided to sew up my wrists there, rather than take me to the local hospital. They put me in a straitjacket and transferred me into a solitary cell. Now things were even worse. Every day was the same, locked up all alone with only my thoughts for company, and my movements restricted by the straitjacket. There wasn't much light in the cell; cockroaches ran across the floor, there was a heavy smell of disinfectant and the only sounds were the screams and shouts of other inmates whose nerves were giving way. It was the darkest time of my life, and I felt totally alone.

It was while I was in the Remand Centre that I first began to think about God. I didn't have any concept of a loving God who cared about me; I just thought of God as someone who was "up there" ready to punish me for all my wrongdoing. When I was at Barnardo's they used to take us to church, but I really hated the way the vicar patted us on the head and said, "Good morning, children," and we all had to reply "Good morning, Vicar". He wore a strange big black frock and gave boring sermons; I spent most of the time thinking about what we'd do when we got home, and whether I could dive off the viaduct into the river. Now, shut up in the Remand Centre, I chose to go to church – really just to get out of the cell. I didn't take a lot of interest in religion. I believed in God, but I didn't think he believed in me. At the time my life was in such a mess that I couldn't imagine anything else, and I was sure it wasn't the sort of life God would approve of. I thought I was too far gone for God to be interested in me.

I remembered all the crazy things I'd done, getting into fights and jumping off bridges to escape the police. Once I'd been in an arcade when another gang cornered a young Asian lad and beat him over the head with a crowbar. The next day a man in traditional Sikh dress, turban and all, came over to me in the shopping centre. He reached inside his coat and pulled out a huge knife.

"Was it you and your friends who beat up my brother?"

"No, it wasn't us!" I said desperately.

"My religion says I can kill to take revenge for him," he said. "I'll slice you up or anybody else if I find who did it."

I was petrified and ran away faster than I'd ever run in my life.

When I thought about things like that, my life felt like a jungle – I never knew what was lying in wait for me. It was full of dangers that I couldn't predict or control, and I was afraid all the time. I hated being locked up, but the outside world was even more frightening.

Eventually my case came up – there were lots of charges and it was too serious for the Magistrates' Court, so it went to the Crown Court where the sentences are heavier. I knew you couldn't be tried twice for the same offence, so it was in my best interests to make a clean breast of things to the police now. There were already so many crimes listed on my record that a few more couldn't make it much worse, but if they were all included, "taken into consideration", they couldn't be brought up again in the future. I made a really thorough job of confessing! I told the police about crimes they hadn't even known about, just to be sure I'd got rid of everything! I knew I could be facing a long sentence, and I wanted to get it over with. After being in the Detention Centre when I was fourteen, and the last few weeks in the Remand Centre, I knew that what lay ahead of me wasn't going to be easy.

When I got to court I was terrified. I didn't know what was going to happen to me. I was pretty sure I was going to end up in prison, but a bit of me thought there was a chance I might get off. I had one strong card to play – my unfortunate background. I often told people I was an orphan, because it seemed to get more sympathy than "I grew up in the care of the local authority". I thought I could make a real sob story out of that: poor little orphan me, brought up in children's homes, no proper family. I had a real chip on my shoulder, and a bit of me still thought that everything that had happened to me was unfair. After all, the arson had been an accident, I hadn't meant to set fire to anything, yet I'd been punished really harshly. And I still thought the crimes I'd been committing recently weren't that serious – after all, we didn't really hurt anyone, did we? The insurance paid. I was full of self-pity, and I hoped I could persuade the judge to feel sorry for me, too.

It didn't work: I was sentenced to 18 months in Borstal. However, it was going to take a while to sort out which Borstal I was going to, so in the meantime they took me off to prison. In fact, they moved me around, and over the next few weeks I spent time in three different prisons. I'd thought the Detention Centre was awful, but I was in for the shock of my life.

In Armley Prison I was put in a special wing with the others who'd been sentenced to Borstal. At first there was a lot of shouting from them – they felt hard done by, too – but being in the big man's prison you soon learnt to keep your head down. The adult prisoners wouldn't put up with us throwing our weight about. There were beatings and abuse, and lots of people couldn't stand it: there were more suicides. There were fights in the exercise yard, and one day some lads broke the legs off a chair and smashed them over a rival's head; prison officers had to come with dogs to break it up. I had a quick temper and I was used to fighting, so I got involved, too. In the end I got locked up all the time. I used to look out of my window and see the buses bringing visitors for other inmates. I longed for someone to visit me, but no one ever came except my solicitor. I'd been going out with a girl at the time of my arrest, but she lost interest when I was put inside. Anyway, I'd wrecked that relationship, like so many others. I was resigned to being alone. They moved me on to Durham and then to Strangeways Prison before I finally ended up at Borstal in County Durham. It was 1981, and I was still only 18 years old.

Rumours Of Another World

Philip Yancey

Philip Yancey is one of the most fearless, provocative and yet readable Christian writers at work today and his staggering popularity bears witness to that status. In his most recent book, Yancey explores what he calls the 'borderlands of belief', seeking to discover traces of the supernatural in our everyday world.

Zonderman
RRP £14.99
HB / 0 3102.5524 4

£6 OFF
£8.99 with voucher

Other titles by the same author

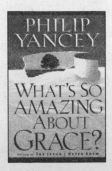

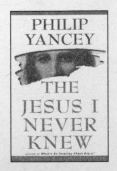

PHILIP YANCEY

rumours
OF ANOTHER WORLD

WHAT ON EARTH ARE WE MISSING?

Out of order

Imaginary evil is romantic and varied; real evil is gloomy, monotonous, barren, boring. Imaginary good is boring; real good is always new, marvellous, intoxicating.

SIMONE WEIL

A question has been looming in the background – a series of questions really, colliding and agitating each other like thunderheads in a summer sky. If this is God's world, why is it such a mess? And why do so few people experience good things, like sex, in the way God supposedly intended? And why must we pay attention and actively search for God? Why only rumours and not proofs of another world?

In short, if there is another world out there, shouldn't this one give more evidence of it? Obviously, a great rift has opened up between the ideal world Christians describe as God's creation and the world we actually inhabit. We stand at the edge of a precipice and peer into a fog for guidance. Some enthusiasts wave their arms and point, convinced of a reality beyond eyeshot, but the rest see only the milky white of clouds.

Christians explain the rift with a three-letter word, "one little, flat, deadly word that covers a lifetime," as novelist Evelyn Waugh put it.

Something in me recoils against that word sin, for reasons I will explain. Yet who can doubt that the world has undergone a kind of breakdown, the cosmic counterpart to a psychological breakdown in an individual. As a species we have lost a sense of self and of meaning, and we struggle to put life together in a coherent whole. A sly, chronic disease prevents us from relating to creation and each other, let alone God, as we should.

We have a deep intuition about how the world should operate and how it should not. Where did we get that sense?

Investigators of an airplane wreck assemble every fragment, poring over the blackened shards of metal in search of how the machine failed to fulfil its original design. Something went badly wrong, bringing instant chaos to a well-ordered system. In a similar way, the introduction of evil disordered the world's original design.

In a few brush strokes, the book of Genesis paints a scene of few rules, no shame, bountiful joy, and an unlimited range of pleasure and creative work. Despair, drought, sickness, death, conflict-all that has cursed human history-did not exist in Eden. John Milton bravely tried to render scenes from paradise, of a naked Eve serving Adam ambrosia and cups of pleasant liquors ("... in those hearts Love unlibidinous reigned, nor jealousy was understood"), though most critics judge him more successful at depicting the fallen state all too familiar to us his readers.

The Hebrew prophets predict a return to Paradise, a time when the elderly can sit safely in the streets watching children play, when vineyards gush wine and deserts gush water, when carnivores and herbivores lie side by side and human races too live in peace-in other words, exactly the opposite of what transpires in the land of the prophets today. Modern Jews still greet each other with the gentle word used by the prophets to describe such a time, *shalom*, the salutation nowadays an aching reminder of how faraway is that state.

When I hike through a field of wildflowers toward a snowfield on a brilliant Colorado summer day, when I sit for hours with an old friend revealing parts of myself that no one else knows, when I add the final satisfying touches to a project that has taken me months or even years at such times a memory stirs, a vestige of the world God intended.

And when I hear the relentless, dreary news of more human cruelty and global conflict, or come face to face with my own stubborn selfishness, I recoil because of that same memory. Something is wrong. As Lewis Smedes put it, Christians must forever pick their way between delight in creation's gifts and sorrow for sin's distortions."

Genesis records that in Paradise a great severing took place. Adam and Eve reached too far, trusting themselves rather than God to set the rules. They tasted of the tree of the knowledge of good and evil, and ever since, human beings have known evil as a daily reality and good as a daily longing. Christians believe that sin, arguably the most "natural" human act, is from God's viewpoint distinctly *un*natural, the very opposite of God's intent for the planet.

I found a website, *wwwnotproud.com*, in which visitors anonymously post confessions of their sins. Listen to these voices of sadness and remorse, reproduced with their original spelling and grammar:

- If I could smack every co-worker and take their responsibilities and salaries, I'd do it. If I could take all competitors incomes and services, I'd do it. If I could hit your face and steal your wallet without looking you in the eye, I would do it.
- Sloth: I should be working now, but I am doing this instead.
  When my father was in a pschatric hospital after a suicide attempt, I wouldn't visit him in order to get back at him.
- i go to college. i used the money iI should have spent on housing to buy dope, alcohol, entertainment, and food. i am bad, i know it, but stopping is soooo hard.
- I wish I was rich. I want to buy things I don't need with money I can afford to waste.
- I want one laptop, one cool flip phone, one Mercedes, two beers

everyday for the rest of my life, and one million bucks in my bank account, thats it all I want.

- i lie about things i have done to hide the fact that my life has been a meaningless timeline of uninteresting events, characters and experiences. i lie to make up for the fact that i have no soul ...

Sin tempts us to choose the artificial over the real, the fleeting pleasure over the lasting good. We follow our longings, only to find them disordered and unquenchable. Thomas Merton wrote about his own disquiet, "The sense of exile bleeds inside me like a hemorrhage – it is always the same wound, whether it is a sense of sin, or of loneliness, or of one's own insufficiency, or of spiritual dryness: they are all really the same, in the way we experience them."

Morton Hunt's book on the human mind, The Universe Within, explores the limits of artificial intelligence. Cognitive scientists, he explains, recognize a restlessness in the human mind, a need to do something with our thoughts and to pursue goals. Being human means grasping for something more, just as Adam and Eve did. "The computer, in contrast, is a passive system: its goals and the strength of its drive to reach them are those given it by the designer. Left to itself, it will sit inert, awaiting further orders. We will not; we look for new goals, and, to reach them, are forced to solve problems we did not have before; we do not let well enough alone."

Artificial intelligence researchers doubt whether they can build a similar restlessness or curiosity into a computer. They can program a computer to seek new avenues and investigate new problems, but it does so because of its program, not because it wants to. Computers don't "want." Hunt concludes, "Maybe the biggest difference between artificial and human intelligence is just that simple: we care about the things we choose to do. Solving a new problem, discovering some new fact, visiting a new place, reading a new book, all make us feel good; that's why we do them. But how would one make a computer feel good?" Perhaps, he speculates, that mystery suggests why computer compositions of music and poetry so far fail to impress: the computer is neither pleased nor displeased by its own creation, unlike every human artist.

The challenge facing computer programmers may shed light on the choices God faced in creating human beings. Presumably, God could have designed a human brain more like a computer CPU, leaving out any neurological restlessness. Animals seem content living out the singular goal of survival, without the need to reflect on themselves or grasp for more. Yet when God created a being in God's own image, he built in restlessness, along with curiosity and desire, in full awareness they could lead the human to choose the wrong path.

That freedom, a reflection of God's image and our greatest "advantage" as human beings, can turn into a terrible disadvantage. Like Adam and Eve, we too can overturn the order of creation. I am not an ordinary man, and the laws of morals and of custom were never made for me," said Napoleon. At times, who doesn't think something similar on smaller scale?

I have read critiques of God's decision to grant such freedom. Couldn't God have set tighter boundaries around our freedom so that people like Adolf Hitler would self-destruct if they exceeded those boundaries? More to the point, couldn't God have created human beings who would always choose good rather than evil, in a world that combines perfect freedom and perfect goodness?*

Maybe not. Most of the science fiction films I have seen circle around the same basic plot. Human beings, weak, error-prone, fools of passion, dangerously "free," encounter aliens who at first glance seem superior: the unflappable *Star Trek* Vulcans, the miracle-working Starman, the allwise Yoda, the bureaucratic Agents of *Matrix*. Yet somehow by the end of the movie it is the humans, not the extra-terrestrials, who save the universe.

---

*Using the complex language of symbolic logic, in the essay "God, Evil and the Metaphysics of Freedom" Christian philosopher Alvin Plantinga offers compelling reasons why it is logically impossible for God to control the amount of evil in a world that also includes free will.

In many of these films, the "superior" beings begin to feel a strange attraction for our humanoid qualities. Even Superman falls in love. As the movie plots suggest, despite our complaints we deeply cherish our humanity, notable for its freedom. (And to Christians, whose faith centres in Jesus, the God who became a man, it seems clear that God cherishes humanity as well.)

In a satire titled "The Wireless Wizard of Wonder," Karen Mains described a new electronic gadget that attaches to a person's arm. It works something like a lie detector, though with much greater sensitivity. Whenever any evil thought crosses the wearer's mind, the machine sets off a warning buzz. Unfortunately, the magazine article carried nothing labelling it as satire, and soon the publisher received a letter from a high school teacher wondering where she could purchase the Wizard Wonder for her students. The teacher missed the point of the article entirely: God, a respecter of our freedom, does not use such overt behaviour-modification techniques.

Apparently God did, in earlier times. Intriguing stories from the Old Testament tell of the prophet Elijah who called down fire from heaven on each company of soldiers that came to arrest him (2 Kings 1); both a king and a servant who contracted leprosy when they defied God (2 Kings 5; 2 Chronicles 26); and another king, Jeroboam, whose hand promptly shrivelled when he outstretched it to do wrong (1 Kings 13). These rebels experienced immediate punishment for their mistakes.

I grew up hearing the Old Testament stories, and they helped form my early image of God. As I read them now, however, what stands out is the contrast between their pattern of instant punishment and Jesus' style. He refused to call down fire from heaven on a town that rejected him. He healed, rather than afflicted, people with leprosy. When opponents took up arms against him, he did not fight back, and even restored a servant's ear severed by an overprotective disciple. I can only conclude that God mercifully changed his style of relating to cantankerous human beings. Although we may deserve instant punishment for rebellion, God has chosen a gentler, freedom-enhancing way.

Once, while celebrating with notorious sinners, Jesus fielded criticism from religious people scandalized by his dinner companions. In response he said, "It is not the healthy who need a doctor, but the sick. I have not come to call the righteous, but sinners [to repentance]." I heard the fiery stories from the Old Testament as active warnings: if I disobeyed, God might strike me down with leprosy. Somehow I missed the change introduced by the Great Physician, a change from judgement to grace.

Jesus' famous parable of the prodigal son paints the picture clearly. By any standard of good and bad behaviour, the prodigal son failed, squandering his inheritance and cavorting with prostitutes. He deserved punishment, not celebration. But the father, representing God, had eyes only for healing and restoration: "This son of mine was dead and is alive again; he was lost and is found." God's method with evil is cure, not prevention.

In Chinese opera, heroes wear a certain colour of face paint with a few simple strokes, while villains wear a different palette in complex patterns. In real life, unlike Chinese opera, we cannot tell the heroes and villains by the colour of paint on their faces. Medieval saints spoke of the Fiend with his stench; more often evil appears as a friend with a smell like perfume.

We can identify some villains, to be sure: suicide bombers who target civilians, priests who abuse children, drug lords in Latin America. The problem is, evil rarely announces itself so brazenly. Like citizens of an industrial city who no longer notice the pollution, we cannot detect more subtle evils in our cultural atmosphere. Consider the seven deadly sins, a moral checklist that emerged from centuries of reflection. We live in a modern world so disordered from the original design that the entire notion of what is good for us has turned upside down.

In the modern United States, at least, the seven deadly sins might be renamed the seven seductive virtues:

Pride: In music, sports, and business, we reserve our applause for winners, and those who flaunt it with an attitude tend to garner the most publicity. We strut our medals at the Olympic Games, lavish rewards on winners, and read management books patterned after Machiavelli and Attila the Hun.

Envy: Our entire advertising industry is built on inciting envy of colleagues and neighbours, so that whatever new electronic marvel or body shape my neighbour has, I want too.

Anger: We must get in touch with and express our anger, counsellors tell us. Encounter groups, television trash-talk shows, town meetings, and political debates offer ample opportunity to do so.

Greed: The economic engine of our nation, and indeed the world, depends on a constant sense of discontent that motivates each consumer to desire ever more.

Sloth: Find an island with a beach, retire early, relax, slow down, feel good — it's all part of the American dream.

Gluttony: Every year the "big gulp" drinks and supersize French fries get bigger, as do the waistlines. Currently 64 percent of Americans are overweight, with half of that percentage qualifying as obese.

Lust: From Lycra-clad professional cheerleaders to dancing babes on MTV videos, lust is ubiquitous in modern America, the single most profitable industry on the Internet.

In the modern world, sin approaches in camouflage. Too late do we realize that it blocks the path to shalom, to wholeness and health. We miss the hidden dangers that prompted the ancients to regard these sins as deadly. I have learned that these sins diminish me and bring disorder to my life. Pride is a kind of addiction, a yearning for ego strokes that will never be satisfied. Greed tempts me to move my focus from people to things. Lust keeps me from connecting in the most meaningful way, diverting that desire in a direction that ultimately does not satisfy. God wants to set me free; evil attempts to enslave.

A Jewish friend once told me he found the list of seven deadly sins unsatisfactory. They seemed so inward-looking, he said – a list compiled by people who spent their lives cloistered in monasteries. In contrast Jews emphasize outward sins, like mistreatment of the poor, injustice, and racism.

At first I agreed with him that the seven deadly sins do not seem nearly as lethal as some others omitted from the list. I grew up among proponents of the Victorious Christian Life who worked hard at personal piety while ignoring the Jim Crow racism of the South and paying little attention to poverty. (Our ancestors didn't let slavery disturb their spiritual equilibrium either.) I know Christians who took more offence at Richard Nixon's profanity captured on the Watergate tapes than at the criminal acts themselves.

On reflection, though, I saw the wisdom of the monks who located the root problem of disorder in the human heart, from where it spreads outwards like a stain. Greed leads corporate executives to reward themselves with bonuses while their company lurches toward bankruptcy, and politicians to grant tax breaks to the rich while doing nothing to help the poor. Pride creates a feeling of superiority that devalues another race, or class, of human beings, as the caste system in India, apartheid in South Africa, and racism in the U.S. have demonstrated only too well. Anger, allied with power, can motivate a dictator like Saddam Hussein to gas his own citizens, or inspire a terrorist to blow up a building. Lust leads to the child sex-slaves of Southeast Asia.

Sinful people create sinful structures, which may then take on a life of their own. Human rebellion has spread across the planet so that every human institution – government, family, church – has been soiled. In some ways a structure or group of people is more inclined to evil than an individual and less inclined to love.

Heinrich Himmler, head of the SS during the Nazi reign in Germany, gives one example:

What happens to the Russians, what happens to the Czechs, is a matter of utter indifference to me.... Whether the other nationalities live in comfort or perish of hunger interests me only insofar as we need them as slaves for our society; apart from that, it does not interest me. Whether or not 10,000 Russian women collapse from exhaustion while digging a tank ditch interests me only insofar as it affects the completion of the tank ditch for Germany.

I have called desire a good thing, a rumour of another world that points back to the Giver. Yet at least four of the seven deadly sins (greed, envy, lust, and gluttony) suggest what may happen when desire becomes disordered. Of these, Jesus spoke most often against the commonplace sin of greed.

"Watch out! Be on your guard against all kinds of greed; a man's life does not consist in the abundance of his possessions," Jesus pronounced with a tone of alarm. He went on to tell of a rich man who built bigger and bigger barns to hold his grain, only to die with little to show for his life but a succession of large barns. Jesus' concern over the seductive power of greed shows in the fact that one-sixth of his sayings in the Gospels centre on money and its dangers. As the rich man demonstrated, wealth offers a glittering short-term satisfaction that obscures the real purpose of living.

Greed led Saddam Hussein to spend billions of dollars on massive, luxurious palaces while thousands of children in his country were dying from malnutrition (and a perverse inversion of greed prompted him to burn up Kuwait's oil fields when he lost control of them). Greed led Enron executives to pillage their company's assets by awarding themselves $745 million in bonuses while proposing a maximum of $13,500 in compensation for each laid-off employee.

"Greed is good," said Michael Douglas in the movie *Wall Street*. "Greed is right. Greed works." Indeed, in consumer economies such as the United States and Europe, greed drives the economy. We want more and more, and advertisers play on our fears that we never have enough. ("There are two ways to get enough," said G. K. Chesterton; "one is to continue to accumulate more and more. The other is to desire less.")

Greed exerts its power on those who have little as well as those who have much. The memoir *Shantung Compound* includes Langdon Gilkey's account of sharing a prison camp with other foreigners during Japan's occupation of China in World War II. Food supplies shrank so that eventually each prisoner received only 1,200 calories per day: six slices of bread, boiled water, and a bowl of stew. All the prisoners were losing weight and feeling malnourished. They dreamed of little else than food.

One day a shipment of two hundred parcels arrived from the American Red Cross, one for each American prisoner. The Americans felt they had struck gold. Each fifty-pound parcel contained a pound of powdered milk, four tins of butter, three of Spam, one pound each of cheese, chocolate, and sugar, as well as cans of powdered coffee, jams, salmon, and a package of dried prunes or raisins.

Gilkey recalls, "After a diet made up largely of bread, low on meats and oils, and lacking in sweets of all sorts–in fact, without real taste–fifty pounds of this sort of rich, fat-laden, and tasteful food was manna from heaven." In addition to the food, the parcels supplied much-needed clothing, far more than the Americans could use. They generously distributed the extra food and clothes to the more numerous prisoners of other nationalities.

Six months later, all the food was gone and conditions had deteriorated. Winter had set in, and morale in the camp hit an all-time low. A few days after Christmas, a donkey train suddenly appeared at the gates like a mirage, bearing more Red Cross parcels, this time too numerous for the prisoners to count. The Japanese commandant catalogued 1,550 parcels in all, and calculated that he could distribute one parcel to each of the 1,450 prisoners, and an extra half-parcel to the two hundred Americans. Joy and excitement gripped the camp: It was as though everyone were living through every Christmas Eve of his lifetime all rolled into one."

The next morning, to their dismay, the prisoners read a notice that no parcels would be distributed. A small group of Americans had protested the arrangement, insisting that only they were entitled to

the gifts from the American Red Cross. In other words, they
demanded seven-and-a-half American parcels for each American,
with none for the other prisoners. Disgusted, the commandant
appealed to Tokyo for a decision, and for ten days Gilkey and the
other Americans had to face the resentment and hostility of prisoners
from other nations. Gilkey reports,

> It was the same story all over. A community where everyone had long
> forgotten whether a man was American or British, white, Negro, Jew,
> Parsec, or Indian, had suddenly disintegrated into a brawling, bitterly
> divided collection of hostile national groups. Ironically, our wondrous
> Christmas gift had brought in its wake the exact opposite of peace on
> earth, The massive mounds of life-giving parcels lay inert in the centre
> of the camp, while gusts of human conflict and ill will swirled turbu-
> lently around them.
>
> For the first time, I felt fundamentally humiliated at being an
> American.

The Japanese authorities, not known for their sense of justice, in this
case showed more of it than the prisoners. Tokyo ordered that each
prisoner receive one parcel, with the extra hundred parcels to be distributed instead to other camps.

From that experience and others, Gilkey learned a painful lesson.
He had entered the camp with a liberal-optimist view of human
nature. After spending two-and-a-half years in a prison camp, among
missionaries, priests, educators, and business people, he emerged with
a much darker view and a new understanding of selfish humanity. He
saw firsthand the enormous consequences of a simple sin like greed.

Greed, like all sin, has its root in disorder. Human freedom allows
us an ambiguous privilege not granted to the rest of creation: we can
throw the balances of nature out of joint. We can accumulate in such
a way as to deprive others, and through wars to destroy them as well.
The entire planet shudders at the results of our attempts to make
ourselves and not God the centre of existence.

And to try to be happy by being admired by men, or loved by women, or warm with liquor, or full of lust, or getting possessions and treasures: that turns you away, soon, from the love of God; then men, women, and drink and lust and greed take precedence over God; and they darken His light.... And then we are unhappy and afraid and angry and fierce, and impatient, and cannot pray, and cannot sit still. That is the bitter yoke of sin: and for this we leave the mild and easy yoke of Christ.

THOMAS MERTON

The Life: A Portrait Of Jesus

J. John & Chris Walley

There is no denying that Jesus was an important
historical figure with an immeasurable impact
on the last two millennia. But is there more to
Jesus than that? This is a highly readable yet
serious exploration into the whole life of Jesus,
which is suitable for both Christians and those
exploring the Christian faith.

Authentic Lifestyle

£8.99

HB / 1 8602.4283 9

£2 OFF

£6.99 with voucher

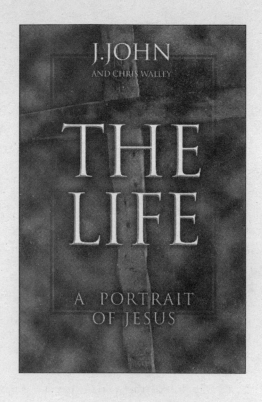

J.JOHN
AND CHRIS WALLEY

THE
LIFE

A PORTRAIT
OF JESUS

First published 2003 by Authentic Lifestyle, a division of Authentic Media.
9 Holdom Avenue, Bletchley, Milton Keynes, Bucks MK1 1QR, UK

Who Was Jesus?

Jesus talked a great deal about the Kingdom, but he also spoke much about who he was. In considering Jesus' identity we are faced with two questions. Who did Jesus claim to be? And was that claim true?

Evidence for who Jesus thought he was can be seen in various areas: his views of his mission, the titles he used for himself, the actions he performed and the claims that he made.

JESUS' VIEW OF HIS MISSION

How Jesus saw himself is reflected in the way that he saw his mission; that can be summed up in four images:

Royal Rescuer

To a Jew, the high point of the Old Testament was when God, through Moses, rescued his people from slavery in Egypt. Jesus saw himself as doing something very similar: he too was someone who had come to set people free. The words 'save', 165 'salvation', 'saviour', 'redeem' and 'redeemer' which occur throughout the gospels all express a series of ideas related to being rescued, whether physically or spiritually.[1]

Jesus' name is significant: Jesus ('Yeshua') means 'Yahweh saves'.[2] At Jesus' birth we are told that he is the promised Saviour and the one who will save his people from their sins.[3] Jesus defined his mission with the following words from the Old Testament:

'The Spirit of the Lord is upon me,
for he has appointed me to preach Good News to the poor.
He has sent me to proclaim
that captives will be released,
that the blind will see,
that the downtrodden will be freed from their oppressors,
and that the time of the Lord's favour has come.'[4]

Jesus saw himself as the great rescuer and deliverer of his people.

Loving Leader

If the image of a royal rescuer seems too military for us, it is balanced by another picture of Jesus as the one who lovingly leads and protects his people. Jesus came to a people who had lost their way and offered to lead them back to God. We read: 'When he saw the crowds, he had compassion on them, because they were harassed and helpless, like sheep without a shepherd.'[5]

Jesus saw himself as the great shepherd, the one who came to guide, recover and protect the lost. There is no contradiction between this caring leadership and that of the royal rescuer; after all, shepherds fight to defend their sheep. As leader, Jesus offered his gentle rule as a lighter load to those struggling with the unbearable burden of keeping the religious laws and traditions.[6]

Jesus claimed he had come to be a ruler who protected and guided his people.

Perfect Provider

Jesus also declared that he was the one who provided for all his people's needs. The feeding of the five thousand, the healing of the sick, the deliverance from demonic oppression, the raising of the dead: they are all examples of how Jesus provides perfectly in every situation. The idea that Jesus is the one who completely provides for his people's needs is summed up by the seven great statements he makes about himself that are recorded in John's gospel:

- 'I am the bread of life. No one who comes to me will ever be hungry again.'
- 'I am the light of the world. If you follow me, you won't be stumbling through the darkness, because you will have the light that leads to life.'
- 'I am the gate for the sheep. . . . Those who come in through me will be saved.'
- 'I am the good shepherd. The good shepherd lays down his life for the sheep.'
- 'I am the resurrection and the life. Those who believe in me, even though they die like everyone else, will live again.'
- 'I am the way, the truth, and the life. No one can come to the Father except through me.'
- 'I am the vine; you are the branches. Those who remain in me, and I in them, will produce much fruit. For apart from me you can do nothing.'[7]

These seven statements show Jesus claiming to be the complete answer to our every requirement, both now and for ever. Whether there is a need for guidance, comfort, protection or an answer to issues of guilt and death, Jesus is the one who is able to help.

Suffering Servant

The fourth image of Jesus in the gospels is one that is particularly remarkable. Jesus talked about himself as being a servant and suffering in the place of those he served. So, after rebuking his followers for their pride and selfishness, Jesus said: 'For even I, the Son of Man, came here not to be served but to serve others, and to give my life as a ransom for many.'[8] Jesus claimed to be Lord and King; but he also declared that he was a lowly servant and, more amazing still, one who would willingly suffer for others.

Behind this saying of Jesus lies one of the most significant of all the Old Testament prophecies. In Isaiah there is a description of a Servant of the LORD, a mighty figure who would come and, despite his high rank, be rejected, suffer and die on behalf of others.[9]

The astonishing idea that Jesus saw himself as this Servant, who had come both to serve and to die for others, occurs in all the gospels. In John's Gospel, Jesus says: 'I am the good shepherd. The good shepherd lays down his life for the sheep.'[10] John the Baptist even referred to Jesus in terms of a sacrificial animal, calling him 'the Lamb of God who takes away the sin of the world'.[11] Jesus claimed by his words and his actions that he was the Messiah, God's king, yet he chose to serve and suffer for his people.

HIS TITLES

The various titles either used by Jesus of himself or given to him are vital in understanding who he saw himself to be. Here are some of the main titles used:

Messiah

The first Christians were so certain that Jesus was God's promised king or Messiah that the names 'Jesus' and 'Christ' (from *Christos*, the Greek translation of 'Messiah') became almost interchangeable. Jesus, however, rarely used the title 'Messiah' of himself, presumably because of its nationalistic and revolutionary overtones. When he did, it appears to have only been where it was practical for him to do so. So, for instance, Jesus declared to a Samaritan woman that he was the Messiah; but the Samaritans were hardly going to cause trouble in Jerusalem. And when Jesus did accept the title 'Messiah' from the disciples, he gave them a warning to keep it private.[12] Linked with 'Messiah' is the title of 'Son of David',[13] a reference to the promised king who would come from the line of David.

Son of God

Jesus directly referred to himself as 'the Son of God' and taught parables that implied that title for himself.[14] At Jesus' baptism and at the transfiguration, a voice from heaven confirmed that Jesus was God's son. In the gospels other figures, including demons, Satan and a Roman centurion, also call Jesus the 'Son of God'. These references link to the promises in the Old Testament that one day God would install a king who would be 'his son'.[15]

But what does 'Son of God' mean? In Jesus' culture, the closest human relationship was that between father and son. Strange as it may seem to us with our knowledge of genetics, it was felt that a son was effectively the continuation of his father; there was a direct and undiluted link between the two. What a father was, his son was.

So how was Jesus the Son of God?

First, *Jesus stands in the place of the Father.* Even today in many traditional Middle Eastern countries if you go to meet an important man and only meet his son, there is no reason to feel disappointed. The son can stand in the place of the father and be relied on to speak for him; any promises that he makes will be honoured by his father. Jesus represents this situation exactly: he is one with his Father and can say:'Anyone who has seen me has seen the Father.'[16]

Second, *Jesus knows the Father perfectly.* Jesus has such an intimate personal fellowship with God that he can call him '*Abba*, Dear Father'. So close is this relationship that Jesus knows exactly his Father's thoughts and wishes. He can say 'My Father has given me authority over everything. No one really knows the Son except the Father, and no one really knows the Father except the Son and those to whom the Son chooses to reveal him.'[17] Jesus could speak for his Father because he knew him.

Third, *Jesus is faithful to the Father's will.* As the perfect son, Jesus does exactly what the Father wants and shows perfect obedience and trust. At both Jesus' baptism and the transfiguration, God announces his pleasure at his son's obedience.[18]

Fourth, *the Father loves the Son.* The gospels clearly show there is a love between the Father and the Son that parallels that which exists between human parents and their children. It is precisely because of this intense love that the Father giving Jesus up to death is so moving. Jesus' death was not some cold and unfeeling transaction but an intense sacrifice by both Father and Son.

Although Jesus taught his followers that they could know God as Father, he made a distinction between his unique relationship to God and theirs. He speaks of 'my Father' and 'your Father'[19] and of himself as God's 'one and only Son'.[20]

Son of Man

The title 'Son of Man' was Jesus' preferred title for himself. At first glance, 'Son of Man' is a rather odd and insignificant phrase. It could be used as an indirect way of talking about yourself or, as '*a* son of man', it could simply mean 'a man'. Certainly, to the Roman authorities, the term would have been utterly meaningless and totally unthreatening. Yet to Jews who knew their Scriptures, it was a very different matter. Jesus referred to himself not as 'a son of man' but '*the* Son of Man'. In doing so, he was referring to one of the most significant passages about the Kingdom in the Old Testament. In the Book of Daniel there are several visions and in one of them Daniel sees God − 'the Ancient One' − sit on a throne and begin to judge the world.

> As my vision continued that night, I saw someone who looked like a Son of Man coming with the clouds of heaven. He approached the Ancient One and was led into his presence. He was given authority, honour, and royal power over all the nations of the world, so that people of every race and nation and language would obey him. His rule is eternal − it will never end. His kingdom will never be destroyed.'[21]

This Son of Man is an awesome figure who is worthy of worship. He is also associated with the Kingdom of God coming with power: this universal and eternal kingdom is his. In some places, Jesus' use of the term 'the Son of Man' for himself is unmistakably linked with this passage, as when he is tried before the Sanhedrin: there Jesus' declaration that he is the Son of Man who will sit 'at God's right hand' provokes uproar and cries of blasphemy.[22]

By saying he was 'the Son of Man' Jesus was claiming to be the king of the eternal Kingdom.

Lord

The Greek word translated as 'Lord' has several meanings in the gospels. Sometimes, when people call Jesus 'Lord' they are simply being respectful and the word means no more than 'Sir'. Yet the word 'Lord' was also used as a term for God and, in some cases, when it is used of Jesus it is a divine title. This is particularly true when Jesus refers to himself as 'the Lord'. 23

The first Christians were in no doubt that to call Jesus 'Lord' was to give him the very highest title. So, early in Acts, Peter concludes a speech with this claim: 'So let it be clearly known by everyone in Israel that God has made this Jesus whom you crucified to be both Lord and Messiah!'[24] In the early church, the most basic statement of belief was to call Jesus Christ 'Lord'.[25]

Other titles

Other titles are used in the gospels for Jesus. On one occasion, Jesus was referred to as 'God'. When the resurrected Jesus confronted Thomas the disciple, his response was to exclaim 'My Lord and my God!'[26]

More subtle, but no less powerful, claims are presented when Jesus makes the great 'I am' statements in John's Gospel: 'I am the bread of life', 'the light of the world', 'the living water', etc.[27] Jesus made the astonishing declaration that he *personally* was all these things.

One use of the little phrase 'I Am' goes even further. During a discussion with Jesus, his hostile opponents referred to their ancestor, Abraham. Jesus responded 'Truly, truly, before Abraham was, I Am.'[28] Here Jesus was not just claiming to have existed before Abraham (which would have been remarkable enough); he was using the phrase 'I AM', which was the name that God had used of himself when he spoke to Moses.[29]

HIS ACTIONS

How we act reflects how we see ourselves. A number of Jesus' actions reveal that he saw himself as much more than a good human being or even a prophet:

* Jesus summoned the twelve disciples in a way that indicated that he personally was going to recreate or restore the twelve tribes of Israel. As it was God who had made Israel, Jesus' claim to remake it is very striking.
* Jesus' entry into Jerusalem on Palm Sunday was a deliberate public claim to be the Messiah.
* At the Last Supper, Jesus talked with his disciples about a 'new covenant'.[30] However, as the covenant was the central bond in the relationship between God and his people Israel, Jesus' claim to be replacing that first covenant is breathtaking. It assumes he considered himself to be equal to the maker of the first covenant.

In addition to these actions, Jesus also performed miracles. As we noted in Chapter 9, the range and style of these extraordinary actions point to Jesus being divine.

HIS CLAIMS

In what he said, and how he said it, Jesus made direct and indirect claims about who he was:

* From the extraordinary authority that Jesus claimed it is apparent that he knew he was no ordinary teacher or prophet. For instance, at the end of the Sermon on the Mount Jesus said: 'Anyone who listens to my teaching and obeys me is wise, like a person who builds a house on solid rock.'[31] Someone who was only a prophet would have mentioned God here: Jesus mentions himself.
* Jesus frequently used the word 'Amen' or 'truly' to introduce his sayings. This is something that seems to have been unique to Jesus and a way of claiming absolute and ultimate truth for his words. It suggests that Jesus believed he was equal to God.
* Jesus claimed to be able to forgive sins.[32] Since every Jew knew

that only God could forgive sins, to say this was to make a claim to be God.

- Jesus claimed the right to make definitive interpretations of the Law of God.[33] He reinterpreted the Law and redefined how it should be applied.[34] Jesus did not even justify his changes: he simply said 'But I say'.
- Jesus saw himself as greater than any figure of the Old Testament. He claimed to be greater than Jonah, Solomon, Jacob and even Abraham.[35] Jesus said that John the Baptist was the greatest man who had ever lived, but implied that he was greater.[36]
- Although the temple was considered to be the dwelling place of God, Jesus claimed that he was superior to it.[37] Jesus even suggested that his own body was the temple.[38]
- The Sabbath day was one of the great distinguishing features of Judaism and considered to be the gift of God. Yet Jesus said: 'I, the Son of Man, am master even of the Sabbath.'[39]
- Jesus claimed that his words would outlast heaven and earth.[40]
- Jesus claimed that total authority on earth had been given to him.[41]
- Jesus claimed that how people responded to him would decide their eternal destiny.[42]
- Jesus stated that he would be the judge on the Day of Judgement.[43]
- Jesus claimed that he must take complete precedence over his follower's family, friends and career.[44]
- Jesus accepted worship, prayer and faith. He commanded people to pray in his name.[45] He invited people to put their faith in him and praised them when they did.[46]
- Jesus taught that what people did to him they did to God.[47]

It is also worth noting that in several places in the gospels Jesus implied that he was not limited by either time or space. When Jesus spoke about his past, he stated that he had come from heaven[48] and had existed before Abraham.[49] Talking of the future, Jesus said that he would return to heaven[50] and promised his disciples that he would be with them for ever.[51] The implication is that Jesus saw himself as eternal, something echoed by John's description of him as 'the Word'.[52] Equally extraordinary was Jesus' claim, when sending the disciples out to the 'ends of the earth', that he would be with them wherever they went.[53]

As only God is eternal and present everywhere, Jesus' claims are very striking.

WHO DID JESUS THINK HE WAS?

If we look at all the evidence, the conclusion is unavoidable that Jesus saw himself as being God. In a variety of ways, Jesus showed that he considered himself to be God; that he was God's Son; the Lord, the Son of Man, the 'I AM'. Certainly, as the letters of the New Testament show, the earliest Christians considered Jesus to be someone who was God and whom they could worship.[54]

In considering this claim, we need to remember that Jesus was speaking in the Jewish world, which fervently believed there was only one God. If Jesus had been an Eastern mystic or a New Age teacher, for him to say that he was God would not have been a big issue; in such belief systems we are all, in some way, divine. But in Judaism there was only one God.

!HOW COULD JESUS BE BOTH MAN AND GOD?

The traditional Christian view of Jesus is that he was both perfectly God and perfectly human. Yet this raises an important issue: how can God and man coexist in the same body? After all, while human beings have limited power and knowledge, God's power and knowledge are unlimited. So how, practically, did it work? For instance, did the young Jesus ever get the wrong answer at school? Did he ever face the frustration that we all face when trying to learn a language?

On the whole, the church has given two answers to such questions: the first is to ignore them and pass on swiftly and the second is to say we don't know and it is pointless speculating. Neither answer is satisfactory. In fact, many people assume that it is quite impossible that Jesus could be both truly God and truly human.

The first thing to say is that this is an undeniably complex area and there is a lot we do not understand. Nevertheless, some helpful suggestions have been made, and we repeat them here because they may help those who find such matters troubling.

The issue of God's power is easier to deal with than God's knowledge, so let's start there. The Bible presents Jesus as someone who was able to exercise divine power and authority, in that he could do such things as calm storms, raise the dead, heal the sick and turn water into wine. Yet it seems obvious that for Jesus to be truly human, he could not be an invulnerable and all-powerful being. Clark Kent may have been the 'Man of Steel' but we aren't, and Jesus wasn't either. And this is not simply something that we deduce from theoretical arguments; the fact is that the gospels portray Jesus as being totally and completely human: he was tired,[55] hungry,[56] thirsty[57] and ultimately he was killed. So presumably, although Jesus had access to God's power, there were times when he did not choose to use it. There is a hint of this when Jesus stops his disciples defending him at his arrest: 'Don't you realize that I could ask my Father for thousands of angels to protect us, and he would send them instantly?'[58] Presumably, Jesus only used such power as he knew his heavenly Father would want him to use.

Such a principle no doubt also applied to the issue of how much Jesus knew. Clearly, Jesus did know many things that ordinary people cannot know,[59] yet there were some things he was not aware of.[60] Luke's reference to Jesus growing 'both in height and in wisdom'[61] implies that Jesus learnt as we do. It seems that while Jesus always had a right to divine knowledge and could have used it, he only made use of such knowledge as he knew his heavenly Father wanted him to. Jesus allowed his obedience to his Father to limit both his power and his knowledge.

Such a suggestion not only helps us make sense of how someone who was God could at the same time be totally human, it also shows us a Jesus who is a helpful model of obedience. The book of Genesis tells how the human race's slip into rebellion began with disobedience against God. The gospels tell us that the answer to this rebellion came when Jesus lived out an entire life of obedience to God.

The New Testament does not try to answer how Jesus is God and how he relates to the Father; it simply 'tells it like it is'. For the gospel writers, the mechanics of how the incarnation worked are not the issue. Ultimately, all we really need to know is that in Jesus, God came to this world to reach out to us.

CONSIDERING THE CLAIMS OF JESUS

Jesus' claims are so awesome and significant that they cannot simply be ignored or overlooked. If Jesus was, in some way, God come to earth, and if our eternal happiness does depend on us giving him our total loyalty, then we are faced with an issue that is without any doubt the most important thing in the world.

Equally, if the claims of Jesus to be God's unique and supreme intervention into our world are to be rejected with any intellectual honesty, then some alternative explanation for them must be found. Yet the alternatives are very limited. One assessment of Jesus sixty years ago by C.S. Lewis was that because of Jesus' claims, there were only two alternatives to him being Lord: he was either a liar or a lunatic. With the passage of time, we might extend and rephrase those alternatives: Jesus was either mythical, misunderstood, mistaken, mentally disturbed or someone who misled his followers.

Was Jesus *mythical*?

This first alternative is an attempt to duck the challenge. This 'escape route' from the claims of Jesus assumes the gospels are unreliable and that the divine figure they portray is fictional. Yet the gospels show none of the hallmarks of myth; they are understated and matter-of-fact accounts and the evidence that Jesus considered himself much more than a man is so diverse (the direct and indirect claims, the titles, the actions) and, above all, so consistent, that it seems far more probable that the figure they portray is authentic.

To maintain such a view a hard question has to be answered: *how did such a mythical Jesus arise*? How did a belief that 'Jesus was a good man' so rapidly evolve into 'Jesus was God'? There are no remotely similar parallels for this sort of development elsewhere, and none at all in Judaism.

Was Jesus *misunderstood*?

This second alternative suggests that, in reality, Jesus never claimed to be God. Rather, his disciples spectacularly misinterpreted what he said and turned his claim to be a faithful prophet of God into that of being an incarnation of God. This view might have some merit if Jesus' claim to be divine rested on one single statement; but given that he presented his claims in so many different ways it seems hard to maintain. It is difficult to believe that Jesus' disciples were so stunningly incompetent that they consistently and repeatedly misunderstood what he said on one of the most fundamental issues of his teaching. The charge of ineptitude can also be extended to the leaders of the early church, for never thinking to check whether the disciples had got it all wrong.

Was Jesus *mistaken*?

A third alternative is that it was Jesus himself who was wrong. On this view, Jesus genuinely thought he was God but, in reality, was sadly mistaken about his own identity. This would mean, however, that far from Jesus being a reliable and authoritative interpreter of the Law, he was breaking the First Commandment – 'you shall have no other gods before me' – in a most breathtaking and blasphemous way. The implications of this view are devastating: if Jesus was wrong about this most fundamental issue, then nothing else that he said can be trusted. If he was wrong here, Jesus was not even a reliable teacher.

Was Jesus *mentally disturbed*?

Another alternative is that Jesus suffered from a delusional psychological disorder. So, for example, the writer George Bernard Shaw considered that Jesus must have suffered from megalomania. Such an explanation has one slight merit: it admits Jesus did make astonishing claims about himself. Yet there is little else to support it. In the gospels, Jesus does not come over as the slightest bit delusional or disturbed.

To hold this view requires you to believe that the greatest moral influence the world has ever seen was a man who was mentally disturbed. That conclusion is so bizarre and unsettling that few people have felt comfortable even considering it.

Did Jesus *mislead* his followers?

A final alternative is that in making his claims, Jesus deliberately misled his followers: he lied to them. Yet it is hard to imagine any motive for Jesus wanting to mislead people in this way; far from leading to fame or fortune, his claims merely led to his death. And the charge of lying hardly seems consistent with everything else that we know of Jesus, including the fact that he started many of his statements by saying 'Truly, I say to you...' To pretend to be God and to accept the worship and praise of devout followers, while you knew you were as human as they were, would be an extraordinary act of deception. To say that it seems out of character with the author of the Sermon on the Mount is an understatement!

CONCLUSIONS

Jesus made extraordinary claims that he was God. If those claims are true then they have awesome and life-changing implications. In Jesus, every search for God comes to its end. In him is found everything that our hearts truly desire and
that our lives really need.

There are alternative explanations for the claims that Jesus made. Yet none of those explanations is without serious flaws. A Christian could easily say that it takes much less faith to believe that Jesus made his claims to be God because that's who he was, than to believe the alternatives. One of Sherlock Holmes' comments to

Watson is helpful here: 'It is an old maxim of mine that when you have excluded the impossible, whatever remains, however improbable, must be the truth.'

One event that we will look at later and that is crucial to Jesus' claims is the Resurrection. If Jesus did rise from the dead, then all his claims are confirmed as true.

Finally, simply saying 'I believe Jesus is God' does not exhaust the significance of Jesus' identity. It is too easy to limit the idea that Jesus is the divine Son of God to some theoretical test-question that identifies true Christianity. Yet to be a Christian does not mean to obey a doctrine or recite a creed, it is to live within a transforming relationship with Jesus. The reality is that the idea that Jesus is God is a truth that should sustain us every day. Jesus was not just the Royal Rescuer, Loving Leader, Perfect Provider and Suffering Servant for his people two thousand years ago: he is all those things for us *today*.

Notes

1:68–79;
2:11; 2:30–32; 5:29–32; 10:29–37; 19:1–10; 23:43
2 Mt. 1:21
3 Lk. 2:11
266
4 Lk. 4:18–19: Jesus is quoting Is. 61:1–2
5 Mt. 9:36 NIV
6 Mt. 11:28–30
7 Jn. 6:35; 8:12; 10:7,9; 10:11; 11:25; 14:6; 15:5
8 Mk. 10:45
9 Is. 42:1–4; 49:1–7; 50:4–9; 52:13–53:12. The last passage is the one most commonly referred to in the New Testament.
10 Jn. 10:11
11 Jn. 1:29
12 Mt. 16:16,20
13 Mt. 9:27; 15:22; Mk. 10:47–48
14 Mk. 12:6
15 2 Sam. 7:14; Ps. 2:7–12
16 Jn. 10:30; 14:9
17 Mt. 11:27
18 Mt. 3:17; 17:5
19 Jn. 20:17
20 Jn. 3:16

21 Dan. 7:13–14
22 Mk. 14:62
23 Mk. 11:3
24 Acts 2:36
25 Rom. 10:9; Phil. 2:11
26 Jn. 20:28
27 Jn. 6:35; 8:12; 10:7,11; 11:25; 14:6; 15:1
28 Jn. 8:58 (NIV)
29 Ex. 3:14
30 Lk. 22:20
31 Mt. 7:24
267
32 Mk. 2:5–7
33 Mt. 5:31–32, 38–39
34 Mk. 7:1–23
35 Mt. 12:38–42; Jn. 4:12; 8:53,56
36 Mt. 11:11
37 Mt. 12:6
38 Jn. 2:18–21
39 Mt. 12:8
40 Mk. 13:31
41 Mt. 11:27; 28:18–20
42 Mt. 10:32–33; 11:6; 25:31–46; Mk. 8:34–38
43 Mt. 7:22–23; 25:31–46
44 Lk. 14:26
45 Jn. 14:13–14; 16:23–24
46 Mk. 5:34; 10:52; Lk. 7:50; 17:19
47 Mt. 10:40; Mk. 9:37
48 Jn. 3:13; 17:5,24
49 Jn. 8:58
50 Jn. 6:62; 16:28
51 Mt. 28:20
52 Jn. 1:1–14
53 Mt. 28:18–20
54 See, for example, Phil. 2:6–11; Col. 1:15–20; Heb. 1:1–3
55 Jn. 4:6
56 Mt. 4:2
57 Jn. 19:28
58 Mt. 26:53
59 Mt. 12:25; Jn. 1:48; 2:24; 16:30
60 Mt. 24:36
61 Lk. 2:52

The Power Of A Praying Woman

Stormie Omartian

Having helped millions of women learn to pray effectively for their husbands, Stormie challenges them to pray for their own lives. Practical and scriptural, this is a powerful tool for all women.

Harvest House Publishers
£7.50
PB / 0 7369.0855 2

£2 OFF
£5.50 with voucher

Other titles by the same author

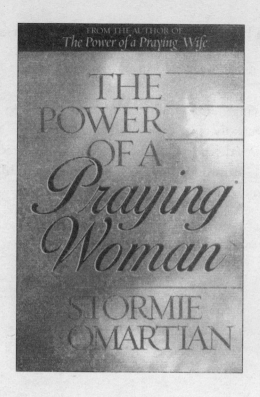

FROM THE AUTHOR OF
The Power of a Praying Wife

THE
POWER
OF A
Praying
Woman

STORMIE
OMARTIAN

Copyright © 2002 by Stormie Omartian

Published by Harvest House Publishers
Eugene, Oregon 97402

The Power

It doesn't matter what age you are, what your marital status is, what the condition of your body and soul is, or how long you have or have not been a believer – if you are a woman, this book is for you. I've been a devoted follower of the Lord for over 30 years and I have not fallen away from Him in all that time, yet I need this book too. In fact, I wrote it for myself as much as I wrote it for you. That's because I'm like you. Many days I find life difficult rather than easy, complex rather than simple, potentially dangerous rather than safe, and exhausting rather than exhilarating. Often it's more like a strong, hot, dry wind than it is a soft, cool, refreshing breeze.

But I have come to know that God can smooth my path, calm the storms, keep me and all I care about safe, and even make my way simple when I ask Him to carry the complexities of life for me. But these things don't just happen. Not without prayer.

In the midst of our busy lives, too often we don't pray enough. Or we only pray about the most pressing issues and neglect to take the time to really get close to God, to know Him better, and to share with Him the deepest longings of our heart. In our pray-and-run existence, we shut off the very avenue by which He brings blessings into our lives. And we risk waking up one day with that empty, insecure feeling in the pit of our stomach frightening us with the thought that our foundation may be turning into sand and our protective armor may be becoming as fragile as an eggshell. This is what happened to me.

A few years ago, I had become so busy with working, taking care of teenagers, trying, to be a good wife, running a home, writing books and traveling to promote them, being at all church meetings, helping people who needed it, and trying to make everyone happy, that I neglected the most important thing—my intimate walk with God. It's not that I stopped walking with Him. To the contrary, I couldn't make it through a day without Him. It's not that I stopped praying. Actually, I was praying more than ever about everyone else on the planet. But I didn't pray about my own walk with Him. It's not that I didn't read His Word. I read for hours as I did research in the Scriptures for different projects I was working on and the Bible study classes I was taking. But I didn't give God time to speak to me personally through it. I was busy doing good and neglected to do what was best. I became Martha instead of Mary without even realizing it (Luke 10:38-42).

I didn't take enough time for God and me alone, and as a result I became so depleted I couldn't go on. I felt like that eggshell, as if I could be crushed with very little outside pressure. I knew I needed more of God in my life, and nothing on earth was more important than that. There wasn't anything else that could satisfy the hunger I felt inside except more of His presence. And I came to realize how important it was for me to guard and protect my personal relationship with God in prayer.

The way to avoid the kind of thing I experienced is to pray about every aspect of our life in such a manner that it will keep us spiritually anchored and reminded of what God's promises are to us. It will keep us focused on who God is and who He made us to be. It will help us live God's way and not our own. It will lift our eyes from the temporal to the eternal and show us what is really important. It will give us the ability to distinguish the truth from a lie. It will strengthen our faith and encourage us to believe for the impossible. It will enable us to become the women of God we long to be and believe we can be. Who among us doesn't need that?

In my previous books on prayer, I have shared the ways husbands and wives can pray for one another, parents can pray for their children, and people can pray for their nation. In this book, I want to share how you can pray for YOU. I want to help you draw close to your heavenly Father, to feel His arms around you, to maintain a right heart before Him, to live in the confidence of knowing you are in the center of His will, to discover more fully who He made you to be, to find wholeness and completeness in Him, and to move into all He has for you. In other words, I want to show you how to effectively cover your life in prayer so that you can have more of God in your life.

Why Is It so Hard to Pray for Myself?

Do you find it is easier to pray for other people than it is to pray for yourself? I know I do. I can pray for my husband, my children, other family members, acquaintances, friends, and people I've never even met whom I hear about in the news far easier than I can pray for my own needs. For one thing, their needs are easy for me to identify. Mine are numerous, sometimes complicated, often difficult to determine, and certainly not easy to label. We women know what we think we need most of the time. We are able to recognize the obvious. But we are often too emotionally involved in the people around us and the day-to-day existence of our lives to be able to figure out how we should be praying for ourselves beyond the immediate and urgent. Sometimes we can be so overwhelmed by our circumstances that our prayer is simply a basic cry for help.

Do you ever have times when your life seems out of control? Do you ever feel pressured, as if your days are so busy that you fear you're missing out on a certain quality of life because of it? Do you worry that you are neglecting one or more areas of your life because you are trying to fill numerous roles and meet many expectations? I've experienced that too.

Have you ever felt as if your life is stuck in one place and you're going nowhere? Or worse yet, you are going backward? Have you had times when you've lost your vision for the future? Or have you never really had one to begin with? Have you wondered whether you can actually move into the full purpose and destiny God has for you? Have you experienced feelings of emptiness, frustration, or unfulfillment? I, too, have felt all those things.

Do you hunger for a greater sense of the Lord's presence in your life? Do you desire to know God in a deeper way? Do you want to serve Him better and more completely but don't feel you have the time, energy, or opportunity to do so? Do you need to spend more time with Him in prayer? Do you want your prayers to be accompanied by greater faith so that you can see greater answers to them? Do you need a more complete knowledge and understanding of God's Word? Do you ever just long to throw your arms wide open and embrace Jesus, white robes and all, and feel His embrace of you? So do I.

The good news is that this is the way God wants you to feel.

God wants you to long for *His* presence. He wants you to find your fulfillment in *Him* and nothing else. He wants you to walk closely with *Him*. He wants you to increase in faith and knowledge of *His* Word. He wants you to put all your hopes and dreams in His hands and look to *Him* to meet all of your needs. When you do, He will open the storehouse of blessing upon your life. That's because these things are *His* will for you.

But none of this happens without prayer.

Where Do I Go to Get My Needs Met?

Every woman has needs. But many of us are guilty of looking to other people to meet them — especially the men in our lives. Too often we expect them to meet the needs that only God can fill. And then we are disappointed when they can't. We expect too much from them when our expectations should be in God.

My friend Lisa Bevere expressed it best when she said that for centuries women have "wrestled and waged war with the sons of Adam in an attempt to get them to bless us and affirm our value. But this struggle has left us frustrated at best .... In the end, it is all a senseless and exhausting process in which both parties lose. It is not the fault of the sons of Adam; they cannot give us the blessing we seek, and we have frightened them by giving them so much power over our souls. We must learn that the blessings we truly need come only from God."*

We will never be happy until we make God the source of our fulfillment and the answer to our longings. He is the only one who should have power over our souls.

We have to put our expectations in the Lord and not in other things or people. I know this is easier said than done. So let's start with the easy part. Let's say to God, "Lord, I look to You for everything I need in my life. Help me to put all my expectations in You." And whenever you are disappointed because your needs are not being met, talk to yourself and say, "My soul, wait silently for God alone, for my expectation is from Hira" (Psalm 623). Then tell God about all your needs and everything that is in your heart. Don't worry, He won't be surprised or shocked. He already knows. He is just waiting to hear it from you.

More Than Just a Survivor

If you're like me, you don't want to live the kind of life where you are barely hanging on. You don't want to merely eke out an existence, find a way to cope with your misery, or just get by. You want to have the abundant life Jesus spoke of when He said, I have come that they may have life, and that they may have it more abundantly" (John 10:10).

We don't want to be women who hear the truth but seldom act in faith to appropriate it for our lives. We don't want to be forever grappling with doubt, fear, insecurity, and uncertainty. We want to live life on purpose and with purpose. We find it boring to live like a baby, feeding only on milk. We want the solid food of God's truth so we can grow into a life that is exciting and productive.

---

*Lisa Bevere, *Kissed the Girls and Made Them Cry*, (Nashville: Tommy Nelson, 2002), pp 189-90.

None of us enjoys going around in circles, always passing through the same territory and coming back to the same problems, same frustrations, same mistakes, and same limitations. We don't want to become calloused, hard-hearted, bitter, unforgiving, anxious, impatient, hopeless, or unteachable. We don't want to end up with a negative attitude that says, "My situation will never be any different because it hasn't been any different for a long time." We want to break out of any self-defeating cycle of repeated pattern, and habits and be able to transcend ourselves, our limitations, and our circumstances. We want to be more than just a survivor.

We want to be an overcomer. We want to be a part of something greater than ourselves. We want to be connected to what God is doing on earth in a way that bears fruit for His kingdom. We want to have a sense of purpose in our lives. We want to abound in God's love and blessings. We want it all. All God has for us. But we can never achieve that quality of life outside the power of God. And then only as we pray.

How Do I Move in the Power of God?

We've all had times when we feel completely powerless in the face of our circumstances. We've proven to ourselves over and over that we don't have what it takes to attain any kind of permanent transformation in our lives. We know without a doubt that our best efforts to change ourselves or our circumstances in ways that are significant or lasting never work. We recognize our need for a power outside of and far greater than ourselves. But there is only one power in the world great enough to help us rise above ourselves and the difficult things we face. That is the power of God.

Without God's power, we can't transcend our limitations or get out of our rut. We can't stand strong in the face of all that opposes us. We are doomed to a life of spiritual mediocrity. Without the power of God's Holy Spirit working in us, we can't be liberated from everything that keeps us from moving into all God has for us.

We don't want to spend our lives waiting to be delivered from all that limits us and separates us from God's best. We want to be set free *now*. But that can't happen if we refuse to acknowledge the Holy Spirit's power. When we deny the Holy Spirit's attributes we become like those people the Bible speaks of who live "having a form of godliness but denying its power" (2 Timothy 33). We become professional Christians who talk "Christianese" with such a slick veneer of superficiality that it makes us untouchable and keeps us untouched. We become all show and no heart. All correctness and no love. All judgment and no mercy. All self-assurance and no humility. All talk and no tears. We live powerless and meaningless lives without any hope for real transformation. And without transformation, how can we ever rise above our limitations and be God's instrument to reach the world around us? And that is what life is all about.

God wants us to understand "what is the exceeding greatness of His power toward us who believe" (Ephesians 1:19). He wants us to know this power that raised Jesus "from the dead and seated Him at His right hand in the heavenly places, far above all principality and power and might and dominion, and every name that is named" (Ephesians 1:20-2 1). He wants us to understand that Jesus is not weak toward us, but mighty *in* us (2 Corinthians 13:3). He wants us to understand that "though He was crucified in weakness, yet He lives by the power of God," and even though we are also weak, we live by the power of God too (2 Corinthians 13:4). God wants us to see that "we have received, not the spirit of the world, but the Spirit who is from God, that we might know the things that have been freely given to us by GoX (1 Corinthians 2:12).

I can't make you see or cause you to comprehend the power of God or the way the Holy Spirit wants to work in you. That is beyond my capabilities and authority in your life. But you don't need me to convince you because the Holy Spirit will do that Himself. Jesus said, "the Helper, the Holy Spirit, whom the Father will send in My name, He will teach you all things" (John 14:26). But you first have to acknowledge the Holy Spirit and invite Him to move in you freely.

We can only move in the power of God's Spirit if we have first received Jesus as Savior. You need to "know the love of Christ which passes knowledge; that you may be filled with all the fullness of God" (Ephesians 3:19). When you have Jesus as ruler of your life, you will come to know Him as the one "who is able to do exceedingly abundantly above all that we ask or think, according to the power that works in us" (Ephesians 3:20). Because of His Holy Spirit in us – or His *power* in us – He can do more in our lives than we can even think to ask for. How great is that?

Being filled with the Holy Spirit is not something that happens against our will. It is something we have to be open to, something we must desire, something for which we have to ask. If you then, being evil, know how to give good gifts to your children, how much more will your heavenly Father give the Holy Spirit to those who ask Him!" (Luke 11:13). We have a choice about whether we will be filled with the Holy Spirit or not. We have to ask God to do that.

I am not going to get into the various doctrines of men about the Holy Spirit of God. There seem to be as many of these as there are denominations. All I am asking is that you recognize the Holy Spirit of God as the power of God, and that you ask God to fill you with His Holy Spirit so He can empower you to move into all He has for you. The Bible says, "be filled with the Spirit" (Ephesians 5:18). Life works better when we do what the Bible says.

The Power to Become All God Made You to Be

Today, more and more believing women are being given an open door to become all they were created to be. They are moving out in different areas of expertise and ministry and making an important difference in the lives of those whom God puts in their realm of influence. They are learning to rely on the power of God to prepare them and open the doors. They are also realizing that they are not just an afterthought in the order of God's creation, but they were created for a special purpose. They might not know exactly what that purpose is or all that it entails, but they know that it is to do good for others and glorify God.

An important reason more women are rising up to fulfill the destiny God has for them is because men are rising up to their place of spiritual authority and leadership. This is an answer to the prayers of countless women and something for which we must praise God. Women need this spiritual covering. When it's done right – with strength, humility, kindness, respect, and understanding-and not with abuse, arrogance, self-promotion, cruelty, harshness, or lovelessness, it becomes a place of safety for a woman. Being in right order in our lives is something to be desired.

The Bible says that "the woman ought to have a symbol of authority on her head" (1 Corinthians 11:10). This means spiritual authority, and it is very important. Everyone is supposed to be submitted to divinely appointed authority. It's part of God's order. God won't pour into our lives all He has for us until we are in right relationship with the proper authority figures whom He has placed in our lives. They are there for our protection and benefit. God's power is too precious and too powerful to be let loose in an unsubmitted soul. (This is something to *pray* about, not *worry* about, so we'll do that in chapter 9.)

God's Promises to You

So often we don't move into all God has for us because we don't understand what it is He has for us. We may know He has given many promises for our lives, but if we don't know exactly what these promises are, we can't get a clear perspective on our situation. God's "divine power has given to us all things that pertain to life and godliness, through the knowledge of Him who called us by glory and virtue, by which have been given to us exceedingly great and precious promises, that through these you may be partakers of the divine nature" (2 Peter 1:3-4).

We need to know these promises well enough to keep them perpetually in our minds and on our hearts. In fact, the *deeper* they are etched in our souls the better off we will be. That's because the enemy of our soul will try to steal them from us. He doesn't want us to know the truth about ourselves. So we must grab on to these promises with all our might. We must cling to them like life and refuse to let them go.

For this reason, at the end of each chapter in this book there is a section called "God's Promises to Me." In it I have listed important promises from God's Word that are applicable to that particular subject. I want us to declare these promises out loud in the face of all obstacles in order to erase any doubt about those priceless truths for our lives. As you read each one, determine what God's promise in that particular Scripture-means specifically for you and your life.

In some instances, determine what promise is *implied* in that Scripture. Take for example the verse, "Watch and pray, lest you enter into temptation. The spirit indeed is willing, but the flesh is weak." (Matthew 26:41). The implied promise here is that if you pray and are watchful, you won't fall into temptation.

While most of God's promises are pleasant and positive, some are not because they are warnings to us. It's like saying to a child, if you do *this*, there is this reward. But if you do *that*, I *promise* you there will be these unpleasant consequences." Because God keeps all of His promises, it's important to know them well.

Time to Move On

Although it may often feel like it, there is never a time when *nothing* is happening in your life. That's because whether you realize it or not, you are never standing still. You are either going forward or you're sliding back. You are either becoming *more* like Christ every day or you're becoming *less* like Him. There is no neutral position in the Lord. And that is the very reason I wrote this book. I want you and me to keep moving forward. I don't want us to wake up one morning and realize we never laid a good foundation in the things of God or we didn't protect the foundation we had with prayer. I want us to move forward by spending quality time with the Lover of our soul every day. I want us to become *passionate* about God. I want us to find out what we are supposed to be doing and then do it. This is not about getting things *from* God, although He has much He wants to give to us. It's about getting *into* God and allowing Him to get into us. It's about letting *Him* make us complete.

When we live this way, according to God's Word and by the power of His Holy Spirit, then we can trust that we are in the right place at the right time and that the Lord is working His perfect will in our lives. We can trust that He is moving us into the life of wholeness and blessing He has for us. Shall we get started?

My Prayer to God

Lord, You have said in Your Word that whoever believes in You will have rivers of living water flowing from their heart (John 7:38). I believe in You, and I long for Your living water to flow in and through me today and every day that I'm alive. I invite Your Holy Spirit to fill me afresh right now. just as a spring is constantly being renewed with fresh water so that it stays pure, I ask You to renew me in that same way today.

Your Word says that "the Spirit also helps in our weaknesses. For we do not know what we should pray for as we ought, but the Spirit Himself makes intercession for us with groanings which cannot be uttered" (Romans 8:26). Lord, I realize I don't know how to pray as I need to, nor as often as I want to, but I invite You, Holy Spirit, to pray through me. Help me in my weakness. Teach me the things I don't know about You.

I am desperately aware of how much I need Your power to transform me and my circumstances. I don't want to live an ineffective life. I want to live in the dynamic power of Your Spirit. I don't want to be a spiritual underachiever. I want to be an overcomer. You paid a price for me so that I could be owned by You. Help me to live like it. You planned out a course for my life so that I could be defined by You. Help me to act like it. You made it possible for me to defeat my enemy. Help me not to forget it. You sent Your Holy Spirit so that I could live in power. Help me to fulfill that promise. You gave Your life for me because You loved me. Help me to do the same for You.

I put all my expectations in You, Lord. I repent of the times I have expected other people or other things to meet my needs when I should have been looking to You. I know that You are the only one who can complete me because You are everything I need. All that I have ever wanted in my life can be found in You. Help me to remember to live not in my own strength, but by the power of Your Spirit living in me. Forgive me for the times I have forgotten to do that. Enable me to grow in the things of Your kingdom so that I can become a whole, properly functioning, contributing, productive child of Yours who moves forward in Your purpose for my life

GOD'S PROMISES TO ME

We have this treasure in earthen vessels, that the excellence of the power may be of God and not of us.

2 CORINTHIANS 4:7

The message of the cross is foolishness to those who are perishing, but to us who are being saved it is the power of God.

1 CORINTHIANS 1:18

My grace is sufficient for you, for My strength is made perfect in weakness.

2 CORINTHIANS 12:9

God both raised up the Lord and will also raise us up by His power.

1 CORINTHIANS 6:14

When the helper comes, whom I shall send to you from the Father, the Spirit of truth who proceeds from the Father, He will testify of Me.

John 15:26

Heaven Bound

Selwyn Hughes

Heaven – we all talk about it, but how many of us know what to expect when we get there? And how should the knowledge of heaven affect our day-to-day lives?

CWR
£6.99
HB / 1 8534.5267 X

£2 OFF
£4.99 with voucher

Other titles by the same author

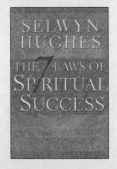

SELWYN HUGHES

HEAVEN BOUND

Living in the light of eternity

Published 2003 by CWR
Waverley Abbey House, Waverley Lane, Farnham, Surrey GU9 8EP

We Have His Word

Matt. 16:21–28;
John 3:1–16; 8:48–58; 14:1–14

'In my Father's house are many rooms; if it were not so I would have
told you. I am going there to prepare a place for you.'

John 14:2

We turn now to ask ourselves the question: Is the longing for heaven
which God has placed within our hearts (though with many it is
ignored, modified or denied) enough evidence that there is a heaven?
Those with a more scientific mindset will say that subjectivity is not
enough. You need more objective proof otherwise you may be
deceiving yourself.

A young scientist once put it to me like this: those who have
travelled across a desert know the deception of the mirage. A person
sees water in front of him. He would bank his life on it being there,
but as he reaches out to drink, it fades away. This shows how our
human senses are subject to illusions. When we long for something
our mind sometimes persuades us that it is available. So how do we
know the longing for heaven isn't just a mirage, that it isn't a form of
self-delusion? I pointed the young scientist to John 14 verse 2 in
which Jesus says, 'I am going there to prepare a place for you.' We
have the best proof possible: Jesus has told us there is a heaven and
that a place in it is reserved for the men and women who believe in
Him.

What better evidence do we need
than the words of Jesus?

Of course, if a person doesn't believe in Jesus or accept His credibility then that is another matter. Jesus' word is good enough for me, however, and I am sure for most of you who are reading these lines. He has told us in the clearest of terms that He will meet those of us who are His one day in heaven. The One who said, 'I am the truth' has given us His word.

Memories!

The only person ever to have lived in this world and possessed first-hand knowledge of heaven is our Lord Jesus Christ. Suppose someone appeared on our television screens and professed to be able to give us a reliable report of life on some other planet. What would our initial reaction be? Would it not be: How do you know? How can you tell if you have never been there?

In John 8 verse 58 we see quite clearly that Jesus was aware of His pre-existence. But how much did He remember of the glories He left behind? How conscious was He of the life He had lived in heaven? Some say Christ had no remembrance of the splendour He had relinquished. The reason He knew of His pre-existence was because it was revealed to Him by God His Father. Others maintain He had a full and complete memory of His days in heaven.

I think the truth lies somewhere between these two schools of thought. Christ had some memories of heaven but only enough to enable Him to fulfil His redemptive mission. There were certain things He did not know in His human state because He had freely chosen to be ignorant of them, one being the day and hour of the second coming (Matt. 24:36). But He was aware, I believe, to a degree appropriate to His human condition, of the atmosphere, the glory and the delights of heaven. If He had no memories of His pre-existence and what heaven was like how could He have declared, 'If it were not so, I would have told you' (John 14:2)?

Engaging honesty

Let's linger a little longer on the words 'if it were not so, I would have told you' as there is more in them than we might suppose at first glance.

We have accepted that these words indicate Jesus had some remembrance of heaven. How else could He have said, 'If it were not so, I would have told you'? But they reveal something more: they tell us about our Lord's engaging honesty. Can those of us who are Christ's followers believe that He would allow us to labour under a delusion concerning the future life? Do you think He would permit us to put faith in a falsehood? From all that we know of Him we are compelled to say that in every circumstance He would tell us the truth.

Christ was as much a realist as an idealist – He never pretended that things were other than they were. Look at how He dealt with the man who said, somewhat enthusiastically, 'I will follow you wherever you go' (Matt. 8:19). Christ's reply was chilly in its realism, 'Foxes have holes and birds ... have nests, but the Son of Man has nowhere to lay his head' (v.20). Our Lord went to great pains to make sure that people understood Him. But He went to great pains also to make sure that He was not misunderstood.

Frank and fearless

We have another example of our Lord's ability to get to grips with actualities and His refusal to allow His disciples to labour under any delusion.

As Jesus talks about going to Jerusalem and suffering many things at the hands of the elders, chief priests and teachers of the law, Peter remonstrates with Him and tries to steer Him away from the subject. Peter and the other disciples – let's face it – were somewhat taken up with dreams of imperial power despite our Lord's oft-repeated declaration of the true character of His kingdom. Does our Lord, in the interests of expediency, allow the minds of His disciples to be dominated by such dreams? He does not. He turns to Peter and says,

'Get behind me, Satan! You are a stumbling-block to me; you do not have in mind the things of God, but the things of men' (Matt. 16:23). Strong words.

One commentator suggests that the phrase 'Jesus turned' indicates that *Jesus turned pale* at the thought of one of His disciples trying to deter Him from the very purpose for which He had come to earth. Somewhat fanciful perhaps, but there can be little doubt that Peter's remonstration had a great effect on our Lord and evoked from Him an extraordinary response.

> *Jesus was a completely frank and fearless Person.*

Therefore, because He said 'If it were not so, I would have told you' in connection with the existence of heaven, we can be sure that He meant what He said and that we can take Him at His Word. 'I would have told you.' He would indeed.

We can trust those words to be true. And why? Because we can see that in His relationship with His followers He was always frank and fearless. He would never hide the truth from them to spare their feelings. Yet another example of this is the story in Mark 10:17–31.

A very rich young man runs up to Jesus, falls at His feet and asks, 'What must I do to inherit eternal life?' Our Lord's answer is clear and pointed: keep the commandments, do not murder, do not commit adultery, and so on. The young man claims that as far as keeping the commandments is concerned he is a rigid observer. However, Jesus looks into his soul and sees that even though on the surface he may pass the test of being a commandment-keeper there is entwined around his heart the love of riches.

Now note what it says in verse 21: 'Jesus looked at him and loved him.' But His love is not a sentimental type of love; it is a love that is strong enough to confront. With a characteristic thrust of His rapier-like logic, Jesus cuts right to the core issue and says, 'Go, sell everything you have and give to the poor' (v.21). The young man is nonplussed. His true god is his wealth and he is not prepared to give it up. Yet again our Lord demonstrates that His love is the kind that never hides the truth even though it may hurt a person's feelings. He is candid no less than kind.

No concealment

It would be easy to go through the Gospels multiplying examples to prove the realism and candour of Christ, but I think the three examples we have looked at are enough. When we deal with Jesus we deal with One who will never allow us to be misled, labour under a delusion or put our faith in a falsehood.

But just in case I have painted a one-sided picture of Jesus by showing Him to be a tough realist, let me introduce you to the thought that He is not just the Christ of candour but also the Christ of compassion. To put it another way: He is not just tough but tender. And the tenderness of His heart would not have allowed Him, while in possession of the facts, to conceal them from His followers. He knew full well how men and women longed for some sure word concerning the curtained future; He knew that the question of what lies beyond the grave was something that weighed heavily on their souls; He understood the concern and feelings of their hearts when they contemplated death.

How could Christ, with such a heart of compassion, have remained silent when He was the only One in the world who could pierce the veil and enlighten people on what lay beyond? How could He withhold the truth when to utter it would bring such solace to troubled souls? He, being who He was, simply had to speak out, to say, 'If it were not so, I would have told you.' Not to have done so would have been unthinkable.

Can you imagine Columbus after having discovered America wanting to keep the matter to himself? Or Captain Cook after exploring New Zealand wishing to leave the world ignorant of his findings? Both of these situations are unthinkable given the character and ideals of the men concerned. Likewise, it is unthinkable that Jesus, having spent eternity past in the presence of His Father, would not want to tell His followers something of the glories of that wondrous world. He says in effect, 'If seventy years of life, more or less, is all you could expect, I would be frank with you and urge you to make the most of it, but in My Father's house ...'

It is said that Professor T.H. Huxley, the famous agnostic (who, by the way, invented the term 'agnostic' and applied it to himself), reversed his views prior to his death and came to believe in God and a future life. As he lay dying (so his nurse reported) he raised himself on his elbows and gazed into the distance as if surveying some invisible scene, then dropped back on his pillow and murmured, 'So it was true! So it was true!'

We, who follow Christ, need no such revelation to convince us of the reality of heaven. It is enough that we have heard Him say, 'In my Father's house are many rooms; if it were not so, I would have told you' (John 14:2). He needs no vision who has heard that word.

Further Study

Luke 10:1–18; John 1:1–18
1. What did Jesus declare He had witnessed?
2. What did John declare about the pre-existent Christ?

Matt. 5:13–18; 18:3–4; 18:13
3. What did Jesus often link to the phrase 'I tell you the truth'?
4. What else did He link to heaven?

John 6:25–38; 3:31; 8:23; 13:3
5. What did Jesus say of His origin?
6. What did Jesus know?

Keeping Heaven in View

Hebrews 11:1–10;
2 Corinthians 4:5–18;
Philippians 1:12–26

'So we fix our eyes on not on what is seen, but on what is unseen. For
what is seen is temporary, but what is unseen is eternal.'

2 Corinthians 4:18

We move on now to consider the suggestion that heaven should
never be far from our minds as we make our way through this world.
Some might respond to this by saying: Surely the constant consideration of heaven will interfere with work we have to do here on earth.
Well, of course it can, but what I am talking about is a balanced view
of the matter – not too little and not too much.

My reading of Christian history has brought me to the conclusion
that the Christians who did most for this world in which we live
were those who thought a good deal about the next. It could be
argued, and argued successfully I think, that Christians who never
allow themselves to think of the world that lies beyond are largely
ineffective in this. If the truth be known, most of us go through life
with our eyes cast downwards. We neither look nor long for heaven.
Those whose eyes are never lifted up to see what lies ahead should
not be surprised if they find the things of earth becoming more
important to them than heaven, time becoming more important than
eternity.

The constant remembrance that we are bound for 'a city whose architect and builder is God' will help us keep matters in perspective. It will enable us to hold onto things loosely, knowing that they are merely temporal. I think it was Cardinal Newman who said, 'Only those work with full effectiveness for the new Jerusalem below who see the New Jerusalem above. They make it after "the pattern which has been shown to them on the mount".'

Between two gardens

Why is it that, generally speaking, we do not walk through this world with the prospect of heaven central to our thinking? One reason could be that we reckon we can have heaven now. A large percentage of believers appear to hold the view that being a Christian means we will no longer have to wrestle with problems or struggle with our finances and that we will never get sick.

Now let me say right away that I have seen too many miracles not to believe in them, and I am convinced that many of us are slow to avail ourselves of the resources of the abundant life found in Jesus Christ. God is willing to bless His people; indeed He delights in it. It is not wrong to ask God to resolve a difficult problem, to heal a serious sickness, or even work a miracle to help you when in financial difficulty. I have seen Him work in my own life in all of the ways I have just mentioned, and expect to see Him do the same in the future. That said, however, our view of the Christian life will be an unbalanced one if we think that life in Christ means that we never have to face problems or struggle with difficulties.

When Adam and Eve were expelled from the Garden of Eden, God put a 'Celestial Bouncer' at the entrance to stop them getting back in. Now we live outside the garden in a world that is cursed because of sin. Meanwhile we must live in a garden that, though still quite beautiful, has thorns and weeds. Those who ignore this fact have a very unbalanced view of Christianity.

We were designed for a world different to the one in which we are presently living. God never intended for us to struggle with sickness, wrestle with guilt, undergo deep bouts of melancholy and gloom or face the awful fact of death.

Another garden awaits us, but that lies up ahead.

It is true that because of what Christ did for us on the cross, which was endorsed by the resurrection and the ascension, we have forgiveness for our sins (a sure remedy for guilt) and the promise of the Holy Spirit's help and comfort as we make our way through this world. But the world we inhabit is still fallen for all that – it is a world for which we were not designed. This is why even when we are joyful the joy we experience is a 'marred joy'. By that I mean that even in our happiest moments we will experience a degree of sadness that arises from the fact we are in an unnatural environment – unnatural in the sense that a departure from God's intentions is unnatural.

We must get to grips with this fact or else we will become disillusioned and disappointed. Oswald Chambers was right when he said, 'Life is more tragic than orderly.' This is a tough world – a world still reeling from the effects of the Fall. Not to recognise or understand this means our expectations will be higher than they should be and our disappointments deeper than they need be.

Think with me for a moment before we continue discussing some of the points we have made. The prospect of heaven is something we should always keep before us. It helps us gain a right perspective on everything. Some believe we can have heaven now: 'Health and wealth until the day we die.' This is nonsense, of course, and quite unscriptural. Yes, God does answer prayer in the way we desire and does work miracles – but not always. Sometimes He lets His people suffer. And it is no good saying the ones who suffer have no faith. That is a cop-out. And a cruel cop-out. The Church needs a theology of suffering to balance its theology of miracles.

We live in a world for which we were not designed – hence we experience a marred joy. At our best moments we are aware that what we are experiencing is not the fullness of what we were made for.

This is not negative thinking; it is realism. And facing the reality does not diminish the joy; rather, it helps prevent us pretending that what we have is better than it is. This is Christian realism – a factor missing in many sections of today's Church.

Consider the apostle's statement in 2 Corinthians 4:5–18. Clearly he was struggling but he was struggling well. Though he was crushed and perplexed (I wonder what about?) he kept his eyes on the unseen (v.18). He knew there was a better world to come, and the prospect of that helped to nerve him forward. It always does. The critics of Christianity call this escapism. But you could never call Paul an escapist. He faced the reality of heaven that he might better face the realities of earth.

Think with me about this: after Christ had ascended to heaven the disciples might well have wondered how they could continue the work He had vouchsafed to them now that He was no longer with them. They had been a vacillating bunch even during the time He had been amongst them. How would they fare now that He was in heaven?

To their credit they obeyed the Lord's command to wait in Jerusalem until they were endued with divine power (Acts 1:8), and when He, the Holy Spirit came, the results were astonishing. The men who just a few weeks previously had deserted their Lord were filled with a new courage. The rabbits became ferrets. And from that day forward the staggering thing is this – not once do we read of the disciples crying out, 'If only the Master was with us now.' In some of the situations in which they found themselves it would have been natural for them to have expressed that wish – but on no occasion did it happen. They lived and acted as if the Master was there with them, right at their side.

Was it merely an illusion? No, for He was right there with them. Not physically of course. His body was in heaven but the Holy Spirit made His presence universal. It is a mystery of course, but what a blessed mystery.

Further Study

Col. 1:1–8; Titus 2:1–14; Heb. 6:19
1. How did Paul link time and eternity?
2. What does the hope of heaven give us?

Rom. 8:18–27; 15:4; Heb. 6:18
3. What does Paul say about the whole of creation?
4. What does he set against this?

Heb. 11:31–40; Psa. 42:1–11
5. What were some of the experiences of these men and women of faith?
6. How did the psalmist talk to himself on such occasions?

Eternal Seasons

Ed. Michael Ford

Henri Nouwen loved the liturgical year. Extracts from a selection of his writings are brought together in this book to provide a unique spiritual companion to the seasons of the church.

Darton, Longman & Todd Ltd
£7.95
PB / 0 2325.2516 1

£2 OFF
£5.95 with voucher

Other titles by the same author

Eternal Seasons

A Liturgical Journey with

HENRI NOUWEN

Edited by Michael Ford

First published in 2003 by Darton, Longman and Todd Ltd
1 Spencer Court, 140–142 Wandsworth High Street, London SW18 4JJ

Easter – Season of Hope

EASTER

The Easter mystery of Christ's death and resurrection lies at the heart of the Church's liturgical life. In the spirit of the Risen Jesus, we are urged during the next fifty days to journey, as one liturgical prayer book puts it, 'on a high plateau'. The way is 'smooth and peaceful, full of joy in the certitude that the Lord is living.' It is a season of joyous thanksgiving. After the ceremonies of Holy Week, it can sometimes seem like an anti-climax. But Easter should be proclaimed as a time for celebration and companionship on the Emmaus Road, an opportunity for dispelling doubt and bringing reassurance to all we meet along the way.

Henri Nouwen was realistic about this season of hope. He acknowledged that there can still be a painful awareness of sinfulness as well as fear but there is also light breaking through. Something new is happening, he once explained, something that goes beyond the changing moods of our life. The stream of God's presence runs beneath our undulating waves of temperament. Nouwen felt that Easter brings the awareness that God is active even when his presence is not directly noticed.

Whatever the headlines, Easter announces the news that evil has ultimately been overcome by good.

This season embraces Ascensiontide when the Church commemorates the return of Jesus to heaven. It is a feast centred round a separation sustained by a blessing. At this time of year I always think of the late leader of the British Labour Party, John Smith. He died suddenly on Ascension Day. I remember praying for him that evening during a service for Ascension broadcast on BBC Radio 4. He was buried on Iona, an island of wild beauty off the west coast of Scotland held by tradition to be 'nearest to heaven'. In a later interview, Elizabeth Smith told me how she and her husband had fallen in love with Iona and spent their holidays there. It was one of the few places where the politician could unwind and relax almost instantaneously. It had been a particular honour for him to be buried there because the graveyard was usually reserved for islanders.

Like many bereaved families (and the disciples themselves), the Smiths went through a period of great shock, numbness and incomprehension after John's death. But Elizabeth revealed that at the time she felt 'an incredible feeling of peace and calm' which she had not expected. It had given her great strength to cope with the sense of loss and separation.

Easter is about acknowledging the breaking in of eternity into the ordinary patterns of our lives. In this selection of writings, we share Henri Nouwen's undisguised joy in the resurrection, symbolised so resplendently by the sun in the paintings of van Gogh.

Easter is a bodily experience, celebrating in every fibre new life, new hope and ecstatic liberation.

EASTER DAY

Dear Lord, risen Lord, light of the world, to you be all praise and glory! This day, so full of your presence, your joy, your peace, is indeed your day.

I just returned from a walk through the dark woods. It was cool and windy, but everything spoke of you. Everything: the clouds, the trees, the wet grass, the valley with its distant lights, the sound of the wind. They all spoke of your resurrection; they all made me aware that everything is indeed good. In you all is created good, and by you all creation is renewed and brought to an even greater glory than it possessed at its beginning.

As I walked through the dark woods at the end of this day, full of intimate joy, I heard you call Mary Magdalene by her name and heard how you called from the shore of the lake to your friends to throw out their nets. I also saw you entering the closed room where your disciples were gathered in fear. I saw you appearing on the mountain and at the outskirts of the village. How intimate these events really are. They are like special favours to dear friends. They were not done to impress or overwhelm anyone, but simply to show that your love is stronger than death.

O Lord, I know now that it is in silence, in a quiet moment, in a forgotten corner that you will meet me, call me by name and speak to me a word of peace. It is in my stillest hour that you became the risen Lord to me.

Dear Lord, I am so grateful for all you have given me this past week. Stay with me in the days to come. Bless all who suffer in this world and bring peace to your people, whom you loved so much that you gave your life for them. Amen.

A Cry for Mercy

PEOPLE OF THE RESURRECTION

After the Gospel reading I reflected on the significance of our faith in the resurrection of the body. As a community of people conscious of our disabilities, we are held together not so much by the Word as by the body. Although we may use many words and there is a lot of 'talk' among us, it is the weak bodies of our core members that create community. We wash, shave, comb, dress, clean, feed, and hold the bodies of those who are entrusted to us and thus build a communal body. As we claim our faith in the resurrection of the body, we come to see that the resurrection is not simply an event after death but a reality of everyday life. Our care for the body calls us to unity beyond organization, to intimacy beyond eroticism, and to integrity beyond psychological wholeness.

Unity, intimacy, and integrity are the three spiritual qualities of the resurrected life. We are called to break through the boundaries of nationality, race, sexual orientation, age, and mental capacities and create a unity of love that allows the weakest among us to live well. We are called to go far beyond the place of lust, sexual need, and desire for physical union to a spiritual intimacy that involves body, mind, and heart. And we are called to let go of old ways of feeling good about ourselves and reach out to a new integration of the many facets of our humanity. These calls are calls to the resurrection while anticipating it in our daily lives through spiritual unity, intimacy, and integrity.

As I talked about these things it seemed that those who were present at the vigil could recognize some of what I spoke about in their daily Daybreak life.

As we received the Body and Blood of Jesus, I was struck by the *real* quality of the paschal mystery. We are the people of the resurrection, living our lives with a great vision that transforms us as we are living it.

Sabbatical Journey

INTIMATE ENCOUNTERS

It was not a spectacular event forcing people to believe. Rather, it was an event for the friends of Jesus, for those who had known him, listened to him, and believed in him. It was a very intimate event: a word here, a gesture there, and a gradual awareness that something new was being born — small, hardly noticed, but with the potential to change the face of the earth. Mary of Magdala heard her name. John and Peter saw the empty grave. Jesus' friends felt their hearts burn in encounters that find expression in the remarkable words 'He is risen.' All had remained the same, while all had changed.

The Road to Daybreak

SPIRITUAL EMPOWERMENT

Today I was thinking how nobody recognizes Jesus immediately. They think he is the gardener, a stranger, or a ghost. But when a familiar gesture is there again – breaking bread, inviting the disciples to try for another catch, calling them by name – his friends know he is there for them. Absence and presence are touching each other. The old Jesus is gone. They no longer can be with him as before. The new Jesus, the risen Lord, is there, intimately, more intimately than ever. It is an empowering presence. 'Do not cling to me … but go … and tell' (John 20:17).

The resurrection stories reveal the always-present tension between coming and leaving, intimacy and distance, holding and letting go, at-homeness and mission, presence and absence. We face that tension every day. It puts us on the journey to the full realization of the promise given to us. 'Do not cling to me' might mean 'This is not heaven yet' but also 'I am now within you and empower you for a spiritual task in the world, continuing what I have begun. You are the living Christ.'

While many question whether the resurrection really took place, I wonder if it doesn't take place every day if we have the eyes to see and the ears to hear.

Sabbatical Journey

A SIGN OF LOVE

The resurrection of Jesus was a hidden event. Jesus didn't rise from the grave to baffle his opponents, to make a victory statement, or to prove to those who crucified him that he was right after all. Jesus rose as a sign to those who loved him and followed him that God's divine love is stronger than death. To the women and men who committed themselves to him, he revealed that his mission had been fulfilled. To those who shared in his ministry, he gave the sacred task to call all people into the new life within him.

The world didn't take notice. Only those whom he called by name, with whom he broke bread and to whom he spoke words of peace, were aware of what happened. Still, it was this hidden event that freed humanity from the shackles of death.

Bread for the Journey

NEW LIFE

When Jesus appeared to his disciples after his resurrection, he convinced them that he was not a ghost but the same one that they had known as their teacher and friend. To his frightened and doubtful friends he said: 'See by my hands and my feet that it is I myself. Touch me and see for yourselves' (Luke 24:39). Then he asked them for something to eat, and later, when he appeared to them for the third time, he offered them breakfast, bread and fish (see Luke 24:42–43 and John 21:12–14).

But Jesus also showed them that his body was a new spiritual body, no longer subject to the laws of nature. While the doors of the room where the disciples had gathered were closed, Jesus came and stood among them (see John 20:19), and when he offered them breakfast, nobody dared to ask: 'Who are you?' They knew it was Jesus, their Lord and teacher, but they also knew that he no longer belonged to their world (see John 21:12). It was this experience of the risen Jesus that revealed to his disciples the life in the resurrection that was awaiting them. Are there any experiences in our lives that give us a hint of the new life that has been promised us?

Bread for the Journey

THE MYSTERY OF ART

A Reflection on Rembrandt's *The Pilgrims of Emmaus*

Jesus sits behind the table looking up in prayer while holding a loaf of bread in his hands. On his right, one of the pilgrims leans backwards with his hands folded; while on his left, the other has moved his chair away from the table and gazes with utter attention at Jesus. Behind him a humble servant, obviously unaware of what is happening, reaches forward to put a plate of food on the table. On the table, a bright white cloth only partially covers the heavy table rug. There are very few objects on the table: three pewter plates, a knife, and two small cups. Jesus sits in front of a majestic stone apse flanked by two big, square pillars. On the right side of the painting, the entrance door is visible, and there is a coat stand in the corner over which a cape has been casually thrown. In the left corner of the room, a doglike figure can be seen lying under a bench. The whole painting is in endless varieties of brown: light brown, dark brown, yellow-brown, red-brown, and so on. The source of light is not revealed, but the white tablecloth is the brightest part of the painting ...

As we looked at the painting [in the Louvre, Paris], many people passed by. One of the guides said, 'Look at Jesus' face, in ecstasy, yet so humble.' That expressed beautifully what we saw. Jesus' face is full of light, a light which radiates from his head in a cloudlike halo. He does not look at the men around him. His eyes look upward in an expression of intimate communion with the Father. While Jesus is in deep prayer, he yet remains present; he remains the humble servant who came to be among us and show us the way to God.

The longer we looked at the painting, the more we felt drawn into the mystery it expresses ... As we continued to let the painting speak to us, we were amazed that we both came to see it more and more as a call to worship Christ in the Eucharist. The hands of Jesus holding the bread on the white altar table cloth are the centre not only of the light, but also of the sacramental action. Yet if Jesus were to leave the altar, the bread would still be there. And we would still be able to be with him.

For an instant the museum became a church, the painting a sanctuary, and Rembrandt a priest. All of it told me something about God's hidden presence in the world.

The Road to Daybreak

VAN GOGH'S MOUNTAIN

Dear Lord, after your resurrection you opened the minds of your disciples to understand the Scriptures. You made it clear to them that Moses, the prophets, and the psalmist had spoken about you. You revealed to them the great mystery that it was ordained that you should suffer and so enter into your glory.

Tonight I pray to you for an always deeper understanding of the

Scriptures and an always greater awareness that you are in the centre,
or – to say it with the words of Vincent van Gogh – that your Gospel
is the top of the mountain of which the Old Testament and the letters
of the Apostles are the slopes. Let me see your presence in the psalms,
in the prophets and in the great story of the people of Israel, and let
this insight help me better understand my own history, my own
struggle and my own pain.

Please, Lord, join me on the road, enter into my closed room, and
take my foolishness away. Open my mind and heart to the great
mystery of your active presence in my life, and give me the courage
to help others discover your presence in their lives.

Thank you, Lord, for this day. Amen.

A Cry for Mercy

VAN GOGH'S SUN

Dear Lord, free me from my dark past, into which I often feel myself
falling as if into a deep cistern. You are the light that has come into
the world so that whoever believes in you need not stay in darkness
any longer. Do not allow me to sink back into my own dark pit, O
Lord, but let your warm, gentle, life-giving light lift me from my
grave. Vincent van Gogh painted you as the sun when he painted the
resurrection of Lazarus. In so doing, he wanted to express his own
liberation from a dark, imprisoning past. Lord, keep showing me your
light, and give me the strength to rise and follow you without ever
looking back. You are my Strength, my Refuge, and my Stronghold.
As long as I keep my eyes on you, there is no reason to return to past
events, past patterns, past ideas. In your light all becomes new. Let me
be fully yours. Amen.

A Cry for Mercy

LIVING IN ECSTASY

Jesus connects joy with the promise of seeing him again. In this sense,
it is similar to the joy we experience when a dear friend returns after
a long absence. But Jesus makes it clear that joy is more than that. It

is 'his own joy', flowing from the love he shares with his heavenly Father and leading to completion. 'Remain in my love ... so that my joy may be in you and your joy may be complete' (John 15:9b, and 11).

The word 'ecstasy' helps us to understand more fully the joy that Jesus offers. The literal meaning of the word can help to guide our thinking about joy. 'Ecstasy' comes from the Greek 'ekstasis', which in turn is derived from 'ek', meaning out, and 'stasis', a state of standstill. To be ecstatic literally means to be outside of a static place. Thus, those who live ecstatic lives are always moving away from rigidly fixed situations and exploring new, unmapped dimensions of reality. Here we see the essence of joy. Joy is always new. Whereas there can be old pain, old grief, and old sorrow, there can be no old joy. Old joy is not joy! Joy is always connected with movement, renewal, rebirth, change – in short, with life.

Joy is essentially ecstatic since it moves out of the place of death, which is rigid and fixed, and into the place of life which is new and surprising. 'God is God not of the dead but of the living' (Matthew 22:32). There is no tinge of death in God. God is pure life. Therefore living in the house of God is living in a state of constant ecstasy, in which we always experience the joy of being alive.

In the House of the Lord

HUMMING IN THE DARKNESS

Hope means to keep living
amid desperation
and to keep humming
in the darkness.
Hoping is knowing that there is love,
it is trust in tomorrow
it is falling asleep
and waking again
when the sun rises.
In the midst of a gale at sea,

it is to discover land.
In the eyes of another
it is to see that you are understood ...

As long as there is still hope
There will also be prayer ...

And you will be held
in God's hands.

With Open Hands

FEASTS OF EASTER

THE ASCENSION

Dear Lord, at the end of this Ascension Day I am filled with gratitude. I realize that on this day you concluded your stay among us and the great mystery of your incarnation became visible in its fullness. Your earthly life, which began with Gabriel's visit to your Mother, was concluded when you were lifted up in a cloud and taken from the sight of your disciples. You, O Lord, Son of God, Son of Man, Emmanuel, Messiah, Redeemer of all people, you indeed shared with us all that is human and led our humanity to the right hand of your Heavenly Father. When you were no longer seen by your friends and had left them behind, you had fulfilled your divine mission. You taught us all we need to know; you did all that could be done; you gave us all that you had.

What would my life have been without knowing you? All my joys and pains are connected with your having come into this world.

Thank you, Lord, for your life on this earth and for calling me to tell the story of your life to all people. Amen.

A Cry for Mercy

GEORGE, MARTYR, PATRON OF ENGLAND, C. 304 (23 APRIL)

Good shepherds are willing to lay down their lives for their sheep (see John 10:11). As spiritual leaders walking in the footsteps of Jesus, we are called to lay down our lives for our people. This laying down might in special circumstances mean dying for others. But it means first of all making our own lives – our sorrows and joys, our despair and hope, our loneliness and experience of intimacy – available to others as sources of new life.

Bread for the Journey

MARK THE EVANGELIST (25 APRIL)

The contemplative life is a life in which time slowly loses its opaqueness and becomes transparent. This is often a very difficult and slow process, but it is full of re-creating power. To start seeing that the many events of our day, week, or year are not in the way of our search for a full life, but rather the way to it, is a real experience of conversion. If we start discovering that writing letters, attending classes, visiting people, and cooking food are not a series of random events that prevent us from realizing our deepest self, but contain within themselves the transforming power we are looking for, then we are beginning to move from time lived as *chronos* to time lived as *kairos*. *Kairos* means *the* opportunity. It is the right time, the real moment, the chance of our life. When our time becomes *kairos*, it opens up endless new possibilities and offers us a constant opportunity for a change of heart.

In Jesus' life every event becomes *kairos*. He opens his public ministry with the words, 'The time has come' (Mark 1:15), and he lives every moment of it as an opportunity. Finally, he announces that his time is near and enters into his last hours as *the kairos*. In so doing he liberates history from fatalistic chronology.

This really is good news because now we know that all the events of life, even such dark events as war, famine and flood, violence and murder, are not irreversible fatalities but rather carry within themselves the possibility of becoming the moment of change.

Clowning in Rome

PHILIP AND JAMES, APOSTLES (1 OR 3 MAY)

Dear Lord, your apostle Philip joined an Ethiopian pilgrim returning from Jerusalem to his country. As you did when you joined the men going to Emmaus, so your apostle explained the Scriptures to this pilgrim and made it clear that they were speaking about you. I pray that this will be my ministry: to join people on their journey and to open their eyes to see you. Many people are searching. Often they are studying, reading, discussing, writing, and performing to find an answer to their most intimate questions. But many remain groping in the dark. Give me the courage to join them and say to them as Philip did, 'Did you understand what you were reading?' Give me the intelligence and conviction to speak to them about you, who are the Way, the Truth, and the Life. Give me the discernment to know when they are ready to be baptized by water and the Holy Spirit.

But, please, Lord, also give me the encouragement you gave to Philip when you said to him, 'Go up and meet that chariot.' You know that I am shy and fearful. Let me be confident and free. Amen.

A Cry for Mercy

Probably no New Testament writer is as explicit about the importance of concrete acts of service as James. He writes, 'Pure, unspoilt religion, in the eyes of God our Father is this: coming to the help of orphans and widows when they need it, and keeping oneself uncontaminated by the world' (James 1:27). With considerable irony, James shows to the 'twelve tribes of the Dispersion' – i.e., the Jewish Christians scattered all over the Graeco-Roman world – the importance of concrete acts of service.

Compassion

MATTHIAS THE APOSTLE (14 MAY)

Each of us has a mission in life. Jesus prays to his Father for his followers, saying: 'As you sent me into the world, I have sent them into the world' (John 17:18).

We seldom realise fully that we are sent to fulfil God-given tasks.

We act as if *we* have to choose how, where and with whom to live. We act as if we were simply dropped down in creation and have to decide how to entertain ourselves until we die. But we were sent into the world by God, just as Jesus was. Once we start living our lives with that conviction, we will soon know what we were sent to do.

Bread for the Journey

THE VISIT OF THE BLESSED VIRGIN MARY TO ELIZABETH (31 May)

Two women [Mary and Elizabeth] who felt oppressed and isolated suddenly realize their greatness and are free to celebrate their blessing. The two of them become community. They need each other, just to be together and protect each other, support each other, and affirm each other. They stay together for three months. Then each of them is ready to face her truth without fear, willing to suffer the consequences of her motherhood.

I can hardly think of a better way to understand friendship, care, and love than 'the way of the visitation.' In a world so full of shame and guilt, we need to visit each other and offer each other a safe place where we can claim our freedom and celebrate our gifts. We need to get away once in a while from the suspicious voices and angry looks and be in a place where we are deeply understood and loved. Then we might be able to face the hostile world again, without fear and with new trust in our integrity.

Sabbatical Journey

I am deeply moved by this simple and mysterious encounter. In the midst of an unbelieving, doubting, pragmatic, and cynical world, two women meet each other and affirm in each other the promise given to them. The humanly impossible has happened to them. God has come to them to begin the salvation promised through the ages. Through these two women God has decided to change the course of history. Who could ever understand? Who could ever believe it? Who could ever let it happen? But Mary says, 'Let it happen to me,' and she immediately realizes that only Elizabeth will be able to affirm her 'yes.' For three months Mary and Elizabeth live together and encourage each other to truly accept the motherhood given to them. Mary's presence makes Elizabeth more fully aware of becoming the mother of the 'prophet of the Most High' (Luke 1:76), and Elizabeth's presence allows Mary to grow in the knowledge of becoming the mother of the 'Son of the Most High' (Luke 1:32).

Neither Mary nor Elizabeth had to wait in isolation. They could wait together and thus deepen in each other their faith in God, for whom nothing is impossible. Thus, God's most radical intervention into history was listened to and received in community.

The story of the Visitation teaches me the meaning of friendship and community. How can I ever let God's grace fully work in my life unless I live in a community of people who can affirm it, deepen it, and strengthen it? We cannot live this new life alone. God does not want to isolate us by his grace. On the contrary, he wants us to form new friendships and a new community — holy places where his grace can grow to fullness and bear fruit.

The Road to Daybreak

Pentecost: Season of the Spirit

PENTECOST

Pentecost is a dramatic moment in the liturgical year when the Spirit of God, 'aflame with his fire', fills the universe and tells of a new heaven and a new earth. Fifty days after Easter, the Spirit showers down on the apostles, signifying the birth of the Church and salvation for all in Jesus Christ. Whit Sunday inaugurates a season of joy, hope and mission, a time when the Church comes 'alive with a new breath'.

These quotations written by a Benedictine monk give a sense of the energy and passion released at Pentecost, signifying not only an historical event or a revealed truth but a spiritual reality. The red tongues of fire sometimes depicted by artists and iconographers are reminiscent of van Gogh's evergreen cypresses which grow upwards 'like green flaming tongues' as one commentator describes them. Their unbridled growth and untamed energy unleash a natural force of cosmic potential.

Pentecost is the season of spiritual energy and political dynamism.

Henri Nouwen believed that if people lived the spiritual life radically, it would affect everything they touched. Not only would it have an impact on personal growth and relationships, it would also influence economics, politics and social structures. But, none the less, one didn't live the spiritual life with the deliberate intention to make political changes or induce social transformation.

'The people who have most influence in politics are often those who are least directly focusing on it,' he told me, citing the witness of St Benedict, whose feast day falls at this time. 'Benedict changed the whole European culture not by trying to be a politician but by trying to be faithful to God and to his community. The Benedictines had an enormous effect on the social and political structures of Europe but not because they were interested in changing political structures. They were interested in being obedient to God, not being politically relevant. A lot of great saints and great spiritual people have had enormous political effect but not because they were after the effect themselves.'

I saw something of this same spirit of humility and influence in the late Cardinal Basil Hume, a Benedictine monk of Ampleforth who became leader of the Roman Catholic Church in England and Wales. Sometimes the Spirit impelled him to intervene on political issues: 'When good and evil are at stake, or when it's a question of what is good for these particular human beings, then they become moral questions. I think there is a way of trying to win other people to your point of view in a manner which respects the other person and recognises that the other person is probably carrying great burdens as well.'

Pentecost is the season when we are called to witness to the ends of the earth, no matter the political, cultural or religious obstacles that might compromise our spiritual integrity. We might even be impelled to speak out in the name of truth and justice, knowing that derision or isolation might be our only rewards. In the following selections, Henri Nouwen invites us into the inner life of God and encourages us to claim the Spirit as the guiding light of our lives, burning away our fears and anxieties and setting us free to move wherever we are sent.

THE RE-CREATING POWER OF LOVE

Pentecost is the coming of the Spirit of Jesus into the world. It is the celebration of God breaking through the boundaries of time and space and opening the whole world for the re-creating power of love. Pentecost is freedom, the freedom of the Spirit to blow where it wants.

Without Pentecost the Christ-event – the life, death, and resurrection of Jesus – remains imprisoned in history as something to remember, think about, and reflect on. The Spirit of Jesus comes to dwell within us, so that we can become living Christs here and now. Pentecost lifts the whole mystery of salvation out of its particularities and makes it into something universal, embracing all peoples, all countries, all seasons, and all eras. Pentecost is also the moment of empowering. Each individual human being can claim the Spirit of Jesus as the guiding spirit of his or her life. In that Spirit we can speak and act freely and confidently with the knowledge that the same Spirit that inspired Jesus is inspiring us.

Sabbatical Journey

THE BREATH OF LIFE

When we speak about the Holy Spirit, we speak about the breath of God, breathing in us. The Greek word for 'spirit' is *pneuma*, which means 'breath'. We are seldom aware of our breathing. It is so essential for life that we only think about it when something is wrong with it.

The Spirit of God is like our breath. God's spirit is more intimate to us than we are to ourselves. We might not often be aware of it, but without it we cannot live a 'spiritual life'. It is the Holy Spirit of God who prays in us, who offers us the gifts of love, forgiveness, kindness, goodness, gentleness, peace and joy. It is the Holy Spirit who offers us the life that death cannot destroy. Let us always pray: 'Come, Holy Spirit, come.'

Bread for the Journey

RENEWING THE WORLD

Dear Lord, when your Spirit descended upon your disciples, they spoke the languages of those who came to hear their witness. Tonight I pray that in our time your Spirit will also break through the many

barriers that divide nations and people. Let there be unity among us
who inhabit this world. Give us the strength to transcend our
physical, emotional, and psychological differences and recognize that
it is your Holy Spirit who unites us by making us all participants in
your own divine life. Let your Spirit open our eyes and ears to your
ongoing presence among us. Let us recognize you when we serve
each other, work together for reconciliation and peace, and unite our
talents to build a better world. Without your Spirit we are powerless,
but with and in your Spirit we can renew the world. Do not leave us
alone, but let your Spirit enter into our hearts so that together we can
prepare the day of your glorious return, and can praise you, thank
you, honour you, and love you all the days of our lives. Amen.

A Cry for Mercy

THE INNER LIFE OF GOD

'The Descent of the Holy Spirit,' a Russian icon painted toward the
end of the 15th century, has reminded me forcefully that a life in the
Spirit is in essence a life in community. Although I have always
known this intellectually, a long and deep encounter with this
Pentecost icon from the Russian Novgorod School has gradually
allowed this knowledge of the head to become a knowledge of the
heart.

That God reveals the fullness of divine love first of all in
community, and that the proclamation of the good news finds its
main source there has radical consequences for our lives. Because
now the question is no longer: How can I best develop my spiritual
life and share it with others? but Where do we find the community
of faith to which the Spirit of God descends and from which God's
message of hope and love can be brought as a light into the world?
Once this question becomes our main concern we can no longer
separate the spiritual life from life in community, belonging to God
from belonging to each other and seeing Christ from seeing one
another in him.

As I spent more time with this Pentecost icon, I gradually saw many new aspects of the spiritual life that other icons had not revealed to me. First, I saw how God is revealed to us at Pentecost as the God within. Then I perceived how this God within creates a new community of faith in which unity and diversity deepen each other. Finally, I discovered how this community of faith forms a vital centre from which the liberation of the world can proceed.

... Pentecost completes the mystery of God's revelation as Father, Son and Holy Spirit, and invites us to become fully part of the inner life of God. By becoming not only a God-for-us and a God-with-us, but also a God-within-us, God offers us the full knowledge of the divine life according to the promise of Jesus:

> 'The Holy Spirit,
> whom the Father will send in my name,
> will teach you everything.' (John 14:26)

The Pentecost icon draws us into the heart of the mystery of God's self-revelation. The way the apostles and evangelists are gathered together manifests the presence of the God-within. The open space portrayed between the central figures of Peter and Paul, as well as the open space created by the half oval in which the twelve are seated, indicate the new, inner space where the Spirit dwells. Jesus is no longer with his disciples. He is risen. But his absence is not an emptiness. On the contrary, his departure has created the space in which his followers can receive the fullness of the Spirit. Jesus himself had prepared them by saying,

> 'It is for your own good that I am going,
> because unless I go
> the Paraclete [the Spirit] will not come to you;
> but if I do go,
> I will send him to you ...
> He will lead you to the complete truth.'
>
> (John 16:7, 13)

With these words Jesus points forward to the new life in the Spirit that will be revealed at Pentecost. It will be a life lived in 'complete truth.' Closely related to the word 'betrothal,' the 'complete truth' means full intimacy with God, a betrothal in which the complete divine life is given to us.

Behold the Beauty of the Lord

GIVING AND RECEIVING

The fruits of the Spirit of God — joy, peace, patience, kindness, goodness, trustfulness, gentleness, and self-control (Galatians 5:22-3) — cannot be limited to interpersonal relationships. They have dimensions which far exceed the small circles of friends, family, and community. They carry in themselves a worldwide dynamic that we call mission ...

One of the most compelling qualities of life in the Spirit of Jesus is that we are always being sent out to bring and receive the gifts of God to and from all peoples and nations. It is spiritually impossible to enter into the house of God and to meet there all of humanity without coming to the inner awareness that the fruits of the Spirit grow and mature in a worldwide process of giving and receiving.

In the House of the Lord

Blood Brothers

Elias Chacour with *David Hazard*

First published in 1984, this is the moving true-life story of a Palestinian Christian striving for peace in the Middle East in the midst of one of the world's most bitter conflicts. This expanded edition includes a new epilogue.

Chosen Books, a division
of Baker Book House
£9.99
PB / 0 8007.9321 8

£3 OFF
£6.99 with voucher

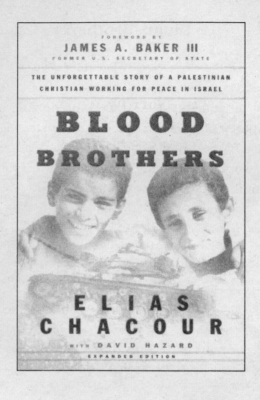

FOREWORD BY
JAMES A. BAKER III
FORMER U.S. SECRETARY OF STATE

THE UNFORGETTABLE STORY OF A PALESTINIAN
CHRISTIAN WORKING FOR PEACE IN ISRAEL

BLOOD BROTHERS

ELIAS CHACOUR

with DAVID HAZARD

EXPANDED EDITION

Published by Chosen Books, a division of Baker Book House Company
PO Box 6287, Grand Rapids, MI 49516-6287

The Narrowing Way

The bombing of our homes was a sharp blow that knocked the wind and spirit out of the people of Biram.

In the scant news I heard from Mother and Father came reports that a few more families were leaving Gish each month for the cities. Perhaps they would be better off hidden among the poor masses in a large city than perched on the open hilltops of Galilee. Understandably, they no longer wanted to stand by the elders in their continuing appeals for the return of our land. With the bombing, they had despaired.

Unbelievably, Father and my brothers continued caring for the fig trees in our confiscated orchard, which had escaped bombing. I pictured Father walking stoically past the ruins of our house. Rudah had said it was nothing but a tumble of stones and charred beams. Father, I knew, would keep his eyes and his heart set on one thing: tending the fig trees – at least for a little while longer. Silently he would plod on, hoping that his sons would follow him in bearing the cross of persecution. It was all he knew to do. Even as I admired his courage, I detected in Father a growing twinge of hopelessness. For the first time, I think, I realized that my father was human, a man with weaknesses and a limited understanding of this bewildering conflict in which we were embroiled.

As for me, I entered my second year of studies in Haifa with great listlessness. I had been away from home more than a year, and that nagging, rootless feeling left me empty. Because I was not an orphan, I was never fully accepted by the other boys. This, my early adolescence, was a bad time to be hit with so many crushing blows to my self-worth. A sense of loss – a deep mourning – threatened to cripple my spirit.

Once again, it seemed that I was not to be forsaken. In my loneliest moment, I was given the gift of a special friendship.

During the first week of classes that fall, two new boys came to study at the Bishop's school. They were Faraj and Khalil Nakhleh, and they came from a fairly well-to-do family in Ramah, another village in Galilee where there was no longer any school.

From the first moment I met Faraj, the older of the two, I sensed a special quality about him. He had a certain politeness, a joy, something quite rare that I could not touch, and yet it felt familiar. He was thirteen also, and the first thin wisps of mustache shadowed our upper lips. Though he was about my height, he was thinner, and I tended toward broad shoulders, a barrel chest and angular bones. He had a quick, easy laugh and the ability to draw me out of my grayness of spirit. Even under the heavy load of lessons, there remained a flicker of fun in his eyes. Such an immediate bond sealed between us that I, rather than Khalil, might have been taken for his brother.

What most amazed me was Faraj's unusual sensitivity. Once, when we were taken as a group to swim in the nearby Mediterranean, I drew apart from the splashing playfulness. The other children were used to my occasional solitary habits. But Faraj appeared at my side, sticking close as I trailed along the hot sand. He listened quietly, nodding and studying my face as I rambled over my confused thoughts about the plight of our families and our own future under the new government.

"'What do you think will happen to us?" I pondered aloud.

"I don't know, Elias," he replied. 'We can't go to university, that's for sure. They aren't accepting –" he stumbled over the words – "aren't accepting *our kind*."

I knew he meant Palestinians. "So what do you plan to do when we're through here? Work in a factory?"

He stopped. A sweep of white foam raced up the beach and splashed warmly over our bare feet. 'I'm not sure," he said in a moment. Sure I believe that someone will take care of us. That much I know."

Who did he mean? The Bishop? I wasn't sure what his vague answer meant, but did not pursue it.

At the moment, I needed to be alone to think. Faraj had somehow developed, in a few short weeks, the uncanny ability to read my moods. If he was boisterous and funloving, he was also sensitive. He left me to wander and trotted back down the beach to where the others were playing in the crashing waves. I found a quiet spot and sat watching the restless surf, imagining that the great swells were the hills rising around Biram.

Biram that lay in ruins.

The home and church — those two "cradles" that had taught me about the Man of Peace — now in ruins. Destroyed by the violent.

In that silence of spirit, sitting before an eternity of blue sea, a vivid image flashed before me. An image of Biram resurrected beneath the ancient olive trees, of all the ransacked homes restored and the women safe within. Palestinian and Jew — sipping coffee together again in tranquil conversation. The church was rebuilt. Each man, woman and child was like a stone — a living stone — in the rebuilt village.

For a split second, it all seemed so real — so *possible* — that my heart leaped.

Then the image was gone.

Shouting at the far end of the beach shook me from my thoughts. Three or four boys had plunged into the surf. With arms flailing, they raced while those on shore cheered. Now I could see that the one about to take the lead was Faraj. All the girls were cheering him on, which made me smile. Our interest in girls was just dawning, but Faraj was the one whose charm was already landing him in one brief romance after another. I felt a sudden surge of brotherly admiration for him.

I got up and shuffled through the sand to rejoin the group. Faraj had waded up onto the beach again where the others clapped him on the back. His chest heaved as he caught his breath, and his lips were parted in that handsome smile the girls loved. The victor.

Faraj would be a success at whatever he chose to do at school, in business. He was that sort of boy. And his family had a bit of money. Maybe they would send him to America when he was old enough. And me? What would I do?

Throughout that year and into 1953, Faraj and I grew closer together, sharing late-night secrets when we ought to have been asleep, and studying in the same classes. My grades, in fact, were quite high, which pleased the Bishop. Occasionally, he would mention to me a minor seminary he was planning to open in Nazareth, a school for young men who were seriously considering service to the Church. It would be ready to receive students the following year, in 1954. Since I would then be fifteen, he thought I was old enough to be considered.

In the fall of 1953, on one of my very rare visits to my family in Gish, I mentioned the Bishop's offer to Mother and Father. They were subdued when they met me at the bus, still grieving over the recent deaths of both my grandparents. Father, now in his fifties, had finally stopped tending the fig orchard. It had become too emotionally draining, and this heaviness showed through his usual, easy smile. But at the suggestion of seminary they both brightened a little.

"And what do *you* want to do?" Father asked.

I was about to reply, but stopped in mid-breath. It suddenly occurred to me that the decision was up to me. Three years before, it had been Father's decision that sent me to Haifa. Suddenly, I felt that I was stepping through the opening door to manhood, free and trusted and mature in the eyes of my father. I could not answer him just then, but my way was slowly becoming more clear.

Shortly after my return to Haifa, I was summoned to the Bishop's office. I knew what his question would be and yet I was in for a surprise.

When I reached his office door I paused, and he beckoned me with a wave of his hand. "Hello, Elias," he said, seated behind his desk. "Sit beside your friend."

I entered and was amazed to see Faraj sitting in one of two straight, wooden chairs in front of the Bishop's desk. We exchanged surprised looks as the Bishop began to address us.

"You've both had some time to reflect since I last spoke with you," he said, his kind, penetrating eyes moving from Faraj to me. 'Now I want to hear your decision. Are you willing to study in Nazareth, and further consider a life of service to the Church? Elias," his eyes riveted on me, "what is your decision?"

I opened my mouth and heard myself answer: "Yes. I want to study in Nazareth."

Without waiting to be asked, Faraj spoke up. "Yes. It's what I want, too."

I could not believe it! Faraj, who was so popular, so charming and such a leader – he had no idea that he was considering a contemplative life within the Church. I would have thought it of his brother Khalil – he was sometimes quiet and meditative. And yet I felt at once that Faraj's choice was right. He was so kind toward others, so keenly sensitive. Somehow I had mistakenly thought that his light, good humor excluded him from interest in spiritual things, as if anyone who wanted to serve God had to be an unhappy drudge. I certainly didn't think of myself in those terms.

The Bishop was still speaking, though now he was staring down at his hands which lay folded on the desk. "I will be honest with you boys. It is not an easy life. It requires obedience to God and to your superiors. In Nazareth you can see what it will be like. It's a challenge I extend to you."

He continued talking to us for a few minutes, telling us about our soon-coming transfer to Nazareth. I was hardly listening. Faraj shot me a quick wink, and inside I was about to burst. If the minor seminary would be a challenge at least Faraj and I would face it together.

Our transfer to Nazareth, early in 1954, marked another sharp turning point for me. Distinctly, I began to feel that my path was carrying me into the service of the Church. Strangely, this was both comforting and disturbing.

On the afternoon of our arrival at the new school, St. Joseph's Minor Seminary, Faraj and I were shepherded into a still-unfinished dormitory by a gray-robed brother. As we marched behind him, I noticed that our accommodations would be far less homey than the orphanage in Haifa. The unglazed windows were not even protected by curtains, and a brisk wind blew steadily through the room. It gave us a sharp view of Nazareth, sprawling over the valley below us – the presumed site of Mary's well and Joseph's carpentry shop. But the room was like ice. I might have known then that our days of warm nurturing by the housemothers were really over. Though life in the orphanage had been regimented out of necessity, for order and convenience, the priests and brothers at St. Joseph's would soon impress us that the rule here was regiment at all cost.

As the brother left us to stow our few belongings beside our newly assigned beds, he said brusquely, "You are expected at prayers soon. Be sure you are not late."

We settled our things, bantering and joking with the few other boys who had arrived before us. There would be just thirty-four students in all that first year. When it was time for prayers we bounded to the church that stood beside our dormitory. Noisily we burst through the entryway and were halted immediately by a stem frown from one of the brothers. Tiptoeing, we slid noiselessly onto a bench near the back.

Up at the front of the sanctuary, a brother was reading the Bible aloud in a rich, sonorous voice that echoed through the dim vastness. The last light of day edged through the windows, warming the stone-gray interior with a certain, faint glow. I glanced up at the high-vaulted ceiling, and drank in the exotic scent of incense that hung in the air. A deep silence seemed to engulf even the voice of the brother – the wonder-filled silence of eternity.

I felt a familiar thrill. To me it was like the comfortable silence between friends, a moment of quiet when nothing needs to be said–when you simply dwell in the warmth and joy of each other's presence. Yes, that's what I felt – that *familiar presence*. The hushed and worshipful atmosphere was drawing from the wells of memory in me. I was bathed again in the wilderness peace that had steeped the hills of Biram. I was reliving, in a split second, those endless days when it seemed that I was actually walking alongside my childhood Champion, Jesus. Unmistakably, I felt a rush of joy stirring in my spirit.

I sat in this inner silence, swaddled in the feeling that in this place – this church, this very bench – I was home. Here, in this presence. I had dignity again. I thought of the words of Jesus which Mother had loved to repeat time and again: "*Peace I leave with you. My peace I give you. Not as the world gives . . .* "

Now I thought I understood the longing for solitude that had become so clear in Haifa. It was not a call to abandon humanity – but a heart cry to stand alone before God. And alone with Him I could find perfect serenity. It was so comforting. Surely this was what Father had intended when he first sent me off to be trained by the Bishop. For me, the service was over too soon. I wanted to bask in the stillness forever.

As we started into our rigid school schedule, I searched for spare moments when I might slip away into the engulfing quietude of the church. There I felt close to the Fatherheart of God. Many times Faraj would join me, which I did not mind at all. I enjoyed his company, for, even when we were in the middle of a hectic day or studying for a test, he seemed to carry inside him a rare tranquility. And when we sat together in the rich quiet of the church's interior he was perfectly still. Sometimes I would open one eye and watch him. Without so much as a fluttering eyelash, he sat as if sculpted in deep contemplation.

Once while we were alone in the church, he opened his eyes and caught me watching him. He grinned at me, with that charming smile that lit up his dark eyes, and he said, "You feel Him, too – don't you?"

I was surprised. I had thought that the overshadowing presence was mostly a product of my own childhood. I did not expect the feeling to be shared by anyone else.

Apart from our visits to the church together, I began to experience a most unusual phenomenon on my own.

Many nights I would curl under the covers on my bed, listening to the rhythmic, slow breathing of the other students until I dropped off to sleep, too. Then, some time around midnight, I would wake up as if I had been shaken by someone. I would blink into the darkness, and my first thought while swimming up from the ocean of sleep was always the same: *Come to the church.* It could not have been more distinct if Faraj or one of the others were whispering in my ear.

One such night, several months after our arrival in Nazareth, I rose and dressed quietly. Then I slipped out into the mysterious and cool-moving airs of midnight. A bright moon had risen, nearly full. I entered the still sanctuary where a silver radiance glanced off the stone pillars. The glow seemed to mirror and gather high above me near the vaulted ceiling, drawing my gaze upward. I slipped quietly onto a bench, still shaking myself awake, absorbed in the beauty of the chill and echoing sanctuary I expected to find the joyful solemnity that I so often met there.

That night I felt uncomfortably on edge.

While the moon cast shadows about me, my thoughts turned to memories of Mother and Father. Of course I thought of my family often, but this night I felt something stronger than mere sentiment. In the quiet spaces of my heart, I seemed to hear a voice repeating familiar passages from the New Testament. It had been nearly eight years since I last sat on Mother's lap listening to these beautiful phrases pour from the treasure-store of her memory. Now they were not just memories, but burning words. I found myself stuck on one passage: the Beatitudes.

As a boy I had sometimes thought them enigmatic, though they had comforted me. Suddenly they were terribly disturbing. Why did they sound so embarrassingly contradictory?

How could you be meek and inherit anything in this power-hungry world? And if you tried to live in happiness and peace, wouldn't someone just kick you out of your home, bomb it and sell off your land? What did it mean to hunger and thirst for righteousness? Were the Beatitudes impossibly beyond reconciliation – uttered by Jesus merely to exercise pious young scholars?

I was amazed as these questions – gentle but provoking – barraged me. They almost seemed to be coming from outside my own thoughts.

My eyes traced the curve of an arch until it disappeared in the blackness above me, and the irony of my situation struck me: I had just found, in my midnight ventures to the church, a haven of tranquility – only to have it disturbed by this growing inner restlessness. Why was this thread of inner peace always being stretched to the breaking point?

I had stayed in the sanctuary too long, wrestling with my thoughts when I should have been back in bed asleep. All at once, I felt greatly exhausted. Instead of getting up immediately, however, I sprawled across the bench, pulling my jacket tightly about me, and tried to shut off my turbulent mind which had gone somewhat hazy with fatigue. Maybe if I lay still for a few minutes the disturbing thoughts would go away. Then I would slip back to the dormitory. I closed my eyes to rest them, just for a minute....

Someone was shaking me by the shoulder. Not the gentle shaking that had seemed to wake me at midnight, but a rough, insistent hand. I blinked. The rose glow of early sunlight colored the stone walls. I looked up into the frowning face of one of the brothers.

'What are you doing here?" he demanded.

I sat up stiffly, a little dazed, hardly knowing what to reply. I came to be alone. To pray. And I guess I fell asleep."

He seemed not to hear. "You are supposed to be in the dormitory – not out wandering in the night. There is no excuse for this."

I was stunned. Didn't he believe me? I tried to protest: I was not wandering. Nor was I making up an excuse.

In response, he lifted me by the collar. As an adolescent I was almost the same size and height as he, but I never thought to resist. Tome. We're going to the principal," he said, shoving me ahead of him.

The principal, Father Basilios Laham, was normally a kind, if somewhat strict man. This morning he peered at me questioningly from across his desk. Quickly my story tumbled out. I had gone to pray, that was all. Surely I had done no harm. Somehow I failed to impress him as a saintly, young visionary.

"I'm sorry, Elias," he replied gravely. "You have broken the rules. What would happen if we allowed every student to do just as he wished? As I am bound by the laws of the Church, so you are bound by the rules of the school. You must be punished."

For the first time, I stood face-to-face with the unbending rules of the Church as an institution. I could not understand why strict obedience to a rule was more important than a heart seeking God. Unhappy though I was, I could not fault the principal. He was just a man carrying out his job to the best of his ability. In the end I submitted, more or less quietly, to my punishment: forty days of restriction.

Unfortunately, this would not be my last exposure to the side of the Church that seemed to have forgotten the humanity it was intended to serve. Unfortunately, too, my quick tongue, which had so often gotten me in trouble as a small boy, had only gotten quicker with adolescence. On one occasion, I was sentenced to forty days of silence for disagreeing with the brothers. I wanted more Bible study and less sports activities. I was judged insubordinate and unsubmissive.

My timing was especially bad at the most obvious moments.

One day late in 1954, we were informed that the Archbishop was coming to inspect our school. Accompanying him on this visit was a very distinguished foreign dignitary, the new Ambassador from the United States to Israel. The Bishop would be coming from Haifa to be with them, eager, of course, that the very best impression be made.

Our dormitory was to be spotless, and we were warned again and again to be impeccably polite.

About a week later, in the middle of a morning lecture, there was a loud knock at the classroom door. Father Laham swept into the room along with the Bishop, the Archbishop and the Ambassador. The brother who was lecturing paled slightly, looking almost as gray as his robe. Nervously he brushed chalk dust off his fingers and extended a trembling hand to greet the dapperly dressed Ambassador. The Archbishop, who took special pride in knowing each of the prospective seminarians by name and by village of origin, began introducing us one by one. As his name was called, each student would hop to his feet, bowing his head respectfully.

After several introductions, the Archbishop turned to me and smiled warmly. I was on my feet at once. 'This is Elias Chacour," he announced broadly. "He is from Gish."

"Sorry, Archbishop," I spouted without thinking. I'm not from Gish. I'm from Birarn."

Suddenly everyone was staring at me. Even Faraj, who was used to my outspokenness, gulped. The brother, the principal and the Bishop colored in unison – though the Ambassador smiled and did not seem to notice my indiscretion. One never corrects an Archbishop.

"Biram does not exist," the Archbishop snapped piquantly. All his warmth was gone.

Bristling, I announced loudly, "But I have hopes it will exist again one day." I could not allow the suffering of my people to be erased so blithely, even in respect for an Archbishop.

Sit down!" he ordered, gritting his teeth.

After a brief, somewhat stiff chat with the poor, fidgeting brother, the visitors swept out of the room and on to tour the rest of the school. I hoped my comment would be forgotten – but no. Later I was treated to a prolonged tongue-lashing for "insolent remarks."

Alone in the dormitory, I chastised myself for not keeping a closer guard on my tongue. Why did this stubbornness persist about Biram? After all, the Archbishop was right in one sense – it *was* destroyed and

our land confiscated. What was it that refused to let me forgetto brush
it aside as the Archbishop did? He was a man of God after all. I
wished I could be more like him – or more like Faraj, who was so
agreeable. I vowed that I would try to be more quiet, more respectful and obedient to my superiors.

On one hand I felt this growing desire to serve my Church; on the
other hand a certain voice was calling me to-what? Something more?
I didn't know.

During the four years of our study at St. Joseph's, the tension would
slowly strain within me. I continued in my resolve to learn
obedience, absorbing the teachings and rules of the Church, trying
hard to mold myself into a pliable, acquiescent seminarian.

An influx of new students swelled our ranks and crowded the
dormitory, so that a few of us were asked if we would like to sleep
inside the church. I quickly volunteered, as did Faraj. Ironically, I was
then able to carry on all the latenight meditations I wanted with
impunity.

In 1955, the Zionist forces invaded Gaza, and a year later the Sinai,
that huge, wedge-like peninsula between the new state and Egypt.
With the Sinai takeover, the United States intervened, insisting that
Israel withdraw to the 1948 armistice lines. Though Prime Minister
Ben Gurion and his defense ministry conceded, they insisted that the
invasion was necessary because Israel needed a buffer zone between
itself and Egypt, whose new President Nasser was talking of uniting
the Arab nations to "liberate" Palestine. The Israeli press was flooded
with outcries against Arab aggression which reverberated around the
world. The question of Palestinian refugees – both in and out of Israel
– was obscured by sympathy for the "beleaguered" young nation.

At St. Joseph's, we watched the conflict escalate and subside, discussing the political implications with the intensity of opinionated
young men. When the fighting ceased with Israeli withdrawal, some
of the students expressed a relief that it was done with, and moreover,
that the war had been fought in the south. Though we had experi-

enced some tightening of the "emergency laws," the trouble had not touched us or our families this time. To a few of them. personal safety was all that mattered.

Such thinking bothered me greatly.

Were we really safe just because we were gathered under the protecting wings of the institutional Church? Or were we being lulled to sleep by our own personal security? Why were we not angry – or at least pained–at the suffering of our people in the hills and refugee camps?

All of this added to my continued inner conflicts. I wished I could remain serene–aloof and undisturbed by worldly conflicts as was Father, as were Faraj and the brothers of St. Joseph's. It did not occur to me then that my unquiet heart was not a bad thing. It was like a delicate balance that had been forcefully tipped and wanted righting. It produced in me a drive – like a hunger – that would carry me to the fiery heart of our land's vast conflict.

As my final two years in Nazareth passed, one conviction flickered dimly and grew: Being a servant of God meant more than drifting above earth's struggles in an other-worldly realm like some pale figure in an icon. In this, I found encouragement from an unexpected source.

Father Ghazal was a stricter teacher than most at St. Joseph's. His voice could sharpen to a metal edge when you gave the wrong answer, making him sound more like a career man in the military than a priest. Most of the students feared him. Somehow, beneath his bristly exterior, I thought I could detect a wonderfully sensitive heart, a true concern for our spiritual and intellectual progress.

I was seated in his lecture one day toward the end of 1957, when another student posed a question: How could one be a good Christian if, well – if certain people bothered you? If, he stammered hastily, you often got angry or impatient?

For a moment Father Ghazal was absolutely frozen, staring off into space in search of the right words.

Then he replied simply, "It's not enough to try to be good – to try to be some sort of 'saint.' You must let God occupy your body. You must be tamed by Him. He may put you through many hard things – and it is these struggles that will tame you. Then you will be ready to do His good pleasure."

How, I do not know, but I suddenly recalled the prayer I had uttered years before, just after we were exiled to Gish. Then I had asked God to use my hands and feet as His own. And now Father Ghazal was saying that a servant of God is never asked to do more than that – or less.

I smiled wondering if it were really possible that God had taken me up on my childlike prayer, guiding me first into the care of the Bishop and then here to St. Joseph's. And more than that, I wondered if God had allowed me to feel His own heart's concern for the Palestinian people. But whenever I thought about the war, the bombing or my beating, some awful twisting thing burned inside of me – something that had yet to be tamed.

Despite the feeling, I had a flicker of conviction: I was to study, not just for ordination in the Church, but as a messenger to my people. Even so, I was amused at the thought. What was my message? That everyone should leave their villages and become contemplative in cloisters?

I glanced across the room at Faraj. His brows were knit in intense thought. I wished I could read his expression and know his response to Father Ghazal's comments. Since we were nearing the end of our schooling in Nazareth, we would both be expected to declare our intentions formally. Would he feel as I did?

Our entire last year was one in which I pondered my direction. A tingle of indignation burned inside me each time I heard of another tightening of the "emergency laws" that governed Palestinians in Israel – each time another village had its farm land confiscated for a *kibbutz*. At the edge of my thoughts, I wondered how I could deliver a message of heavenly peace to people – Jew or Palestinianwhen they lived daily with war.

One evening in the spring of 1958, as we moved into our final semester at St. Joseph's, Faraj and I were alone in our church quarters, studying for a test. I sensed him watching me and looked up from my page.

Faraj shut his book abruptly and a sheaf of paper fluttered to the floor. He sat up and braced his long, willowy arms across his chest. We were both nearly nineteen, and while I had continued to thicken at the chest and shoulders, he had stayed slender as he grew. He stretched out his lean legs, and I retrieved his paper from the floor. Curious, I asked, "What is it? What are you thinking?"

"Elias," he began, "we've grown up just like brothers. Do you know we've been together for almost six years? And it won't be long until St. Joseph's is through with us."

"That's true. And ... ?" I smiled, wondering what my alter-ego was getting at. He lay back on his mattress, hands braced behind his head. Suddenly he unfolded a vision of the future-our future.

"You know the Bishop is making inquiries at the seminary in Jerusalem. If things work out, we can go there together. Won't that be great? We can go together as brothers, Elias. We are brothers, aren't we?"

My heart leaped at his words: "seminary ... together ....."

He went on. 'And after seminary – after we're ordained – we can have a church together maybe. I've been thinking of the things Father Ghazal said about letting God occupy your body. That's what we can do. We can live simply, sharing all things in common, fifty-fifty, just like the early Christians. We can live peacefully among the poor. We can give our lives to serving them ......"

He talked on for some time, building a bright dream. It touched my deepest wound-the need for a home, a sense of *place*. It sounded so comforting, so easy. When he finished, I found myself agreeing to his plan, eagerly trying to fill my emptiness with someone else's dream. And in that moment, I shoved aside the unsettling thoughts and the challenging voice that beckoned me.

Daily we talked with increasing excitement about the vows we would take to live lives of charity, humility, obedience, extending

God's hand of love through the villages of Galilee. We would live, I thought, as Father did, in poorness of spirit, holding everything we had in open hands before God.

However, our dream flickered once, chilled by a harsh breath of reality.

During our last weeks at St. Joseph's, while we struggled under the pressure of final examinations, the Bishop delivered one more bit of hard-hitting news. Holding back tears of pain and anger, his eyes welled as he told us evenly, "You cannot go to Jerusalem. The authorities will not allow you to cross the border to the seminary."

The seminary, a very old Melkite school, lay outside the borders of Israel in the part of Jerusalem apportioned by the United Nations to the kingdom of Jordan. The Jordanians, the Bishop explained, did not want "contaminated Palestinians from occupied territories" coming to study in their sector of the city. Although it was the closest seminary, and though our expressed intent was to serve the Church, the Bishop had no power to sway the authorities. We were barred from entering Jordan's territory. And once again our people had been maligned with a variation of that hideous phrase, "dirty Palestinians." How I hated that!

The Bishop, in his resourcefulness, was not about to let this snag tear his net, allowing two live seminarians to get away. He quickly made inquiries through his connections in the Church hierarchy, and in a week he announced, "Elias. Faraj. You will go to study at Saint Sulpice. A good school, a very good school – in Paris. I've made all the arrangements."

In Paris? We were stunned. Neither of us had been outside of Galilee, except for our sheltered schooling in Haifa, let alone to far-off hinterlands such as Europe. But the Bishop had decided. That was that.

When I returned to Gish after graduation, the reaction of my family was as mixed as my own. Mother and Father were delighted that one of their sons would study for ordination. But in Paris? In their thinking, no one ever went to Europe and returned. As all my remaining relatives gathered to see me off, I saw the sadness behind their smiles.

When it was time to leave, Wardi and my brothers hugged me one by one. Mother and Father clutched me close to them one last time, and then released me — as parents have always set their children free in the world — with a mixture of happiness and heartache. And now I had a sense — comforting and challenging at the same time — that my way was narrowing before me.

A week later, Faraj and I tried to get our sea legs on the rolling deck of the ship that carried us away from the port at Haifa. We stood side by side like two brothers, tall, eager and still quite sheltered about things of the world. The Bishop had given us a little money — the equivalent of ten dollars — to get us from our European port of entry in Naples, Italy, to Rome. There, he had assured us, one of his contacts would be waiting to help us. Holding onto the rail for balance, we stared in silence as the green shoreline of our land faded and was gone.

"More than six years, Elias," Farajs voice broke the concentration. "That's a long time to be away."

I felt a tightening in my throat ánd could not answer. Once again the raging conflict that was Israel had driven my family apart.

I could not guess the pressures that would slowly grind and pulverize our already crippled villages. In my heart was the shining plan to return and live simply, quietly among my people, dispensing the charities of the Church. I had no thought that my life was about to take another sharp turn-that my dream of a peaceful life in service with Faraj would never be. An astonishing awakening lay ahead of me.

When we left the deck, our mood lightened a bit. And then our conversation turned to Paris.

The Lost Message Of Jesus

Steve Chalke & Alan Mann

In his new book, top Christian communicator Steve Chalke invites the reader to rediscover the real Jesus in his own world, challenging many of our preconceptions about who we think he is. Focusing on key incidents as recorded in the gospels, readers will be challenged afresh by the radical, life-changing message of Jesus.

Zonderman
£8.99
PB / 0 3102.4882 5

£2 OFF
£6.99 with voucher

steve chalke
& alan mann

the lost
message
of Jesus

Right Here, Right Now

One of the most harrowing images of the twentieth century was caught on film in 1972 on the outskirts of the Vietnamese village of Trang Bang. The now-famous photograph captures Kim Phuc, a nine-year-old girl, running down a road with outstretched arms, her face etched with terror and pain. The naked girl is screaming in agony from the terrible burns inflicted on her just minutes earlier by a napalm attack on her home. It was a picture that shocked the world, bringing the pain of war momentarily home to tens of millions of ordinary people. But for John Plummer, one of the helicopter pilots involved in that fateful raid, this image would haunt him daily for the next twenty-four years.

On Veterans Day in 1996, hundreds of former soldiers gathered at the foot of the Vietnam Memorial in Washington, DC to remember their colleagues lost in a war fought a quarter of a century earlier. Among them stood John Plummer, still unable to come to terms with what he had done, his life destroyed by inner turmoil. But unknown to him, this day would change his life forever. As he watched the ceremony unfold, to his and everyone else's surprise, a Vietnamese woman stepped forward to lay a wreath alongside the others at the foot of the memorial. She turned to address the crowd. Kim Phuc told the hushed audience her story, one of tortured years of psychological and physical suffering. Then, as if it were the easiest thing in the world, Kim gently added that she now no longer held any bitterness towards the men responsible for bombing her village. At last, she had found a sense of peace through the act of forgiving them.

Weeping uncontrollably, John found himself pushing through the crowd. He knew that he desperately needed the forgiveness, acceptance and peace that only Kim. could grant him. Somehow, despite the mass of people and Kim's police escort, he managed to get her attention. "Kim saw my grief, my pain, my sorrow," he later recalled. "She held out her arms to me and embraced me. All I could say was 'I'm sorry; I'm sorry over and over again. And at the same time she was saying, 'It's all right, I forgive you.'" As Plummer went on to testify, the twenty-four years of torment he had endured were wiped away forever in those two short minutes.

Kim's story is powerful. How did she find the strength to forgive the men who had killed so many members of her family and had sentenced her to a life of emotional and physical pain? From where did she get the courage to come to Washington, DC to lay down that wreath? Or the grace to embrace John Plummer?

Our culture is fascinated by such accounts of forgiveness against the odds. Lifestyle magazines run countless articles about the power of forgiveness, while daytime television chat shows regularly invite guests to reveal their deepest emotional scars and explore the benefits of learning to forgive. Meanwhile, we nod in agreement with the experts who tell us unforgiveness is a cancer that eats you from the inside and that the act of forgiving is healing and renewing. It may be a hard pathway to tread, but it is ultimately easier than any of the alternatives.

So when we read Jesus' question to the religious leaders of his day," Is it easier for me to tell this crippled man that his sins are forgiven or to tell him to get up and walk?" (Luke 5:23), the answer to us is obvious. Living in an age that struggles with the concept of the "miraculous", for us telling a crippled man to get up and walk seems an infinitely more difficult option than the comparatively simple act of granting forgiveness, especially when the "sins" committed in the first place were not against us personally. Yet in first-century Israel, things were very different, clues to which can still be found in modern times.

In 1985, the then President of the United States, Ronald Reagan, caused huge offence to many in the American Jewish community when he visited the military cemetery at Bitburg, Germany, where several SS officers are buried. In the resulting media frenzy, the question was raised as to why many Jewish people remained unforgiving so many years after the Holocaust. One eminent rabbi, reflecting the Jewish law passed down through the ages, replied, "Even if I were asked by a perpetrator to forgive him for this crime, a rabbi is not empowered to give absolution or to be a pardoner. Only God has the right to forgive."

In Jesus' culture, forgiveness was a prerogative of God alone. Ordinary people couldn't go around just granting forgiveness. But that didn't seem to bother Jesus. He gave forgiveness away with an authority that rocked the foundations of his world to the core. As the Pharisees gasped, "Jesus must think he is God!" (Luke 5:21).

A One-Man Temple System

To grasp why the Pharisees and the chief priests were so angered by Jesus' actions and statements, we need a fuller understanding of the Jerusalem temple. According to the renowned New Testament scholar E. P. Sanders, it is impossible to overvalue the role of the temple in the lives of Jesus' contemporaries. It was the nerve-centre of the Jewish religious faith, a hive of activity where the daily ritual of sacrifice dealt with the sins of individuals as well as the whole nation.

At the centre of this "sin-busting", forgiveness-bestowing machine was what was known as the Holy of Holies, where God's presence was believed to be enshrined. According to the Jews, this was literally where heaven met earth, a belief that led to their claim that Israel was at the very heart of Creation and that from there God reigned over the entire universe. This "Israel-centric" or "Zionist" view of the cosmos put them in a pretty key position in terms of the unfolding of history. To put it bluntly, the temple was very good for the Jewish elite's sense of self-worth (not to mention their bank accounts!). In fact, it had become their central cultural icon; a social, political and religious symbol of hope; a constant reminder that God had not deserted them, that he would one day rid them of their enemies and grant them the freedom they so desperately craved.

When Jesus started forgiving people on hillsides, in their own houses and out on the streets, it was as though total anarchy had broken out. His actions amounted to nothing less than a massive threat to the entire religious, political and social fabric of Israel. By offering forgiveness of sins, "right here, right now" and for free, he was deliberately bypassing the entire temple system. In effect, he was announcing that it was redundant, irrelevant and obsolete. No-one could doubt that not only did Jesus see himself as a rival to the temple, but that with each act of forgiveness he was declaring war on it and the massive bureaucracy that surrounded it. Upon reaching Jerusalem he decided to take the whole system on, head-to-head.

The temple had become a huge filtration system for the religious leaders and chief priests to bar and exclude any who were deemed undesirable from access to God. For a start, non-Jews could only get as far as the outer square – the Court of the Gentiles, where the moneychangers worked. Though Jewish women could get a little further into a specially designated area (the Court of the Women), they were still kept clear of the centre of things. Jewish men – at least those judged not to be physically disfigured or disabled – were allowed to go one level deeper, into the Court of Israel, but beyond this point only priests could enter. Finally came the most sacred point, the Holy of Holies, which could only be entered by the chief priest once a year on the Day of Atonement. In fact, in the eyes of Israel's religious elite, the distance you were allowed to travel towards the heart of the temple directly related to your status in society.

So when Jesus overturned the tables of the money-changers in the outer court of the temple (Matthew 21:12-17), his point couldn't have been clearer. This group of men were responsible for exchanging the normal currency for special temple money known as Tyrian Shekels. Without this no animal or bird could be bought for the purpose of sacrifice in order to obtain forgiveness. Jesus' act of vandalism and his judgement that these henchmen of the teachers of the law and the chief priests had turned the temple into "a den of robbers" (Matthew 21:13 NIV) echoed that of Jeremiah, "Be fair and honest with each other. Stop taking advantage of the foreigners, orphans, and widows ... You are thieves, and you have made my temple your hideout" (Jeremiah 7:5-6, 11).

Much of the Jewish leaders' wealth was derived from the exploitation of those they were actually supposed to be helping. They used the temple to both justify and perpetuate their pocket-lining practices. However, Jesus' greatest complaint against the temple officials wasn't the bad exchange rate; it was that they had dared to put a price on forgiveness at all, when God had always intended it to be free.

Jesus singled out the money-changers for special attention because they were the "turn-stile" keepers everyone had to get past in order to stand a chance of being forgiven and accepted back into the worshipping community of Israel. They were effectively the temple's bouncers, security men armed with a list of undesirables issued by the religious leaders. If your name was on that list, you were barred access and no amount of money or sacrifices would ever get you in. So, for Jesus, although the temple was supposed to be a "house of worship for all nations" (Isaiah 56:7) and a place of inclusiveness and welcome for all, it had become the exact opposite. It had become a symbol of jewish exclusiveness and discrimination – and as such it had to go!

Jesus' outburst, however, was no spur-of-the-moment, hotheaded protest. His action was not only pre-planned (Mark 11:11), it was designed to render the whole temple system temporarily obsolete. As the money-changers groped around on the floor for their spilled coins and the salesmen chased pigeons that were intended for sacrifice, the "official" vehicle of forgiveness became non-operational

– closed for business. And what's more, as N. T. Wright has pointed out, in the confusion Matthew tells us that "blind and lame people came to Jesus in the temple, and he healed them" (21:14). Those deliberately excluded by the Pharisees had somehow pushed passed the distracted officials and got into the temple precincts, perhaps for the first time in their lives.

The Spittle of Forgiveness

Among the Masai of East Africa, a son can perpetrate no greater crime than to offend his father by committing a direct sin against him. The magnitude of this offence is reflected in the fact that such a sin is believed to be in danger of destroying the whole community, not just the relationship between the father and the son. As a result the son becomes an outcast, banished from his tribe, shunned by family and friends, who are afraid of being cursed by the sin that has taken hold of him. This is taken so seriously that the son can find himself an outcast for months, years or even an entire lifetime. But, as the missionary Vincent Donovan discovered, there is hope.

Spittle is a very sacred element to the Masai. It represents the actual life of a living, breathing human being. Though in our culture, to spit on someone is an insult, for the Masai it is a sign of forgiveness and love. But, just like the Jews, the Masai believe that only God can forgive. Therefore, a father can spend hours, even weeks and sometimes months praying and pleading for God to provide him with the spittle of forgiveness so he can then forgive his wayward son. If and when the word is given, it has to spread fast. The son is tracked down and brought to the father, who waits with the elders back in the village. The two meet at the very centre of the village where the son is expected to ask for the father's forgiveness. Then, and only then, will the father spit on his son and so forgive him. The act of the forgiveness is then marked by a great celebration that the son has returned.

In the parable of the Prodigal Son in which Jesus tells how the wayward sibling, after effectively wishing that his father was dead by arrogantly asking for his share of the family inheritance, leaves home and heads off to discover what the world has to offer (Luke 15:11-32). The story is well known – how he squanders his money, ends up homeless and hungry and is forced to take a menial job feeding pigs – hardly the greatest career move for a Jew.

However, when the son finally comes to his senses and beats a pathway home, he doesn't find an angry father waiting for him, but nor has his father had to wrestle for months for the spittle of forgiveness. The son found that he couldn't barter or bargain his way back into his father's heart because the father's heart had been held in a permanent, unwavering attitude of forgiveness since day one. Likewise, there were no punishments or tasks to undertake in order to receive forgiveness, because his father had never removed his love for his son in the first place. And furthermore, there were not even any lectures to face, because when it comes to the God of the Bible there is only one kind of sin in the world -forgiven sin. As Martin Luther King Jr, once said," Forgiveness is not an occasional act; it is a permanent attitude."

But another character in this story seldom gets a mention when we retell it in our Sunday schools or preach it from our pulpits – the father's other son, the prodigal's elder brother. He finds himself unwilling or unable to accept that his father has not only forgiven his younger, "sinful" brother, but that he has also been received back into the family with great fuss and honour. While we may gloss over him, it is this character that Jesus' audience would have picked up on. Jesus often took well-known Jewish folk stories or sayings and used them to make a telling point by adding a startling twist. In this case, he extends the story beyond what was likely to have been the traditional ending (the celebration of the return of the wayward son) and adds the details of the elder son's response to the homecoming of his younger brother.

The point Jesus was making is startlingly clear: God's attitude to the prodigals of Israel (the "sinners") was completely different to that of the religious leader's (the older brother). The spittle of forgiveness was free and available at any time, for all who came seeking it. And though the parable of the Prodigal Son makes the point as plain as daylight, Jesus' constant offering of "free forgiveness" out on the streets, and in the episode at the temple, said it louder than ever.

An Exceptional Case

In the Gospel of Luke, the story is told of a man with leprosy who, seeking to be healed, approached Jesus. Jesus, we are told, had compassion on him and cured him. But then he adds, curiously, to us: "Don't tell anyone about this, but go and show yourself to the priest. Offer a gift to the priest, just as Moses commanded, and everyone will know that you have been healed" (Luke 5:14). This is the only time that Jesus sends anybody he has healed or forgiven to the temple – but why? Is it because he is having second thoughts? If he really does believe in free forgiveness, right here, right now, out on the streets, then why is he compromising by sending this man to the temple?

The answer parallels a current practice in the UK. If you are sick for an extended period and have to take time off work, an employer will require you to obtain a certificate, a "sick-note", from your doctor to prove the genuineness of your illness. There's no time-out without the necessary paperwork. In Israel the situation was the exact reverse. If a person who was sick or disabled wished to be accepted back into the community, they had to have proof that the source of their original exclusion was gone – that they had been cured or healed of their infirmity. For someone who had been blind or lame and could now walk, the evidence was obvious to all. But for someone suffering from leprosy, only the signed word of a priest was good enough for the people to believe that the disease was actually and permanently cured.

Jesus knew precisely how the system worked. People were so fearful of this disease that anyone suffering from leprosy was forced to scrape out an existence totally isolated from the rest of society. Only a recognized certificate of proof from someone in authority would get them what they really wanted and desperately needed – acceptance and social inclusion. So there was no point in this man boasting of his healing to his family, friends or the wider community – no matter how well he now appeared to be and no matter how much they believed him. Unless he was given the official okay from the priest, he would still suffer as an outcast.

One Temple, One God

Jesus' early followers didn't have any doubt that he was human – after all they had seen him, spoken to him and eaten with him. Their big question was whether he was God. In contrast, twenty-first century Christians have the opposite problem – we are convinced Jesus is God, but we too often forget that he was human. But interestingly, when we are actually pinned down as to why we believe in Jesus' divinity, we begin to struggle. We end up scrambling around for the odd verse where we are semi-confident that Jesus was claiming that this is the case. But trying to find verses where Jesus explicitly says he is divine is like trying to find needles in a haystack. As we have already seen, the kind of verses we cling to (Peter's declaration in Matthew 16:16, "You are the Messiah, the Son of the living God," and Jesus' reply, "You're right! I am"; or the Jewish authorities' challenge to Jesus, "Are you the Messiah?" and his response "Yes I am" in Mark 14:61-62) had nothing to do with a claim to divinity. In staking his claim to be the Messiah, he wasn't claiming divinity

Ultimately, while there is a distinct absence of short, sharp "I am God" sound bites from Jesus, the Gospels are simply loaded through his actions with explicit evidence that unambiguously declare over and over his divinity. Indeed, people could hardly be in Jesus' presence for as long as a day without having to face up to the reality of his "outrageous" claim. His actions were designed to send a very clear message to the temple, its officials and the whole religious system: "This town ain't big enough for the both of us!"

As far as Jesus was concerned, he was the real temple and as such, forgiveness belonged out on the streets, available to all without cost through him. The presence of God wasn't to be trapped behind the stone walls of some grand building, only accessible to the privileged few. God was living with the ordinary people in their villages and towns, not in the Holy of Holies where those born into privilege could only access him once a year. To everyone who encountered him, Jesus' message was becoming inescapable: "The Kingdom, the in-breaking shalom of God, is available now to everyone through me, because I am the living temple, I am God on earth."

The Provocative Church

Graham Tomlin

A new edition of the book that has helped many churches rethink their attitudes to evangelism. The author argues for a church that takes seriously the need to be intriguing to the outside world.

SPCK
£9.99
PB / 0 2810.5641 2

£2 OFF
£7.99 with voucher

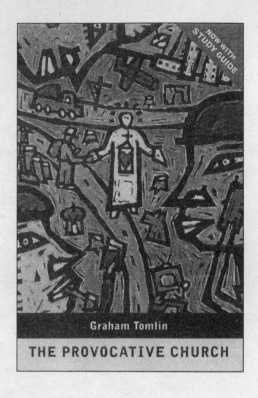

NOW WITH STUDY GUIDE

Graham Tomlin

THE PROVOCATIVE CHURCH

Published by Society for Promoting Christian Knowledge
Holy Trinity Church, Marylebone Road, London NW1 4DU

Evangelism that Works and Evangelism that Doesn't

John Diamond was a journalist for the London Times. He died of cancer in March 2001, and became widely known in the UK for a series of penetrating and disarmingly honest articles on his struggles with the disease. Along with his book *C: Because Cowards Get Cancer* too, these helped many people discover a new approach to dying. Two months before his death, he wrote in characteristically courteous tones about the many Christians who had read his column and e-mailed him with spiritual answers.

> There is no level at which the evangelists and I can engage. They tell me about their spiritual product as if I might not have come across it before . . . as if in 47 years of living in a Christian country I might not yet have stumbled upon the concept of Christ as redeemer. . . They don't seem to understand that I can't force myself to believe what I don't believe. Which is the point at which agnostics usually say 'I only wish I could believe', and I used to say that myself. But I've discovered that it's not true. I'm happy not believing, and that's what the evangelists don't seem to understand.[1]

The words are worth pondering slowly. Sometimes Christians assume that people 'out there' are eager to listen to what the Church has to say. The only problem is learning how to say it louder and more clearly. Yet, over the past few decades, indications suggest that more and more people are exactly like John Diamond. Not hostile to or uninformed about Christianity, often interested in spiritual questions and prepared to face the difficult issues of mortality and meaning. And yet the Church is the last place they would look for answers. With a note of sadness, the journalist Paul Vallely (himself a practising Christian) says: 'For most people today, the Church no longer says anything worthwhile.'

Churches around the country are working hard at turning this around and slowly but surely, many are finding ways of reaching those outside their walls. Alpha, Emmaus, Christianity Explored and other 'process evangelism' courses have proved excellent tools to pick up those people, often on the fringes of church life, who are interested to find out more about Christianity. Yet what about those like John Diamond, who are simply 'happy not believing'? Those who are not particularly interested to find out more? Those who wouldn't choose to come on an Alpha course, even if they were invited to do so? Those whose point is not that they don't believe, but that they don't want to believe? What would provoke them to think the Church had anything worth listening to?

So far, so bleak. However, God is not dead. Nor has he yet given up on the churches in the West, even if it's the ones in places like South East Asia or South America that are thriving. Despite the well-documented weakness of many of our churches, people still do become Christians today, even from the hard-nosed worlds of the media, journalism and politics. One of the best ways of learning is to listen to people's stories. Another, very different tale perhaps might help us glimpse a way ahead.

Finding Jesus

Derek Draper was a successful political lobbyist who subsequently worked behind the scenes for the Labour government in London. A bout of clubbing, cocaine and Ecstasy tablets in the mid-1990s, along with a very public scandal about political corruption, led to depression and resignation from his government work. Having been told by therapists that he needed some kind of 'spirituality' to balance his life, and finding yoga, New Age remedies and Buddhism all lacking something, a powerful experience on a visit to Westminster Abbey was followed up by an invitation to his local church, a high Anglican parish with an attractive mixture of the solemn and the informal. The impact is probably best described in his own words:

> I started to discover Jesus Christ, his life and teachings. I'm still learning about the liturgy, and there's no doubt that as I read I struggle both with aspects of the Bible, especially the Old Testament, and with the actions, past and present, of the organized church. What I know, though, is that none of that matters too much. The core of my Christianity is a belief in the wisdom of Jesus' words as told in the Gospels. Now I look back on that time of excess in the mid to late nineties (work, money, drink, drugs, sex, power) with horror. I'm going to try to live my life according to what Jesus laid down 2,000 years ago. I used to live a shallow, materialistic life. I was impatient and intolerant. Now, I try to think and act with others in mind. It's a nauseous idea to many, but there is no other way of putting it: 'God is love,' says the Bible, and that is what I bear in mind now – love for everyone I meet, unconditional, patient and kind.[2]

Interesting. In fact there are quite a few fascinating things about this account. First, Derek Draper was drawn to the spiritual search by a moment of crisis. Depression and drugs are a potent combination, and usually add up to despair. While he was living his successful political career, high on adrenalin, narcotics and power, Christianity was not remotely even on the horizon. It took something to stop him in his tracks, to make him think again. It's a fairly typical Prodigal Son story, substituting advertising and politics for the far country, and a rehabilitation clinic for the pigsty, but it follows a well-trodden route – through despair to discovery, through sleaze to salvation. Despite affluence, financial security and even the pleasures of family and friends, crises still hit people's lives now as much as they ever did. The questions of why there is life at all, what it means and how it is to be lived have still not gone away, even if the Christian answers seem less obviously true than they used to.

However, cancer too is a moment of crisis and, as John Diamond teaches us, crises on their own don't inevitably lead someone to God. The question is whether and how Christians can offer something at moments of such crisis to open up a viable way ahead, which satisfies the restless soul, and which answers the questions that are being asked, rather the ones we Christians like answering. This leads us to the second thing: it happened through a church – a provocative church.

We sometimes say these days that people don't tend to drop into churches very often. Maybe it's true. Maybe they don't do it as much as they used to. However, at least Derek Draper did, and the key question was what he found there when he turned up. At that stage his interest in Christianity was on a par with his interest in yoga, Buddhism and ancient Japanese healing. In other words, pretty standard for someone on the spiritual search today. Like many others, he dipped his toe into the water of each of these pools and, naturally enough, was drawn to the one which felt right.

A number of years ago I was given the difficult job of organizing a study day for students in two very different church institutions, without it ending up in theological warfare. I decided to get them all out on the streets, using a basic questionnaire to ask ordinary people about their impression of church. One finding that surprised us all was the very high number of people who had been inside a church within the past year. Whether it was a baptism, a funeral, a wedding, invited by a friend, just dropping in for some peace and quiet, or just trying it out, we were amazed by how many people had drifted in. The other side of the coin, however, was that they had also drifted out. Presumably there was little there to make them want to come back. Derek Draper's church was different. There was something about it which gripped him:

That Sunday, I walked into a church service for the first time since I was thirteen. I had stumbled upon the perfect church for me . . . the splendour of the robes, the incense and the beautiful choir mix with an informality that was summed up on All Saints' Day, when two altar boys mounted the steps with day-glo trainers showing under their vestments. That first Sunday, the vicar managed to combine a sermon addressing fear with a genuinely funny joke . . . I was hooked.

The point is not the style of worship – similar stories can be told of less liturgical churches. The point is rather that he sensed something real, different and distinct in the life of that church as they met together: something provocative. It makes me ask the question of my local church – if he had dropped in there, would it also have made him come back for more?

Third, what interests me is the word he uses to describe what attracted him about Jesus: What appealed to him was the practical *wisdom* of the teaching of Jesus. We might have wanted him to come armed with a number of key theological questions, such as 'Where can I find forgiveness for my sins?' or 'Is this logically coherent?' but, doctrinally at least, it wasn't as clearly formed as that and it rarely is.

He was looking not for a guaranteed place in heaven, or guilt forgiven, but quite simply a better and less superficial way of life. It was the prospect of learning a style of life steered by the priority of love, which seemed so much better, richer and more fulfilling than anything he had found elsewhere. It was not so much the ideas and intellectual content of faith that were at issue, but Christianity as a way of life. Christian doctrine and the Bible became valued not primarily because they could be shown to be objectively 'true', but because they were the foundations of a healthier and more rounded existence. Perhaps this shouldn't surprise us, if we know anything about the postmodern condition with its suspicion of truth, or even the Bible and its vision of an incarnate Word, but here was a search for something spiritually satisfying and practically workable.

Douglas Coupland is a perceptive Canadian author, who wrote the book and coined the term 'Generation X' to describe the children of the 1980s, born into affluence and apathy, committed to nothing, laid back and heavily overdosed on irony. In one of his books, *Life after God*, he writes of this generation as the first to have grown up without any sense of God at all – their parents were at least taught the basics of Christianity as they grew up, only to reject it as adults. Now their children are emerging into life after God. Towards the end of the book, the character at the heart of the story, drifting off alone into the wild in search of something almost indefinable, expresses his heartfelt desires:

> Now – here is my secret: I tell it to you with an openness of heart that I doubt I shall ever achieve again, so I pray that you are in a quiet room as you hear these words. My secret is that I need God – that I am sick and can no longer make it alone. I need God to help me give, because I am no longer capable of giving; to help me to be kind, as I no longer seem capable of kindness; to help me to love, as I seem beyond being able to love.[3]

Over the past few years, I have occasionally heard this quotation used by Christian preachers and apologists: at last here is a true postmodern telling us that God is necessary after all. Yet I wonder if the most important thing here is not the fact that he needs God, but the way in which he expresses his need for God. Like Derek Draper, he doesn't sense a need for God to forgive him, teach him the truth, or to satisfy his curiosity about the origins of the universe. Instead, he needs something or someone who can help him learn how to give, to be kind and to love. Now a Christian would want to say that we learn these things by first learning that there is a God who gives to us, who is kind to us, who loves us with a passion far deeper than we can ever fathom. You can never separate Christian doctrine from Christian ethics. Yet the question is framed in this way – he wants to learn these moral qualities, which he knows are essential to human flourishing, and looks for a place where he can learn them.

These three lessons put together offer some directions for the way ahead. They tell us that the questions are still there; they tell us that the quality of church life is a vitally important issue for evangelism, and they tell us that if Christian faith can offer a radically different agenda, a distinctive style of life to those available elsewhere, it will have a great appeal to many people. Yet, somehow, we have to come clean, and admit that very often, it isn't working.

The Church and the Spiritual Search

It's a commonplace in both church and non-church circles to say that despite all the prophecies of wholesale secularization, interest in spirituality and the spiritual search are growing, not declining, today. Buddhism, yoga, meditation techniques, feng shui and New Age therapies are all suddenly respectable, and have begun to creep into respectable Sunday supplements. Religion and spirituality sections of high-street bookshops are far more likely to stock titles such as *The Spiritual Teaching of the Tao* or *The Dalai Lama's Book of Wisdom* than the most recent volumes in Christian theology. Yet the secularists are right in that this spiritual search has not seen a mass return to Christianity. In fact, church is often the last place that people who read such books would look for something truly 'spiritual'. It's estimated that around two-thirds of those who have become seriously involved in New Agetype practices and beliefs have tried church at some time or other, and found it had nothing to offer.[4] Christianity seems part of the old world being left behind, not the new age that is coming.

If there is this large-scale turning towards spirituality, why then has Christianity not seen the benefit? Two broad reasons might be given. On the one hand, there are things in Christian theology that cut directly across postmodern and New Age concerns. Christians do believe there is such a thing as truth and that it can be found. They believe that there are kinds of behaviour that are objectively right or wrong. And what is more, the Christian faith has always declared that Jesus is the one and only Lord of heaven and earth, a claim most postmoderns would shudder at.

More important perhaps is the second reason, which is that, as

Bishop Nigel MacCulloch puts it, 'the issue that the churches must face up to ... is not so much that people do not believe in God, but that they do not find the churches credible'.[5] There is something missing, something that a postmodern generation looks for but fails to find in church life. Jean Baudrillard, commenting as he so often does on the way in which postmodern culture is dominated by the surface image, writes some prophetic words: 'None of our societies know how to manage their mourning for the real.'[6] A sense of a lack of depth, a lack of reality pervades this culture so much that no one quite knows any more what is real and what is fake. For Baudrillard, this nostalgia for reality is one of the key hallmarks of a postmodern world.

Graham Cray, a perceptive commentator on postmodern culture, tells of a student who commented after a presentation of the Christian gospel: 'It doesn't seem real. It seems true, but it doesn't seem real.'

George Monbiot, the author of the influential book *Captive State*, and a key figure in the anti-globalization movement, describes himself as 'not religious'. Yet he speaks for many when he offers his reasons for drifting away from church:

> I was brought up with the classic middle-class Anglican stance, which effectively means plenty of form, and very little function, and just a semblance of belief – going through the ritual of going to church on Sunday morning but not allowing your professed belief to interfere in any way with the way you lead your life. It's a very easy ethos to shed, because it isn't really an ethos at all ... What counts is what churches do, much more than what they profess ... they must match the positive things they say with action.[7]

Put Baudrillard, the anonymous student and George Monbiot together and again we find another clue to why the churches don't seem to appeal. It's not so much a lack of truth (there are many words in churches, claiming and even demonstrating truth) but a missing connection between the words uttered and the style of life that results from it: a lack of authenticity, of depth, of correlation between words, images and reality.

To put it bluntly, church attendance sometimes doesn't seem to make any great difference to people's lives. If going to church and calling myself a Christian makes almost no discernible difference to the way I live my life, spend my money or use my time, then it is not surprising if my friends who are not Christians are not that interested in finding out any more about it.

One of the key themes of this book is that unless there is something about church, or Christians, or Christian faith that intrigues, provokes or entices, then all the evangelism in the world will fall on deaf ears. If churches cannot convey a sense of 'reality' then all our 'truth' will count for nothing. Unless someone wants to hear, there's no point in shouting louder. Churches need to become provocative, arresting places which make the searcher, the casual visitor, want to come back for more.

Now this might seem just a pragmatic point about supply and demand. However, there is an important theological dimension to it as well. To put it simply, the Christian God can only be found by those who desire him. The point can perhaps best be explained in the words of the great seventeenth-century Christian apologist, Blaise Pascal.

The God of the Philosophers and the God of Jesus Christ

Pascal never saw his fortieth birthday. He was an anguished, illness-ridden, often lonely man who, at the cutting edge of contemporary scientific experimentation, felt keenly the intellectual ferment of his times. One November night in 1654, he experienced a profound encounter with God, which turned a distant and arid faith into a gripping sense of mission and devotion. He died eight years later in voluntary poverty, leaving behind scattered papers, probably intended as a grand apology for Christianity. These were subsequently gathered together and published by his friends as the famous *Pensées*: 'Thoughts on religion and various other subjects'.

Among these fragments, two simple points are made again and again. First, Pascal pointed out that because of basic human sinfulness, we only tend to believe what we want to believe. If we don't want something to be true, we are remarkably good at thinking of reasons why it isn't. Second, he argued that the Christian God doesn't stand at the end of an argument, ready to be proved, then ticked off as something known and then ignored. He is an intensely passionate God who, when he comes into relationship with people, 'unites himself with them in the depths of their soul . . . and makes them incapable of having any other end but him'.[8] You either have this kind of intimate personal encounter with God, or you don't have him at all. Those who are idly curious, who don't really want this kind of God and are only playing theological games, will not find him. It is only those who hunger for him deep within themselves, who are desperate to know him, who will find what they are looking for.

So, for Pascal, presenting someone with a list of proofs for Christianity or evidence for faith is probably a waste of time. If someone basically doesn't want to believe, no amount of proof (or proof texts) can ever convince her. And even if she were convinced, then it wouldn't be the Christian God she had come to believe in, but only what Pascal called 'the God of the philosophers'. The crucial factor in persuading someone to believe, then, is not to present evidence, but first to awaken a desire for God in them. In other words, when commending Christianity to people, 'Make it attractive, make good men wish it were true, and then show that it is.'[9] Such arguments as there are for Christianity can convince those who hope it is true, but will never convince those who don't.[10]

Pascal would probably have thought that many of our assumptions about evangelism start in the wrong place. I have been on (and even led!) many evangelism training courses that have spent quite a bit of time persuading Christians that they need to know how to answer lots of complicated apologetic questions, such as 'Why does God allow suffering?' and 'Don't other religions also lead to God?' Now these are important questions, not least for Christians to work out; after all, they puzzle us sometimes too, not just our non-Christian friends. Or again, evangelism training often focuses on learning a memorable 'gospel presentation' that can be explained to people, often with diagrams drawn on the back of an envelope. In themselves, these are useful things, good for helping Christians to understand the basics of their faith, and sometimes perhaps for explaining it as well.

Yet perhaps we need to start a stage further back. It is not just a case of shouting a bit louder, or explaining a bit more articulately. The truth is that it doesn't work like that in the twenty-first century any more than it did in the seventeenth. Pascal's point is that before we ever get to the stage of explaining or convincing, there needs to emerge in people the desire, the question, the hunger to discover more, to find God. Now Pascal, like the great St Augustine before him, was fully aware that only God does that, only God can touch the heart and make it long for himself; yet he also knew that God often uses people like himself and ourselves to awaken that desire in people.

Creating the Desire for God

If all this is anywhere near true, the first stage in a church's approach to its non-Christian neighbours may not be in thinking 'how can we persuade them that it's true?', but by asking 'how can we make them want to know more?' This might involve questions of personal lifestyle: 'How different are my values, my home and my behaviour from those of my neighbours and friends who are not Christians? Is there anything there that might make them want to know more, to want what I have?' It also involves frank and honest questioning of church lifestyle: 'Is our church just another little club for likeminded people who happen to enjoy singing, religious emotion and sermons? Or is there anything in the life or worship of our church that would make an outsider looking in want to have what we have?' An evangelistic lifestyle then becomes one that simply makes other people think. It stirs a faint echo of desire to discover what it is that makes the difference. And this cannot be done alone. To maintain a lifestyle that is different from the culture around is lonely work. It can't be kept going for too long without the strong support and encouragement of a few other people committed to living this way. Derek Draper's story teaches us that when the Church does live by and display a different wisdom, then God can use even something as small as a sermon which helps people conquer fear, or even day-glo trainers, to create the desire for himself.

In other words, a community of people that lives by God's ways, that has learnt to place love, humility, compassion, forgiveness and honesty right at the centre will make people think. To put it differently, a church that lives its life under the kingdom of God cannot help but provoke questions. And when it does that, then is the time for evangelism. That is the time for the simple explanation of the good news of Jesus Christ.

But that is to get ahead of ourselves. Before we step out on the path of understanding 'how', we need to ask the question 'why'. Why do we do evangelism? Why, in a cool postmodern world, would Christians want to make themselves unpopular by forcing their views on others in the first place? Wouldn't it just be easier to keep quiet? These are important questions. The next chapter goes back to basics to try to give some answers.

Notes

1   *The Times Saturday Magazine*, 6 January 2001.

2   *The Times*, 21 February 2001.

3   Douglas Coupland, *Life after God*, London: Simon & Schuster, 1994, p. 359.

4   Nigel McCulloch, *A Gospel to Proclaim*, London: Darton, Longman and Todd, 1992, p. 84.

5   McCulloch, *Gospel*, p. 46.

6   Jean Baudrillard, 'Simulacra and Simulations' in *Modernism/Postmodernism*, ed. Peter Brooker, London: Longman, 1992, p. 159.

7   George Monbiot, *Third Way*, August 2001, p. 22.

8   Blaise Pascal, *Pensées*, translated by Alban J. Krailsheimer, *Penguin Classics*, Harmondsworth: Penguin, 1966, p. 169.

9   Pascal, *Pensées*, p. 34.

10 For more on Pascal's Apologetics, see Graham Tomlin, *The Power of the Cross*, Carlisle: Paternoster, 1999, pp. 207–55. 15

God's Big Picture

Vaughan Roberts

Unless you've been to Bible college, the Bible can be a very difficult book to understand. This book helps to show how it all fits together and points to its ultimate subject – Jesus.

IVP
£5.99
PB / 0 8511.1298 6

£2 OFF
£3.99 with voucher

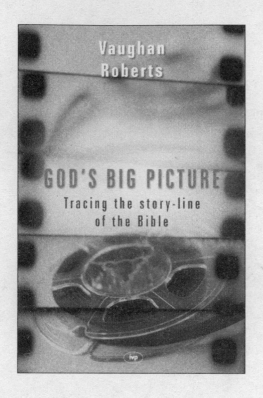

Vaughan
Roberts

GOD'S BIG PICTURE
Tracing the story-line
of the Bible

ivp

Inter-Varsity Press, 38 De Montfort Street, Leicester LE1 7GP, England

The Present Kingdom

The time has come

At first sight we may feel that a genealogy is an uninspiring way to start the New Testament, but, if we remember God's promises, we will be on the edge of our seats as soon as we read the words: 'A record of the genealogy of Jesus Christ the son of David, the son of Abraharn.' (Matthew 1:1). He is the one who fulfils the promises to Abraharn in Genesis 12 and to David in 2 Samuel 7. The apostle Paul expresses it clearly: 'no matter how many promises God has made, they are "yes" in Christ' (2 Corinthians 1:20).

Mark begins his Gospel by quoting from Malachi and Isaiah:

> 'I will send my messenger ahead of you,
>   who will prepare your way' –
> 'a voice of one calling in the desert,
> "Prepare the way for the Lord,
>   make straight paths for him.'"

(Mark 1:2-3)

Both prophets foretold that a herald would appear in advance of God's king, to announce his imminent arrival and to urge people to get ready for him. Mark identifies John the Baptist as that herald: 'And so John came, baptising in the desert region and preaching a baptism of repentance for the forgiveness of sins' (1:4). The message is clear: the waiting is over; the exile is about to end and the time of fulfilment is soon to come. And then Jesus appears, 'proclaiming the good news of God. "The time has come," he said. "The kingdom of God is near. Repent and believe the good news!"' (1:14-15).

'The kingdom of God' is not an expression the Old Testament uses, but Jesus speaks of it often in his teaching. it sums up the prophetic hope. He understands that he has come in fulfilment of all that the Old Testament pointed forward to. He tells his disciples, '... blessed are your eyes because they see, and your ears because they hear. For I tell you the truth, many prophets and righteous men longed to see what you see but did not see it, and to hear what you hear but did not hear it' (Matthew 13:16-17). Speaking of the Old Testament, he says, 'These are the Scriptures that testify about me' (John 5:39).

Fulfilment in Christ

The New Testament never leads us to expect that there will be any fulfilment of the Old Testament promises other than their fulfilment in Christ (Figure 29). We are not encouraged, for example, to look for their fulfilment in the State of Israel and to expect a new temple to be built there. That is to expect a renewal of the model that has now been dismantled. The permanent reality is found in Christ. Graeme Goldsworthy has put it like this:

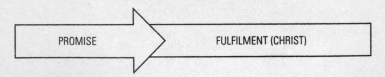

PROMISE   FULFILMENT (CHRIST)

Figure 29. Fulfilment in Christ

'For the New Testament the interpretation of the Old Testament is not "literal" but "Christological". That is to say that the coming of

Christ transforms all the kingdom terms of the Old Testament into gospel reality.[1]

Another writer draws an analogy with a father a century ago, who promises his young son that he will give him a horse on his twenty-first birthday. Cars are subsequently invented, and so, when the birthday finally comes, the boy is given a car instead of a horse. The promise has still been fulfilled, but not literally. The father could not have promised his son a car because neither could have understood the concept. In a similar way, God made his promises to Israel in ways they could understand. He used categories they were familiar with, such as the nation, the temple and material prosperity in the land. But the fulfilment breaks the boundaries of those categories. To expect a literal fulfilment is to miss the point: 'To look for direct fulfilments of, say, Ezekiel in the twentieth-century Middle East, is to bypass and short-circuit the reality and the finality of what we already have in Christ as the fulfilment of those great assurances. It is like taking delivery of the motor car but still expecting to receive a horse.[2] All the promises of the kingdom of God are fulfilled in Christ; he is God's people, God's place and God's rule.

God's people

Adam, the first man, failed in his role as the image of God and was evicted from the garden. God made a new start with the Israelites, who were called to be his holy people, reflecting his character as they obeyed his law. They too failed and were sent into exile. But, where Adam and Israel failed, Jesus succeeds. He is what the people of God were meant to be: the true Adam and the true Israel.

Jesus is the true Adam

The Gospels stress that Jesus is a real human being. He is born as a baby; he sleeps, weeps, gets tired and even dies. He is descended from Adam (Luke 3:23-38) and identifies with Adam's race in his baptism (Luke 3:21-22). But, unlike Adam, when he is tempted he does not sin. He is the only human being who perfectly obeys God, his Father.

He is, therefore, the one person to have lived who does not deserve
to be banished from God's presence. But on the cross he willingly
faces the punishment that we all deserve, as sinners who are bound
up with the first Adam. As a result, if we trust in him, we enter into
a new humanity, headed not by Adam, the sinner, but by Jesus, the
righteous new Adam. Paul writes, '... just as through the disobedience
of one man [Adam] the many were made sinners, so also through the
obedience of the one man [Christ] the many will be made righteous'
(Romans 5:19; see Figure 30).

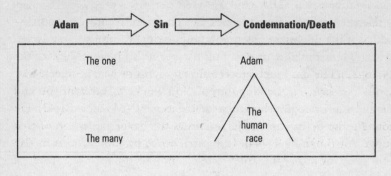

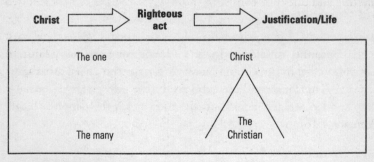

Figure 30. Romans 5:19

Jesus is the true Israel

When Jesus is a child, Joseph and Mary take him to Egypt to protect
him from Herod's persecution. Matthew comments: 'So was fulfilled

what the Lord had said through the prophet: "Out of Egypt I called my son" (Matthew 2:15). Some commentators suggest that this is an unprincipled use of Old Testament prophecy. The quotation is from Hosea 11:1, which is not a messianic promise referring to an individual. The original context makes it very clear that it refers to the exodus of the nation of Israel. But Matthew is neither naive nor unprincipled. He knows exactly what he is doing. He is deliberately identifying Jesus with Israel. But Jesus is different. He too is tempted, as the Israelites were in the wilderness, but, unlike them, he does not fall (Matthew 4:1-11).

He then calls his first disciples. His choice of twelve is no coincidence; it is a deliberate statement. He is calling together a new Israel, with twelve disciples as the foundation, rather than twelve tribes (4:18-22). The old Israel rejects Jesus and will, in turn, be rejected by God. Jesus says, '. . . the kingdom of God will be taken from you and be given to a people who will produce its fruit' (Matthew 21:43). He foretells the destruction of Jerusalem as the awful expression of that judgment (Luke 19:43-44). It is carried out by the Romans in AD 70. From now on the true Israel is not focused on the land of Palestine and does not consist of those who are physically descended from Abraham. It rather consists of his spiritual descendants: those, both Jew and Gentile, who follow his example and place their trust in God's promise fulfilled in Jesus: '... the promise comes by faith, so that it may be by grace and may be guaranteed to all Abraham's offspring – not only to those who are of the law [i.e. Jews] but also to those who are of the faith of Abraham. He is the father of us all' (Romans 4:16).

God's place

Adam and Eve enjoyed God's presence with them in the garden before the fall – God also drew near to the Israelites, living in their midst in the tabernacle and then in the temple. But the temple in Jerusalem was just a shadow of what we can receive in Christ. He is the true temple, the place where we may enter perfectly into God's presence. He is not just the true human being; he is also the true God. In Christ, God himself has drawn near to us.

Jesus is the true tabernacle

'The Word became flesh and made his dwelling [or "tabernacled"] among us' (John 1: 14).

Jesus is the true temple

After he has cleared the temple of those who had set up their own businesses there, some Jews challenge Jesus to prove his authority to do it. He replies, 'Destroy this temple, and I will raise it again in three days' (John 2:19). They assume he is speaking about the building, but John tells us that 'the temple he had spoken of was his body' (2:21). The temple in Jerusalem is soon to be destroyed. If we want to meet with God we must go, not to a building, but to Jesus (see John 4:21-24). Standing in the temple courts, he says, 'If anyone is thirsty, let him come to me and drink. Whoever believes in me, as the Scripture has said, streams of living water will flow from within him' (John 7:37-38). He is surely thinking of Ezekiel's promise of the new temple, from which a river would flow, bringing life to all (Ezekiel 47). He is that temple, and the water is the Spirit he gives to all who trust in him.

God's rule and blessing

Jesus introduces the new covenant

He has come, not to abolish the law, but to fulfil it (Matthew 5:17). He perfectly obeys its demands, and therefore, uniquely, does not need to face the curse of judgment that must be met by all law-breakers. But on the cross 'Christ redeemed us from the curse of the law by becoming a curse for us'. He dies to take the penalty we deserve so that we may receive the blessings of the covenant through faith in him (Galatians 3:13-14). He lives a perfect life for us and then dies our death for us. As a result, 'the righteous requirements of the law' are 'fully met in us' (Romans 8:4). A wonderful swap takes place.

If we have trusted in Christ, we can be sure that he has taken our sin and its judgment, so that he can give us his perfect righteousness: 'God made him who had no sin to be sin for us, so that in him we might become the righteousness of God' (2 Corinthians 5:21). The death of Jesus thus introduces the new covenant: 'Christ is the mediator of a new covenant, that those who are called may receive the promised eternal inheritance – now that he has died as a ransom to set them free from the sins committed under the first covenant' (Hebrews 9:15).

Jesus is the new king

The prophets made it clear that God's promises would be fulfilled by a new king, a descendant of David. He would establish God's rule and introduce a new age in which the evil effects of the fall are undone. The miracles of Jesus point to the fact that he is that king. They are signs of the new creation he has come to establish. When Jesus heals a demon-possessed man, who is also blind and mute, an astonished crowd asks, 'Could this be the son of David?'

The Pharisees reply: 'It is only by BeeIzebub [Satan], the prince of demons, that this fellow drives out demons.'

Jesus points out the logical contradiction in their explanation: why would Satan drive out Satan? 'But if I drive out demons by the Spirit of God, then the kingdom of God has come upon you' (Matthew 12:22-28). The kingdom of God has come because God's king has come. At times he does not look much like a king, not least when he dies in weakness on the cross. But that is the moment of his greatest victory, when he defeats his enemies and sets his people free (Colossians 2:13-15). And then, on the third day, he is raised to life again and later ascends to the right hand of the Father. The resurrection proclaims beyond doubt that he is not simply the son of David; he is also the Son of God (Romans1:4).

Jesus is the source of God's blessing

He says, 'Come to me, all you who are weary and burdened, and I

will give you rest' (Matthew 11:28). 'Rest' was the goal of God's
creation. That does not mean that we were designed to do nothing,
but rather that God wants us to share in his rest, the Sabbath day,
which symbolizes the perfection of God's creation. Adam. and Eve
enjoyed that rest before the fall, as described in Genesis 2; but everything was spoilt by their sin. The Israelites then knew something of
it in the promised land in the partial kingdom. But that was just a pale
reflection of what God now wants to give us in Christ. By his resurrection he introduces a new age. He faces the penalty of death and
comes out the other side. The resurrection marks the beginning of a
new age. If we trust in him, we too can pass from death to life. We
can experience life as it was designed to be lived by the loving
creator: '... if anyone is in Christ, he is a new creation; the old has
gone, the new has come' (2 Corinthians 5:17).

The cross: salvation through substitution

There is no hint of embarrassment among the first Christians that
their Lord has been killed as a common criminal by a degrading
method of execution. Paul even says, 'May I never boast except in the
cross of our Lord Jesus Christ, through which the world has been
crucified to me, and I to the world' (Calatians 6:14). He knows that
the cross is no tragic failure; it is a triumphant success. God's kingdom
could have come no other way. Something had to be done about sin
and God's anger against it. He could not simply stop being angry; if
he did that, he would cease to be God. God's justice demands that he
cannot turn a blind eye to evil; it must be punished. God in his grace
sent his own Son to take that punishment in our place. He died as a
substitute, instead of others, facing God's anger against human sin. He
is the one to whom the Passover lambs and all the sacrifices of the
Old Testament pointed. As a result, God's righteous wrath is satisfied
or I propitiated', and, if we trust in Christ, we need no longer face it.
'Christ died for sins once for all, the righteous for the unrighteous,
to bring you to God' (1 Peter 3:18; see also Romans 3:21; 1 John
2:2).

The kingdom of God	The pattern of the kingdom	The perished kingdom	The promised kingdom	The partial kingdom	The prophesied kingdom	The present kingdom
God's people	Adam and Eve	No-one	Abraham's descendants	The Israelites	Remnant of Israel; inclusion of nations	*Jesus Christ:* new Adam; new Israel
God's place	The garden	Banished	Canaan	Canaan (and Jerusalem and temple)	New temple; new creation	*Jesus Christ:* true tabernacle; true temple
God's rule and blessing	God's word; perfect relationships	Disobedience and curse	Blessing to Israel and the nations	The law and the king	New covenant; new king; great blessing	*Jesus Christ:* new covenant; rest

Figure 31. The present kingdom

The salvation Christ won for us is so wonderful that no one image can fully express it. The New Testament uses several, all of which result from the fact that Christ died in our place to take our punishment.

Redemption

We have been set free by the payment of a price: 'it was not with perishable things such as silver or gold that you were redeemed from the empty way of life handed down to you from your forefathers, but with the precious blood of Christ, a lamb without blemish or fault' (1 Peter 18-19).

Reconciliation

We were God's enemies but now we are his friends: 'AD this is from God, who reconciled us to himself through Christ and gave us the ministry of reconciliation' (2 Corinthians 5:18).

Justification

We were under God's condemnation but now we are righteous in his sight: '... all have sinned and fall short of the glory of God, and are justified freely by his grace through the redemption that came by Christ Jesus' (Romans 3:23-24).

Conquest

We were powerless in the face of evil spiritual forces who had us in their clutches. But Christ's death releases us from bondage to death and therefore sets us free from Satan's power: 'Having disarmed the principalities and powers, he made a public spectacle of them, triumphing over them by the cross' (Colossians 2:15).

Figure 32. The achievement of the cross

The four Gospels

There are many verbal similarities between the 'synoptic' Gospels (Matthew, Mark and Luke). It seems that there is a literary relationship between the writers, although no-one knows exactly who copied from whom and whether or not any of them relied on another common source. John's Gospel is written in a very different style and contains much material that is unique to him. The Gospels do not contradict one another, but rather give us complementary accounts of what Jesus said and did. Although they have much in common, they each provide their own distinctive contributions to our understanding of Jesus.

Matthew: Jesus is the Christ of the Old Testament Scriptures

Matthew has a primarily Jewish audience in mind and stresses that Jesus came to fulfil the Old Testament. There are over a hundred references to the Old Testament in the Gospel. Twelve times Matthew introduces a quotation by saying something like, 'This took to place to fulfil what the Lord had said through the prophet ...' (e.g. 1:22; 2:15, 17).

Mark: Jesus is the Suffering Servant who calls us to suffer too

Mark is a gospel in two halves. The first half concludes when Peter recognizes that Jesus is the Christ (8:29). The second half focuses on the cross: 'He then began to teach them that the Son of Man must suffer many things ... and that he must be killed' (8:31). And his disciples are to walk the path he trod: 'If anyone would come after me, he must deny himself and take up his cross and follow me' (8:34).

Luke: Jesus is the Saviour of the world

Salvation for Luke consists of two great blessings: the forgiveness of sins and the gift of the Holy Spirit. This salvation is not limited to religious people or to Jews; it is for all types and all nations. We see men and women, children and adults, rich and poor, Jews and Gentiles all receiving grace from Jesus. Luke's second volume, Acts, shows how the good news about him spreads all over the world.

John: Jesus is the Son of God who gives eternal life

John's characteristic description of Jesus is as the eternal, unique Son of God the Father. As such, he makes some staggering claims about himself in the 'I am' sayings, such as 'I am the light of the world' and 'I am the way and the truth and the life' (8:12; 14:6). These claims are supported by a series of miracles, or 'signs'. They are designed to promote faith in Jesus: 'These [signs] are written that you may believe that Jesus is the Christ, the Son of God, and that by believing you may have life in his name' (John 20:31).

The conductor returns

When I go to a classical-music concert, I am always amazed that an orchestra, which consists of so many individuals with very different instruments, can combine to produce such a beautiful sound. They depend on two vital ingredients: a score, which tells them which notes to play, and a conductor, who directs them when they are to play them. it would be disastrous if the orchestra tried to get rid of the conductor: they would not know when to come in or what speed to play at. It would be even worse if they tore up the score.

That is what we humans have done. God is the composer who created this world, and he gave instructions about how we should live; the score he wants us to play. But we ignore them. We would rather play our own notes in our own time, so we dismiss him and tear up his score. It is hardly surprising that there is no harmony in the world. How can there be, if we all insist on playing our own tune? The result is a terrible cacophony. We desperately need a conductor if we are to begin to play the right notes again. There is no hope for the world otherwise.

Jesus is both the composer and the conductor. He has come to restore order. He wants to change the ugly discord of our lives and our world into the beautiful music they were designed to make: a symphony of praise to the Creator. He himself played that perfect music as he lived in perfect submission to God his Father. By his death on the cross he made it possible for us to return to God's orchestra, despite the way we have treated him. Then, by his resurrection, he was established as the eternal conductor. If we take our lead from him we will find our proper place in God's world once more. Our lives will make sense and will begin to produce beautiful music again, bringing praise to God.

But we do not have to be very humble to admit that at the moment we still also produce many discordant notes and we live in a world that is full of discord. The conductor has come, and yet we still disobey him, and many refuse to acknowledge him altogether. To use the language of the Bible, the kingdom of God has come, and yet it has not come in all its fullness. Jesus taught his disciples that he would leave the earth and that there would be a delay before he returned. it is only when he comes again that everything will be put right and all discord will be banished for ever. Our next chapter looks at what the Bible teaches about what we can expect in the meantime, between Jesus' first and second comings.

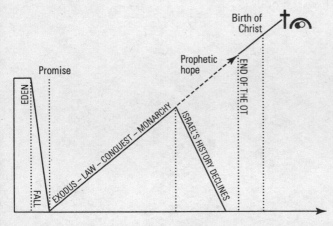

Figure 33. The story so far: the birth of Christ

Bible Study

Luke 1:39-80; 2:25-32

What do the words of Mary, Zechariah and Simeon teach us about the salvation Jesus brings?

How do they point to the fulfilment of the following Old Testament passages?

- Genesis 12:1-3
- 2 Samuel 7:11-6
- Isaiah 9:2-7
- Isaiah 42:5-7
- Isaiah 49:5-7
- Jeremiah 31:31-34
- Malachi 3:1

How should we respond?

God And Us

Keith Warrington

All of us hunger to know more of what God is really like. This easy-to-read study of his character is sure to lead to greater reverence and worship of our great God.

Scripture Union
£6.99
PB / 1 8599.9698 1

£2 OFF
£4.99 with voucher

First published 2004 by Scripture Union
207-209 Queensway, Bletchley, Milton Keynes, MK2 2EB, England

He's always saying 'Hello'

Have you ever wondered:

- how God is involved in prayer?
- whether prayer is one-way or two-way communication?
- whether God's role is to listen while I talk, or whether I am supposed to listen as well?
- how to listen to God?

I hate sermons on prayer. They fill me with guilt and drive me to despair. The preacher describes prayer as able to move mountains; as interaction with the Almighty; as the springboard to a God-anointed life. He reminds me that revivals are born in prayer.

I say 'Amen' to it all, but inwardly I cringe. Satan creeps on to my shoulder and whispers 'Fraud!', while my conscience reminds me that as a prayer warrior I'm a failure. My most common prayers are fairly short: 'Thank you' and 'Sorry'.

If the preacher asks me if I want to develop a better prayer life, or even a prayer life that has some hope of improvement, he can't lose. With prayer, I'm at my weakest. What does he want me to do? Come to the front, receive prayer, stand on my head? I'll do it, if only I can clamber over this prayer mountain, this hurdle that's too high – just so that next time he preaches on prayer I can look him in the eye and say, 'It's OK now. I've got this prayer problem under control.' If only!

My experiences so far have not always helped me. Three issues used to dominate my prayer life in my early years as a Christian – methods, the Bible and guilt. The Quiet Time was a part of my daily life – a time of reading the Bible and prayer. It was foundational to my development, but rarely an easy task. And that was the problem: it was a task, a discipline. In fact, when I thought of prayer, I quickly associated it with the word 'discipline'. Prayer was something one had to do; a discipline to be learnt; a practice to be worked at. Strangely enough, words like 'liberty', 'joy' or 'Wow!' did not come to my mind when I thought of prayer. I learnt how to engage in 'Seven Minutes with God' and other methods developed to help people like me through the tiresome battlefield of prayer. Don't misunderstand me – prayer wasn't always hard work, and neither is discipline (a word that should not be far from a disciple who is developing in prayer). The problem for me was that it was the *only* word I associated with prayer.

Prayer that didn't have a significant element of sacrifice about it was somehow questionable, deficient, if not counterfeit. Prayer that took place in the early hours when all my friends were asleep was worth more than the prayer offered during the lunch break. During my youth, a famous evangelist came to my city. He prayed at 6 am and he was a successful evangelist. His early prayer time was surely an important key to his effectiveness. Sure enough, even though he did not encourage anyone to follow his pattern for prayer, I got up at 6 am to pray. But I fell asleep somewhere in the middle of the prayer. The next morning I was determined to do better, but I didn't. The following morning I gave up. Maybe I should have persevered. There was another of my keywords when it came to prayer: perseverance. People who pray must be passionate and persevering, and too often I lacked both characteristics. I lived with the guilt of those failures for many years. Only later in my Christian journey did I realise that prayer is very personal, and that many of the burdens we carry concerning it are self-imposed.

We are often misled into trying to follow the agendas and guidelines that God has given to others, without first checking whether they are appropriate for us. If they are, we can learn from the experiences of those who are following a similar pattern. If they are not, we should discover the prayer pilgrimage that is appropriate for us and follow it faithfully, learning to develop it along the way. For some Christians, the morning is the best time to be with God; for others, the best time may be last thing at night. Others try to build time with God into the course of their day. Prayer is not a competition; it's a conversation, a way of life. That means it's very personal to each Christian.

Something else that increased my frustration with myself was what I read in the Bible. It shone its spotlight on me and what it showed up wasn't pleasant. Jesus spent whole nights in prayer! Now, I've done that in my time. I was a missionary for a year. Every Friday my team spent the night in prayer. But somehow Friday nights didn't seem to match up to the nights Jesus spent in prayer. Paul didn't help either; he told the Thessalonian Christians to pray continually (1 Thess 5:17), and they'd only been Christians for a few months! Paul was expecting them to do what I could only dream about – though it was more of a nightmare than a dream! What did Paul mean, anyway? How can anyone pray continually?

All this deepened my reservoir of guilt while my surface Christian face betrayed none of it. How could I share such failings with other Christians, who seemed not to experience my battles with prayer? Older Christians sometimes plunged me under the waters of guilt until I nearly drowned with such encouragements as these:

'If the Queen was here, your mind wouldn't wander!'

'Jesus died on the cross for you and you can't even stay awake for a few minutes to pray!'

'What do you think you're going to do in heaven if you don't pray now?'

The thought of heaven as one eternal prayer meeting didn't help me, until I began to rethink prayer.

And so began my journey as a prayer pilgrim. This chapter shares some of the lessons I'm learning along the way.

Prayer is primarily an encounter with God

For most of my life, I've identified prayer with talking to God. Of course, that's part of prayer, and I endorse the importance of prayer meetings and personal conversational prayer. But I'm learning that talking to God is only a part of prayer. I am learning to define prayer as a God-conscious event; it's a time when I'm conscious of God, when heaven breaks into my life on earth, when the transcendent God who created the universe opens a window in my world and says, 'Hello, Keith.' God's interruption establishes an encounter with him and, in that encounter, a prayer is born. No words need to be spoken; it's enough that I have become aware of God. I am learning to define those encounters as prayers. It's not the only form of prayer, but it's still prayer, initiated by God. The psalmist appears to be speaking of a similar experience when he encourages his readers to be quiet and, in that stillness, to acknowledge the presence of God. 'Hush – God's here' (see Ps 46:10).

Sometimes I work at home. Picture the scene. I'm engrossed in my studies, but later in the day a key turns in the lock of our front door. My wife Judy has come home. I've not seen her yet; no words have been spoken but a range of emotions, thoughts and feelings have been sparked off within me. At that moment, words are not as important as the fact that I am conscious of her presence. An encounter has already taken place in my mind. I'm learning to see prayer like this, as encounters with God when he opens a door into my life and, without words, I'm aware that he's there. One of the most sobering verses in the Bible is Genesis 28:16, in which Jacob says, 'Surely the LORD is in this place, and I was not aware of it.' We need to learn not to miss God when he visits us.

A poor man sat in church. He'd been there for hours, just sitting. The minister came up to him and asked if he was all right. He said that he was, and explained what he had been doing. 'I've been looking at God, God's been looking at me, and we're happy together.' He had learnt to encounter God without spoiling that intimacy with speech.

Prayer doesn't have to be frenetic or hard work. Prayer is the excitement of encountering God, of experiencing a God-conscious moment. It may involve words; it may not. This is what I'm learning.

Prayer is learning to encounter God in his world

I am learning to listen for the key in the lock when God opens a door into my life and says, 'Hello, it's me again.' It happens more times than we realise. I remember seeing my daughter sitting in church with her friends. As I saw her, I had an encounter with God. Anna-Marie was laughing, full of life, fresh, pretty, vivacious – and then she saw me looking at her through the ranks of people in church, and she smiled. It was a father–daughter moment and I felt proud, but I also felt God. It was as if he said, 'I've made her the girl she is; the person she's going to be.' It was a God-conscious moment; when God said 'Hello' and, in effect, 'Relax, I'm in charge.'

I think of times when my students and I have explored the Bible. We have asked questions and even perhaps discovered answers. Sometimes, the answers surprise and stimulate us. In those times, we are encountering God. We often respond to those encounters with words that don't seem to belong to prayer, such as 'Wow!' or 'That's remarkable!' or 'Mmm – I've never thought of that before.' God has opened his Word and said 'Hello', and we've replied 'Wow!'

With colleagues and students, I have often explored aspects of God and his dealings with us. In our creative probing we have tried to tap into the inexhaustible nature of God. As we do, before we know it we find that, while we are encountering each other as Christians in our quest of God, we are encountering God himself. We haven't prayed, and yet we have, for we have encountered God. We haven't stopped to pray, but he has stepped in to say 'Hello'.

One of my students came to our college from Korea. Before her arrival she had suffered a major accident that caused a severe loss of memory. Nevertheless, throughout her time as a student she was conscientious and caring, faithful in the smallest details, which few others noticed. I noticed. She now serves the Lord in an isolated region of

Northern Ghana. When I think of In-Hee, God speaks to me and
says 'Hello'.

I am learning to recognise that prayer is to encounter God and to
listen for his 'Hello' in people around me, in circumstances good and
bad (2 Cor 1:9; 1 Thess 2:2), in his creation, in his Word, and even in
me. This is probably the kind of prayerconsciousness Paul had in mind
when he encouraged his readers to be faithful in prayer (Rom 12:12).

Prayer means responding to God as well as speaking to God

In his book *Working the Angles*, Eugene Peterson speaks of 'the overwhelming previousness of God's speech to our prayers'. Prayer is not
always a matter of me saying 'Hello' to God; it's often God who's the
first to say 'Hello'. Many of my prayers do consist of me saying
'Hello', and, of course, that's fine. But how many times does God start
the conversation and we just don't hear him?

When my daughter was very young, I was driving to the airport
with her to pick up Judy. 'Why doesn't God speak to me?' Anna-
Marie asked. I knew what she meant. As Christians, we talk about
God speaking to us but we have very limited notions as to how he
does so. Perhaps he will speak through a sermon, a prophecy or our
personal Bible-reading. Few of us expect an audible voice or an
angelic visitation. But the fact is, he's everywhere, and I'm learning
the importance of identifying where he is so that I can respond to
him, whatever he says, however he says it. Paul anticipated this when
he wrote to the church in the bustling metropolis of Rome and
reminded the believers that God whispers his presence throughout
his creation (Rom 1:20).

I remember reading a book that offered many guidelines for
getting God's attention. But we don't need to learn how to get God's
attention. He's already perfectly attentive to us. Instead, I am learning
how to listen for him.

You may have heard the old story of a group of radio operators
turning up for an interview and being shown into a crowded

waiting-room to await their turn. The call never came. After some uncertainty, one man jumped out of his chair and ran into the interview room, emerging a few minutes later to announce that he had been offered the job – to the astonishment of those present. He told them to listen and, sure enough, a message was being tapped out in Morse code, informing them that the first person who responded to it and came into the interview room would be offered the job. But only one man was listening.

I've often assumed that God is to be encountered in the magnificent, the extraordinary, the sensational and the atmospherically charged (and sometimes he is). But I'm learning that he is also encountered in the ordinary events of life.

Prayer is very personal

God loves us individually and perfectly. He loves us uniquely and differently. He therefore encounters each of us differently. He says 'Hello' to each of us, countless times every day. But he does so in different ways, depending on who we are and how we are. That's the way a good father relates to his children, and God is the best father there is.

So rejoice in your individuality. Refuse to be driven to feel that you have to relate to God in any way other than that which he has chosen for you. Don't let God's agenda for others burden you. Be true to yourself as the person God is making you. Listen out for God, for he speaks to us in our own accents so that we can recognise him.

The Bible reflects a remarkable variety of forms of prayer, depending on who is praying and what the circumstances are (1 Kings 8:54; Ps 35:13; Matt 26:39). Some of us encounter God in loud worship, others in silence; some in the magnificent, others in the ordinary; some in written prayers, others with songs of praise, and yet others with tears. Be aware of who you are and listen for God to speak to you in ways that he knows are appropriate for you. Then be creative in your response to him.

Have you ever wondered whether we'll pray in heaven? We'll certainly encounter God there – in each other, in the angels, in our conversations, our excitement, our humour, our discussions, our plans, our memories and our dreams. Everything will reflect God. In heaven he will be reflected perfectly, but even in this dark world he's still God and it's still his world and he still sparkles in it. At times, his light rushes towards us like a searchlight; at other times, it's like a candle beckoning us softly to follow. In all these ways God is saying, 'Here I am; I've just called to say "Hello".' And when we say 'Hello' to God in response, a prayer is born as we encounter him in our lives.

> *I can't begin to imagine what God's got in store in heaven for me,*
> *but it'll keep me content for eternity*
> *for God will be in it, I'm sure.*

> *I want to explore and gaze at the places I've never been to before.*
> *I want to climb the mountains on the moon and paddle to the distant shore*
> *of a desert island, and then explore some more, a*
> *nd all I see will reflect God, I'm sure.*

> *I want to talk to Paul and James and talk and talk some more.*
> *I want to speak with the angels, put my cheek to a lion's paw,*
> *and watch the films of the exodus and the flood*
> *from the heavenly video store.*
> *I want to see how creation occurred, and yet there's so*
> *much more;*
> *and in it all, I'll encounter God; of that one thing I'm sure.*

> *But will I have time for prayer in heaven? Surely that's the reason I'm there.*
> *Yet, there's so much to do, I'm not sure I'll have time to spare.*
> *But still, I should pray. There must be a time to stop and say*
> *a few words to the Lord in prayer.*

> *But I sense him saying that my whole life there*

will be one big encounter with him.
Wherever I go, he'll have been there
before, and his perfume will fill every place,
and the people I see and talk to will reflect all the time his grace
and although I'll not see his face, God will still embrace me and trace
within my heart and mind the finger of love, the finger of grace.

I won't need to pray in heaven. Prayer won't bring me to God.
He'll be in everyone, everything, every sight, every song that I sing.
He'll be there in the acts and the deeds.
He'll be there in the sights that I see.
He'll be there in the plans that I have for the future,
the talks that I have about the past.
The places I'll go to, he's been to, and he'll be in the bits in between.
Everywhere I go, God will say 'Hello'.
I'll encounter him without trying.
Without prayer, he'll still be there;
the consciousness of God will be like the air.

Maybe there'll be no prayer meetings in heaven
but prayer as it was meant to be;
responding to God in encounters he's planned
with me in mind, a mere speck in the sand.
For all eternity, he'll be whispering 'Hello'
in everyone around me and everywhere I go.

Questions for discussion

1. Does God enjoy it when we pray to him? (Deut 4:7; Job 33:26; Acts 10:4; 1 Pet 3:12)
2. Can we change God's mind when we pray? (Matt 26:39,42; 1 John 5:14)
3. What are some of the purposes of prayer? (Ps 32:6,7; Jer 42:3; Dan 6:11; 9:4,5; Acts 1:24; 6:6; 28:8; Phil 1:9–11; Col 4:3,4; James 5:16; 1 John 1:9)

4. What kinds of prayer does God appreciate? (1 Chron 5:20; Prov 15:8,29; James 5:16)
5. Where is God speaking today? (Ps 19:1–4)

Questions to think about

1. Should we pray to the Father, to Jesus, or to the Spirit, or doesn't it matter?
2. Why is prayer important for Christians?
3. Does it matter how long we pray or when we pray?
4. Is praying together more significant than praying on your own?
5. How should Christians listen for God in prayer?

Why Me Lord?

Michael Apichella

In this disarmingly honest book, the author provides valuable and biblical insights into the thing many of us find hardest to deal with – failure – and help us respond with faith.

Kevin Mayhew
£6.99
PB / 1 8400.3902 7

£2 OFF
£4.99 with voucher

Other titles by the same author

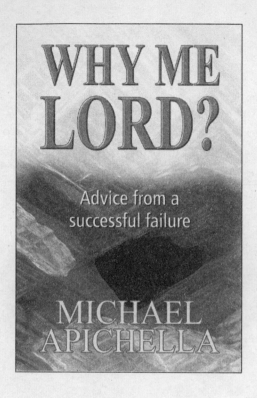

WHY ME LORD?

Advice from a
successful failure

MICHAEL APICHELLA

First published in 2002 by Kevin Mayhew Ltd
Buxhall, Stowmarket, Suffolk IP14 3BW

Man of passion

Dawn is breaking. A silent figure steals along narrow backstreets in a large Middle-eastern city. He wears a heavy woollen cloak, hitched high on his neck to obscure his familiar profile. In his fevered mind, every bump, every footstep means he's surely being followed.

At the shrill yowl of a cat, the man dodges down an alley, breaking into a canter until at last he reaches his secret destination.

There he frantically taps on the door then pauses.

In the agonising seconds that pass, a curse catches in his throat. Growling, he now pounds his fist on the door, grazing his hairy knuckles on the rough oak door.

At last a timid voice from within calls, 'What do you want?' 'Open up, you fool. It's me!' he whispers through clenched teeth.

An iron bolt slams back and the door opens to reveal a gaunt man with a thick brown beard. The red rims and dark semi-circles under his eyes show he hasn't slept that night, and his lined face is the colour of a flounder's belly.

'Peter, where have you –?' Grabbing James by his bony shoulders, Peter cuts off the question. 'This time I've really failed the Master,' he wailed.

'Do you hear me?' 'I've failed him, too. Remember, I was in the Garden when they took him away.'

'No, for God's sake! It's worse than that, James! Not an hour ago, I was with him at the house of the high priest.'

A look of hope crosses James' face. 'Did you speak up in his defence?' Peter buries his face in his large callused hands and cries, 'No. I denied even knowing him, three times, just when my testimony might have helped the Master. *Three* times!' Peter's baritone suddenly boomed into the frosty air, 'I denied him once for each year I knew him.'

James' eyes widened in terror. Taking Peter by the arm, the younger man pulls him inside, scolding, 'Will you pipe down, you old fool. Do you want the centurions to find us?' With that, the door slams shut and the bolt rasps back in place.

Why me, Lord?

When our performance is so unspeakably bad it disgusts even us, it's very tempting to give up — just as Peter did after Christ was arrested and accused of crimes he never committed. Since even knowing Jesus would have been suicide, who could blame Peter for failing to acknowledge his relationship with the Lord? (Matthew 26:69-75).

On reflection, though, it's surprising that Jesus selected Peter among the twelve apostles to be the leader of the first church considering this craven act of betrayal (Luke 22:31- 32). It was not the first time Peter failed his Lord. And it wasn't to be the last time, either. To be sure, the other apostles had their fair share of failures – Thomas was a sceptic (Luke 20:24-25); James and John were hungry for glory (Matthew 20:20-28); Nathaniel was a racist (John 1:46); and all had abandoned Jesus at his arrest. However, because the Gospels are so full of Peter, and because Jesus speaks most often to him, let's focus on this flawed man.

Certainly Peter was honoured among all the followers of Christ. For instance, the very first time Jesus came into Peter's home, Peter's mother-in-law was seriously ill and languishing on her deathbed. To everyone's utter delight, Jesus asked to see the woman and healed her of a fever (Luke 4:39). Although in the months that followed, Peter saw Jesus cure other sick people, his mother-in-law's healing must have left a deep and lasting impression on him and his family. Thus it's easy to understand that when Peter subsequently gave up his successful fishing business to follow an itinerant preacher, there was little or no protest from his family, even though they were partners in the business! Peter was a man bred on the water, and it made sense to him when Jesus said, 'Follow me and I'll make you a fisher of men!' Not long after, however, Jesus and his twelve followers were out in a boat crossing a lake. As the men navigated, Jesus became weary and stretched out in the sun for a nap.

But while he was asleep, a squall came up and the wind began to thrash the small sailing craft. Although Luke doesn't mention any names, it's more than likely that it was Peter, the implied leader of the band, who shook Jesus awake, calling, 'Master, Master. We're sinking!' Christ turned his bearded face into the gale and growled, 'Quiet down!' with the firm authority of a man secure in his power to control the elements. Then turning to the twelve, and no doubt glaring at Peter, Jesus demanded, 'Where is your faith?' Whatever they replied outwardly, inwardly they were filled with dread for Jesus, asking themselves, 'Who in the world is this man that even the wind obeys his commands?' (Luke 8:22-25).

One day in a crowded square, Peter deftly inserted his foot in his mouth after a woman suffering from chronic haemorrhaging touched the hem of Christ's dusty robe, knowing Jesus would heal her. Pivoting, Christ queried, 'Who touched me?' Peter, who felt more at home on an isolated beach among his nets, was probably agitated by the throng of urbanites milling about Jesus like bees in a hive. He tugged at his beard and exploded, 'Master, there are hundreds of people here to see you!' Jesus' reply once again put Peter in the dog house. 'No, it was someone who deliberately touched me because I felt power go out from me.' Seconds later, Peter learned that a woman had been healed by her faith in Jesus, although she had been diagnosed as incurable by the best doctors of that day (Luke 8:45-48).

After witnessing Christ's authority time and time again, one might think that Peter would have known better than to question the Master's behaviour. Certainly, Peter had more than an inkling of who

Jesus was. After all, it was he who spoke for the twelve when he answered Jesus' question, 'Who do you say I am?' Peter answered correctly when he replied, 'You are the Messiah' (Luke 9:20).

Yet Peter continued to get it wrong. For example, when Jesus decided it was time to explain to the apostles what men would do to him, he referred to the scriptures teaching that the leading religious experts would reject him. He spelled out that he would be arrested, tortured, and finally killed. But, he assured them, he would also rise from the dead three days later (Mark 8:31). This was not new to Peter or the others, for the texts were ancient – Isaiah 52:13; 53:1-12. Yet, Peter clearly missed the point Jesus was making, for he took Jesus aside and reprimand him. It's not hard to imagine the scene: 'Lord. A little while ago you were telling us that you were about to be killed. Did I understand you right?' 'Yes, Peter, you certainly did. My time is short and –' Grabbing Jesus by the arm, he explodes, 'Hang on a moment, Jesus. If I were you, I'd be careful not to go around saying things like that.' Glancing over his shoulder at the other apostles, he adds, 'You know, some of the lads like John there, or Judas. They're a little sensitive, like. They might not know what you mean. I'm not sure I understand you either.' Puffing out his chest, he continues, 'Anyway, Lord, you got me to look after you so you can go on doing all your miracles and what not. And as long as I'm with you, you'll be safe.'

Looking ruefully at the blank faces of the apostles and then back at Peter who is still preening himself, Jesus spits, 'Satan, get behind me!' Peter twists around but there's no one there but him.

'Who are you calling Satan, Lord? Me?' 'Yes, Peter.' Sighing, Jesus tries to explain. 'You are only seeing this from a human point of view. I'm seeing it from my Father's.'

Imagine Peter's mortification. Yet again he spoke out of turn, and this time he even had to endure Christ calling him *Satan* in front of the others. I'm certain that Peter wanted the earth to open up and swallow him. He may even have begun to think about quietly slipping away and going back to his nets and the sea where life was so much simpler for a crude loudmouth like him. Although no scripture records this, it is easy to see Peter confronting Jesus tearfully, saying, 'You appointed the wrong man to lead the group, Master.

Why not make John the leader? You love him and he never seems to get it wrong. Or how about Philip? He's so *reliable*.

I'm sure he'll understand you when you talk about these spiritual things.' As always, an ever-lurking demon would be right at Peter's elbow, egging him on and grinning to hear Peter fall for the old trick of comparing himself unfavourably with others.

Still, Jesus would be unmoved. He knew exactly what qualities he wanted when he selected Peter to lead. For all his flaws, Peter had something that God wants in all his leaders. Peter had *passion*.

When you look at the great saints, you will notice two things. All were prone to failure, and all had great enthusiasm in following Christ. Peter was certainly ready to do anything and go anywhere for God. For me, one of the most touching examples of Peter's fidelity to Jesus is recorded in John 6.

Here Jesus has told his Jewish disciples that he is the bread of life. Speaking metaphorically, he explains, 'He who eats my flesh and drinks my blood has eternal life, and I will raise him up at the last day' (John 6:54). This was spoken in a synagogue. When he said it, there was an outburst of disagreement. Some said Jesus was a blasphemer. John tells us that that day, Jesus lost a significant number of his followers.

When the crowds dwindled to only a handful of disciples, Jesus glanced sadly at the apostles and said, 'Do you also wish to go away?' (67). Peter alone replied, 'Lord, to whom shall we go? You have the words of eternal life; and we have believed, and have come to know that you are the Holy One of God' (68).

While Peter did not have any formal theological training, he did know the truth thanks to John the Baptist. Peter had been a disciple of John during his ministry along the Jordan River. This is what Jesus saw when he looked at Peter: a man of conviction, not a dreamer. He didn't see a failure; he saw a man who one day would organise the first missionary movement, a man who would inspire other saints to dare to attempt great things for the Kingdom, a man who would muster the faith to perform the first of many miracles in the name of Jesus of Nazareth, healing a cripple at the Beautiful Gate of the temple (Acts 3:2-10).

You may be feeling like a failure right now. If so, don't allow Satan to accuse you of the obvious. Remember that God sees us as we can be. This means that to serve God well you don't need a perfect track record (who can claim that, anyway?) If success were a prerequisite, then all of the saints of the Old and New Testament would have been eliminated systematically.

The death of failure

Through plentiful examples, I have aimed to prove that Christians are bound to err, sin, and fail – sometimes miserably – as they attempt to serve God with the gifts and talents God has given us. Whatever the circumstances, we must not lose sight of this fact: We may often lose skirmishes and small battles in this life, but we have already won the war through Jesus Christ our Lord and Saviour. In the eternal sense, we are winners. Romans 8:37 proclaims: 'In all things we are more than conquerors through him who loved us.'

The conflict is won and Jesus is victorious. We may have this assurance even as we look discord squarely in the eye.

This is our hope, the one thing that makes Christians the happiest people in the world. As Paul wrote nearly 2000 years ago: '"O death, where is thy victory? O death, where is thy sting?" The sting of death is sin, and the power of sin is the law. But thanks be to God, who gives us the victory through our Lord Jesus Christ' (1 Corinthians 15:55-57).

Christ's Sermon on the Mount makes it clear that being a Christian requires great humility. Let's look at Peter again. The best known incident where he failed to understand the authority we each possess as followers of Christ is the time he saw Christ walking towards his boat across rough seas (Matthew 14:22-23). Peter wanted desperately to show Jesus that he had faith. Peter asked the Lord to call him out of the boat onto the water. When Jesus complied, Peter clambered over the side of the boat and to the amazement of his companions, began to walk on the water towards Jesus. Certainly it was not through Peter's own ability that he accomplished this feat. That he could even have stood on water and not sink is a wonderful object lesson illustrating Mark 10:27 – with God *all* things are possible. Clearly, Peter had managed for one bright and shining moment to demonstrate the awesome power we have as the children of God.

Two men stood on the surface of a rough sea. But I am convinced by what happened next that there was an unwelcome but ever-lurking third person on the waves that day, although Scripture doesn't point him out. It was a demon.

And that demon was determined to trip up Peter.

I am aware that many Christians feel that when anyone mentions demons, they may be guilty of ascribing too much power to Satan, who is, after all, a defeated enemy.

Defeated or not, he is still a dangerous enemy. Jesus warned Peter of satanic activity in Luke 22:31: 'Satan wants to sift you like wheat'. Later on, Paul and Peter write to other Christians warning them about the powers of darkness that have one goal in mind – to do battle with the Church. Paul states categorically that Christians are up *against powers and principalities* in the spirit realm (Ephesians 6:12-18). Peter writes of demonic attacks, adding that demons are like wild beasts seeking *to devour* naïve Christians (1 Peter 5:8).

C. S. Lewis shows clearly in *Screwtape Letters* that Satan is not able to be in two places at one time, so he must depend on a lowerarchy of fallen angels to help him get up to mischief in London and in San Francisco on the same day.[1] Fortunately, evil spirits and demons do not dominate the spirit world. There are also angels which encamp around the faithful as David wrote in Psalm 34:7. That means if we could picture the unseen realm, we would see a host of spiritual creatures anxiously looking on to see how the Church is doing

(Hebrews 12:1; 1 Peter 1:11-12; Ephesians 3:12).

Here is how the demon on the sea might have prompted Peter to stop trusting Jesus and to start trusting in himself: Demon: Peter, my good man, you're a fisherman and well acquainted with the properties of water and the laws of nature. Don't you know it's impossible for you to, *ahem*, walk on water? Peter: (To himself) Uh oh! My toes are getting wet. What was I thinking of when I jumped out of that boat? Demon: Well, you're out here now and all of your mates are looking at you. Whatever happens now, Old Boy, you mustn't blow it. Do hurry up before you begin to sink! Peter: Good grief, what'll the lads think of me if I muck this up? Maybe I should start to run.

Demon: Jesus will never let you forget it if you blow it again. I tell you what. Have faith in yourself and you can do it.

Peter: I can do it. I *know* I can do it. I – Aaahiii! But it was too late. Peter's faith wavered, fear set in, and the rest is history. Peter began to sink. 'Help me, Lord,' he sputtered as salt water filled is eyes, nose and mouth. 'I'm drowning!' And once again, Jesus had to criticise passionate Peter for setting out in faith, but then giving in to the human temptation of trying to please God in his own strength.

Peter's problem here is twofold: He initiated a task that Jesus had not asked of him, and then he set out to complete it under his own strength.[2] The result was inundating! Peter's anxiety to succeed created a climate of fear and God cannot or will not honour fear. He honours only that which is undertaken in faith. Romans 14:23 says he who doubts is condemned even before he starts.

Peter also fell for the old sin of humanism or self-actualisation – the belief that we may do anything provided we try hard enough. This is, of course, nonsense, but it has permeated our society through mass education, the media, pop-psychology, and the New Age Movement. Fortunately, Peter called out to Jesus whom he knew and loved. Indeed, it was his passionate love for Jesus that saved his life on that occasion. But note that that love did not prevent Peter from failing; nevertheless, Jesus loved Peter back because the Lord saw something deep inside this man whom he called 'The Rock' (or

Rocky, as I like to think of him!) At the opening of this chapter, we saw Peter during the lowest point of his life — the day he denied Jesus three times. Writing from the comfortable distance of 2000 years, and with the benefit of hindsight, it's tempting to imagine that if I had spent three years in the intimate company of the Messiah, I would have been bold enough to say to Pilate at Jesus' trial: 'You bet I know Jesus. And so do you, you old hypocrite! And I also know he's being framed, so let my pal go!' Or would I? Actually, I wouldn't bet my life on it.

---

1. I am not one to use the word 'prophetic' loosely, but having recently reread *Screwtape Letters*, I am certain that Lewis was writing in a prophetic mode, particularly in Letters 8–12. If you have never read *Screwtape Letters*, do so.
2. This was the same error I had made when I was trying to become a missionary. See Chapter 1.

Travelling Well

Stephen Cottrell & Steven Croft

Ideal for those who have recently found faith
and are seeking to learn more about the
Christian walk, this book explores themes such
as worship, reading the Bible and prayer.

Church House Publishing
£7.95
PB / 0 7151.4935 0

£2 OFF
£5.95 with voucher

Also by the same author

Travelling Well
A Companion Guide
to the Christian Life

Steven Croft
Stephen Cottrell

Published 2000 by National Society Enterprises Ltd
and in 2003 by Church House Publishing
Church House, Great Smith Street, London SW1P 3NZ

Preface by the Archbishop of York

If we reflect on our human relationships, especially those with people to whom we are very close, we recognize that their characters change over time. The pressure to talk at great length about all manner of things can pass naturally into a depth of communication where words are fewer, though laden with shared meaning.

As we reflect on our relationship with God, we will also be aware of such changes. Sometimes this can be disorientating. A pattern of prayer that once seemed to bring a great deal of help and comfort can come to seem somehow unfulfilling. The sort of worship we find uplifting can begin to change. Aspects of ourselves that once felt uncomfortable begin to trouble us and we feel called to deeper change and conversion.

These changes are natural. Jesus called us to perfection (Matthew 5.48) but as Cardinal Newman reminds us, 'to obtain the gift of holiness is the work of a life'.

It is a work in which we seek to cooperate more and more fully with the Holy Spirit as he seeks to make Christ ever more present to us, and changing us in the process. It is my hope that Travelling Well will be of help to you as you seek to respond ever more deeply to God's call in your life and will assist you at those times when the outer or inner journey can seem perplexing, as well as when it is deeply joyful and consoling.

David Ebor

How to use this book

Travelling Well is a companion for your Christian life. We've written it mainly for people who have recently completed a short course learning what it means to be a Christian and have been baptized or confirmed or made an affirmation of faith as an adult. We hope it will also be a useful companion to those who have been Christians for a longer time.

Our aim has been to give you some help and resources for the next part of the journey.

Each short chapter provides an introduction to the theme to guide you and then a selection of readings and prayers.

The sections can be tackled in any order. We've begun the book with a chapter on what it means to be baptized, based around the words of the service and one about the lifelong business of being changed by God. There are then four chapters on the inner journey, exploring prayer, the Scriptures, Holy Communion and belonging to the Church. Then four chapters on what we have called the outer journey: seeking the kingdom; faith in daily life; serving God and Christian witness. At the end you will find two final chapters: one for times of difficulty and the last on Christian hope.

Both of us have been privileged to walk alongside other people as they have begun their Christian journey at different times and in different places. This book is, in part, the fruit of those experiences.

May God give you grace to travel well on the great Christian journey.

Stephen Cottrell
Steven Croft

Learning to Pray

Pray as you can, not as you can't.

Dom Chapman

One of the disciples said to Jesus: 'Lord, teach us to pray, as John taught his disciples.'

Luke 11.1

Why do we pray?

To be a Christian means to be in a close and growing relationship with God, Father, Son and Holy Spirit, a relationship the Bible dares to call a friendship. That friendship develops in part through worship, reading the Scriptures, fellowship with other Christians and through serving God and others but it develops also through personal prayer.. time we spend with God on our own. Prayer is about far more than asking God for things on behalf of other people or ourselves: it is about building this relationship with God.

As we pray we are following the example of Jesus, whose pattern in the gospels is to set aside time regularly for solitary prayer. We are also following his teaching. In the Sermon on the Mount Jesus tells his followers to pray in secret:

Whenever you pray, go into your own room and shut the door and pray to your Father who is in secret; and your Father who sees in secret will reward you.

Matthew 6.6

As we pray, we strengthen and develop our relationship with God. We remember who we are before God. We re-orientate our lives, our desires and our will once again around God rather than ourselves.

Jesus gave the Lord's Prayer to his disciples as a pattern for prayer as well as words to learn and to use in prayer: it is a prayer which is meant to be prayed each day by a disciple of Christ ('Give us *this day* our daily bread'). Through the Lord's Prayer we learn to pray: 'Your will be done, on earth as it is in heaven' *before* we pray for our own needs.

Different Christians find different ways of praying helpful. Sometimes a person's pattern for prayer will be stable for long periods of their lives; sometimes there will be change and development as we change and develop as people. However long we have been Christians and however long we have been praying, we still have more to learn.

Establishing a foundation

For those who are new to faith, the most important thing is to begin to pray in the way which is most natural and helpful to you. If you can, work towards setting aside a time each day which is a regular time for prayer. It's better to begin with a short time and grow from there than to aim for too much too soon. Experiment with prayer at different times of the day. For most people, the very beginning of the day or the very end work best. For some, finding even five minutes when you are undisturbed can be very difficult, although it's still important to try.

Praying at the same time each day and in the same place is helpful to most people so that our prayer becomes a regular routine, just like our meals. Good habits can be as hard to establish as bad habits are to overcome so be prepared to keep going. Aim for a healthy discipline, in which you can be flexible without feeling guilty if you miss a prayer time. A place in the house where you can be on your own is easy for some people and hard for others. You may have a church nearby which is open for prayer; or you may be able to make a corner of your room into a prayer place with, perhaps, a candle or icon and a Bible and prayer book ready to hand. Our bodies are important: for most people sitting or kneeling will be the most natural posture. You need to be comfortable – but not too relaxed, especially if you pray last thing at night.

Most of us find it helpful to give a basic shape to our prayers which contains a balance of different elements and also to use at least some words written by other Christians or from the Scriptures. At the back of this book you will find a suggested outline for daily prayer for either the morning or the evening. It follows a basic structure: a time of preparation, reading the Bible, reflection upon the readings and prayers.

Praying at a set time each day doesn't mean, of course, that this is the only time when we might pray. Practising the presence of God at other times in the day can be extremely helpful. So can short prayers in difficult or dangerous situations; before meals; when the telephone rings or the doorbell goes or when the unexpected happens.

Find the natural rhythms of your day and develop a life of prayer which goes with the grain of your routine.

Learning to listen

Prayer is about listening to God as much as talking to him – or at least it should be. We listen as we read the Bible and reflect on what we read. We listen and try to discern God's voice as we write down our thoughts and reflections. We listen in the quietness of our own hearts to that still, small voice speaking within us: to affirm us; to call us; to guide us.

There are many different ways of listening to God. Through the years the Church has developed sensible and much needed guidelines

for discerning when a Christian may be genuinely hearing God and
when he or she may be hearing either simply their own desires or
temptations from outside. These are some of the most important of
these guidelines:

HOW DO WE RECOGNIZE GODS VOICE?

1. *Is what you have heard consistent with the Scriptures?* If it is, then it may
   be from God. If it isn't then you should discard it.
2. *Does what you have heard lead to an increase of faith, hope or love in
   yourself or in other people?* If the answer is yes, this may be God's
   word to you.
3. *Does what you hove heard draw you towards God or away from him?*
4. *If God is saying something to you for someone else, is that word for their
   upbuilding, encouragement or consolation* (1 Corinthians 114.3)? If it is
   not then you have no right to share it.
5. *Is what you have heard consistent with what you believe God has said to
   you on, earlier occasions?*
6. *Are you wilting to subject what has been said to the discernment of other
   Christians?*

Emotions in prayer

Our emotions and feelings are part of being human and therefore
part of our life of prayer and our wider relationship with God. Most
Christians find that there are at least some periods in their life when
they are aware of God's presence in terms of how they feel: people
experience a sense of inner peace, of warmth, of joy or of security.
These times are a gift from God and are to be appreciated and
enjoyed. Many also find that at least some of the time God seems very
distant or far away and prayer becomes dry routine and, occasionally,
very difficult. There may be an obvious reason (such as an emotional
turmoil in óur lives like failing in love, bereavement or moving
house) but sometimes there is no obvious cause that we can see. The
wise counsel of Christians down the centuries has been that in these
dry and difficult times when there are no obvious signs of God's

presence it remains very important to keep going and to maintain our basic rhythms of prayer and worship. God is teaching us new lessons in faith, trust and perseverance. However, if such times persist, it may be the right time to talk with a trusted Christian friend or minister.

Answers to prayer

The Bible encourages us to pray for many different situations: for governments and those in authority; for the kingdom of God to be realized on earth; for those who are sick or in trouble; for Christian ministers and for the worldwide church; and for those who are our enemies or who we do not naturally like or get on with.

In many of these situations we are joining our prayers with those of the Church around the world for particular situations: we may not be able to see instant answers to prayer in what are often enormous situations of need. Our prayer is made in obedience and trust that somehow prayer which is sincerely offered will make a difference.

In situations closer to us, we should expect, often, to see prayer make a difference in the lives of those around us and in our own lives. The answers to prayer may seem to others to be nothing more than coincidence – it's just that when we don't pray the coincidences stop happening! It is good to share the answers to prayer with other Christians to build up our own faith and strengthen that of others.

However, not every prayer we pray will be answered. Praying is not like wishing with a magic lamp. Sometimes we will need to think again about what we are praying for. 'God, help me to win the lottery'. 'God, I know he's married but please let him ask me out for a drink'; 'God, let the Inland Revenue overlook my affairs this year' are prayers we need to think hard about not praying. Sometimes though, good and sincere prayers we pray for those we love or for ourselves are not answered: people we care about suffer dreadfully or else they die and God seems to do nothing.

At those times, which we all experience, we will be angry with God; we will want to ask him very hard questions indeed, especially the question 'why?' As with any close friend, it is much better to be honest than to be polite. The Book of Psalms in the Bible is full of prayers which express every human emotion in prayer to God: anger, hatred of others, jealousy, loneliness and deep hurt and sorrow. These emotions may not all be 'correct', but if they are part of the way we feel we need to be able to put them into words to God and sometimes talk them through with others.

Finally, at other times, we may be the answer to our own prayers. What use is it praying to God for the welfare of our parents or children and then neglecting them ourselves? Or praying for the relief of poverty and not being prepared to work, to give or to shop in such a way that the poor are given practical help? Or to pray for someone to lead the youth group at the church and not be prepared to ask whether God may be calling you?

Going further and deeper

There are many books and guides to take you further into the different ways of prayer. Your own church may have courses on offer. The rhythm of the Church year gives opportunity for a deepening of the life of prayer, especially in Lent and Advent (the seasons of the year which come before Easter and Christmas). Many Christians are helped through occasional quiet days or residential retreats of different kinds. It can be helpful to talk through your life of prayer from time to time with your minister or someone who acts as a spiritual guide or director. You may be helped by meeting to pray regularly with one or two others either in a shared form of prayer or in your own words. There are many different ways forward. The important thing is to keep moving on and to keep growing in this most important of relationships with Almighty God, Father, Son and Holy Spirit.

Readings and prayers

O Lord, my heart is not lifted up,
my eyes are not raised too high,

I do not occupy myself with things
too great and too marvellous for me.
But I have calmed and quieted my soul,
like a weaned child with its mother;
my soul is like the weaned child that is with me.

Psalm 131

Be still and know that I am God.

Psalm 46.10

A reflection on prayer

Your prayer will take countless forms
because it is the echo of your life,
and a reflection of the inexhaustible light
in which God dwells.

Sometimes you will taste and see how good the Lord is.
Be glad then, and give Him all honour,
because His goodness to you has no measure.
Sometimes you will be dry and joyless
like a parched land or an empty well.
But your thirst and helplessness
will be your best prayer
if you accept them with patience
and embrace them lovingly.
Sometimes your prayer will be an experience
of the infinite distance that separates you from God;
sometimes your being and His fullness
will flow into each other.
Sometimes you will be able to pray
only with your body and eyes;
sometimes your prayer will move beyond words
and images;

sometimes you will be able to leave everything
behind you
to concentrate on God and His Word.
Sometimes you will be able to do nothing else
but take your whole life and everything in you
and bring them before God.
Every hour has its own possibilities
of genuine prayer.

So set yourself again and again
on the way of prayer.

Rule for a New Brother

A prayer to repeat over and over, like breathing ...

Lord Jesus Christ, Son of the living God, have mercy on me, a
sinner.

Lord, make me an instrument of your peace;
where there is hatred, let me sow love,
where there is injury, let me sow pardon,
where there is doubt, let me sow faith,
where there is despair, let me give hope,
where there is darkness, let me give light,
where there is sadness, let me give joy.

O divine master, grant that I may
not try to be comforted but to comfort
not try to be understood but to understand
not try to be loved, but to love.
Because it is in giving that we are received,
it is in forgiving that we are forgiven,
and it is in dying that we are born to eternal life.

Ascribed to St Francis of Assisi

Thanks be to you,
my Lord Jesus Christ,
for all the blessings and benefits
which you have given to me,
for all the pains and insults
you have borne for me.
O most merciful Friend
my Brother and Redeemer,
may I know you more clearly,
love you more dearly
and follow you more nearly
day by day.

St Richard of Chichester

Christ be with me, Christ within me,
Christ behind me, Christ before me,
Christ beside me, Christ to win me,
Christ to comfort and restore me,
Christ beneath me, Christ above me,
Christ in quiet, Christ in danger,
Christ in hearts of all that love me,
Christ in mouth of friend and stranger.

St Patrick's Breastplate

Go before us, Lord, in all we do
with your most gracious favour,
and guide us with your continual help,
that in all our works
begun, continued and ended in you,
we may glorify your holy name,
and finally by your mercy receive everlasting life;
through Jesus Christ our Lord.

The Christian Year: Collects and Post Communion Prayers
for Sundays and Festivals (Fourth Sunday Before Lent)

God be in my head and in my understanding
God be in my eyes and in my looking
God be in my mouth and in my speaking
God be in my heart and in my thinking
God be at my end and at my departing.

                                        The Sorum Primer

Be thou a bright flame before me,
Be thou a guiding star above me,
Be thou a smooth path below me,
Be thou a kindly shepherd behind me,
Today — tonight — and forever.

                                        St Columba of Iona

A General Thanksgiving

Almighty God, Father of all mercies,
we your unworthy servants give you most
   humble and hearty thanks
for all your goodness and loving kindness.
We bless you for our creation, preservation,
   and all the blessings of this life;
but above all for your immeasurable love
in the redemption of the world by our Lord Jesus Christ,
for the means of grace, and for the hope of glory.
And give us, we pray, such a sense of all your mercies
that our hearts may be unfeignedly thankful,
and that we show forth your praise,
not only with our lips but in our lives,
by giving up ourselves to your service,
and by walking before you in holiness
   and righteousness all our days;
through Jesus Christ our Lord,
to whom, with you and the Holy Spirit,

be all honour and glory,
for ever and ever. Amen.

Common Worship: Daily Prayer

Prayer

Prayer the Church's banquet, Angel's age,
  God's breath in man returning to his birth,
  The soul in paraphrase, heart in pilgrimage,
The Christian plummet, sounding heaven and earth;
Engine against th'Almighty, sinners' tower,
  Reversed thunder, Christ-side-piercing spear,
  The six-days world transposing in an hour, A kind of tune,
which all things hear and fear;
Softness, and peace, and joy, and love, and bliss,
  Exalted Manna, gladness of the best,
  Heaven in ordinary, man well drest,
The milky way, the bird of Paradise,
  Church-bells beyond the stars heard,
  the souls blood
  The land of spices; something understood.

George Herbert

Pure Joy

R. T. Kendall

In his thoroughly biblical and down-to-earth manner, R. T. Kendall explores the 'inexpressible and glorious joy' that God gives his children. What does this archaic-sounding concept mean for us here and now?

Hodder & Stoughton
£7.99
PB / 0 3408.6194 0

£2 OFF
£5.99 with voucher

Other titles by the same author

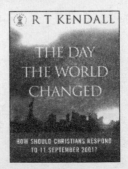

R.T. KENDALL

Pure Joy

First published in Great Britain in 2004
Hodder & Stoughton
A Division of Hodder Headline Ltd
338 Euston Road, London NW1 3BH

The Joy of God's Esteem

How can you believe if you accept praise from one another, yet make no effort to obtain the praise that comes from the only God?

(John 5:44)

This verse has influenced me, and probably governed me, more than any other verse in the Bible. I have probably quoted it more than any other verse in all my preaching ministry next to Romans 8:28. When someone asks me to sign a book or write my name in their Bible I tend to put Romans 8:28 after my name. I tried using John 5:44 a few times, but it confused people; some thought I was trying to send them a direct message or hint that I thought they needed that verse; so it did not edify them, and I stopped using it for that particular reason. But this *is* the verse that means more to me than any other. If I have an unfulfilled dream when it comes to writing a book, it would be an elaboration of this verse with a very full and detailed study of the glory of God.

The Authorised Version translates this verse, 'How can ye believe, which receive honour one of another, and seek not the honour that cometh from God only?' This suggests that we should seek only the honour of God and that there is an honour that comes from him that is distinct from the honour that comes from people. It is this idea that grips me most – because it indicates a promise that there is a special honour God delights to give to those who esteem it above the praise that comes from people.

Not that I myself have successfully or consistently sought to obtain the honour Jesus had in mind, or that I have even come close to receiving it. Hardly! I can only say that the depth to which this verse stirs me and grips me has left a longing in my heart that is so earnest that I have spent the last forty-five years endeavouring to understand and experience this verse for myself. Perhaps this verse has spoken to me so much simply because I have an acute weakness in wanting people's approval. I have always been convicted by Paul's words, 'Am I now trying to win the approval of men, or of God? Or am I trying to please men? If I were still trying to please men, I would not be a servant of Christ' (Galatians 1:10). This last sentence haunts me – that I might still be trying to please men – and so not be a servant of Christ. If this is true without any conditions or mitigating circumstances, I fear that I have been disqualified from being called a servant of Christ many times. For if I made a list of my greatest weaknesses, I am quite sure that this would be at the very top of the list: I want to please people too much.

None the less, I can say that I have tried hard over the years to exemplify the principles inherent in John 5:44, whether in small things or big things. Small things would refer to fishing for a compliment (when I should wait and let others say what they feel without any hints from me); big things would refer to major decisions at crucial stages in my life (like whether to endorse a controversial ministry or to accept a particular invitation).

It is interesting to note that Jesus did not rebuke the Jews he was addressing because they had not *obtained* the honour of God; he rebuked them because they had *made no attempt* to obtain it. It was not even in their minds to think in this manner. The implication is, they should have done so; they should have known better. Hundreds of years of teaching about the honour and glory of God should have resulted in their seeking it above all else. Indeed, had they been bent on seeking the honour that comes from God, they never would have missed the Messiah in the first place. They missed the Man that God sent to them because it was not a part of their way of thinking or doing things. This is the reason Jesus said, 'How *can* you believe…if you make no effort to obtain the praise that comes from the only God?' Not to make an attempt to obtain God's praise is what removes the possibility of true faith. Their seeking the praise of people apparently rendered faith an impossibility in one stroke.

This is a warning and an encouragement to you and me. The warning: if you and I do not make an attempt to receive the praise that comes from God rather than the praise of people, we too will find it impossible to exercise genuine faith. The encouragement: we are not required to have obtained the honour and praise of God, but only to *make an effort* to obtain it. God's commands are not burdensome (1 John 5:3). He is not demanding that we perfectly repudiate the praise of people and absolutely receive his praise; he is only asking us to make an effort to obtain his praise. Nothing can be more reasonable than that.

Jesus therefore asked, 'How *can* you believe…' if no attempt is made to seek solely the honour of God. The conclusion is: if you are not seeking God's honour but only the praise of people, it is not possible to have true faith. If you seek people's applause rather than God's praise, you render the possibility of believing out of the question, says Jesus. This, then, is how they missed their promised Messiah.

What is so scary about this implication is that you and I could continue to miss what God may be up to in his church generally and in our lives in particular. If I choose the praise of people over God's approval, I will be a victim of unbelief. I will render myself incapable of believing God, as he wants me to. I will likewise miss whatever God has chosen to do at the moment. Jonathan Edwards taught us that the task of every generation is to discover in which direction the Sovereign Redeemer is moving, then move in that direction. But if I am found being enamoured with the praise of people during the time God is at work in my day or in my area, I will miss seeing his glory – even if it is right in front of me. That is what happened to the ancient Jews in Israel and it can happen to us today. I can think of nothing worse than that.

This verse therefore contains an immense encouragement, namely, if I but *seek* – or make an effort to obtain – his honour, I will be able to believe and see what he is up to. That way, I won't miss his activity. I won't miss what he is doing, where he is at work and how he is moving. God has implicitly guaranteed in this verse that if you and I will set as a goal his honour and glory in all our thinking and decision-making, two things will follow: (1) we will be people of genuine faith, and (2) we will see him work – whenever, however, and wherever that may be.

This verse thus contains a promise of joy – a joy that no purer can be conceived. That joy is actually, personally and consciously receiving the praise of God. It is when he esteems me. He affirms me. He approves of me. He lets me know it in a definite way. There is no greater joy on earth than this.

We all grow up wanting parental approval. My desire to excel when I was a small boy in school was motivated almost entirely by the look on my dad's face when he saw my report card. I am not sure I ever outgrew that! During the last seven years of his life he had Alzheimer's disease, but just a year or two before this illness set in, when he was in his eighties, his approval meant the world to me. But how much more do we need our heavenly Father's approval. There is no greater joy to be had on this earth than the conscious awareness of his praise. Nothing compares. It is pure joy.

It was no small thing for Jesus to hear the words, 'This is my Son, whom I love; with him I am well pleased' (Matthew 3:17). That was at Jesus's baptism. Later on, when he was transfigured before Peter, James and John, he used the same words again, 'This is my Son, whom I love; with him I am well pleased. Listen to him!' (Matthew 17:5). These words thrilled Jesus to his fingertips. It is all he wanted to hear; to know he was pleasing his Father. That is all he lived for.

'...I always do what pleases him' (John 8:29). This is what gave him joy.

It is what will give us joy as well. Pure joy. The best feeling in the world. The most satisfying and fulfilling feeling in the world. It means a good conscience. It means you are walking in the light (1 John 1:7). It means God can use you. It means you won't miss anything he may want to do in your life and that you will be 'in' on it should he be pleased to move in your time. You won't be left out. All he envisages for you will be yours.

None of us wants to be a 'has been' – or a yesterday's man or woman. A horrible spiritual position is to be in a place where you can't hear God speak any more (Hebrews 5:11 – 6:6) or where you cannot be changed from glory to glory any more (2 Corinthians 3:18). But when you have God's definite praise and approval, believe me, that is as good as it gets. You know you haven't missed what God wants to do with you and that he can put you anywhere he pleases. Of course, because he is sovereign and all-powerful, he can put anybody anywhere he pleases – regardless of whether they have been pursuing his glory. But the *promise* of experiencing this honour is given to those who maintain good communication with him. I wish that all of us in his family did this.

The word 'esteem' means to think highly of; it means respect or favourable opinion. Can anything be more fantastic than to have God esteem you – to think highly of you? This, it seems to me, is somewhat different from love. It is wonderful to be loved by God, but God loves the world (John 3:16). God moreover loves all his people – his elect – with a particularity and security that is not the same as for those who are not his. Likewise, being esteemed by God suggests that one is not only loved by him, because you are a member of the family, but that you are honoured in a special way that not all in the family enjoy.

God said to Gideon, 'The LORD is with you, mighty warrior' (Judges 6:12). Three times the Lord said to Daniel, 'You are highly esteemed' (Daniel 9:23; 10:11, 19). Moses and Abraham had in

common that each was called God's friend (Exodus 33:11; Isaiah
42:8). God said of Hezekiah, 'There was no-one like him among all
the kings of Judah, either before him or after him' (2 Kings 18:5).
God did not say this of every king, because not every king was
obedient as Hezekiah was. God said of Josiah, 'Neither before nor
after Josiah was there a king like him who turned to the LORD as
he did – with all his heart and with all his soul and with all his
strength, in accordance with the Law of Moses' (2 Kings 23:25). King
David was called a man after God's own heart (1 Samuel 13:14; Acts
13:22). The fact that a man as vulnerable as David could be called that
shows us that perfection is not required to have God's esteem! No
human being on earth is without sin: '...there is no-one who does
not sin' (1 Kings 8:46). Sinless perfection has never existed except in
the person of Jesus Christ (Hebrews 4:15).

What is required of us is not perfection, but *seeking* – making an
effort to obtain – his praise and esteem. It must be something you
want in your heart of hearts. It must be pre-eminently important to
you. It must regulate your life and the decisions you make. What is
the reward? Pure joy.

How much time and energy is required on our part? It all depends.
If we *want* his esteem, it follows that we are going to walk in any ray
of light he gives to us along the way. We prove we want his esteem by
the decisions we make. The honour of God is therefore at our fingertips. It is closer than our hands or our feet, closer than the air we
breathe. It is centred in the mind, heart and will. In the mind, that we
perceive the difference between the praise of people and the commendation of God. In the heart, that we sincerely want his honour and
approval more than we want anything in this world. In the will, that
we demonstrate what we say we want in our hearts by what we say
when faced with the temptation to desire earthly praise more than we
want his smile. One could say, therefore, that to have the esteem of God
is the easiest thing in the world to achieve because he is eager to show
it. And yet to feel that esteem and hear his 'well done' comes to those
who show that it is really what they want by their words and deeds.

God had already esteemed Israel. The Jews were special. They were the primary object of God's affections. God has always had a 'soft spot' for Israel, but they had developed a preference for the praise of one another. This is why Jesus asked them, 'How can you believe if you accept praise from one another, yet make no effort to obtain the praise that comes from the only God?' They accepted praise from one another because this was where their hearts were. '…for they loved praise from men more than praise from God' (John 12:43). Jesus said of them, 'Everything they do is done for men to see' (Matthew 23:5). This is why they announced their almsgiving with trumpets – 'to be honoured by men' (Matthew 6:2). They prayed in public for the same reason (Matthew 6:5), and it is what motivated them to fast (Matthew 6:16). The concept of doing these things utterly and totally for God alone was not something they apparently even considered. This, then, is why they could not believe, and this unbelief was the bottom line in their failing to spot the Messiah.

It is a powerful and wonderful thing to have God's esteem. This is possible not because of our profile, our importance or performance, but because we want it more than anything else. This means that *you* – whoever you are – can have God's esteem. You don't have to be Daniel the prophet. Daniel was called highly esteemed not because he was a prophet, but because he loved God more than the approval of people (Daniel 6:10). It was his love for God's honour that put him where he was; he could be trusted with a high profile *because* it meant less to him than God's honour.

You or I may not be given the privilege to prophesy before royalty or heads of state, but we can be just as esteemed by the Father as Daniel was. Profile does not mean that God is pleased with you. There are people who are rich and famous, but they will never experience God's commendation. All that is required is to want it – more than anything. That's all. Our acts and words will prove that we really want it.

Therefore high profile on earth has nothing to do with receiving God's esteem in heaven. You can be royal or a head of state and never get it, be an ambassador and never get it, a merchant banker or a wealthy stockbroker and never know God's 'well done'. For these things mean little in heaven. Jesus went so far as to say that 'What is highly valued among men is detestable in God's sight' (Luke 16:15). Of course, this does not mean that if you are royal or a head of state, you will *not* have the knowledge of God's esteem. God loves to show his approval to all people. But it has nothing to do with their position or earthly prestige. It has all to do with their preference for his applause rather than that of men and women.

If you say that you really do want the knowledge of his esteem more than you want the praise of people, I can give you a prophecy I know will be fulfilled! My prophecy to you is, you will have an opportunity *soon* – very soon – to show which means more to you: people's praise or God's praise of you. Do not be surprised if my prophecy to you is fulfilled before another day passes!

Signs Of The Times:
Modern Icons And Their Meaning

Peter Graystone

This highly original and timely book asks, what is the spiritual meaning of the icons of youth culture, such as tattoos, body piercing, logo-loyalty, sport and celebrity status?

Canterbury Press
£7.99
PB / 1 8531.1566 5

£2 OFF
£5.99 with voucher

SIGNS
OF THE
TIMES

THE SECRET LIVES OF TWELVE EVERYDAY ICONS

PETER GRAYSTONE

First published in 2004 by the Canterbury Press Norwich
(a publishing imprint of Hymns Ancient & Modern Limited, a registered charity)
St Mary's Works, St Mary's Plain, Norwich, Norfolk, NR3 3BH

The Tattoo

The answer to your first question is: 'No I haven't.'

I don't think I would either, not even if I was twenty years younger and it was the ultimate fashion statement of the moment. Which, of course, it is! It is the commitment I couldn't cope with. Now that is very twenty-first century!

Commitment comes no more easily to me than to anyone else whose values are shaped by the age in which we live. If I am in a job for more than three years I convince myself that I have gone stale. I am frequently bored with all my clothes, all my music, and I can't find a single book on my overflowing shelves that I want to read. I have even found myself complaining to God that there are not enough colours in the spectrum because I have seen the ones I like already. It is a miracle, which I put down to grace alone, that I have kept a relationship with God alive for two decades, so you can imagine how unlikely it is that I will decorate myself with something that is absolutely never going to go.

But Bjork has got one. It is on her arm and it is a Norse symbol like a snowflake. It signifies seeking strength for the future in the cultural hinterland of your ancestry. Drawing on Iceland's rich mythological heritage, it seems appropriate to her. However, my cultural heritage is Croydon, and it is difficult to know what kind of strength one is supposed to draw from that!

Robbie Williams has many. His arm looks like a cheese grater. He has got two with words in them. One reads 'Elvis grant me serenity' and the other reads 'Born to be mild'. It is interesting that in both cases he has chosen words that allude to Christian sayings. I wonder what he yearns after.

David Beckham has five. At least, he has five that you could see in that infamous publicity shoot, and it is difficult to imagine where he would put one that isn't already on show. He has got his son's name, Brooklyn, at the base of his spine. He has got his wife Victoria's name on his forearm, written in Hindi (although apparently there is an embarrassing mistake in one of the characters). I won't tell you what is on his chest because I think there are some things that ought to remain private between a man and his one million readers of the *News of the World*.

Mika Salo, lead driver for the Toyota Formula One team, has one on his finger. It looks like a twig about to burst into leaf, and it encircles the fourth finger of his left hand in the place where one might expect to see a wedding ring. His wife Noriko has one too, in exactly the same position. They were tattooed together on the day of their marriage.

Tom Cruise has reputedly paid a fortune for laser treatment to have NK removed from one buttock, but the gossip columns have not revealed whether PC has appeared on the other.

Geri Halliwell's tattoo disappeared overnight, which seems slightly unfair on the legions of teenage girls who managed to scrape together enough money from their Saturday jobs to copy her first decision, but will never earn enough to copy her second decision. This leads to the strange prospect, sixty years hence, of a generation of elderly ladies in nursing homes with grey and wrinkled smudges that they assure the nurses used to be roses and birds.

Lloyd Cole sings of the ultimate embarrassment – the girl who promised that the relationship would last forever, but moved on and became just an indelible 'Jennifer' written in blue underneath a heart and an arrow on his arm.'[1]

Could anyone have predicted ten years ago that the tattoo would become the major fashion statement of the beginning of the twenty-first century?

Obviously tattooing has an honourable tradition. Every culture in the history of the world has at some point found it attractive to decorate the body by marking it or piercing it or stretching it in some way. And I have no doubt that our Celtic ancestors hunting on the mountains in wode would recognize in the tattoos of today the spirit of what was found beautiful centuries ago. We now deplore Victorian missionaries who went to Africa and were so shocked by what they saw that they insisted new converts to Christianity combed their hair and hid their body-painting under skirts. Through the goodness of God some lessons have been learnt from history. Perhaps that is why there are no Christians picketing tattoo parlours denouncing what is going on inside as the work of Satan.

However, tattooing also has a dishonourable history. It has been used to brand slaves and to number prisoners or workers in concentration camps. It has become useful to people who perpetrate evil as a way of dehumanizing others, permanently diminishing their dignity until they cease to be personalities and become someone else's numbered property. It may be in this context, or simply to make the worship of the Hebrews distinct from heathen practices, that the Old Testament Law forbade the practice: 'Do not cut your bodies for the dead or put tattoo marks on yourselves. I am the Lord.'[2]

The kind of tattooing we know today has its roots in eighteenth-century Polynesian society, and Europeans first encountered it when the accounts and pictures of james Cook's voyage to Tahiti came to Britain. joseph Banks, the naturalist who accompanied Cook on his first voyage to the Pacific Ocean recorded this:

> I shall now mention their methods of painting their bodies, or tattow as it is called in their language. They do this by inlaying black under their skin in such a manner as to be indelible. Everyone is thus marked in different parts of his body according to his humour or different circumstances of his life . . . I saw this operation performed on the

buttocks of a girl about fourteen years of age. For some time she bore it with great resolution, but afterwards began to complain, and in little time grew so outrageous that all the threats and force her friends could use hardly obliged her to endure it.[3]

In the islands of the South Pacific, tattooing was not mere decoration, but had a deeply spiritual significance. The tiny, detailed flecks and curls of patterning that made up Samoan tattoos were held to protect the bearer from the dangers of the spiritual world by sealing all that was sacred within the body. In Tahiti, broad areas of black imposed on the buttocks and around the genitals were a rite of passage, indicating that boys and girls had reached puberty and could enter certain social and sexual relationships without risking spiritual injury to themselves or others. It seems that the pain involved in achieving the tattoo was as vital a part of the experience as the finished result. The bravado required is doubtless still part of people's motivation today, although it is worth remembering that in Polynesia the tattoo was created with a chisel, hammer and crude ink with only the encouragement of watching friends as an anaesthetic!

Christian missionaries arrived first in the Polynesian islands in 1797, and by 1850 the islanders were largely converted to Christianity. The London Missionary Society, as you would anticipate, saw tattoos as indicative of a sinful life and urged converts to repent of them. Because of their permanence, the islanders bore the guilt they felt for what they'd done innocently in early life in a very obvious way. However, children brought up in the Christian faith were kept free from tattoos. Those who broke the prohibition were punished by being scoured with sandstone until their skin was torn away. The missionaries encouraged the association between tattooing and sin by changing its use. They used the techniques to brand criminals as a punishment, for instance imposing the word 'thief' on an offender's face. There is a line of shame that stretches indelibly from concentration camp commandants to Christian missionaries.

However, as fast as European Christianity was putting converts into trousers, a cultural exchange was happening of its own accord. It took less than thirty years for a tattoo to become essential fashion for sailors world-wide. A new kind of imagery developed, making less use of abstract designs and more of recognizable shapes and pictures – often maritime images. At the trial following the mutiny on board the *Bounty*, Captain Bligh used tattoos which had been gained in Tahiti to identify the mutineers. For the record, Fletcher Christian had a cross on his chest and an anchor on his buttock.

In the nineteenth and early twentieth centuries it became a widespread practice for sailors to have an image of the crucifixion of Jesus tattooed across their backs. The thinking behind this was that a sea captain, no matter how harsh, would not dare order the lash to be administered to the image of Christ. The spiritual protection which the indigenous Polynesian religions had offered through tattoos had been absorbed in a much more practical way by the Christian religion – not as taught, but as lived. (Tattooed images of Jesus have endured in popularity. Phil Taylor, who has been darts world-champion ten times, sports the crucified Jesus on his right calf. Curiously, the footballer Diego Maradona has Fidel Castro in exactly the same place.)

In 1882 the future King George V created a remarkable precedent by having the image of a dragon tattooed while he was in the Far East. (He was seventeen. Under presentday legislation he would have to wait another year to be tattooed in the UK.) For a brief period, high-quality tattoos became fashionable among the upper classes as a result of this. However, this was much against the tide of belief about the appropriateness of the practice. In fact, criminologists such as Cesare Lombroso interpreted the desire to brand oneself in this way as evidence of 'a degenerate and primitive mentality that arose from the bad breeding of the socially and biologically inferior classes',[4] and the presence of a tattoo was sometimes offered in court as evidence of criminally inclined character.

For fifty years after the turn of the century tattooing was almost exclusively associated with the navy or the military – a badge of pride in your ship or patriotic fervour, or a tribute to your lover back home. It was something accepted and perhaps respected (an unspoken acknowledgement of having served one's country during war). However, it was definitely a male adornment, and almost exclusively working class again. In fact John F. Kennedy had one that he picked up as a young subaltern of which he was ashamed later in life because he felt it was beneath the dignity of someone who had risen to become President of the United States.

It was during the second half of the twentieth century that groups on the fringes of society adopted tattooing as a mark of clan identity. Anyone who was in his or her heyday in the 1960s or 1970s associated tattoos almost exclusively with Hell's Angels, or later with skinheads. It was part of a revival in the art which emanated from California (again, starting in the seaports). By the 1980s it was almost entirely associated with the tribal instincts of urban youth, and with being aggressively at odds with society.

So it would have been difficult to anticipate that this was going to develop, in the last few years, into a fashion worn with dignity across a large demographic range – a mainstream style accessory spotted by a broad spectrum of the population. And it would have been well-nigh impossible to foresee that its main appeal would be to the middle classes, and that women would be inclined to decorate themselves with a tattoo as much as (and amongst hardcore nightclubbers, more than) men. But that is the case, and any lingering doubts about it were swept aside in June 2003 when Selfridges department store in London, that shrine to respectable middle-class aspiration, opened its own booth – Zulu Tattoo.

Jon Simmons runs a tattoo parlour in Central London. Not only does he see himself as an artist, he has a degree to prove it. There is not a centimetre of pink left on him! His suite is not dingy or threatening, as one might have expected ten years ago. It is bright and clean, with magazines to read in the waiting room and high-class advertising on the walls. In fact, it looks like a dentist's waiting room. It is a place designed to make a middle-class consumer feel at home.

I say hallo to him every time I walk past, because he stands outside to smoke a cigarette. Obviously, for hygiene reasons he is not allowed to smoke inside his studio. However, environmental health regulations will not allow smoking in the waiting room either, because his assistant serves cappuccino there.

In 1992 he visited New Zealand to research traditional Maori designs and techniques of body decoration, which were undergoing a revival. In remote places such as Samoa the practice had never been completely suppressed, despite the best efforts of the missionaries. Jon Simmons speaks zealously of the function of the tattoo (and specifically of designs with spiritual significance in the traditions of indigenous peoples) as running counter to the materialist culture of developed nations. The tone of his voice is almost religious as he describes the experience of getting and giving a tattoo as transcendent. It has, he says, grounded his sense of 'home' in his own body. He sees it as a way of surrendering one's body to a mark of something higher and of more value than consumerism. 'A mobile phone is for show, but a tattoo is for life.'

Jon sees the renaissance of the tattoo as one part of a 'modern primitivism' which, feeling let down by organized religion, seeks inspiration in aboriginal religions and paganism. However, he scorns those who seek motifs that have significance in the heritage of ancient peoples solely because of their aesthetic value. (In this respect Celtic, Maori and Chinese designs are of the moment.) He is proud, he says, to mark people with images that they have chosen 'not because they are pretty, but to create a beautiful cultural exchange'. And his cheeks glow blue with admiration when he reflects on the decoration of Robbie Williams' shoulder, which was described earlier: 'Not static, but a living thing – curling and spiralling.' It is, he reveals, the work of the Polynesian artist Te Rangitu Netana, regarded as the greatest living exponent of his craft. (I should not have described it so dismissively in the opening paragraphs!) Looking to the future, Jon points out that being incorporated into a fashion system that expresses identity and spirituality, the present role of the tattoo might be understood sympathetically by men and women who lived in the South Pacific islands two hundred years ago.

Nicholas Thomas, however, doubts that the tattoo will ever be accepted as a 'safe' fashion accessory. In his book Skin Deep he points out that, historically, a period of acceptance of tattoos has always prompted new ways of shocking people with the imagery:

> Urban youth is creating new tattoo styles that draw their imagery ... from graffiti. These kinds of development indicate that tattooing has not simply become incorporated into some fashionable system that threatens or offends no one.[5]

In what way is it a sign of the times that the concept of tattooing, which may be as old as time itself, is suddenly the nation's hottest fashion? Thinking about that question has drawn me back to the Bible. Tattooing is a biblical metaphor. Its most memorable use is by Paul, who employed it to describe a characteristic of the Holy Spirit:

> You were included in Christ when you heard the word of truth, the gospel of your salvation. Having believed, you were marked in him with a seal, the promised Holy Spirit, who is a deposit guaranteeing our inheritance until the redemption of those who are God's possession – to the praise of his glory.[6]

'Marked with a seal' is the Hebrew word for tattooed or branded. Christians have been tattooed with the Holy Spirit, an invisible but absolutely permanent mark of belonging to God. Shoppers in the market place thirty years after Jesus did not purchase their goods from Tesco in prepacked containers containing just enough for two; they bought goods in substantial quantities! Sackfuls of produce, livestock still live and refusing to be stock still, and perhaps even humans! Goods bought at the beginning of a day would be tattooed with a personal brand. Being indelibly and permanently marked with a sign showed that they belonged to one owner and were unavailable to anyone else until they were collected by the customer at the end of the day. The tattoo was a deposit that guaranteed ownership.

Committed ownership is the concept about which Paul is talking. As Christians purchased by God at enormous expense – it cost the life of his Son – we can never, absolutely never, be taken from him to belong to anyone else. How can anyone tell? Because we have been tattooed with the Holy Spirit – invisible, but straightforwardly obvious to God, and increasingly obvious to anyone who sees that the influence of God's ownership of our lives changes us for the better. It is God's deposit on us guaranteeing that, on the day we meet him, he will be able to say without fear of contradiction: 'That man, that woman, that child is mine – and there is the sign which proves it.'

For the Christian that is an exhilarating truth. Somewhere hidden about your person is a mark invisible to everyone but God – a unique and extraordinary tattoo which is your guarantee that you will join him in Heaven. You can't roll up your sleeve and point it out to people. You have to find other ways of showing them. Old fashioned ways like 'love, joy, peace, patience, kindness, goodness, faithfulness, gentleness and self-control'.[7] Against such things there is no law, and against such things there is no stereotypically British reserve. And there never will be!

There never will be, because a tattoo is totally permanent. It is never going to change without extreme and expensive difficulty. So, as a sign of the times, it can speak to us of God's irrevocable commitment to us. To ordinary and undeserving members of a changeable and fashionconscious society! That commitment is never going to weaken until we are his own close possession, as Paul remarkably puts it: 'to the praise of his glory'.

However, the biggest surprise about the rise and rise of the tattoo in the last few years is that it has happened at a time when we are led to believe that commitment of any kind is a diminished concept. Young people, so it is said, are not prepared to commit themselves to marriage. They are not prepared to commit themselves to relationships over a long term. The concept of a job for life is yesterday's. The concept of living in one town for life is that of a previous generation. We have disposable everything. We recycle into something new and different. We make dates and then text people to change the arrangements at the last minute because we get a better offer.

Commitment, so we are told, simply does not figure in the make-up of our society. Except for tattoos! A person who is in every way a child of this generation will freely make a decision to commit himself or herself for all time to a fashion statement.

As a Christian that thrills me! Sometimes I feel that we are on the verge of giving up expecting people to commit themselves in faith for a lifetime because it runs against the spirit of the age. But the tattoo tells us not to give up hope in the gospel message which we hold out – that the way God intended us to live is in permanent, life-enhancing commitment to him. There are still some things that people deem so valuable that they are prepared to invest their whole lives in them. A new tattoo is one. The gospel of new life, new hope, new expectations, new joy can be another.

What is it that can draw out of people this heroic, all-embracing commitment to God? It is his gratuitous, all-forgiving commitment to us. And if we ever have cause to doubt it the Holy Spirit, his deposit within us, is the guarantee that he is our owner.

Alison Lyon has a tattoo. I haven't seen it, but several years of working as colleagues have made me sure that I can take her at her word. And besides, I joined thousands of others to hear the whizz of the drill on Radio 4's *Home Truths*. She wanted to mark the twentieth anniversary of her recovery from cancer. Among the few physical signs left of her fight against the illness were the irremovable blue marks that had been put on her torso, front and back, to line up the machines that delivered therapeutic radiography. They themselves were tattoos, and they were a memory of a bad thing. So she decided to have the marks incorporated into a design of her own choosing that would be full of symbolism as a sign of thanksgiving.

Ali told me, 'The little dots that remain from my treatment are not that unsightly, but they are quite obvious and they are not self-explanatory. One reason for the tattoo was to draw attention away from them on to something that doesn't require a medical life history to explain. It is a green spiral which, for me, is a very godly symbol. Both the shape (in and out, out and in, on and on) and the colour (fertility, which technically I do not have because my ovaries were wrecked by the treatment) are important to me.'

Her friends have found it inspiring that she has chosen to redeem something scarring and indelible into something beautiful and full of meaning. It is a reflection of the God in whom we believe – faithful through bad times and good, and always at work on a project to bring good out of evil on earth. And he is ultimately intent on 'bringing all things in heaven and on earth together under one head, namely Christ', as Paul puts it when he writes about being tattooed by the Holy Spirit.[8]

Throughout history, the way the body has been presented has never been wholly natural. It has always been modified and groomed for social reasons. And in equal measure, the way it has been manipulated has been either to express social norms or to exclude a person from them. But tattooing is unique in this because of its enduring quality – not just adorning people but creating illustrated men and women.

There is, however, one word of caution to add before we rejoice in the possibility of commitment in the twenty-first century. Just recently something insidious has sneaked its way into fashion. It is called the temporary tattoo. It looks like the real thing, but after six weeks it fades away to leave not a mark behind. It is made with henna, or from some kind of chemical transfer, and it is only applied to the surface instead of being drilled indelibly into the skin. People who want the style but not the commitment can have a tattoo safely in the knowledge that if they change their mind, they can change their appearance too. In fact, looking at some of the rock stars who are so conscious of moving with the fashion of the moment, one cannot help but wonder whether some of them have cheated! Is it possible that when we see the shoulders of some celebrities after the craze has moved on their tattoos will mysteriously have faded away? Who can tell? Let's wait and see!

There is an insidious brand of spirituality around as well. It is one which says that I can choose what works for me today – a bit of Eastern mysticism, a bit of Buddhism, a bit of Celtic Christianity – knowing that when it stops working I can scrub it away and move on. That is not the gospel of 'hope in Christ for his praise and glory'; that is the gospel of hope for the best because you never know what might happen. It is in startling contrast to what God has done for us. But astonishingly the facts remain the same – even when a person's commitment to God turns out to be a six-week wonder, God's commitment to him or her goes on and on. He is a God of permanence – the Bible calls him 'the Rock', the great unchangeable 'I am'. 'Although we may be faithless, he remains faithful.'[9]

God, the unchangeable one. Jesus, the one whose commitment to us went as far as death itself. The Holy Spirit, who is the tattoo that has marked us out as God's until the day we meet him face to face. A sign of the times? A sign for all times! Don't be scared to expect commitment in a generation which is obsessed with style, because God was committed first!

Notes

1 'Jennifer She Said', Lloyd Cole and the Commotions, SBK Songs Ltd., 1987.
2 Leviticus 19:28.
3 Joseph Banks, recorded in *The Journals of Captain James Cook*, 1769.
4 Cesare Lombroso, *Crime, its Causes and Remedies*, 1899.
5 Nocholas Thomas, *Skin Deep: A History of Tattooing*, National Maritime Museum, 2002.
6 Ephesians 1:13.
7 Galatians 5:22, 23.
8 Ephesians 1:10.
9 2 Timothy 2:13.

So You Think You're
A New Testament Writer

Mike Coles

Ever wished you could put the gospel and epistle writers on the spot and ask them what they really meant? Well, in this innovative book you can, through 'interviews' with the writers.

BRF
£6.99
PB / 1 8410.1183 5

£2 OFF
£4.99 with voucher

Other titles by the same author

MIKE COLES interviews some biblical celebrity
guests in front of a live audience in the chat show...

SO YOU THINK YOU'RE A
New Testament writer

Text copyright © Mike Coles 2004

Published by
The Bible Reading Fellowship
First Floor, Elsfield Hall, 15–17 Elsfield Way, Oxford OX2 8FG

Introduction

Before the show begins, there are a few points that you will need to bear in mind.

First, the show is actually 'outside time'. In other words, there is no exact time when the show takes place. All you need to know is that it is some time during the first century ad. The actual date is not important. Each show begins in the late afternoon / early evening.

Second, the venue. Here, you need to imagine the show taking place at the home of a wealthy person living in Jerusalem. The house has a huge courtyard, with two or three rooms built around. The large courtyard is set up with a small stage at one end, and stools and backed chairs facing it for the audience.

Finally, when the Bible is quoted, no one translation is ever used. It will often depend on who is quoting the text and what style is appropriate. And so, straight on to the show.

Standing in the middle of the stage, Mike begins:

'Hi there, folks. Welcome to this brand new and exciting show. What a great honour it is for me to be able to chat to some of the chaps who were responsible for writing those books that make up the New Testament. That's right, folks, those 27 wonderful books!

Now, we all know that there would be no books, no New Testament and no show here tonight, if it had not been for that most remarkable man, Jesus. Jesus didn't leave us any writings, but we know that his life and ministry, and what he said it all meant, were preserved and passed on by some of his main followers. Despite absolutely awful persecution, these followers spread the message far and wide. Their message was simple: God had become human in Jesus Christ. This Jesus came to show us all what God is like, how he would save us, and how we should live.

My special guests, the New Testament writers, show Jesus as the person who fulfils centuries of promise and hope, of wonderful prophecies that echo throughout the Old Testament. My guests also write about how Jesus will return a second time to establish a kingdom of love, justice and truth. They tell us that Jesus invites us to say sorry for all our sins, to turn to God, to accept that Jesus died on the cross to wipe away all our sins, and that we should make Jesus central in our lives and ask him to help us in our everyday lives to please God.

Well, folks, what a powerful message this New Testament contains. I am delighted to say that over the next five weeks, I will have the honour and pleasure to speaking to – wait for it – Matthew, Mark, Luke, John and last, but by no means least, Paul!

Episode 1

Mike Coles chats to Matthew

Musical introduction

Just before the show proper begins, a small group of musicians walk on to the stage. They are mainly singers, male and female, but some of them play rhythm and melody instruments. You'll hear more about music during biblical times later in the show.

The group begins the show by singing the words of Mary in that amazing song of praise recorded in Luke, chapter one, verses 46 to 55.

These words were used as a great hymn in worship at a very early date. The audience also join in, as most of them know the words, and they make a glorious sound.

At the end the audience applaud and cheer. The music group exit the stage. Mike thanks the group as they leave.

MIKE: Now, ladies and gentlemen, without any further ado, I would like you to welcome this week's guest, that one-time dodgy tax collector turned good – Matthew, son of Alphaeus!

The audience gives Matthew a very warm welcome, with plenty of enthusiastic applause, although there are one or two heckles, and a few 'boos' can be heard.

MIKE: Matthew, welcome to this brand new show. I'm sorry about the hecklers. There are obviously a few folk in the audience who still remember you as a tax collector!

MATTHEW: God bless you, Mike. It's great to be here. Don't worry about the hecklers. I can totally understand their anger. In fact, I do remember one or two of their faces from back in Capernaum, where I was a greedy man. I hope that later in the show I'll get a chance to explain myself and apologize for my pretty awful past.

MIKE: Most definitely, Matthew. In fact, I look forward to chatting about your tax collecting days a little later.

You know, I have to say, you really are looking remarkably well. What's your secret?

MATTHEW: Plenty of olives and olive oil, Mike. That's the secret – and fish when I can afford it!

MIKE: Sounds like great advice to me!

So, Matthew, tell me a little about your upbringing. You're quite an educated chap, aren't you?

MATTHEW: My dad was a strict man. He made sure I became fluent in both Aramaic and Greek, and from a young age I was quite skilled in arithmetic.

Someone shouts from the audience, 'You can't have been that good at maths, mate! You used to charge me far too much as a bloomin' tax collector!'

MIKE: Oh dear, we're back on that again. OK, then, let's talk about those days. Why tax collecting?

MATTHEW: It was simply for the cash, Mike. I was greedy. The Roman government saw me as an educated man, skilled in maths. They told me I'd make a fair bit of money, and I did.

MIKE: Matthew, tell us why tax collectors are so hated. Try to explain why you've got a few enemies in the audience tonight.

MATTHEW: Well, obviously, nobody likes to pay taxes at the best of time. But there are three reasons why we are so unpopular.

First, the Romans employed us, and they're hated by the Jews because they're occupying our land. I'm Jewish myself, of course, so my fellow countrymen thought I was a traitor for working for the Romans.

Second, we have a reputation for being dishonest. The Romans let us charge a rate of tax that would also provide a living for ourselves. Some of us, including me, interpreted this privilege more liberally than others.

Finally, as tax collectors, we often come into contact with Gentiles (that means anyone who's not Jewish), which according to the Jewish faith makes us 'unclean'.

But of course, that's all in the past. I am so sorry to all those I cheated. Those of you in the audience whom I've offended, I beg your forgiveness. Since meeting Jesus, my whole life has changed. I was a wicked man, and I am really sorry.

At this point there is a huge round of applause from the audience.

MIKE: Thanks for being so honest. You've certainly won all the audience over now. This brings us on nicely to one of the biggest questions I wanted to ask you this evening. We've talked a little about your past, but what we're all dying to know is, what happened? One minute you're a lousy tax collector, making money, partying every other night, making all sorts of enemies, and the next minute you give all this up. Your whole life just turned upside down. Matthew, could you please tell us how this man Jesus changed your life?

MATTHEW: As a tax collector on the big toll road running through Capernaum, I used to get to hear about everything that was going on in the area. I started to hear about this man called Jesus. People were describing him as a rabbi with a real difference. I heard folk saying that he had performed miracles, healing folk all over the place. I'd heard that he was a wonderful storyteller. People were saying that he wasn't like the other Jewish teachers they knew. He didn't walk around thinking he was all it, trying to look really holy and important like some religious teachers and leaders I've come across!

The other thing that really interested me was that I'd heard that he mixed with anyone and everyone; apparently, he didn't go around telling people how wicked they were. As a tax collector I was criticized almost every day by the other Jewish leaders and teachers of the Law. To hear about a teacher who didn't try to make people feel guilty fascinated me. I began to look forward to coming across this Jesus from Nazareth.

The other thing I would like to say is that, during this stage in my life, I wasn't really happy. Yes, I had money, I threw parties every other night, but I wasn't happy. Who can be totally happy when they're hated by nearly everyone around? The only friends I did have were people like me, fellow tax collectors and other dodgy people.

That's why this chap Jesus really interested me. If he turned up one day while I was collecting taxes, what would he say to me? Would he just condemn me like all the other teachers that used to walk by? I began to think about this a lot.

MIKE: I notice in your Gospel, chapter 9 verse 9, your first meeting with Jesus is described. It's in Mark's Gospel as well, chapter 2 verses 13 and 14, and Luke chapter 5 verses 27 and 28. These Gospel accounts say what happened, but not what was going through your mind. Tell us about it.

MATTHEW: Like I mentioned before, Mike, I was not a happy chap, and I had been hearing a great deal about this man Jesus, the rabbi. Deep down, I really was hoping that I might get the chance to meet him. I'd heard how he had changed people's lives, and that's what I wanted – some sort of change in my life. Exactly what change, I didn't know. But things were not right.

It was one afternoon in Capernaum when I heard a large crowd walking towards me. I began to hear people shouting out the name of Jesus. I can tell you now, my heart starting beating like the clappers. This was the man I had heard so much about, and before I knew it, he was standing in front of me. He stared at me. I expected to get a load of abuse as per usual – to be told what a terrible sinner I was. Instead, I heard the two most amazing words I'd ever heard, two words that were to change my entire life. Jesus simply said to me, 'Follow me.'

Well, Mike, you can only imagine my reaction. At that precise moment, my life was turned upside down. A rabbi had spoken to me kindly, not judged me as a sinner. But not only that, I was being given the opportunity to follow him – this great man, the talk of the town. I had tears in my eyes; a great weight was lifted from my heart. I knew at that moment, I couldn't spend another second collecting taxes. I was aware that if you gave up your rights as a tax collector, you could never go back to the job, but I didn't care. Jesus had called me.

At this point there is a huge round of applause from the audience. Many members of the audience are clearly moved after listening to Matthew's words.

MIKE: It's a real pleasure to have you share that experience with us, Matthew. Did you literally just drop everything and follow Jesus?

MATTHEW: That's exactly what I did! I wanted to start everything again, there and then. I was just rotting away inside. Jesus saying, 'Follow me' was all I needed. There was nothing to hold me back. The money, the partying, all of that just made me more and more miserable. This man Jesus, and what he had to offer, was all I wanted.

MIKE: Many folk already thought that Jesus was crazy asking you, a dodgy tax collector, to join him. Didn't he then go on to your house later that evening and mix with a whole load of down-and-out 'sinners'?

MATTHEW: He certainly did. Once I'd walked out of my office, I immediately asked Jesus if he'd like to have supper with me that evening. I did it as a little gesture of hospitality.

I was a tax collector, and Jesus still spoke to me and cared for me, so I also invited loads of other tax collectors along, and all sorts of 'sinners' – mainly what you might call non-observant Jews, the ones who didn't follow the teachings of the Law.

We had a great evening! Many of my guests were really moved that Jesus, this great rabbi, dared enter a house full of so many disreputable people. I can tell you now, it wasn't just my life that changed that day, but many of my guests thought very deeply about their own lives after listening to Jesus talk and teach.

MIKE: You mention in your Gospel that during this meal some Pharisees turned up and started moaning about Jesus. Who were these people and what actually happened?

MATTHEW: The Pharisees were the teachers who were really keen on keeping all the tiniest details of the Law, so I think you can all probably guess why they weren't happy. They simply asked Jesus' disciples why Jesus, the rabbi, was mixing with all these sinners. How could Jesus, if he was in his right mind, eat with us lot? Jesus heard what they were saying, and what he went on to say in reply was wonderful.

MIKE: That's right. Didn't he say something about needing a doctor and being sick?

MATTHEW: What he said, Mike, was brilliant, as it always was! He said to the Pharisees, 'People who are well do not need a doctor, only those who are sick.' The great thing then was that he gave them some homework to do.

The audience laugh.

MATTHEW: He said to them, 'Go and find out what is meant by the scripture that says: "It's kindness that I want, not animal sacrifices." I haven't come to call respectable people, but all the outcasts.'

MIKE: Excellent stuff! I presume that Jesus was making the point that what really counts is human relationships, not just religious rule-keeping.

MATTHEW: Yes, what we see here is Jesus expressing his compassion for sinners. That's why he came, that was his mission — to save sinners. Jesus was also having a go at the self-righteousness of the Pharisees. They weren't all bad, but many of them walked around so full of themselves. They didn't realize that they too were sick and needed a doctor.

Big cheers from the audience here.

MIKE: I think most of tonight's audience have come across some of these dodgy Pharisees from time to time!

At this point in the show, Matthew (and I hope you don't mind), I'd like to go over to the audience and ask them if they've got any questions for you.

MATTHEW: I'd be delighted to answer any questions, Mike, as long as they're not too tricky!

Audience laugh.

MIKE: So, ladies and gentlemen, boys and girls, who would like to start the ball rolling?

OK, the lady in the third row, wearing the blue tunic with the embroidered edges around the neckline.[1] Yes, you're the one. Could you tell us your name, where you're from, and what's your question?

'Good evening. My name is Rebekah from Caesarea Philippi. First of all, I'd like to say how excited I am to be here tonight. God bless you, Matthew. Could you please explain why it is that, in your Gospel, you quote from the Old Testament 41 times, which is a great deal more than the other Gospel writers?'

MATTHEW: Well, good evening, Rebekah. I'm just as excited as you about being here, and may God bless you too! Thanks for the great question – was it really 41 times? My immediate answer to you is to point out where my Gospel has been placed in the Bible. It follows immediately after the Old Testament, and stands at the beginning of the New. In other words, it's like a link between the two. One of the main reasons why I wrote my Gospel was to show that Jesus is the Messiah – the great leader promised in the Old Testament. You may all have noticed that in the 41 times I quote from the Old Testament, I nearly always say, '... so that it might be fulfilled'.

Also, to answer the question, I need to remind you that in the first place I wrote my Gospel for Jewish Christians, to help strengthen their faith that Jesus truly is the Messiah. The 41 times I quote from the Old Testament are to show that Jesus is the fulfilment of all Old Testament prophecy. Christ was not only born as a Jew, but he was sent, first, to the Jews. As the prophet Isaiah said (oops! Here I go again), 'Unto us a child is born, unto us a son is given.'

A big round of applause from the audience.

MIKE: A great question, Rebekah! Thanks for that, and thank you, Matthew, for that very interesting answer. I think we'll take one more question from the audience, and then we'll have a little break and listen to some great music. More about that in a moment. Now, would anyone else like to ask Matthew a question?

OK, the man at the back who has just arrived with his mule – the one that has just made a big mess on our floor, but never mind. Yes, you, sir. What's your name, where are you from, and what's your question for Matthew?

'Good evening, Mike, and good evening, Matthew. Sorry about the animal; he's not been feeling himself recently. My name is Joshua, from Bethlehem. Matthew, it's great to be here this evening listening to you. Could you tell me a little about Jesus' "Sermon on the Mount", as we all like to call it today. We know that Moses gave the Ten Commandments to the Israelites years ago. Is Jesus to be seen as the "new Moses", giving his commandments to the people?'

MATTHEW: Good evening, Joshua. Thank you for your kind words, and I do hope your mule feels better soon. In fact, I think we all do! So, you're from Bethlehem. Can I repeat the Old Testament quote that I used in chapter 2, verse 6 of my Gospel?

'Yes!' the whole audience shout.

MATTHEW: 'Bethlehem Ephrathah, you may be one of the smallest towns in Judah, but from you I will bring a ruler who will guide my people Israel.' That, of course, was Micah's prophecy about the birth of our Messiah.

So, the 'Sermon on the Mount'. You are quite right, Joshua. My aim is to show Jesus as the new Moses giving the new law to the new Israel on a new mountain. We Jews always expected our Messiah to fulfil the Law of Moses, or to give the Law some sort of deeper meaning. That's why I quote Jesus in chapter 5, verse 17, when he says, 'Do not think that I have come here to get rid of the Law or the

Prophets; I haven't come to abolish them but to fulfil them.' I'm trying to show Jesus as the great teacher, teaching with real authority about the true meaning of the Old Testament Law. To many people, the Law was simply something written on stone – hundreds of rules to obey. But Jesus brought the Law alive; instead of laws written on stone, the law is now written in our hearts. It has been fulfilled – brought to life in our own experience.

Jesus' great sermon is not a collection of laws, because, let's face it, some of the ideals he sets out are virtually impossible to keep. The sermon simply teaches us ways to behave which we should be able to apply to any situation.

MIKE: Matthew, you mention that some of the ideals Jesus teaches are virtually impossible to keep. Do any examples spring to mind?

At this moment, Matthew quickly leans over, and lightly slaps Mike on his right cheek. Mike is a little shocked, as are many of the audience.

MIKE: Good grief, Matthew! I certainly wasn't expecting that. I presume you're going to make a point.

MATTHEW: Indeed I am, Mike. Could I now please slap you on your other cheek?

MIKE: You must be joking!

Audience laugh.

MATTHEW: Listen to the words of Jesus that I recorded in my Gospel, chapter 5, verses 38 and 39.

'You know how the Law said, "An eye for an eye, and a tooth for a tooth." But now I tell you this: do not take revenge on someone who does wrong to you. If anyone slaps you on the right cheek, let him slap your left cheek too.'

MIKE: Wow! Powerful stuff. I see what you mean about Jesus teaching ideals that are pretty impossible to keep. You know, if I hadn't known you, and you just slapped me on the cheek like you did, I'd have given you a good slap back!

The audience are still laughing.

MATTHEW: Those of us who follow Jesus have to be peacemakers, and we are not to return evil for evil. We are to absorb it and change it into love. Jesus actually went on to say, 'You must be perfect, just as your Father in heaven is perfect.' Jesus didn't come to give us rules – he showed us perfection. We can never be perfect, but we can try. Constantly trying – talking to God in prayer, getting support from other followers and help from the Spirit of Jesus himself – that's what it's all about!

'Amen to that,' shout out many of the audience.

MIKE: Great stuff! If we have time, we may talk about this amazing sermon in a little more detail later. But now, as promised, we have some great entertainment for you. This evening's music will be performed by that wonderful group of musicians, Zebedee and his Magic Singers and Harps! They'll be singing Psalm 23 and Psalm 60 for us. A big, warm welcome to the band!

The audience cheer, clap and whistle as the band arrives.

While they're playing, it might be worth telling you a little about the band, what instruments they use and so on. Musicians at the time of the New Testament were very important. Music was a vital part of religious life.

Some of the instruments Zebedee's group play are the Hazora, a trumpet made of silver or bronze. The sound it makes is quite sharp. Some members of the band also play the Kinnor, a stringed instrument shaped like a harp. Then there is the Menanaim, a percussion instrument made of metal plates that make a sound when moved. Finally, some of the band play the Tof, another percussion instrument that has a membrane like a drum. There were different sizes of drum, which could be played with the hands or with sticks.

Hebrew music at this time was more concerned with rhythm than melody. There weren't actually very many melodies around, and those that did exist were very popular. Many were folk songs, and they were used to sing some of the Psalms. (For example, Psalm 60 was set to the tune 'Shushan Eduth', which means 'The Lily of Testimony'.)

Well, the music is almost over, and so we go back to the show.

As the band finish Psalm 60, there is a huge round of applause!

MIKE: Fantastic! Thank you so much, Zebedee and the band.

MATTHEW: They were excellent!

MIKE: Matthew, so far this evening, we've heard how you describe Jesus as the person who fulfils all Old Testament prophecy and the Law. In writing your Gospel, you have made it clear that Jesus in his life and death has, in a way, made Judaism complete. Certainly, compared to the other Gospels, you really do emphasize the importance of Jewish teaching and the Law of Moses. In the light of all this, what would you say to those who might think you're suggesting that the good news is only for Jewish people?

MATTHEW: I would say to them, absolutely not! The good news (which, of course, is what the word 'gospel' actually means) may have grown out of what God did in the Old Testament, but this good news is for the whole world, and that means it's for Jews and Gentiles. In my Gospel, I make this point very clearly. In chapter 8, verses 5 to 13, I recall the story of Jesus healing a Roman officer's servant. Jesus was amazed by that man's faith. He was a Gentile, who would not have had any training in the Jewish scriptures, and yet he recognized Jesus as the Messiah.

I have also recalled Jesus' parable of the tenants in the vineyard, in chapter 21, verses 33 to 46. In that story, after the tenants had killed the owner's son, Jesus said that the owner would kill those evil men, 'and let the vineyard out to other tenants'. Jesus then quoted from Psalm 118 and said, 'The stone which the builders rejected as worthless turned out to be the most important of all. This was done by the Lord; what a wonderful sight it is.'

All of this clearly refers to the fact that Gentiles could be accepted into the Church – the worldwide group of Jesus' followers. Last but not least, Mike, are the words I use to end my Gospel, when Jesus says to his disciples, 'Go now to all peoples everywhere and make them my disciples. Baptize them in the name of the Father, the Son, and the Holy Spirit. Teach them all to obey everything that I have commanded you. I will be with you always, to the end of the age.'

'Alleluia! Alleluia!' shout most of the audience.

MIKE: Thanks, Matthew. Now, I have a letter here sent in by a viewer. Her name is Deborah, and she lives in Capernaum. We need to go back to the Sermon on the Mount again. She would like you to explain Jesus' words in chapter 5, verses 3 to 10, which are the 'Happy are they...' sayings. Deborah is really quite confused about these sayings. For example, she writes, 'How on earth can anyone be happy who is in mourning? How can you be happy if you're poor and down and out? Maybe I'm missing something here, but I really would love it if Matthew could shed some light on these sayings of Jesus.'

Well, Matthew, quite a tough one if you ask me. I'm glad you're answering it and not me.

MATTHEW: Well, thanks very much, Mike! Deborah, thank you very much for your letter. I will do my very best to try to explain the real meaning and beauty of these sayings. If it's OK with you, Mike, could I just recite the sayings first, before explaining them?

MIKE: To think you were actually there, Matthew, when Jesus spoke these words is amazing. We would all love to hear you recite these 'Happiness' sayings of Jesus, wouldn't we, folks?

'Yeah!' shout the whole audience.

MATTHEW: 'Happy are all those folk who know they are spiritually poor, because the kingdom of heaven belongs to them.

Happy are those people who mourn; God will comfort and help them.

Happy are those people who are humble; they will receive all that God has promised.

Happy are those who really hunger and thirst to do what God requires; God will totally satisfy them.

Happy are those who can show mercy to others; God will be merciful to them.

Happy are those who are pure in heart; they will truly see God.

Happy are those who work for peace; they will be God's children.

Happy are those who are persecuted because they do God's work; the kingdom of heaven belongs to them.'

Many of the audience are moved to tears when they hear these beautiful words of Jesus. There is also some applause.

MATTHEW: If I could just begin by explaining that many folk call these sayings 'the Beatitudes'. The sayings start 'Blessed are...' or 'Happy are...' and Beatitude comes from the Latin word beatus, which means 'blessed'.

MIKE: Well, strike a light! I never knew that. What do you think Jesus actually meant when he used this word 'blessed'?

MATTHEW: It's a really powerful word, Mike. This 'blessedness' that Jesus spoke about was a type of deep inner happiness that nothing will ever be able to touch. If you were to ask the average person in the street what would make them happy, they might say, 'more money,' or 'a nice house' or even having a healthy mule!

(Matthew looks at the chap at the back. Audience laugh. Joshua gives a little wave.)

But Jesus turns upside down the average person's idea of happiness. The happiness Jesus speaks of in these sayings is the most wonderful thing any of us could ever experience.

I'd like to explain just briefly the true meaning of each saying now, to try to help Deborah truly understand what it was that Jesus was saying.

The first saying, about those who are spiritually, poor means, quite simply, that until someone realizes they need God, God cannot help them. It's a bit like saying that a doctor can only help someone who knows that they are ill and wants to be cured. It's exactly the same if you want a relationship with God. You can turn your back on God, but if you let God know that you need him, he will be there for you, and you will know true happiness.

MIKE: But next comes the Beatitude that really troubled Deborah – the one about mourning. What's that one all about, Matthew?

MATTHEW: The immediate response, Mike, is to think, 'How on earth can I feel true happiness when I am mourning, when my heart is in pieces?' We all know that grief is always a terrible thing, but in fact we can learn a great deal when we have bad experiences.

Whenever we want really good advice about something, it's always best to turn to people who have been through similar circumstances; they always share real wisdom. If we are to truly grow as human beings, we need to experience suffering in our lives. When we look at it like this, Jesus' saying means exactly what it says. We should also remember that going through awful times can be a great blessing, as then we turn to God for help, and he gives us the greatest help and comfort of all, and helps to put joy back into our hearts.

MIKE: I once heard someone say, 'Storms make a strong tree; testings make a strong Christian!'

MATTHEW: Beautifully put!

MIKE: I must admit, Matthew, that that saying about 'happy are they who mourn' did confuse me a little, but the way you've explained it was wonderful. I really hope Deborah and all of you watching found that as inspiring as I did.

Big round of applause at this point.

MATTHEW: Could I just quickly zoom through the other sayings and their meanings? Of course, the next saying refers to people who were 'humble' or 'meek'. I remember the promise given to the humble in Psalm 37 verse 11: 'the humble will possess the land and enjoy prosperity and peace'.

Humble people, who know their needs rather than boasting about how they can cope all alone, are the spiritually strong ones.

'Happy are those who hunger and thirst to do what God requires,' Jesus said. Quite simply, folks, Jesus was making the point that people who are desperately hungry and thirsty for righteousness, and who want to be close to God, will be totally satisfied. God will fill their hearts with a joy they've never experienced before.

'Happy are those who can show mercy to others.' Mike, I hope you can forgive me for the slap in the face earlier!

MIKE: Why, of course!

MATTHEW: Remember, folks, if we expect God to forgive us (and we can be pretty bad sometimes), then we have to forgive other people. It can be tough to do this sometimes, but we must try, and with God's help we can learn to forgive others even in really difficult situations.

'Happy are the pure in heart.' When Jesus spoke these words, he was talking about our motives. Purity does not come from performing loads of rituals, or from not eating certain types of food. It's all about motives. Many of us may behave generously or kindly, but what are our motives for doing this? To make sure other people see us doing the right thing? I think if we are all honest with ourselves, Mike, there aren't many of us who could say that our motives are always pure. Those that are pure in heart will see God face to face.

This reminds me of a passage in 2 Esdras 7 verse 98: 'The greatest joy of all will be the confident and exultant assurance which will be theirs, free from all fear and shame, as they press forward to see face to face the One whom they served in their lifetime and from whom they are now to receive their reward in glory.' [2]

We're lmost at the end now. 'Happy are the peacemakers,' Jesus said. This is not just about people who are non-violent, it's about those who have truly found peace with God and try to share and pass this peace on to others.[3]

Finally, while I was writing my Gospel, the Church was suffering terrible persecution, and many Christians were facing death. Jesus said that this would happen, and this gives us great encouragement. The more the Christians were persecuted, the more Christianity flourished.[4]

MIKE: Matthew, thanks very much for that. You know, I heard someone the other day refer to these sayings as the 'Be happy attitudes', which I thought was very clever.

'I heard someone call them the "Beautiful attitudes",' shouts someone from the audience.

MATTHEW: I think they're both wonderful ways to describe these sayings of Jesus.

MIKE: OK. It's that time of the show when we have a quick advert. Back in a moment for more fascinating conversation with Matthew.

Two men walk across the stage carrying a large piece of fairly smooth wood. On it are painted the words:

Best Cast Nets in Israel!

A third gentleman then appears and says:

'Yes, ladies and gentlemen, my name is David, and I know that many of you here this evening are involved with fishing in one way or another. If you're fed up with your old nets, then look no further. My cast nets are the best you'll find. They're bigger than ever and superbly weighted all around. I'll be here after the show this evening should you wish to come and haggle a price. You won't get a better deal anywhere!' [5]

MIKE: Thanks very much, David. In fact, that reminds me. Matthew – didn't you write in your Gospel that Jesus told a parable about one of these cast nets?

MATTHEW: Well remembered, Mike. It was in chapter 13, verses 47 to 50. Jesus was telling us about God's kingdom and how God was going to judge us all. He described how some fishermen threw out their net in the lake and how they caught all kinds of fish. When the net was full, they pulled it to shore and sat down to divide up all the fish. All the good fish were put in their buckets, and the rubbish and useless fish were thrown away. [6] Of course, the point he was making is that, at the end of time, the angels will separate out all the evil people from the good, and the evil ones will be thrown into the fire.

MIKE: Always makes me shiver a little, Matthew, when I hear about that Day of Judgment.

MATTHEW: Nothing to fear, Mike, and everyone listening. Just keep your faith in God; try to be faithful. Remember our chat about the Beatitudes? Just try to follow those teachings, and you will most certainly be seen as someone who is righteous in God's eyes.

MIKE: Well, that's all we can do. Thanks for that, Matthew. Now, we have another letter here, but sadly there is no name with this one. But this is a great question for you. 'Matthew, can you tell us a little about the other disciples, and what it was like suddenly being in a group of twelve totally different people.' That's the question our anonymous letter writer would like to ask you, and to be honest, I think all of us here would love to hear you answer it.

MATTHEW: My, my; now there's a tricky one! It's interesting, actually, because only last week someone asked me why Jesus bothered having any disciples, because if you read about us in the Gospels, we do come across as being quite thick. We never seem to understand what Jesus is talking about!

Audience laugh.

It's true, we didn't understand many of Jesus' parables, or miracles, or many of his sayings. But the whole point is that we were just twelve ordinary men – pretty dodgy people before we met Jesus. We were chosen to be disciples, which, as most of you know, means 'pupils – people who learn'. Jesus chose us for a reason. Mark mentions it in his Gospel, when he quotes Jesus saying, 'I've chosen you lot to be with me. I'm going to send you out to preach and drive out evil spirits.' [7] OK, we may appear to have been a little dopey at times, but we were there to learn. Jesus was training us to do his work.

---

1 In many cases, one could often tell from what village or area the women came from, by looking at the style of the embroidered edges around their neckline.

2 This passage is from a book in the Apocrypha, which dates from between the Old Testament and the New Testament periods.

3 The best way this can be summed up is through the words of Francis of Assisi.
Lord, make me an instrument of Thy peace;
Where there is hatred, let me sow love;
Where there is injury, pardon;
Where there is discord, union;
Where there is doubt, faith;
Where there is despair, hope;
Where there is darkness, light;
Where there is sadness, joy.

4 Tertullian was to say, 'The blood of the martyrs is the seed of the Church.' Tertullian was an ecclesiastical writer in the second and third centuries. A pagan until middle life, he was converted around AD197 and became a priest.

5 These cast nets were circular nets, often about five metres in diameter, and they had little weights all around the edges. A very long rope was attached to the centre. Whenever a large shoal of fish was seen, the net was dropped over it. Of course, the weights pulled the net down and the fish were trapped underneath. The net was then pulled into shore. In fact, Peter and Andrew were using their cast net when Jesus called them to join him.

6 Cast nets actually dragged everything in from the bottom of the lake, so it was always necessary to separate the good fish from all the rubbish.

7 Mark 3:14–15

Now in paperback!

Pride And Perjury

Jonathan Aitken

This is the sensational story of Jonathan Aitken's slide from one of the country's most promising MPs to convicted criminal. His dramatic conversion while in prison testifies to God's amazing grace.

Continuum
£8.99
PB / 0 8264.7274 5

£2 OFF
£6.99 with voucher

Also by the same author

JONATHAN AITKEN

PRIDE AND PERJURY

First published in Great Britain in 2000 by HarperCollins*Publishers*
Reprinted by Continuum 2003
The Tower Building, 11 York Road, London SE1 7NX
and 15 East 26th Street, New Yorrk 10010, USA

Deep Calls to Deall

Having decided to launch the battered ship of my soul into the deeper waters of the sea of faith, I soon discovered that I was pitifully short of plans for how to navigate in them.

Some fortunate believers evidently find it simple to steer towards salvation. They talk with confidence about how they have 'seen the light', 'formed a personal relationship with Jesus', and 'been saved'. I respected such fast-track conversions, but because of the heavy barnacles of sinfulness still stuck on my conscience, I felt that if I set my compass towards similar havens of redemption the voyage would be a rougher, longer and slower haul. This was frustrating at first because I was impatient to achieve 'results'. I was also under the erroneous impression that such results would be related to the work I put in at the traditional disciplines of prayer, meditation and Bible study. I therefore made the mistake of trying to do too much too soon, until another letter from Chuck Colson calmed me down with these wise words:

> I would have to say that the process of metanoia is always a gradual one. Somehow we think of conversions as being instantaneous. The moment when God regenerates us is. There is certainty about the fact that we are now His. But the conversion, that is the transformation from the old man to the new man, sometimes takes us a long while. There are lots of struggles that we inevitably go through. That is par-

ticularly true for strong willed, able individuals like you and me. We have been so accustomed to thinking that we can do it on our own that it is very hard to release everything and simply trust God. But that is precisely what we must do. And we only learn to do that as we stumble and often grope in the dark. Don't be impatient with yourself..[1]

Learning to be patient became one of the hardest struggles of my new journey. Throughout my career I had been in one long, energetic rush to set agendas, achieve targets, make deliveries ahead of schedule, claim the first-past-the-post winner's bonus, and then accelerate ahead to the next milestone. This style of existence had been exciting but ultimately unfulfilling. Long before my world fell apart I knew that there should be more to life than the onwards and upwards drive of the ambitious careerist. Now that the pace of my life had slowed from a sprint to an amble, I had the time to discover what that phrase 'more to life' might mean. Gradually I came to recognize that if I wanted it to mean anything at all in the spiritual domain of God's work, that could only be started when the fever of impatience had been conquered.

The message that I must quell my impatience was reinforced by what I can only describe as a supernatural experience. It happened on an early autumn walk along the beach at Sandwich Bay. The weather was idyllic, for it was an Indian summer of an afternoon. The westering sun was blazing as if it was still July, while on the eastern horizon a pale September moon was beginning to rise over the Channel. There was not a cloud in the sky or a breath of wind on the sea. Only the tiniest of waves were trickling in over the sands, burbling contentedly like babies at play, reminding me of a line from Keats which describes the sea as 'an untumultuous line of silver foam'. The beach was totally deserted and I was a good two miles from the nearest house, so I was able to drink in this beautiful moment of maritime solitude with deep contentment.

Suddenly, yet quietly, I became aware of someone else's presence on the beach. For a moment I thought I heard the crunch of footsteps on the shingle behind me, but when I turned round no one was there. But someone was — I sensed them, strongly at first, and then overwhelmingly. Again I looked around, particularly on my right, for the presence felt as though it had drawn alongside me, but all I could see was the sun, whose rays seemed to be blazing even more intensely.

'Slow down,' said a gentle voice somewhere inside my head. It was not an audible or even a human voice, but I knew it was speaking to me. So I obeyed and slowed my pace.

The next extraordinary happening was that tears started to trickle down my cheeks for no reason at all except that I was feeling blissfully happy. Once again I felt overwhelmed by the invisible presence that was so close to me — in the sun, perhaps, or beside me, or inside me, but undoubtedly right there with me. And then amidst swelling feelings of joy, that gentle voice spoke again, saying words which were very close to this: 'Slow down. The road ahead of you is longer and harder than you think. But keep on it. Keep praying. Keep trying to find the way. Trust, believe, and you will discover the path. Do not worry about your problems. They will test you but I will guide you. I have work for you to do. I will show you the way. I love you.'

Then I shed a few more happy tears, feeling utterly insignificant yet totally protected and loved as this amazing presence gently faded away and I floated back to reality, wondering what on earth had been going on.

When I got back to our house I literally pinched myself to make sure I was still all there and *compos mentis*. The next thing I did was to sit down and write an account of what had happened. Reverting to my most methodical style of record-keeping, I set out every detail I could remember. Getting it all down on paper (including the words spoken to me as best I could recall them) took about three-quarters of an hour. When I read it through I was so astonished that I called Victoria — the only member of the family with me in the house — into my study and read her my description of what had happened.

She was almost as amazed as I had been.

'What time was all this?' she asked.

'I noted down the exact time just as I came off the beach and put it down at the top of the page,' I replied. 'It was ten to four.'

'What time is it now?' inquired Victoria.

I looked at my watch, an automatic-winding Platinum Rolex which had never stopped in the 12 or more years I had owned it. On this afternoon it had stopped at precisely 3.50 p.m.

To my rational mind this strange experience was inexplicable. In retrospect I was unnerved by it. Hearing voices and feeling presences were the preserve of saints, surely off-limits for a decidedly unsaintly and worldly ex-politician in disgrace. But I was not mad. Everything else happening in my life was down to earth and normal. Yet on that beach I had heard something, felt something, and my watch had unaccountably stopped. All I could fall back on was the term 'supernatural experience', which gave me little understanding but much food for thought. By the time I returned to London a few days later, I had decided that I must strive to be more patient, recognize that my journey was going to be far longer and more difficult than I had imagined, and pray for guidance.

How to pray was another problem. I was not getting particularly far in solving it until by chance I was brought into a series of prayer partnerships. 'When you start to pray, get yourself some company,' wrote the fifteenth-century mystic St Teresa of Avila. I read her words at about the same time as the latest instalment in our correspondence arrived from Chuck Colson, suggesting that I should form a prayer group with Michael Alison, an old friend of his and a former parliamentary colleague of mine.

Although the concept of sharing in oral prayer was alien to me, I felt it might be right. A few weeks earlier I had stumbled into a one-to-one prayer relationship with Mervyn Thomas, the Sales and Marketing Director of Sweet'n'Low plc, the low-calorie sweetener company. On the face of it, Mervyn was an improbable character to become the repository of some of my most intimate confidences of the soul. We came from different social backgrounds, different religious traditions, and had no obvious interests or connections in common. We had corresponded but never met until the late summer of 1997, when he called at my house saying that he had read so much about me in the newspapers that he felt he would like to come and pray with me. I was touched but embarrassed. 'I'll try it once, but I wouldn't like to make this a regular thing,' I told him awkwardly. Yet soon we were meeting two or three times a month, bonding together over prayers and a course of Bible studies.

My Colson-inspired prayer breakfasts were something else again. As Chuck had suggested, I got in touch with Michael Alison. He had been a long-standing friend, though not a particularly close one, in the House of Commons where he had served with distinction as a minister, as Margaret Thatcher's Parliamentary Private Secretary, and as an MP for 33 years until his retirement in 1997. Between us we recruited a further quartet of Christian acquaintances: Alastair Burt, who had been a rising star in the previous Government as Social Security Minister until he lost his seat in the Labour landslide of May 1997; Anthony Cordle, a pastoral adviser with wide-ranging political connections in Westminster and Washington; Tom Benyon, a former MP in the 1980s who now owned an insurance magazine; and Jim Pringle, a retired businessman from Winchester. As we assembled for our first breakfast I was full of misgivings, for I did not feel that we looked like a particularly fraternal or mutually congenial team. How wrong I was.

Over the next few months our Thursday morning prayer breakfasts became a vital and love-giving force in the lives of all six participants.[2] At first we were shy of each other, hesitant at expressing our needs and reluctant to show our feelings — in short, a quintessential group of middle-aged Englishmen. There was initially a tendency to focus the prayers of the group on me as the lame duck so obviously in the worst trouble. But as we gradually opened our hearts to one another in friendship and faith, we not only became a mutual support group for all our respective family and personal problems, we also became increasingly aware of the presence and guidance of God, speaking to us through our prayers and readings of Scripture.

In my case the 30 or so Thursday mornings we spent on an indepth study of the Sermon on the Mount was a cumulative spiritual experience which I found both humbling and enriching. Coming to realize how little I really knew, understood or practised of this most familiar of Gospel passages, I began to look forward eagerly to the weekly interpretations of whichever verses from it we had reached. Through our combined efforts we could (on our good days) produce an interesting mixture in our discussions of humour, theological scholarship, scriptural knowledge, intellectual argument and personal testimony. As I struggled to try and live the Word as well as hear it, I gradually developed a hunger for seeking God which took me into new territory of the soul.

One of the turning points in this new territory was my participation in a week-long 'Christian Teaching Holiday' at Launde Abbey in Leicestershire. At the last minute I almost dropped out of this gathering on the grounds that it sounded too much like a jolly-hockeysticks jamboree for retired gentry, only to discover that it was a deeply spiritual gathering of the active intelligentry. The talks we heard from Doctor Graham Scott-Brown, a former medical missionary, the prayers we shared in Launde's sixteenth-century chapel, and the warmth of the friendships I began to build with one or two people who were to become linchpins of my life in the crises of the next few months, were all very deep and very special.

In the afternoons at Launde I went for long walks with Martin Marriott, the recently retired headmaster of Canford School, and his wife Judith. We had never met before, but we struck up a rapport of intimate communication which deepened as both Marriotts intuitively perceived my pain and gently ministered to it.

After one long afternoon of shared confidences walking across the rolling country of the Cottesmore and Pytchley hunts, we came across a sheep caught in a thicket. It turned out to be a ram, trapped in no ordinary tangle, for he had several strands of heavy bramble twisted round his neck which were cutting deep into his flesh. Assuming the role of two RSPCA volunteers, Martin and I tried to free the wounded animal. It would have been a difficult rescue job at the best of times, but without a knife, gloves, or any means of protecting ourselves from the continuous butting and kicking of the far from grateful captive, the task proved almost impossible. Yet after a considerable struggle, and not inconsiderable pain to all three participants, the ram was eventually liberated and bounced joyfully away towards his lambs and his ewes.

'Very symbolic,' said Martin, wiping the blood and thorns from his hands. The symbolism was not lost on Judith either. From that time on, the Aitken–Marriott friendship steadily deepened – so much so that without the growing strength of this relationship with its loving fellowship, laughter, prayer and good companionship, I might well, like that ram, still be trapped in a thicket of unbearable pain.

It was one of the most remarkable aspects of my inner journey that unexpected people kept popping up to offer me their friendship and prayerful support. I jokingly came to call Judith Marriott 'my guardian angel', but I could well have conferred wings on a small galaxy of old and new Christian friends who visited me, wrote letters to me, prayed for me and sustained me in a multitude of visible and invisible ways. Among these supporters and helpers were several priests from different denominations. The clergy often get a bad press in the modern world, yet those who offered me pastoral guidance showed great skill and sensitivity in their compassionate care for a bruised pilgrim, so I have listed their names with gratitude in the notes to this chapter.[3]

One of these good shepherds was Sandy Millar, the Vicar of Holy Trinity, Brompton. Against all my instincts he persuaded me to do an Alpha course at his church.[4] Not my scene at all, I decided in advance. Happy-clappy evangelicals in the congregation listening to Bible-bashing fundamentalists in the pulpit ... easy-believism and instant salvation ... bringing down the Holy Spirit by turning up the volume of the electric guitars ... I had read all about HTB in magazine articles, which portrayed it as a charismatic circus for the Hooray Henry brigade from SW7, who allegedly swooned in the aisles, confessed their sins in public, Put £3 million a year from their City bonuses into the collection plate, and saved the souls of celebrities. If my anti-HTB prejudices were not quite in the category of 'Pass the sick bag, Alice', they were certainly a case of 'Pass by on the other side'.

So how on earth did I find myself walking into a crowded Holy Trinity, Brompton one Wednesday evening in September 1997 to enrol for the first night of the autumn Alpha course? As 800 pairs of eyes swivelled curiously towards me (I was still near the height of my notoriety), I could think of no explanation other than that I had made a bad decision out of good manners to Sandy. I settled uneasily into my seat, firmly resolved to make this first visit to HTB my last attendance at an Alpha course.

My immediate discovery was that the magazine articles on HTB were a travesty. Nobody clapped, confessed, blessed, swooned or even passed round a collection plate. The electric guitar playing was good once you got used to it. As I listened to the sermon, or 'talk', from Nicky Gumbel, the energetic priest in charge of Alpha, I was struck by his sensible, mainstream theology and by his powerful presentation of the Gospel message. 'Everyone can have a second chance through Christ,' was a phrase that I remember from that evening. I needed one myself. So I condescendingly gave Alpha a second chance, then a third, then a fourth, and ended up completing all is sessions.

About three weeks into the course there was a certain amount of chatter about 'the Holy Spirit weekend'. Apparently it was being suggested that we should set off in groups for two nights at a seaside hotel where someone would call down the Holy Spirit into our hearts. Never had I heard such codswallop! This part of evangelical Christianity was certainly not for me. Moreover, I knew that the Alpha discussion group of which I was a member contained such obviously sensible people, whose feet were so firmly on the ground, that it just would not be possible for our lot to get into this sort of weird activity.

It was therefore another strange surprise that I found myself, still a Spirit sceptic, turning up in the unpromising venue of the Chatsworth Hotel in Worthing with most of the other members of my Alpha group. Our number included the senior partner in a successful firm of London solicitors and his down-to-earth Australian wife; a photographer from Windsor; the owner of a chain of language schools; a successful young tax barrister and his solicitor wife; a Northamptonshire farmer turned horse equipment importer; a merchant banker; two lady university teachers; and myself – an unemployed ex-Cabinet minister in disgrace.

The early part of the weekend passed peacefully and agreeably. The talks were good and the walks over the South Downs were even better. I did a seven-mile hike on the Saturday afternoon with the Northamptonshire farmer and a Lloyd's insurance broker. As we enjoyed the autumn sunshine of a mellow Sussex afternoon, all three of us agreed that Alpha had been helpful, even at times inspirational, but that this 'summoning up the Holy Spirit' business we were going to hear about at 5 p.m. was just too fanciful for experienced men of the world like us.

The keynote talk on the Holy Spirit was given by the leader of our group, Bruce Streather, the founder and senior partner of the solicitors Streather and Co. As I was to discover on my numerous later visits to his firm's Mayfair offices, Bruce has many sterling qualities and talents. Oratory, however, is not one of them. His talk was as far removed from Bible-thumping or hot-gospelling as the Chatsworth Hotel is from Claridges. When he brought his preaching of Scripture to the climax of an appeal to the Almighty with the words, 'Come Holy Spirit, come,' his tones sounded so monotonous that he might as well have been reading out the small print of some dry-as-dust contract in a commercial court.

Nevertheless, as Morely said of Gladstone, 'It was not the words but the character breathing through his sentences that counted.' I already knew that Bruce Streather was one of the most attractive Christian characters anyone could meet. So I listened respectfully to his mumblings and obeyed his instruction to stand with hands outstretched at waist height, palms upwards, praying that the Holy Spirit would come.

Nothing happened. After two or three minutes of standing awkwardly in this posture, the young tax barrister in our group, Tom Adam, came over to me, put his hands on my shoulder and whispered into my ear that he was praying especially hard that the Holy Spirit would descend on me. I cannot now remember exactly what Tom said, but the gist of it was that he knew I needed help, that he and others were grateful that I had contributed to the course from my heart, and that he knew the Lord would now send the Holy Spirit to me.

At this point my palms suddenly began to tingle with a strange physical sensation which strengthened until my hands and wrists became hot and uncomfortable, as though they were being charged with an electric current. Then I began to cry. This should have been deeply embarrassing, for shedding tears in public is anathema to me. I rather pride myself on my stiff-upper-lip stoicism in emotional gatherings, even to the point of trying hard not to cry at the funerals of close friends and relatives. Yet here I was in a room full of people in the lounge of a seaside hotel, letting out not just a trickle but a torrent of tears. To my surprise I felt amazingly warm and good about those tears. The more they flowed, the more I recognized that they were tears of happiness. I smiled, beamed and physically shook with silent laughter. Something extraordinary and uncontrollable was going on inside me.

Meanwhile, the voice of Bruce Streather, still sounding as if it was doing a voice-over in a commercial for dull ditchwater, was reading out more Scripture while Tom Adam kept his hand on my shoulder and continued to pray. Shedding all inhibitions, I hugged both of them with passionate gratitude and joy. It would be difficult to think of three more unlikely characters than these two English lawyers and myself to be taking part in this public spectacle of Holy Spirit calling and receiving, yet that is what was happening.

After about another 10 minutes of high emotion I calmed down, cooled down and reverted to normal. Later that night I was driven back to London by Alphonse Kelly, the language school proprietor. Sitting in bemused silence in his Mercedes, I tried to work out what on earth had gone on. If I could have discovered that the whole episode had been some elaborate conjuring trick, I would have been amused and reassured that my feet were still firmly on worldly ground. But there had been no trick and no conjurors. In all the circumstances there was overwhelming evidence (with two lawyers as my chief witnesses!) that I had received a genuine manifestation of the power of the Holy Spirit.

Despite all the impact that this manifestation had on me, I cannot pretend that my life changed overnight. I did not think I had been 'saved', or that I had seen some blinding light on the road to Damascus. Indeed, in immediate retrospect I felt that my encounter with the force that had shaken me to the core in the Chatsworth Hotel was as much an unnerving experience as an uplifting one. I decided to think about it, pray about it, and ask myself questions about it. Had it been real? Were there any physical or psychic explanations for it? Was I becoming some sort of religious nutter? How could I check it out with the calm and rational thought processes on which I had prided myself in my political career? These thoughts and many others troubled me. So, although I completed the Alpha course, I held myself back from involvement in other HTB services and activities in the following few weeks. I wanted to test my balance and recalculate my bearings.

As part of this process I tried to make daily life as normal as possible. I was looking for a job at this time, so was reasonably busy in talks with companies interested in offering me employment or consultancies. I saw and lunched with worldly friends who had no curiosity about my spiritual dimension. As far as my travels in this realm were concerned, the only progress I made in them at this time was achieved in · Christian settings at the opposite end of the spectrum from HTB. In the mornings I kept a daily rule of prayer from 7 a.m. to 8 a.m. in St Faith's Chapel at Westminster Abbey, often breakfasting afterwards with my special friend Canon Donald Gray and his wife Joyce. My evenings were usually given over to reading authors such as C. S. Lewis, Dietrich Bonhoeffer, John Stott, J. I. Packer, Henri J. M. Nouwen, Michael Ramsey, Dallas Willard, Thomas Merton, Richard J. Foster, Evelyn Underhill, Basil Hume, Augustine of Hippo and, last but by no means least, the books of Charles W Colson.

It was a quotation I read in Colson's Loving God that helped to move me towards a new phase of my inner journey. The words came from a conversation between Alexander Solzhenitsyn and Boris Nicholayevich Kornfeld, the doctor who had treated and testified to Solzhenitsyn in a Soviet prison-camp hospital. In that discussion Kornfeld says:

> On the whole, you know, I have become convinced that there is no punishment that comes to us in this life on earth which is undeserved. Superficially, it can have nothing to do with what we are guilty of in actual fact, but if you go over your life with a fine-tooth comb and ponder it deeply, you will always be able to hunt down that transgression of yours for which you have now received this blow.[5]

Chuck Colson, with whom I was now corresponding regularly, referred to this quotation in one of his letters and linked it to a personal recommendation for me:

> One last piece of advice. Don't look back on the past, the unfairness of the attacks, or the viciousness of the media. That happened. You can't change it. It's part of the travesty of modern life that the press can stereotype a person – that individual can never escape that stereotype. Believe me, I know. So we have to accept it in the same way that you would have to accept it if you were in an accident and lost an arm.

> There's nothing you can do to get it back. So you have to learn how
> to live despite it.[6]

Taking this advice was not easy, but I knew I had to do it. It was soul-destroying to keep looking back in anger on this or that journalistic calumny, or to continue fulminating against particular media tormentors, some of whom were still poisonously active in their writings about me. How much better it would be if I could accept, like Solzhenitsyn's Kornfeld, that I had committed enough general transgressions to deserve all blows, even if some of them had been individually unfair. I prayed for help, and unexpectedly got it from Lolicia. She had been following my spiritual journey through our intermittent telephone conversations, and suddenly she called me from her new flat in France to say, 'I believe you should make a confession.'

'Yes I will,' I heard myself replying, 'but how do I go about it?'

Lolicia suggested going to see Father Norman Brown at Westminster Cathedral, who had been extremely helpful to both of us some years earlier at a difficult stage of our marriage. I duly set off to see Father Norman in his rooms at the Cathedral's clergy house in Francis Street, and after some long preliminary talks with him I came back a few days later and made my confession.

This was far too private and too profound an experience to write about, except to say that the discipline of preparing the confession was agonizing, but the sense of joyful release that flooded over me when I received absolution was glorious. Moreover, when doing the preparation work on what for me (as a non-Catholic) was the difficult and unusual task of formalized penitence, I saw clearly that the whole process would fail unless I first unconditionally cast out all my old demons of the lack of forgiveness I felt towards others. So by prayer and meditation I laid these past burdens of animosity at the foot of the Cross, before coming to kneel there to ask forgiveness for my own sins. When this was granted, as I knew at once it had been from the new surge of joy and peace in my heart, I was sure that a great leap forward in my Christian commitment had happened.

Something that had not happened by the late autumn of 1997, despite the efforts of my just-forgiven media adversaries to make it happen, was any sign of a serious police investigation into the *Guardian's* allegations of criminal activities by me, Lolicia and Victoria. This complaint had been formally lodged by Alan Rusbridger in June. By December there had not been so much as a murmur from the sleuths of Scotland Yard in my direction, nor, so far as I could discover, in the direction of anyone else connected with the case. The only murmurs we could pick up on the gossip grapevine were to the effect that police officers in the department concerned had made dismissive comments about the whole affair, allegedly calling it 'a victimless crime', 'a nine-day media wonder', and 'very difficult to prove in court'.[7]

Although the six months of silence from Scotland Yard could be taken as an encouraging sign that the *Guardian's* perjury charge campaign was faltering, I did not myself share the growing optimism of my friends and advisers that I would soon be out of the woods. This was partly through intuition and partly because of a conversation I had with my most expert friend in the world of criminal law. He was John Nutting QC, a top silk at the Old Bailey who until a few months earlier had held the post of Senior Treasury Counsel – the Crown's chief prosecutor.

Johnny Nutting and I had arrived together as new boys in the same house at Eton in 1956. The Suez crisis was at its height at that time, and Johnny's father Sir Anthony Nutting had recently resigned as a Foreign Office Minister. As the opinionated son of a loyal Tory backbencher who disapproved of this resignation, I took it upon myself to express some criticism of Nutting *père* to Nutting *fils*, who promptly and with admirable paternal loyalty punched me on the nose. A vigorous bout of fisticuffs ensued. After the Captain of the House had pulled the protagonists apart, he was heard to say, 'These new boys are extraordinary. Fighting on their first day here, and then they say it was about *politics!*'

Over 40 years after this initial encounter, Johnny Nutting came round as an old friend to offer me advice. His message was not an encouraging one. He said that the delay might not mean much because it was almost impossible to overestimate the glacier-like slowness of the Crown Prosecution Service. When we went over the outline of the case his reaction was that a perjury charge might be difficult to prove. I said that if one was brought I would certainly plead guilty to it and asked him what the penalty would be.

'Four or five years,' said Johnny.

There was a stunned silence.

'But that's the sort of sentence given to armed bank robbers, rapists, arsonists and so on!' I expostulated, for in my ignorance I had been thinking in terms of a light sentence, perhaps even a suspended one or a community service order.[8]

'I'm afraid the Judges take perjury very seriously,' was the reply, 'and they could decide to make an example of you – although a lot will depend on your mitigation.'

This conversation gave me a nasty shock, an experience which was becoming all too familiar in this saga. But I was not devastated by it. Somehow I had got the message that I was going to be tested in the fire for reasons that were unknown, but surely not unconnected with my deepening faith. Trusting in God does not, except in illusory religion, mean that he will ensure that none of the things you are afraid of will ever happen to you. On the contrary, it means that whatever you fear is quite likely to happen, but that with God's help it will in the end turn out to be nothing to be afraid of.

If my faith had brought me to the point of calm acceptance of God's will, this was real progress. Certainly I had sailed way out into the waters of the deep, far enough to recognize the great truth of St Augustine's words, 'In his will we find our peace.'[9] Yet the dark clouds were gathering and it remained to be seen whether or not I would remain at peace when the storm burst.

NOTES - CHAPTER NINETEEN

1 Charles Colson, letter to the author, 24 October 1997.
2 A year later we were joined by a seventh participant: Derek Foster, MP for Bishop Auckland and a former Labour Chief Whip.
3 The clerical or religious counsellors who helped me in 1997-9 included: my three retreat tutors, Lister Tonge, Madeleine Prendergast and Gerry Hughes; my cousin Stephen Verney, a retired Anglican bishop; Chris Hancock, the Vicar of Holy Trinity, Cambridge; David Mathers, my closest friend at prep school and now Vicar of Thurston; David Stancliffe, the Bishop of Salisbury; Francis Pym, a Parliamentary Chaplain; Roger Holloway, the Preacher of Gray's Inn; Philip Chester of St Matthew's, Westminster; Father James Naters SSJE; Father Felix Stephen OSB; Donald Gray, Robert Wright and Dominic Fenton of Westminster Abbey; Father Norman Brown of Westminster Cathedral; Michael Chantry, Chaplain of Hertford College, Oxford; Colin Dye of Kensington Temple; Canon Bruce Duncan, Principal of Sarum College, Salisbury; Richard Coombs, Vicar of Burford; Dick Lucas, Rector of St Helen's, Bishopsgate; Jeremy Jennings, Nicky Gumbel and Sandy Millar of Holy Trinity, Brompton.
4 Alpha is an informal introductory or refresher course on the basics of Christianity. Pioneered by Holy Trinity, Brompton, the courses now ran in churches all round the country.
5 Charles Colson, *Loving God,* Zondervan, 1983, P. 33.
6 Charles Colson, letter to the author, 24 October 1997.
7 Private information given to the author by police sources.
8 The maximum sentence for perjury is seven years. The average sentence for the 200 or so annual perjury convictions in the courts is four months' imprisonment.
9 St Augustine of Hippo, *Confessions*, Oxford University Press, 1992, p. 61.

The Holy Wild

Mark Buchanan

In this brave new study of God's character, Mark Buchanan asks how we know we can trust God and how trusting in him should affect our lives, work and relationships.

Multnomah Publishers
£12.99
HB / 1 5905.2249 4

£3 OFF
£9.99 with voucher

Other titles by the same author

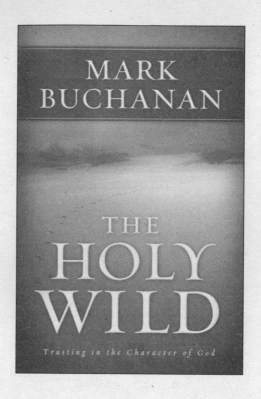

MARK
BUCHANAN

THE
HOLY
WILD

Trusting in the Character of God

Published by Multnomah Publishers, Inc in association with
the literary agency of Ann Spangler and Associates,
1420 Pontiac Road SE, Grand Rapids, Michigan 49506

A Haven for Fools

God's wisdom

Several summers past, the *Vancouver Sun* published excerpts of some gaffes from real-life courtroom crossexaminations:

- "Now doctor, isn't it true that when a person dies in his sleep, he doesn't know about it until the next morning."
- "The youngest son, the twenty-year-old, how old is he?"
- "Were you present when your picture was taken?"

And here are some real responses to lawyers' questions:

Q: Is your appearance here this morning pursuant to a deposition notice which I sent to your attorney?"

A: "No, this is how I dress when I go to work."

Q: "All your responses must be oral, okay? What school did you go to?"

A: "Oral."

And my favorite:

Q: "Doctor, before you performed the autopsy, did you check for a pulse?"

A "No."

Q: "Did you check for blood pressure?"

A: "No."

Q: "Did you check for breathing?"

A: "No."

Q: "So then, is it possible that the patient was alive when you began the autopsy??"

A: "No."

Q: "How can you be so sure, doctor?"

A "Because his brain was sitting on my desk in a jar."

Q: "But could the patient have still been alive nevertheless?"

A: "It is possible that he could have been alive and practicing law somewhere."[1]

God gave us laughter, I think, as a balm to wash the wounds of our own blunders, as a splint to mend the bones we break in our rashness or vanity. But laughter or no, I am amazed at times by my own folly.

And I'm not just talking about how little I know. That in itself is staggering. My children can ask me the simplest questions, questions about things I've spent my whole life observing, and I am stumped.

"Dad, how come there's different kinds of clouds?" Urn, uh, wind and, urn, temperature and the amount of moisture in the air and dust particles and ... I don't know.

"Daddy, how does a television work?" Well, see, there's these, you know, electric sort of thingies that, urn, you can store information in and transfer them to little doohickeys that sort them and ... I'm not sure.

"Dad, why did Grampa have to die?"

The simplest things can throw me. But I'm not talking about my silly mistakes or my plumb ignorance. I'm talking about my folly, my amazing lack of wisdom. Wisdom is more than knowing things; it's knowing what to do with the things you know It's the art of living well, living so that you and all around you benefit. That's wisdom.

And at times I am shockingly deficient in it. I *know* that a cup of coffee at eight o'clock at night will keep me up until three in the morning, and my tossing in the bed will drive my wife to thoughts of torture and murder. I drink it anyhow I *know* that a word of kindness at a crucial moment will bring peace, healing, and reconciliation; it will calm the rage, quell the storm. I speak a word of harshness anyhow I *know* what the Lord requires of me – to do justly, love mercy, and walk humbly with Him. I still sometimes choose otherwise.

Wisdom – at least human wisdom – is the art of living well. By that measure, some of the smartest people in the world are among the stupidest. journalist and historian Paul johnson documented this in his book *Intellectuals,* a collection of minibiographies of leading thinkers of the last two hundred years, men and women whose ideas shaped whole cultures, began revolutions, and toppled civilizations. Karl Marx, Jean-Jacques Rousseau, Bertrand Russell, Henrik Ibsen, Lillian Hellman, others. johnson shows in every instance that these men and women possessed massive intellects but puny souls. They lacked wisdom. They were cruel, shallow, heartless, selfish. They loved humanity but hated people.[2]

I think of sorne of the histories of the Vietnam War – David Halberstarn's *The Best and the Brightest,* Barbara Tuchman's *The March of Folly,* Neil Sheehan's *A Bright Shining Lie.* Each leads to one overriding conclusion: The smartest people in the world are capable of making – no, *prone* to makc-the stupidest choices. Knowledge is no guarantee of wisdom.

The apostle Paul opens his letter to the Romans by describing people like that. They're the people against whom God reveals His wrath. Paul puts it this way:

> For although *they knew God,* they neither glorified him as God nor gave thanks to him, but their thinking became futile and their foolish hearts were darkened. *Although they claimed to be wise,* they became fools.[3]

For although they knew God, although they claimed to be wise, they became fools.

Christians are hardly immune to this. Take Peter, for example. One minute he's declaring that Jesus is the Messiah, and the next minute, Peter is telling Jesus what He can and can't do, provoking this harsh rebuke from Jesus: "Get behind me, Satan!...You do not have in mind the things of God, but the things of men. "[4]

Our mouths — and hearts — mix wisdom and folly freely. Like Peter, we weave together insight and myopia, shrewdness and obtuseness. We're a patchwork of silk and rags, a braid of straw and hemp.

PAUL DESCRIBES IN HIS LETTER to the Romans a world awash in folly. But he ends the letter with this dedication and benediction: "*To the only wise* God be glory forever through Jesus Christ! Amen."[5]

To the only wise God. God is not just the only one who is truly wise, but He is *only wise*. There is no shade of folly in Him. Wisdom saturates everything He is and everything He does.

Which begs the question, *Really?*

In 1999, during a presidential debate, George W Bush was asked, "Who is your favorite political philosopher?"

"Jesus Christ," he answered.

This stunned the audience, and afterward the press had a field day, a carnival of mockery. Douglas Groothuis, in an article in *Books & Culture,* citing that event, notes that in most authoritative encyclopedias of philosophy, Jesus is not listed in the roster of history's great thinkers. Buddha makes the cut. But not Jesus.[6] The irony of this is glaring. The very word *philosopher* means "lover of wisdom." Scripture describes Jesus as "the wisdom of God."[7] Just as God as Father is meant to be the touchstone of all earthly fathers, just as Christ as husband is meant to be our template for all human marriages, so God as the "only wise" One is meant to be the epitome of all philosophers. God in Christ is the Original Thinker.

Apparently, this slipped the notice of the gatekeepers.

It may have slipped more than their notice. The wisdom of God is one of those attributes that we simultaneously have oceans of evidence for and mountains of evidence against. As I write this, Severe Acute Respiratory Syndrome (SARS) is wreaking havoc in various cities in China and in Toronto, Canada. In Beijing, the mayor was fired for failing to deal swiftly and decisively with the outbreak, as if the plague were *his* fault. In Toronto, the mayor is ranting at the World Health Organization for their mismanagement of the situation. Accusations are flying back and forth that health professionals–doctors, nurses, hospital administrators – bungled the matter and turned it into an epidemic.

But where did SARS come from? Or AIDS? Or genetic disease? Or treacherous tectonic plates? Or typhoons?

Who's managing this planet, anyhow? Have any of us witnessed divine wisdom in such a way that we can honestly rest in it – trusting that God knows best and will do what's best? Again, I'm pushing here for more than a knee-jerk reply. All our deephoned creedal instincts, nurtured by hymn and sermon, grandmother's piety and granddad's patriotism, want to rush in and affirm that of course we believe this about God. Of course He is all wise. Of course He knows what to do and when to do it and how to do it, and of course He will do it. Of course.

But its one thing to say that it's so and another to live like it is.

Often, I'm asked by people in my church to fill out character references for them. Sometimes these references are for people applying for jobs that involve working closely with children. Once in a while, they are for people hoping to adopt a child. The people who ask me to do this are good people, people of integrity, discipline, grace. I usually whip through the form. *Describe how this person handles stress.* "With calmness and patience." *Describe how this person behaves with their own children.* "She is a caring and attentive mother, stem when she needs to be, but fair ....."

I skate through those questions, blithely strewing my answers.

But there's one question, always at the end, that gives me pause. It makes me tremble. It causes me to put down my pen and really think and test my convictions and see if I believe in my heart what I speak with my mouth. The question is, "Would you entrust your own children to this person's care?"

Adam. Sarah. Nicola. Twelve, ten, and seven. My children. Some nights, I lie in bed beside my son Adam and we listen to hockey games. His clock radio bristles with static, and at times it's hard to hear, but it doesn't matter. We're both just looking for an excuse to draw near, to press the length of our arms together. Some evenings, after my daughters get out of the bath, they each in turn sit on my knee, and I brush their hair, slowly and gently, with little tugging, jabbing strokes at first to work out the knots, and then with long, sweeping strokes to give it luster.

My children. The ones I would gladly give my own life for. The ones I would fight with all my strength to defend, and cultivate all tenderness to protect. The ones I love.

Would I entrust Adam and Sarah and Nicola to this person's care? It's not a question I've ever answered glibly. And that's the rub. This is the trick question, the lie detector, the one that pins me to the wall and forces me to declare what I *really think*. It's easy to praise someone's character from afar. But when you're called upon to place your priceless and irreplaceable treasures in that person's hands, you find out what you truly believe.

To the all wise God. Would you entrust your priceless treasures to His wisdom? Would you rest fully in this aspect of His character?

GREEK HAS THREE WORDS for wisdom, and all three are used to describe God's wisdom. The first is *sophia,* from which we get our word *philosophy.* It means insight into the nature of things, an ability to see through, to comprehend truly and fully what is going on. It takes sophia, for instance, to see someone's anger as woundedness, as the mask that they've put over their pain. Sophia is not deceived by surfaces, not duped by disguises.

The second Greek word is *phronesis.* Phronesis is insight applied: taking the ability to see through − sophia − and doing the right thing in light of it. Sometimes we have sophia but lack phronesis, and so a moment of wisdom gives way to folly. We may know, This *angry person before me is really in pain*. That's sophia. But phronesis is the decision: I need to quiet them with my love, and not match fire for fire. Many times, sophia is squandered by a failure of phronesis. They must be married to produce the fullness of wisdom.

That brings us to the third Greek word, *sunesis*. Sunesis, often translated "understanding," describes this marriage, this joining of sophia with phronesis. Sunesis is knowing truth *and* acting on it.

To the only wise God. The Bible's claim is that God possesses all these dimensions of wisdom in completeness and perfection – God embodies all wisdom.

But here's the catch: God has hidden His wisdom from the wise and the learned, and revealed it to little children.[8] By design, God disguises His wisdom, and often the disguise is foolishness.

This is especially true in two of the three showcases God has chosen to display His wisdom. One showcase – creation – is obvious. Creation shows off divine wisdom, if not flawlessly, then with panache, with chutzpah, for all eyes to see. But there are two other showcases for God's wisdom, and these conceal it as much as reveal it. it takes an abiding intimacy with the Father through the Son and in the Spirit to see His wisdom in the other two – to see it so clearly that you rest in it deeply.

But more of that later.

For now, let's take the most obvious showcase for God's wisdom first: creation.

> *By wisdom the Lord laid the earth's foundations,*
> *by understanding he set the heavens in place;*
> *by his knowledge the deeps were divided*
> *and the clouds let drop the dew.*[9]

Though much seems amiss in the creation – SARS! AIDS! earthquakes! – the wonder of creation–its infinite bigness, its infinitesimally small detail, its staggering beauty, its harrowing ugliness–is astounding. The simplest things, from worms and stones to eyebrows and fingernails, involve a magnitude of genius humans can admire but never fully imitate. Consider:

> The human body is composed of nearly 100 trillion cells. Think of the skin – while water penetrates the skin outwardly, it cannot penetrate it inwardly. Think of the bones – capable of carrying a load thirty times greater than brick will support. Think of the liver – it breaks up old blood cells into bile and neutralizes poisonous substances. Think of the blood – ten to twelve pints of a syrupy substance that distributes oxygen and carries away waste from tissues and organs, and also regulates the body's temperature. Think of the heart – weighing less than a pound, it's a real workhorse. On the average, it pumps 100,000 times every day, circulating 2,000 gallons of blood through 60,000 miles of arteries, capillaries and veins.[10]

Have you ever tried to create something? Anything – a birdhouse, a go-cart, a cake, a violin? One mistake – a wrong measurement, an extra part, a missed ingredient-and everything else usually goes awry. And how frustrating, even without mistakes, just to get all the parts to work together – dovetails to fit snugly, soufflés to puff without burning, gears to mesh without grinding or release without sticking. And creating things is timeconsuming, a vast temporal pit that devours minutes, hours, days, years. The wheel? Centuries of brooding and fumbling, trial and error, failure upon failure. And after all that, even our most dazzling and innovative works – rocket ships or submarines, tennis balls (I'm not kidding) or zippers – are nothing compared to a single leaf on a single tree in God's creation.

As I mentioned, I recently took up scuba diving. Scuba equipment, over many decades of refining, has attained a high level of durability, reliability, functionality, and simplicity. But it's still unwieldy. The outfit – a constricting rubber suit, a spine-twisting tank, a ganglion of hoses, an armload of valves and gauges – is the best design arrived at to date. But held against the simple elegance of a single guppy, it's gaudy and gangling beyond belief.

Creation is God's first showcase for His wisdom.

His SECOND SHOWCASE – and where God hides His wisdom as much as unveils it – is the church.

The Bible puts it this way: God's intent "was that now, through the church, the manifold wisdom of God should be made known to the rulers and authorities in the heavenly realms."[11]

The church? This ragtag bunch of squabbling, bumbling, rumormongering misfits? Are you kidding? If the church is a showcase of God's wisdom, how wise is that?

Charles Colson opens his book *The Body* with a story about a large and wealthy suburban church that sat next door to a rescue mission. The church, through legal maneuvers, forced the mission to close its doors. The problem? Some of the men and women the mission was trying to help kept wandering over onto the church's beautiful property, smoking in the parking lot, sleeping in the stairwells, littering behind the manicured shrubs, sullying up the place.[12]

The church, rather than being a testimony of God's wisdom, sometimes looks like God's Big Blunder. I once asked my own congregation how many of them had ever been hurt by the church. The air bristled like a staked pit with all the arms that went up. And I know many of these stories. The fist-fight that broke out between two deacons at an annual business meeting. The small posse that split and shattered a healthy, thriving church. The acts of blackmail, the hijackings, the lawsuits, the rumor mills, the gossip-mongering, the personality cults, the factions, the scandals, the squabbles, and the many sordid sundry tales of sexual hanky-panky and financial skull-duggery. It's enough to make you think that the church is the very worst evidence of God's wisdom.

But the Bible insists that the church makes known God's manifold wisdom. Two things are of crucial importance about this. The first is that it is God's *intent* that through the church His manifold wisdom should be made known.

God *intends* for us to be a testimony to His wisdom. But He leaves us the responsibility of whether or not we'll fulfill or thwart His intent. On Sundays, you make a choice whether you'll *go* to church.

But every day, you make a choice whether you'll *be* the church – working out your salvation with fear and trembling, contributing to the health of the whole body, being salt and light, letting no unwholesome word come out of your mouth, having clean hands and a pure heart, loving the least of these. God has not left us to our own devices about this: He freely gives His own wisdom and strength and presence to carry out His intention.

Recently, our church said good-bye to our patron saint, Helen Baker. Helen, nearing eighty and growing frail, was moving away to live with her daughter in another town. Helen never really warmed up to the music at our church. If she had her druthers, we would have sung only hymns in three-quarters time. But she never once complained about it. The week before she moved, someone asked her why she supported this church, year in, year out. She was surprised by the question. I came here with my husband when he was alive. We became members. We made a promise. We said we would commit to supporting this church. Why wouldn't we keep that promise?'"

It's God's *intent* that His wisdom would be made known through the church.

The second crucial thing is that God's wisdom through the church is made known "to the rulers and authorities in the heavenly realms."

The drama of our lives is cosmic more than earthly, not intended primarily for human eyes. The church's chief witness is heaven-bent, vertical rather than horizontal, played out in the presence of demons and angels more than neighbors and colleagues. God's wisdom is refracted through the church, but mere mortals sit cockeyed to it, at an angle that eclipses rather than emblazons it. It's like looking into water: At too close an angle, its surface obscures its depths; only at higher levels does the surface magnify the beauty and intricacy beneath it. To see the church's wisdom fully, in all its many-layered, jewel-like splendor, you have to be higher up. What is foolishness to man, when seen from the right perspective, is the very wisdom of God.

God's ways, seen at ground level, are often puzzling, both to ourselves and to those who gather near. We fumble for explanations, scramble to find some account for why things are the way they are, and still we come up with nothing more than blandishments and balderdash.

God, it turns out, does not stage His wisdom show for *our* friends or enemies. He stages it for *His* — "the rulers and authorities in the heavenly realms." They get front-row seats. They witness His wisdom through the church.

And what do they see? That God takes the most unlikely people — not many of whom are wise by human standards[13] — and by sheer grace and at great cost, makes them His very own. God adopts riffraff and ragamuffins:

> He chose the lowly things of this world and the despised things — and the things that are notto nullify the things that are.... It is because of him that you are in Christ Jesus, who has become for us wisdom from God — that is, our righteousness, holiness and redemption. [14]

The wisdom of God that we can rest in is not first or foremost a demonstration of creative brilliance or managerial competency or technical mastery It is, rather, wisdom disguised as foolishness. It is not aptitudinal, but relational; not a display of divine proficiency, but an unveiling of the Father's heart toward the least of these. Jesus *becomes* wisdom for us. He does in us, through us, and on our behalf what we could never do for ourselves. In a move so reckless and costly and counterintuitive it seems harebrained and laughable to the so-called philosophers of this age,[15] but which makes the rulers and authorities in the heavenly places shudder, God sought those who were nothing and made them, by His choice, His own sons and daughters.

God's wisdom is this: He chose you and me for no better reason than because He wants us for His own. That's enough for me to rest in.

WHICH LEADS TO THE LAST, best thing. The main showcase of God's wisdom is neither the creation nor the church.

It is the Cross.

> For the message of the cross is foolishness to those who are perishing,
> but to us who are being saved it is the power of God.1[6]

Imagine if God assembled the world's experts to help Him answer the question, "How do you deal with sin and evil?"

The Philosopher would speak: "God, it is my considered opinion that we must apply rigorous logic to the problem. it's really an intellectual deficiency. Send them teachers, Socraticlike teachers, men with minds illumined by deep thoughts, whose tongues are blessed with eloquence. Make it dignified. Lofty. Bring the consolation of philosophy. Educate them out of their trouble."

The Moralist stands up: "Mr. God, with all due respect, these people need to strive after the good life more robustly, more vigorously They need to be more circumspect in the way they live. I think you need to devise a carefully calibrated system of reward and punishment and make them cam, by good deeds, their way into heaven."

The Politician interrupts: "No, God. It's policy reform. That's what's needed." And the Militarist finally storms in, gruff with impatience: "Policy reform! God, you simply need to go kick butt. Mobilize the troops. We're gonna do this thing big, just like Iraq. They won't know what hit 'em."

"Hah!" the Entertainer shouts. "They're all wrong, God. What you really need to do is razzle-dazzle them. Lots of music, stunts. Blow up some cars and buildings. Show them power! We can pipe in a Dolby digital soundtrack. Generate some computer graphics. We'll get Peter Jackson to direct. It will be a spectacle!"

And on and on would go the wisdom of the world. And you and I? We'd still be in our sin. Dying, dying, dying.

God didn't consult our wisdom. God said, "This is how I will save them. I will come Myself, in disguise. I'll be born in a barn to an unmarried couple. I will live in obscurity for thirty years, then wander like a vagabond, slum around with a ragtag group of men who are rash one minute, timid the next. I will live in poverty. I will make enemies of the powerful and the influential. I will go to Jerusalem, straight into their snare, and be beaten. I will be killed like a criminal."

From then until now, the pundits and experts have looked on and, like the Stoic and Epicurean philosophers who listened to Paul speak on this subject in Athens, asked, "What is this babbler trying to say?"[17]

For the message of the Cross is foolishness to those who are perishing.

But a few, then and now, see beneath the disguise, that here is true wisdom – the wisdom that doesn't just talk, but which acts, acts with power to save even a wretch like me. *To us who are being saved it is the power of God.*

The book of 1 Kings tells of the great wisdom of Solomon and offers one story to illustrate it. Two women come to the king, each claiming to be the mother of the same baby Solomon says, "I can't tell who's the real mother. Bring me a sword. Cut this child in two, and give half to each woman." One woman cries, "Do it!" The other cries, "No, give the child to her." Solomon knows instantly who the real mother is: the one who would give the child away. That's wisdom, knowing that love would rather see its child alive and whole in someone else's arms than dead and dismembered in its own."

The wisdom of God puts a new twist on this. God wanted to see us alive and whole in *His* arms, but sin was killing us. Sin was the sword that would sever us.

So the King had Himself cut in two instead.

It took the Son of Man, the Son of God, dying on a cross to make us whole and to get us back into the Father's arms. With all the wisdom in the world, we never would have figured that out. But when we see it, when we grasp it, we boast in nothing else. We trust in no one else. At the cross God made a way, and you and I can rest there for all eternity.

To Him, the only wise God, be glory forever through Jesus Christ.

Notes – Chapter Ten

1. "There Ought to Be a Law," *Vancouver Sun*, July 1997.
2. Paul M. johnson, *Intellectuals* (London: Weidenfeld and Nicolson, 1988).
3. Romans 1:21–22, my emphasis.
4. See Matthew 16:15–23.
5. Romans 16:27, my emphasis.
6. Douglas Groothuis, "Jesus the Philosopher," *Books & Culture*, January/February 2003, 38.
7. See 1 Corinthians 1:23–24.
8. See Matthew 11:25.
9. Proverbs 3:19-20.
10. Wilbur Nelson, *If I Were an Atheist* (Grand Rapids, M1: Baker, 1973), cited in *Our Daily Bread*, 6 August 1994.
11. Ephesians 3: 10.
12. Charles Colson, *The Body* (Nashville: Word Publishing, 1992), 11ff.
13. See 1 Corinthians 1:26.
14. 1 Corinthians 1:28, 30.
15. 1 Corinthians 1:18.
17. Acts 17:18.
18. See 1 Kings 3:16–28.

Red Moon Rising

Pete Greig and Dave Roberts

This is the story of the 24-7 Prayer movement, told by Pete Greig, its founder. From Pete's first vision from God about raising up an army of young prayer warriors to the formation of global prayer rooms, this inspiring account testifies to a powerful new work of God around the world.

Survivor
£7.99
PB / 1 8429.1095 7

£2 OFF
£5.99 with voucher

Also by the same author

RED MOON RISING
PETE GREIG // DAVE ROBERTS
THE ADVENTURE OF FAITH... THE POWER OF PRAYER

THE STORY OF 24-7 PRAYER

Foreword

In 1722 a rag-tag band of several hundred young people gathered on the estate of a wealthy count by the name of Zinzendorf. Five years later, God showed up and they began to pray. They prayed in strange and creative ways, but they prayed. They prayed 24-7. Their prayer led to compassion for the poor and those who had never heard of Jesus. Their prayer meeting went on for 125 years without ceasing – the longest prayer meeting in history.

God has decided to do again what he did among the Moravians almost 300 years ago. A 24-7 prayer meeting has started again, but now it has circled the globe overnight. We should not be surprised God chose an unlikely candidate to lead the 24-7 prayer movement. Pete Greig struggled to hear God's voice and wasn't very good at praying, but he was determined to chase the Spirit wherever that took him. The chase led to a blue-haired kid in Dresden, who in turn got him to the home of that first 24-7 prayer meeting started those many years ago. God got through to Pete, and the rest, as they say, is history.

Pete Greig reminds us that prayer doesn't belong to the stodgy or the religious. Nor can prayer be controlled by religious types who think they have a corner on the right words to use and the correct way to stand. *Red Moon Rising* reminds us that prayer is not something to do, but someone to talk to. It stirs faith in us to believe that when we talk to God, he responds.

In his amazing story, Pete Greig takes us with him as he chases the

Spirit, as he dances with God. God initiated the dance, Pete Greig and his wife Samie responded and now God is responding to their response. And what a cool response!

Does this movement have anything to do with the last days? Is there a red moon rising again? Pete Greig believes so. For years, guys like Pete have believed Jesus is coming back very soon. Jesus has not come back. Does that change anything? Not for me. It just means that the Spirit of God is awakening the hearts of young men and women all over the earth. He is creating expectation. Expectation is necessary for Jesus to return. He is not going to come back for a bride who is not prepared. Expectation is a part of preparation. I see expectation growing in the hearts of people like Pete, and it awakens my heart as well.

Red Moon Rising is not just a book; it's an invitation. I have accepted the invitation. I jumped at the offer the first moment I met Pete. I think you will too, once you listen to the Spirit as he speaks through these pages. I invite you to join Pete and myself and many others in giving our hearts to this one thing – to prepare for a great harvest that will usher in the return of Jesus. I would rather throw in my lot with a bunch of crazy lovers of Jesus whose hearts have been awakened, and who are building churches that make disciples who love Jesus, than hang back and be safe. As they say, those who hope, lead.

Why all the fuss with prayer and stirring up expectation? So Jesus will be glorified in the earth. It's about Jesus hear-ing his name in languages he has never heard in heaven. That's the goal. More love for Jesus. More cultures and peoples set free to love him and enjoy him for ever.

When I kneel before the throne of God, I want to look into his eyes and see the joy he receives when I lay crowns at his feet. I found that same desire in Pete and Samie Greig and their friends. They are part of a movement birthed by the Holy Spirit that no one person or organization can claim or control. But anyone can join in. Just listen like Pete did, and start chasing the wind of the Spirit.

Floyd McClung
All Nations Family
September 2003

Introduction

'In the last days, God says, I will pour out my Spirit on all people.
Your sons and daughters will prophesy,
your young men will see visions,
your old men will dream dreams ...
The sun will be turned to darkness and the moon to blood
before the coming of the great and glorious day of the Lord.
And everyone who calls on the name of the Lord will be saved.'

(Acts 2:17–21)

Outside the first great prayer room it is a roughneck fisherman of all people, a guy called Peter, who is preaching to the multicultural crowds of Jerusalem. He's quoting the prophet Joel, explaining with great passion that right here, right now, right before their very eyes, the Spirit of Yahweh is raining down on 'all people'. An era of vision and salvation has begun. Welcome to the last days, he says. Welcome to the end of the movie.

According to the prophet Joel, God's heavenly logo for such an era is the harvest moon, rising blood red and pregnant with possibilities above us. Such a moon rises over every generation awaiting the one that will finally fulfil the Great Commission; taking the good news of Jesus to every culture and ushering in the kingdom of heaven. In our time the Spirit is mobilizing young people with fresh vision, sons and daughters are speaking prophetically to the culture, older generations continue to dream and many people cry out for salvation in every tribe and tongue.

This is a book about a prayer movement; 24-7 is catalysing intercession and mission all over the world and anyone can join in (though no one can join). But the movement has a context and this book will also introduce you to some of the amazing people and surprising places at the heart of this phenomenon. As this 24-7 story unfolds, friendships grow, we often laugh, there are always frustrations and sometimes we are stunned into silence. But in the midst of many emotions, a nameless, faceless army is meeting God on its own in tiny prayer rooms from Alaska to Australia, and emerges with a fresh resolve to help people discover Jesus and the timeless message of his life, death and resurrection.

Signs in the sky

A red moon rose in the winter sky above the nightclub in which we gathered to launch 24-7 prayer. For us it was a sign, reminding us of Joel's prophecy and Peter's great pentecostal sermon. We sensed that this movement of prayer initiated by God, much to everyone's surprise, was somehow something to do with the end times, called to be a portal for fresh vision, a small part of a big picture as the Holy Spirit moves in our time. As we have explored the story of what God is doing through people willing to pray 24-7, we continue to see that red moon rising as Joel predicted and Peter preached.

The book in your hands is not simply Pete Greig's story, although it is told from his perspective and he is involved in it. This is the story of a group of friends in various countries exploring the power of prayer, mission and Christian community together. As you read this book our prayer is that you might somehow be challenged, encouraged and even changed to become more like the Lord Jesus. This story isn't ultimately about 24-7; it's about what can happen when ordinary people dare to dream extraordinary dreams, responding recklessly to the whispered invitations of God. Our prayer is that you will be inspired to say 'yes' to the Holy Spirit, whatever that means for you right now and however inadequate you may sometimes feel.

The prophet Joel predicts that whenever God's people truly surrender to the outpouring of his Spirit in this way (like a surfer to the sea), heaven will speak once again in the tongues of men, as happened on the Day of Pentecost through ordinary people in ordinary places. Prophets will begin to wander the land once more, championing the poor, provoking God's people and calling nations to account. And a rag-tag family of youthful visionaries and seasoned dreamers will conspire together to carry the consequences of the cross to the ends of the earth and into every dark corner of every culture in the name of Christ.

Such, says Joel, are the signs of the end times. But dare we believe that these could be those days? Could a red moon rise once more?

How to Use this Book

You can read *Red Moon Rising* at three different levels. Alongside the main narrative of each chapter you will find additional material either drawing out personal testimonies, poems and quotes (these are called 'Journey') or deeper teaching exploring the themes of the chapter in a bit more depth ('Deeper').

At the back of the book you will also find a set of further articles linked to the Deeper boxes but exploring eight key themes in greater detail and therefore entitled 'Even Deeper'. These are designed to provoke thought, unpacking some of the thinking and theology that shapes the 24-7 movement.

Electrical Storm
(PORTUGAL, GERMANY)

'Let's see colours that have never been seen
Let's go places no one else has been . . .
Well if the sky can crack there must be some way back
To love and only love.'

(U2 – 'Electrical Storm')

Standing on the spectacular cliffs of Cape St Vincent that night, I had
no idea that my life was about to change. We had pitched our little
tent on the most south-westerly point of Europe, far from the lights
of any city and beneath a canopy of unusually bright stars.

For days Nick and I had been travelling west along the coast of the
Portuguese Algarve, camping on cliff tops looking out to sea and
cooking fresh fish on an open fire. By day we would hit the beaches,
often leaving our backpacks on the sand to plunge into the sea.

Having recently graduated from university in London, our futures
stretched out before us like those long, straight, empty roads you see
in photographs of Montana. We were tanned and dirty, the sea had
bleached our tousled hair, and we were having the time of our lives.

After so many days of travelling with the ocean on our left, it had
been exciting to catch the first glimpse of sea to the right as well.
Gradually, over recent days, the land had tapered to the point where
I was standing now, where a solitary lighthouse puts an exclamation

mark on Europe, and the oceans collide in rage.

There is something absolute about Cape St Vincent: its lunar landscape, the ceaseless pounding of the waves against nature's vast battlements and even the black ravens circling majestically below as you look out to sea. Few things in life are so certain as these rocks. It isn't pretty, but it's real with a meaning that everyone senses and perhaps no one can quite express.

People have always been drawn to this mysterious wasteland, which has been battered for thousands of years by the collision of the Atlantic and the Mediterranean seas.

Bronze age tribes buried their dead here and erected standing stones. In AD 304, grieving monks brought the body of St Vincent the martyr here and, according to legend, ravens guarded his bones. The place took on the martyr's name and became a place of Christian and Muslim pilgrimage for centuries to come. The Romans quite simply thought it was the end of the world. Here their maps ran out and their empire marched relentlessly into the endless sea. It would be centuries before Europeans 'discovered' the Americas beyond the blue curve of that deadpan horizon.

But standing there that night I knew none of this history. I only sensed something unfathomably sad and special about the place. Nick and I had pitched our little green tent right there on the cliffs, laughing that we were to be the most south-westerly people in all of Europe for a night. But, unable to sleep, I had climbed quietly out of the tent, leaving Nick gently snoring. A breathtaking sight had greeted me: the vast, glowering ocean glimmering under a shimmering eternity of stars. It was like being lost in the branches of some colossal Christmas tree.

*A faceless army of young people was rising out of the page,
crowds of them in every nation awaiting orders.*

To the south of me the next great landmass was Africa. To the west it was America. But I turned and with my back to the ocean imagined

Europe, rolling away from my feet for 10,000 miles. From where I stood, the continent began with a handful of rocks and a small green tent, but beyond that I could imagine Portugal and Spain, France, Switzerland, Italy and Germany eventually becoming Russia, China and the Indian sub-continent.

Visualizing nation after nation I raised my hands and began to pray out loud for each one by name. And that was when it happened. First my scalp began to tingle and an electric current pulsed down my spine, again and again, physically shaking my body. Nothing like this had ever happened to me before, and it was years before the spiritual excitement associated with the Toronto Blessing would appear to plug millions into the mains. I could hear a buzzing, clicking sound overhead, as if an electric pylon was short-circuiting, and I seriously wondered if I was about to get fried. As these strange sensations continued I received a vision. My eyes were open, but I could 'see' with absolute clarity before me the different countries laid out like an atlas and from each one a faceless army of young people was rising out of the page, crowds of them in every nation awaiting orders.

I have no idea how long that vision lasted – it might have been a minute or as much as an hour – but eventually I climbed into my sleeping bag next to Nick, who was quietly snoring, and with my head still spinning, I drifted into a deep sleep.

My life would never be the same.

★ ★ ★

Two years earlier, in the city of Leipzig in communist East Germany, a 13-year-old was looking around in amazement at all the candles and people crammed into the building to pray for peace. Markus Lägel felt like a small part of something very big – anonymous and special at the same time.

It was hard to be a Christian under one of the most repressive regimes in the world. The ever-present fear of conflict with the West weighed heavily on everyone, so the East German church began to mobilize prayers for peace. They started in 1979, and by 1989 the prayer rally at Leipzig was attracting 300,000 people.

With so many people expressing their protest in prayer, the State was preparing for war. Markus remembers guns on the roofs of churches and tanks in the street. But when the Berlin Wall finally came down one communist official made an extraordinary admission to a journalist: 'We were prepared for every eventuality, but not for candles and not for prayers.'

Markus spent formative years caught up in those peace prayer rallies in Leipzig and when the communist regime finally fell, he became convinced that prayer has the power to undermine any ideology that oppresses. Watching consumerism usurp communism, one form of oppression for another, Markus began a spiritual journey that would one day make him an essential part of the 24-7 story.

★ ★ ★

As Nick and I hitched our way back across Europe, the vision of Cape St Vincent kept replaying in my mind. 'Where is the army, Lord?' I would wonder again and again as we travelled from Lisbon to Valladolid, Bilbao, Bordeaux, Paris and London. 'Where are the signs of such people in these streets, these tenements, these crowded places?' Maybe my vision had meant nothing at all.

It's a question I guess we all ask, looking around our towns and cities, looking at the classroom or the office or the campus, watching TV and even scanning the pews at church. Where are those 'forceful' men and women rising up to lay hold of God's kingdom (Matthew 11:12)? Where are the people of God advancing the purposes of God with militancy and humility in the power of his Spirit today?

And why do we need such an army anyway, when churches abound? What is the urgency that compels us?

To die for

I still remember where I was when I heard the news that Kurt Cobain had killed himself. Somehow it seemed momentous that a world-famous musical genius had stuck a gun in his mouth and pulled the trigger. In his suicide note he simply claimed that he felt 'guilty beyond words'. But, with hindsight, the rock star's suicide wasn't momentous at all; it was just another death of another depressed individual failing to find sufficient meaning in a messed-up world.

After working twelve hours a day copying product numbers into account ledgers, a Japanese man called Wataru Tsurumi wrote a book called *The Complete Manual of Suicide*, advising young people on how to kill themselves. It has sold 1.3 million copies since 1993.

Der Spiegel magazine estimates that in Germany alone there are at least 30 Internet death forums where suicidal teenagers can discuss the best ways to die. A kid called Rizzo wrote on one: 'Hi people! I've bought a 7-metre long piece of cord. Can someone tell me the height of drop to hang myself properly?' A forum master called Markus 'B' left his final message on 11th November: 'When you have a 12-calibre shotgun in your hand, you think differently about death. If you think there's something heroic about shooting yourself, hold a gun in your hand.' Three days later Markus's parents found him dead with the Beatles track 'Let it be' playing on repeat.

With suicide rates among young men soaring, alongside self-harm and eating disorders in women, we can say with some confidence that this generation may well be hurting more profoundly than any other. Amid sparkling creativity, spectacular innovation and unprecedented wealth, growing up in the West means for many a sense of alienation and a craving for intimacy, authenticity and hope.

That, surely, is a heart cry that moves the heart of God as his Spirit intercedes for us in groans beyond talking. It's why he anoints us to preach good news to the poor and to bind up the broken-hearted (Isaiah 61:1). It's why he is sounding the trumpet in our time, summoning his forces to wage war in heaven and declare peace on earth (Ephesians 6). The battle is real, but it's not just to save our souls from an epidemic of rock 'n' roll angst, and it's not simply to refill our lonely pews either. We need an army to arise because the poor and the oppressed are crying out to God for urgent intervention and some ray of hope. 'Though I call for help,' they say, 'there is no justice' (Job 19:7).

JOURNEY: THE POWER OF STORIES

How beautiful on the mountains are the feet of those who bring good news, who proclaim peace, who bring good tidings, who proclaim salvation, who say to Zion, 'Your God reigns!' (Isaiah 52:7)

In New York City a guy called John bought a Big Mac for a homeless man; it was the beginning of a lifelong friendship. In Dublin, Lucy's heart felt as if it were breaking as she prayed for friends who didn't know Jesus. In Tennessee, a prodigal stepped inside a prayer room and began the journey home.

The stories of Jesus are still being told. He is alive and moving powerfully in our generation, still comforting those who mourn, answering prayer and making ordinary lives extraordinary.

Stories are powerful; they can evoke anger, ignite truth, inspire hope or invade a person's loneliness with an empathetic hug. Jesus told stories but he also was the story.

Throughout this book, in these 'Journey' boxes, you'll find short quotes and personal accounts of God on the move. If life is like a video, these are like snapshots capturing particular moments on people's spiritual journeys. Hopefully they will help you to understand God's character better. And when we get our heads around God's character, prayer, devotion and discipleship ceases to be a technique and becomes an instinct.

That's when we can take our place in an army that marches on its knees, fighting for the Prince of Peace.

Black death

'And who is my neighbour?' (Luke 10:29)

We probably never expected to find ourselves living at the time of the worst epidemic in world history, but AIDS has now killed more people than the Black Death. That's why in Africa tonight 400,000 children will lie down to sleep without a mother or father to kiss them goodnight, innocently orphaned by AIDS. History will hold us accountable for our response to such suffering. And yet some countries, like Malawi, are being forced to spend more on debt repayment to countries like ours than they are on preventing and treating HIV/AIDS or feeding their own people.[1] Our governments are effectively making things worse!

In America, 40 years after Martin Luther King's 'I have a dream' speech, if you're black you are nearly twice as likely to be fired from your job than your white co-workers.[2] What's more, the median income of black American families was 54 per cent of the income of white families in 1992, which is significantly worse than it was back in 1969.[3] Something has to change and Jesus says that something *can* change, promising that 'the first shall be last and the last shall be first'. In a world obsessed with celebrity, sex and superficial appearance, he still chooses the lepers and the AIDS victims, the bullied kids from school and the 'fools' of this world to confound the wise with hope and justice. In the company of Christ, the ugly become beautiful and classroom cowards become the bewildered heroes of his kingdom. That, after all, is my story, and I suspect it is yours too:

> Take a good look, friends, at who you were when you got called into this life. I don't see many of 'the brightest and the best' among you, not many influential, not many from highsociety families. Isn't it obvious that God deliberately chose men and women that the culture overlooks and exploits and abuses, chose these 'nobodies' to expose the hollow pretensions of the 'somebodies'? (1 Corinthians 1:25–27, *The Message*)

That is the gospel as much today as it was when Paul was writing to the Corinthians. In fact there may well be more outcasts in our modern industrialized society – slaves of the free market economy –

---

1 www.maketradefair.com August 2003.
2 Even allowing for differences in age, education, job performance and a score of other factors, blacks in the US are fired at nearly twice the rate of whites (*Philadelphia Inquirer*, October 1994).
3 *Ibid.*

than there were in the Roman Empire. When I worked in Hong Kong with heroin addicts as part of Jackie Pullinger's remarkable ministry, she would say, 'If you want to see revival, plant your church in the gutter.' Jesus warned us that the upwardly mobile middle classes would always find it extremely hard to receive him. But among the losers, the freaks and the apparent failures, what one preacher called the 'shrimps and wimps and those with limps'[4] . . . that is actually where the gospel spreads quite easily.

Talking about a revolution

Revolutions always begin in the streets with the dispossessed – never in the corridors of power. Think of the early church, the French Revolution, the Bolshevik Revolution and the American wars for independence. Think of William Booth's Salvation Army and the birth of Pentecostalism in a back street of Los Angeles. Think of the roots of rock 'n' roll, of hip-hop and rap.

Something must change. Something can change. But can the church as we know her rise to the task? The respected researcher George Barna looks in the rear view mirror and makes a tragic obser-vation: 'Recent decades have seen the impact of the Church wane to almost nothing.'[5]

In the company of Christ, the ugly become beautiful and classroom cowards become the bewildered heroes of his kingdom.

The charismatic movement of the last 50 years has, in parts, done more to 'church' a generation into certain ways of thinking and acting than it has to disciple them to think and act like Christ. As a result, teenagers and young adults are finding our meetings and teachings increasingly irrelevant. Every Sunday thousands of our contemporaries leave the pew, never to return. But statistics mask the real story. A 50-year time warp often separates Saturday night from Sunday morning, and faced with such alienation some of our peers have simply retreated from the world altogether, taking up residence in a protective Christian bubble

---

4 Gerald Coates.
5 George Barna and Mark Hatch, *Boiling Point* (Regal, 2001), p. 311.

in which they can avoid meaningful interaction with the challenges of a wider culture. Others send their bodies faithfully to church on Sunday, having stored their brains in a pickle jar at home and left their hearts at the party, the pub or the cinema the night before. And of course many of our friends just avoid church altogether.

Right now, one in five American children are living in poverty and yet, according to the Barna Research Group, 'Half of all adults did nothing at all in the past year to help a poor person' and 'few churches have a serious ministry to the poor'.[6] With such crying needs and such self-absorption among God's people, surely things have never been worse?

Christianity will be forgotten in 30 years

In a message called 'Prayer & Revival'[7] J. Edwin Orr, a widely respected historian, described the situation in America in the 1780s. Drunkenness was epidemic and the streets were judged not to be safe after dark. What about the churches?

> The Methodists were losing more members than they were gaining. In a typical Congregational church, the Rev. Samuel Shepherd of Lennos, Massachusetts, in sixteen years had not taken one young person into fellowship. The Lutherans were so languishing that they discussed uniting with Episcopalians who were even worse off. The Protestant Episcopal Bishop of New York, Bishop Samuel Provost, quit functioning; he confirmed no one for so long that he decided he was out of work, so he took up other employment.
>
> The Chief Justice of the United States, John Marshall, wrote to the Bishop of Virginia, James Madison, that the Church 'was too far gone ever to be redeemed.' The great philosopher Voltaire averred and the author Tom Paine echoed, 'Christianity will be forgotten in thirty years.'

The spiritual state of America's universities at the time concurred with such gloomy predictions, giving little or no hope for the future

6 *Ibid.*, p. 41.
7 International Revival Network: www.openheaven.com

of the faith in that land:

> Take the liberal arts colleges at that time. A poll taken at Harvard had
> discovered not one believer in the whole student body. They took a
> poll at Princeton, a much more evangelical place, where they discov-
> ered only two believers in the student body, and only five that did not
> belong to the filthy speech movement of that day. Students rioted.
> They held a mock communion at Williams College, and they put on
> anti-Christian plays at Dartmouth. They burned down the Nassau Hall
> at Princeton. They forced the resignation of the president of Harvard.
> They took a Bible out of a local Presbyterian church in New Jersey,
> and burnt it in a public bonfire. Christians were so few on campus in
> the 1790s that they met in secret, like a communist cell, and kept their
> minutes in code so that no one would know.

It's hard to believe that this was taking place in America just 200 years
ago, but then, Orr continues, God intervened and he did so by mobilizing his people to pray, first in the UK and then in the States:

> A prayer movement started in Britain through William Carey, Andrew
> Fuller, John Sutcliffe and other leaders who began what the British
> called the Union of Prayer. Hence, the year after John Wesley died
> (1791), the second great awakening began and swept Great Britain.
>
> In New England, there was a man of prayer named Isaac Backus, a
> Baptist pastor, who in 1794, when conditions were at their worst,
> addressed an urgent plea for prayer for revival to pastors of every
> Christian denomination in the United States. Churches knew that
> their backs were to the wall. All the churches adopted the plan until
> America, like Britain, was interlaced with a network of prayer
> meetings, which set aside the first Monday of each month to pray. It
> was not long before revival came... Out of that second great
> awakening came the modern missionary movement and its societies.
> Out of it came the abolition of slavery, popular education, Bible
> Societies, Sunday schools and many social benefits.

DEEPER: VALLEY OF BONES

Consider for a moment some statistics. They're mainly from the UK and USA, but with small variations they might represent any major Western nation. They could so easily be used to posture and condemn, accuse others and parade our virtue. But there is another way to view them. Think of them as the symptoms of a spiritually malnourished generation. Think of them as the evidence of loss, alienation and pain.

*   **Drink and drugs** – Almost a third of UK teenagers have been drunk 20 or more times and more than 35 per cent have experimented with illegal drugs.[1] Why?*

*   **Bullying** – Nearly one-third of the middle school and high school students in one survey admitted being a bully, being bullied or both.[2] Why?*

*   **Priorities** – It currently costs $2.2 million to air a 30-second commercial during the American Super Bowl, while literally hundreds of millions of people are malnourished, homeless and dying of curable diseases.[3] Where are the people crying for change?*

*   **Self-harm** – Children as young as six are cutting themselves. The average self-harmer is aged eleven, and one in ten adolescents are thought to have cut themselves deliberately at least once. A typical 16-year-old girl says that most days she cuts into her arms until they bleed, explaining that 'the pain proves you're human'.[4] Why?*

*   There are never simple one-line answers to such questions.*

Maybe some people are merely rebellious, refusing any constraint. But for how many is sex a search for intimacy, drink and drugs a way of escape, self-harm a demonic self-loathing and bullying a search for power and significance? Only a prophetic community can help people discover the wisdom that will heal these wounds.

---

1 BBC Report, 20/2/2001.
2 *The Journal of the American Medical Association*, 25th April 2001.
3 George Barna and Mark Hatch, *Boiling Point* (Regal, 2001), p. 110.
4 Centre for Suicide Research, Oxford University, 2003.

Utter hopelessness turned to renewal and restoration as God's people turned to determined prayer. Could it happen for a new generation?

UCBONES

'Where, Lord, is the army for today?'

It was a question the people of Israel in captivity asked too. Then Ezekiel found himself in a valley of dry bones — as unpromising a place as any confronting us — only to witness a dramatic transformation. The bones became corpses, 'breath entered them; they came to life and stood up on their feet — a vast army' (Ezekiel 37:10).

We may be tempted to look at youth culture around the world and echo the despair of the people of Israel: 'Our bones are dried up and our hope is gone; we are cut off.' But could it be that as we declare the 'word of the Lord' in our time, the flesh will return, bones will reconnect and the body will breathe again? Could an army arise in Silicone Valley, the Thames Valley or any other modern-day valley of bones?

Years after Markus Lägel's experiences in Leipzig and mine in Portugal, we are friends from different countries walking the journey of faith together. These days you may find us on occasion wearing identical 24-7 T-shirts. On the front they say 'UCBONES' and on the back 'ICANARMY.' We're declaring to those cynics busy writing off our generation, 'You see bones, but I see an army!' We choose to believe that walls can still fall the way they did in Jericho and in Germany. We choose to believe that a heart cry can become a war cry for justice. We choose to believe that the army of the Lord can arise once again in the valley of dry bones.

> Then he said to me: 'Son of man, these bones are the whole house of Israel. They say, "Our bones are dried up and our hope is gone; we are cut off." Therefore prophesy and say to them: "This is what the Sovereign LORD says: O my people, I am going to open your graves and bring you up from them; I will bring you back to the land of Israel . . . I will put my Spirit in you and you will live." ' (Ezekiel 37:11–14)

Oriel's Travels

Robert Harrison

This sequel to last year's Oriel's Diary sees our Archangel hero sent to accompany Paul on his travels, providing a fresh take on the biblical stories of the early church.

Scripture Union
£6.99
PB / 1 8599.9786 4

£2 OFF
£4.99 with voucher

Also by the same author

An Archangel's Travels with St Paul

Robert Harrison

Published in 2003 by Scripture Union
207-209 Queensway, Bletchley MK2 2EB

In my office - free from the unrelenting pressure of time

'I have a challenge for you, Oriel,' my Boss said to me after a thought-filled silence. The word 'challenge' swept through my Angelic being like a great wave.

Serving the author of all creations is a challenge in itself. I shuddered to think what it might be that even he calls a 'challenge'.

'After your excellent work looking after my Son,' he began, glancing at the Heavenly man seated beside him, 'I would like you to look after another human for me.'

I have been responsible for Heaven's Angel guardian scheme since the very first humans stumbled across planet Earth. However, only once have I been a guardian myself and that was for Jesus, my Boss's Son, during his last months on Earth.

Father and Son looked intently at me while I digested their request.

'Who is it?' I asked, suppressing a rising tide of excitement.

'I have been looking for someone to travel to Rome,' my Boss explained, 'and tell its citizens about Jesus.'

I glanced at the Son, seated beside his eternal Father.

'What's so special about Rome?'

'It is the centre of the world's most powerful empire, at the particular moment in Earth's story that we are considering.'

I nodded thoughtfully. 'Who have you chosen?'

'A man called Saul, from Tarsus in Turkey.'

I was confused. 'You have picked a Turk to tell a Jewish story to the citizens of Rome?' I asked. I knew it was unwise to question his judgement but there was nothing to be gained from keeping my thoughts to myself; my Boss always knows them anyway.

'You know me, Oriel,' he replied with a disarming smile that invited me to ask further.

'What is it that makes Saul the right man for this job?'

'That is for you to discover,' my Creator replied, his eyes twinkling.

The Son joined the conversation. 'Saul is a Jew – he got *that* from his mother. And he's also a citizen of Rome – he inherited *that* from his father.'

This was an encouraging start. I waited for more.

'He has spent the last three years studying at the Rabbinical University at Jerusalem.'

'I like the man already,' I interrupted enthusiastically. 'I always said you should choose some followers from the university!'

'You did indeed,' the Son said. Now he was the one with a twinkle in his eyes. 'That's why you are clearly the Archangel for the job.'

'Where and when will I find the man?' I asked.

The communication that holds Eternal Father and Son in perfect unity is too deep for any Angel to fathom, but they allowed me to glimpse a ray of playful amusement that passed between them. I recognised it at once, and it set my spirit on alert. It warned me that there is something about this Saul that does not match the picture I was forming in my imagination. I shall just have to travel down to Jerusalem and meet the man to find out what.

Just outside Jerusalem – around 32 AD   (I always struggle with human dates and calendars)

I arrived at a narrow, private gate in Jerusalem's wall which leads directly into the Temple complex. I spotted my man immediately. A small mob of angry priests were dragging a prisoner out into the sunlight from the labyrinth of passages behind the Temple. My Angelic eye was led directly to the shining spirit of their victim. He shone with the intense Heavenly brightness that illuminates all my Boss's human children. I quickly scanned the minds of the priests, to find out why they had turned against this wonderful man. The source of their anger was obvious: they were jealous of his faith. They were dragging him out of the city with one purpose – to dispose of this follower of Jesus just as they had wanted to get rid of Jesus himself. They were determined not to waste time pandering to the Roman Governor this time; they were going to do the job themselves – with stones.

The group was led by a thin, tight-spirited Pharisee whose mind was consumed by a determination to exterminate all memory of Jesus.

My first task was obvious: to rescue my man from his immediate fate and take him somewhere safe. The angry mob dragged their quarry down into the filthy valley where Jerusalem's rubbish is dumped. There they threw him to the ground and prepared to end his life by the crude method of throwing rocks at his head until his brain could take no more. Before this energetic execution began the priests removed their coats and handed them to their leader. I grabbed my moment.

I stood between hounds and prey, and called for the attention of all 23 Angel guardians present. 'Stop the hands of your charges and don't let them throw a single stone,' I ordered with the authority granted to all Archangels. 'Our Boss has chosen this Saul to tell the story of his Son right in the heart of the Roman Empire. He must not be killed.'

There was an awkward silence. Then a particularly depressed Angel spoke up. He was the guardian of the condemned man. 'This *isn't* Saul,' he said, nodding towards the prisoner.

'But he must be!' I replied.

'This is Stephen. He has just been condemned to death by the Jewish Council for asserting that our Boss's Son is indeed our Boss's son.'

I was confused. I was sure that I had come to the right time and place to find the man my Boss had chosen.

'So which one *is* Saul of Tarsus?' I asked the assembled Angels, while the furious priests were gathering large stones to hurl at Stephen's head.

Twenty three Angelic faces looked in exactly the same direction. I turned round, following their gaze, and to my horror they were looking at the young Pharisee whose arms were laden with his companions' coats – the leader of the mob. As I watched, Saul gave a grim nod and the stones began to fly, crashing into Stephen's skull.

Jesus arrived.

'Ah, Oriel,' he said calmly. 'You've found your man, I see.'

I scowled back. 'We need to talk,' I said coldly.

'Drop into my office when you get back,' Jesus replied.

'They're killing one of your friends,' I pointed out. 'Don't you care?'

'That's why I'm here. I've come to take him home.'

We turned to look at Stephen. His human life was fading rapidly. 'Look!' he called faintly, 'I can see the Son of God.'

This prompted another volley of rocks, thrown with even more force and passion than before. They hit their target. Stephen's skull caved in and fragments of bone pierced his brain. The myriad of messages that had maintained his humanity throughout his life were silenced, his heart stopped pumping. As Stephen's spirit rose from its battered body I did not see the enslaved shadow that I have always seen before, tangled in the knots of its own selfishness. What emerged from Stephen's failing form was a vibrant spiritual body just like that of Jesus himself. With his last lungful of breath, Stephen said, 'Lord Jesus, receive my spirit.'

'I most certainly will,' the Son replied. He grasped Stephen's bright spirit by the hand and took him directly to Heaven.

Saul of Tarsus returned the coats to his fellow thugs and said, 'Good work! Now, come with me, we have much more still to do.'

They disappeared through the small gate in the city wall, leaving Stephen's shattered corpse where it was, on a heap of refuse. I remained there for some time until a group of frightened disciples arrived to remove the body for burial.

I must speak with my Boss.

In Heaven

I marched directly to my Boss's room. He instantly disarmed my fury with a forgiving smile. I knew there was no value in delivering the speech I had prepared during my lonely vigil beside Stephen's human remains, so I waited for him to speak first.

'Oriel,' he said, 'the potential for your mistake has been lurking in you since the day my Son chose a group of humble fishermen to be his first disciples.'

'I know,' I replied. 'I'm sorry.'

He smiled his full, radiant smile which reassured me that my mistake was completely forgiven.

I still needed to be sure that I had found the right man. 'But this man – is *this* the human you wish me to take to Rome,' I asked, 'to tell them about Jesus?'

'Yes,' was the united reply of Father and Son.

'But he hates you,' I said.

'He hates *me*,' the Son confirmed.

'He is utterly devoted to *me*,' the Father added.

I looked at the two expressions of Creative Love before me.

'That doesn't make sense.'

'That, Oriel, my dear friend,' the Son answered, 'is what you must help Saul understand.'

There was a knock at the door. In walked Stephen, liberated from the constraints and complications of time, and resplendent in his new, Heavenly body. On his face were carved the wounds of his bloody execution, but here in Heaven they were not the ugly scars that had disfigured Stephen's corpse. They were an elaborate adornment that proclaimed the beauty of their owner's love for my Boss.

Jesus stood up and hugged his friend. He introduced me. 'Stephen, this is Archangel Oriel, Heaven's chief administrator.'

Stephen embraced me. 'I saw you back there in Jerusalem,' he said, adding, 'I believe you mistook me for Saul.'

'Oriel is going to help Saul understand the truth,' Jesus explained. 'Then he will escort him to Rome so that he can tell my story there.'

'Quite a challenge,' Stephen observed with a wry smile.

'Do you have any hints?' I asked the man who had just experienced the full force of Saul's *devotion* to my Boss.

'Don't quote the Scriptures at him,' Stephen replied. 'He is a bit sensitive in that department.'

I thanked him for his advice and left for my office. I have asked Archangels Michael, Gabriel and Raphael to join me.

Back in Jerusalem, at the place where Jesus died

My three Archangel colleagues responded to my call and we met in my office before I left for Earth. When I explained the situation to them, Michael was the first to comment. 'I don't think our army will be much use to you,' he said. 'Sorry, Oriel.'

We pondered the challenge in shared silence until Gabriel offered, 'I could go down and speak to him.'

'He deserves a fright,' I said to the great messenger, 'but, to be honest, I don't think he would notice you.'

We returned to our separate thoughts, brought back together again by Raphael. 'Before you can make any progress with this man, Oriel,' he said, 'you will have to learn to love him.'

The idea revolted me. I had viewed Saul with the same pure anger that I have for the Angels who have abandoned my Boss's service to join the Opposition.

'Impossible!' I replied.

'When you were looking after the Son during his human life,' Raphael said, 'didn't you listen to what he said?'

Raphael is the most thoughtful of my Archangel colleagues. I had no doubt that he was about to reveal a diamond of divine wisdom. I didn't answer his question but simply waited for him to continue.

'The Son said, *Love your enemies and pray for those who persecute you.* Does that sound familiar?'

Nothing else needed to be said. I thanked my friends for their support and came here, to the place where Jesus was executed. This is where my Boss showed the full extent of his love for his human enemies. Perhaps here I will find something to love in Saul of Tarsus.

I spent the Earth night alone on the barren hillock outside Jerusalem. At dawn, Raphael arrived.

'How are you getting on, my dear?' asked the conductor of Heaven's choir.

'Just thinking'.

'May I join you, Oriel?'

Jerusalem spun round into the yellow rays of the sun. Farmers and merchants leading donkeys laden with produce made their way up to the city's gates and waited for them to open. Nothing seemed to have changed since I was last working within the narrow stream of Earth's time. Two winters of rain had washed away the last traces of Jesus' human blood – they had been replaced with the stains of other men's deaths.

Raphael spoke. 'Cursed is the one who hangs on a tree.'

'What?' I asked, my mind emerging from dark memories.

'It is a line from the Jewish law,' my companion said. 'It may just be part of your Saul's problem.'

'How's that?'

'Jesus was hung on a wooden cross and so he became cursed under Jewish law,' Raphael explained. 'Saul is a Pharisee, so it is impossible – in his understanding – for Jesus to be anything other than an offence to all that is pure and holy.'

I considered Raphael's words. And the more I did so, the more hopeless my quest seemed.

'Is that supposed to help me?' I turned to ask my enigmatic friend. He had gone.

Saul's room - that evening

When the city gates opened, I made my way to the priests' offices behind the Temple and waited for Saul to arrive. Observing his thoughts yesterday, I saw that he's intent on eradicating all Jesus' followers as quickly as possible. So, assuming he would hatch his plans in the same ants' nest of dark corridors where Jesus' death was plotted, I settled into a vantage point that Raphael once used – a stone pillar - from which I could watch the comings and goings of the politician priests who rule the Jewish nation.

I was not disappointed. Saul of Tarsus strode arrogantly into the priestly headquarters as soon as morning prayers finished. He waited at the door to the high priest's office. The high priest, rounding the corner from another direction, was a different high priest to the one who engineered Jesus' crucifixion. He was an older man, Annas. I studied his mind and quickly learned that Annas is deeper and wiser than his predecessor.

Annas led Saul into his room and closed the door. I joined them. Before Annas had settled into his chair, Saul unleashed a tirade of anger against the followers of Jesus.

'These men and women are undermining the very structure of our nation,' he bellowed. 'They say it doesn't matter if you break the Law, because their Jesus will forgive you. The people, of course, lap it all up. They have water poured over their heads and say, *I'm living Jesus' way*. We have to stop them.'

'That's easier said than done,' observed the elderly priest. 'Caiaphas thought that killing Jesus would shut them up; it only made them more fanatical. Now they are claiming he is still alive.'

'We can't simply sit here and do nothing,' the young Pharisee asserted, his fists clenched in his lap.

'I'm inclined to agree with your old teacher.' Annas spoke slowly. 'Gamaliel said that if this Jesus movement is not from the Almighty, it will die out. But if, by some chance, it is blessed by the Almighty, then we will not stop it, whatever we do.'

'Jesus was not, nor ever could have been, the Messiah,' Saul thundered.

I was startled by the picture in Saul's mind. He saw Jesus nailed not to a cross but to a tree. Raphael had hit the mark with outstanding accuracy.

'Everyone who honours Jesus must be silenced.'

'What do you propose, Saul?'

'I propose we arrest everybody found proclaiming that this Jesus was... ' He wouldn't allow himself to speak the words he was thinking. The very idea that Jesus is my Boss's Son is, to Saul, an unutterable heresy. He rephrased his reply. 'We must arrest anyone who claims that Jesus was more than a man, and charge them with blasphemy.'

'I don't want any more martyrs,' Annas said calmly. 'What happened yesterday, with Stephen, was unfortunate.'

Saul looked across the table at the old priest. He was irritated by the man's caution but knew he had to make concessions to get his own way.

'Have it your way,' he declared. 'No deaths. I'll leave them to rot in prison until they lose interest in their Messiah. You have my promise.'

Saul stood to leave. As he opened the door, the high priest said, 'Two more things, Saul.' The young man closed the door again.

'The first is that you and I never had this conversation. What you choose to do is entirely on your own initiative. Do you understand?'

'I do,' Saul said, nodding gravely.

'The second is that I don't want you to go anywhere near the fisherman, Peter.'

Saul scowled.

'I have already arrested him three times,' Annas continued. 'He is mine.'

Saul said nothing, but I saw his thoughts. 'Oh. no he isn't! That loudmouthed Galilean is at the top of my list.'

Saul made his way to the vast outer court of the Temple, to a shaded area called Solomon's Colonnade. A group of people were gathered there, most of whom shone with the spiritual light of my Boss's new-born children. Saul joined them, welcomed with warm smiles. None of those present seemed to know who he was. Matthew, the former tax collector arrived, his expensive Roman coat now worn and faded. A thrill of excitement spread through the small crowd; they were about to hear from one of Jesus' twelve chosen assistants. Saul listened for a while, shaking his head in disagreement at almost everything Matthew said. Then he slipped quietly away. I knew he would be back.

As Saul left I called to his Angel Guardian, Harruel – a tortured-looking spirit – and informed him that I would be taking over the care of Saul with immediate effect.

'You're welcome,' he said, darkly. 'I'm off!'

Meanwhile, Matthew told of the day when Jesus walked into his tax office and invited him to join John and Peter as one of his followers. Matthew described his amazement, a year later, when he told a crippled child to stand up and she jumped into his arms and hugged him. He told the people that Jesus' friendship was the best investment they could ever make, that it would insure their lives against Death and judgement.

Saul returned. He sat at the back of Matthew's rapidly growing audience. At the same time, a group of Temple guards appeared at the end of the colonnade. Saul watched Matthew, and the guards watched Saul. He was waiting for an excuse to have the former tax collector arrested.

Eventually Matthew said, 'Brothers and sisters, whoever believes that Jesus is the Son of Almighty God will be forgiven, no matter how many of the laws they have broken.'

Saul looked to the guards and nodded. Two stepped forward and grabbed Matthew by the arms.

'You're under arrest for blasphemy,' one said, marching Matthew off to the Temple prison.

Undeterred, another of my Boss's shining children stood up in Matthew's place and began to talk of her meetings with Jesus. The moment she said something Saul considered to be blasphemous, he nodded at the guards, and she was escorted to the dungeons.

So the pattern continued throughout the day. Despite repeated arrests, the crowd grew, and every time a speaker was taken away someone else stood up and said what they knew about my Boss's Son. I studied the spirits and minds of these people. The news of Stephen's death had convinced them of the urgency of their cause. It didn't matter to them if they too were stoned to death; they believed they would see Jesus just as Stephen had done.

When the Temple horn was blown to announce the time for evening prayers, seventeen of Jesus' followers were in prison. The remaining disciples assured their audience that they would return tomorrow. They then went further into the Temple to join the service of prayers and readings. Saul accompanied them.

The daily reading from the Book of their Law was an instruction given by my Boss through Moses when he was preparing the Jews to become an independent nation: *I will hand over to you the people who live in the land and you will drive them out. Do not make any deals with them or with their gods. Do not let them live in your land, or they will cause you to turn against me.*

The priest invited any of the men present to comment on the passage. Saul stood up awkwardly and walked to the front. There was about him none of the icy confidence he had shown in the high priest's office. He was intimidated by the size of the congregation and was desperately lacking in confidence in his ability to say what he wanted to say. I was surprised. 'I can't imagine this man speaking up for my Boss in the middle of Rome,' I thought.

Saul began to speak, or rather to mumble. Half of those present couldn't hear a word he was saying – but that was a blessing.

'Brothers and fathers,' Saul began hesitantly, 'our Law demands that we maintain the purity of our nation and of our faith. We have in our midst a greater and more deadly poison than the dumb idols of the Philistines but, like all false religion, we are commanded by our Lord to root it. . . '

I'd heard enough. My Boss has made me responsible for this angry young man; I didn't intend to do nothing while he spread his hatred of Jesus' new family. I grabbed hold of Saul's venomous tongue and wouldn't allow him to speak another word. The congregation waited for him to continue. Saul tried to force his tongue back into action. I held on tightly. The young Pharisee blushed, let out an incoherent gulping sound and fled. I did not relinquish my grip on his tongue until he was safely inside his own home. He collapsed onto his bed, furious, frustrated, desperate and defeated.

I Was Only Asking

Steve Turner

Talented children's poet Steve Turner addresses some of the big questions kids ask in his stunning new collection. Arranged thematically, these are poems that children and parents alike will adore reading.

Lion Publishing
£9.99
HB / 0 7459.4821 9

£2 OFF
£7.99 with voucher

Other titles by the same author

Published by Lion Publishing plc
Mayfield House, 256 Banbury Road, Oxford OX2 7DH, England

Rubbish

You may be rubbish at dancing,
or rubbish at hitting a ball
with a large wooden stick.
You may be rubbish at
     counting,
or rubbish at putting order
into the right words.
But you're not rubbish.

No one is rubbish.
No one is a ball of paper,
or the curly skin of a potato.
No one is a twisted wheel,
or a fridge that no longer
     works.
No one chooses to live
on a scrap heap.
No one wants to be treated
like dirt.

You may be rubbish at
     inventing stories,
or rubbish at remembering
the punch lines of jokes.
You may be rubbish at skipping,
or rubbish at keeping your
     room
free from rubbish.
But you're not rubbish.

The voice that calls
and tells you that you're
     rubbish?
That's rubbish.
The voice in the middle of your
     head
that tells you that you're
     rubbish?
That's rubbish.

You may be rubbish at hearing
the music in your heart,
or rubbish at believing
all the wonders that you are.
But you're not rubbish.
No one is rubbish.

The Me Bit

There's a me bit of me
Inside, somewhere deep,
That never takes time out
Or drops off to sleep.

My features it wears as
Its daily disguise.
It feels with my fingers
And looks through my eyes.

There's a me bit of me
That takes up no space.
You can't say you've found it
In heart, brain or face.

It won't show on X-rays.
You can't cut it out.
But it's there just the same –
Of that there's no doubt.

There's a me bit of me
That's just out of range.
To you it's a puzzle.
To me it seems strange.
It hides in a hollow
Inside my insides

And never gets smaller,
Or older, or dies.

God's Great Studio of Art

I'd love to have been a fly on the wall
In God's great studio of art
When he first had the idea for the world
And planned it all out on a chart.

I'd love to have heard the CRACK! and the POW!
As lightning crashed through his mind
To have seen the sweet smile of pleasure
That came with each sketch and each find.

I'd love to have seen the outlines and drafts
For the whale, the moon and the rose,
For the peacock, the dolphin, the tiger,
The elephant's ears and nose.

I'd love to have been a fly on the wall
In God's great studio of art
When he first had the idea for the world
And decided to give me a part.

Snowmen

Snowmen have nothing to live for
Snowmen just stand still and stare
Snowmen are made for our pleasure
Snowmen just have to be there.

Snowmen don't get bored with standing
Snowmen get used to the cold
Snowmen were never once snowboys
Snowmen are born looking old.

Snowmen don't ask where they come from
Snowmen don't ask where they'll go
Snowmen can't be good or evil
Snowmen can only be snow

Why Am I Here?

Why am I here
rather than there
and why am I here at all?
Why am I bones
rather than sticks
and why not a box or a ball?

Why am I Steve
rather than Sam
and why not Jemima or Jim?
Why am I me
rather than you
and why am I not her or him?

Why am I skin
rather than leaf
and why not a rock or a cat?
Why am I he
rather than she
and why not just 'thingy' or
   'that'?

All the Hours God Gives

I work all the hours God gives.
I work. All the hours – God
  gives.
I work all the hours. God gives.

God gives all the hours I work.
God gives. All the hours – I
  work.
God gives all. The hours? I
  work.

The hours God gives, I work.
The hours! God gives, I work.
I give God all the work hours.

The hours I give God all work.

Be Careful with the World

Don't let it get too hot
Or crumble, rot or break
Be careful with the world
Don't scratch it by mistake.

Keep it clean and tidy
Improve its look and smell
Be careful with the world
Make sure it's working well.

Pass it on to others
Who haven't yet been born
Be careful with the world
Don't leave it wrecked and
  worn.

Love it like a best friend
Love it no matter what
Be careful with the world
It's the only world we've got.

Careers Advice

Johnson.
You're good at staring into space.
You can be an astronaut.

Patel.
You're good at copying other
    people's answers,
especially upside down.
You can be a magician.

Chivers.
You're good at making up
    excuses.
You can be a politician.

Diggory.
You're good at shouting.
You can sell fruit and vegetables.

Matthews.
You're good at absenteeism.
You can be the space
into which Johnson stares.

Washing Our Hands

Sometimes we wash our hands
When guilty of a crime
Quick thinking in the bathroom
Can buy us extra time.

Sometimes we wash our hands
To lift a stubborn stain
Clues that might convict us
Go swirling down the drain.

Sometimes we wash our hands
To bring things to a halt
To let the public know
It's really not our fault.

Sometimes we wash our hands
To get a brand new start
Wanting new scrubbed fingers
And not a new scrubbed heart.

What is Truth?

The truth
is
what's what.
A lie
is
what's not.

TODAY AT THE FORUM
THE MOON.
IS IT MADE
OF CHEESE?

The Vanishing Power Of Death

Erwin W. Lutzer

Christians have nothing to fear from death, writes pastor Erwin Lutzer. This book helps believers renew their confidence in that truth and awakens unbelievers to it for the first time.

Moody Publishers
£8.99
HB / 0 8024.0944 X

£2 OFF
£6.99 with voucher

Other titles by the same author

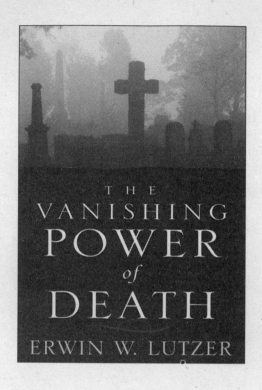

THE
VANISHING
POWER
of
DEATH

ERWIN W. LUTZER

The Friend Who Calls Our Name

Many believers long to visit the Holy Land and "walk where Jesus walked". Those of us who have visited Israel have tried literally to follow in His path; we have made sure that we climbed the steps that Jesus climbed and have prayed in the garden where He prayed. We want the spirit of Jesus to grip us; we want to find Him in a special way right where He lived and taught.

This desire is understandable. Similarly, some who seek Jesus want to find Him in a statue or in the rituals of the church. But when we do this, we're looking in the wrong places. He will not be found in a specific location or among dead things! And sometimes., when we are feeling lost or lonely or grief-stricken, our tears can blind us from seeing Him. In our sorrow, we wonder where He has gone. Just ask Mary Magdalene.

We meet Mary in a text embedded in the book of Luke, a text that reminds us that women always had a prominent role in the ministry of Jesus. "The Twelve were with him, and also some women who had been cured of evil spirits and diseases: Mary (called Magdalene), from whom seven demons had come out" (8:1-2). Other women who supported Jesus out of their own means are also listed.

Mary Magdalene was a victim; she knew the torments of alien spirits in her body. These were not just psychological scars; these were actual, personal beings that harassed her and made her unclean. We don't know how or why she acquired these foul spirits – perhaps through occultism or unrestrained immorality. Or perhaps she was a victim of abuse, and these spirits took advantage of her vulnerability.

Then she met Jesus, who told her, "Your sins are forgiven." For the first time she felt as if her spirit had been washed clean. The torment stopped; the accusing voices ended. Her friends could not account for the difference in her attitude and demeanor. The new Mary was not the woman they knew.

Recently I spoke to a distraught husband who told me that his wife would suddenly "turn into another person," venting anger for no apparent reason. This woman was tormented by some alien spirit who would bring overwhelming guilt and deep feelings of self-hate. She, like Mary, was delivered from these attacks by faith in Christ and the promise that if the Son makes us free, we are "free indeed" (John 8:36).

This was quite possibly the first time Mary met a man who did not misuse her, demean her, or manipulate her. Here was a man with impeccable purity, a man who could be trusted to treat her with love and respect, a man who could forgive and accept her without degrading her with suggestive innuendoes. No wonder she was willing to contribute to His welfare with the little money she had: Those who are forgiven much love much.

Love to the End

This love motivated her to follow Him to His horrific end.

Golgotha was no place for a woman. But Mary wanted to be there, to pray, to meditate, and to grieve. In fact, we are told that she, along with Mary the mother of James and John, stayed until the very end to see where the body of Jesus was laid (Mark. 15:47). The only man who ever loved her was dead. The One who had given her her first taste of dignity, the man who elevated her self-worth by His gracious words, was no more.

We should not be surprised that three days later we see her at the tomb. "Early on the first day of the week, while it was still dark, Mary Magdalene went to the tomb and saw that the stone had been removed from the tomb" (John 20: 1). She ran to find Peter and John and to give them the sad news: "They have taken away the Lord out of the tomb, and we don't know where they have put him!" (v. 2). She cared not to disguise the sobs. With that news, Peter and John raced toward the tomb.

John outran Peter and looked into the tomb first, but did not step in. But Peter, ever brash, actually entered the tomb and saw the strips of linen and the burial cloth; then John followed him into the tomb, and we read, "He saw and believed" (v. 8). But because they still were not clear about the Resurrection, they simply left the area and returned to their homes.

But Mary Magdalene refused to leave.

This woman, bless her, would not be put off; she would try to find the body, or at least find where it was to be found. She loved this man who had set her free; she wanted to honor the memory of a man she could trust. This woman was on a mission to make sure she knew where His body was, and that it had been properly cared for.

She stood beside the tomb, crying. "As she wept, she bent over the tomb and saw two angels in white, seated where Jesus' body had been, one at the head, the other at the foot. They asked her, Woman, why are you crying?"

"'They have taken my Lord away,' she said, 'and I don't know where they have put him'" (John 20:11–13).

We might be surprised at her seemingly calm response to these divine messengers. Keep in mind that in those days people were accustomed to miracles, especially because of the works of Jesus and the prevailing belief that angelic visitors did in fact occasionally bring messages from heaven. Also, Mary was so preoccupied with her grief that she probably did not care about the identity of these messengers. Her loss was too great to be concerned with formal introductions.

Mary did not want angels; she wanted her Lord. In those days, like today, some people believed that angels are more accessible than God; but Mary cared not for their company. She longed only for Jesus, and if she could not have Him alive at least she could honor His decaying body.

Has anyone ever *loved* like this woman?

Has anyone ever *wept* like this woman?

Has anyone ever *cared* like this woman?

She peered into the dark tomb long enough to be satisfied that it was empty. She was contemplating what to do next. Slowly she backed away and straightened herself, her eyes adjusting to the light around her.

The Unexpected Meeting

"At this, she turned around and saw Jesus standing there, but she did not realize that it was Jesus.

"'Woma' he said, 'why are you crying? Who is it you are looking for?' Thinking he was the gardener, she said, 'Sir, if you have carried him away, tell me where you have put him, and I will get him'" (vv. 14–15).

"Tell Me Where You Have Put Him"

She does not know that she is in the presence of the One whom she seeks. Grief-deep griefcan blur reality for us. In our dark moments we cannot see Christ even when He stands beside us.

Why did she not recognize Jesus?

She was looking in *the wrong place*. She was looking for a corpse, not the living Lord. She was "seeking the living among the dead." (see Luke 24:5). She thought that her last act of appreciation would be to care for His dead body. Her hopes rose no higher than to find a corpse.

How sad if Mary had found what she was looking for! What a tragedy if her Master's lifeless body had simply been carried to another tomb! Pity her if she had found a body that needed her care. Thankfully, God sometimes does not let us find what we are looking for.

Mary was also looking in the *wrong direction*. When she was peering into the tomb, she had her back to Him. She must not look *into* the tomb, but *out* of it; she must not look for a dead Christ, but a living one. She was looking for Him in a place where He does not belong.

Bunyan in *The Pilgrim's Progress* tells us about a Christian who would always keep his eyes riveted on the floor and failed to look up. For him, life was but an experience of this world, not the world to come. As long as we are looking down we cannot look up to our Father in heaven. The direction we face determines what we will discover and the destination we shall reach.

The gardener asked her a question, and she turned to reply to this stranger whom she presumed might be able to help her. Think again about her words: "Sir, if you have carried Him away, tell me where you have laid Him and I will take Him away" (v. 15). She did not know that she was speaking to her Lord.

Nor could she have known what she had just said. Even if Jesus had been of slight weight, Mary could hardly have thought that she would be able to carry His body with the heavy ointments wrapped in the linen cloths. But as Donald Grey Barnhouse wrote, "Here is one of the greatest character portrayals of all of literature, human or divine. Here is the heart of a good woman. Here is love, offering to do the impossible as love always does."[1] Jesus no doubt was touched by her devotion.

"Mary."

Now Jesus looks into her eyes and says but one word, *"Mary."*

The voice, the presence ... a second look, and yes, it is Jesus! No one ever said her name just like that!

In a flash she responds, "'Rabboni'" (which means, Teacher)" (v. 16). She falls at His feet, clinging to Him, determined to not let go.

Mary will leave the garden a different woman. Her sorrow has vanished as thoroughly as the darkness in a sun-drenched room. Her grief is a memory a reminder of her failure to recognize her Master standing at her side. Her beloved who was dead is now alive, and knows her by name. Nothing important has changed, yet everything is different.

What a Friend We Have ...

And He called herby name.

"Mary!" He said.

The name *Mary* is a compound of two Hebrew words, which means "exalted by the Lord." The Lord exalted her by giving her the privilege of being the first person to whom He revealed Himself. She sees Jesus before Peter, James, or John does. Imagine the honor of experiencing this first revelation of the living Jesus!

"Your Master Is Here.'

He speaks her name tenderly, for the Lord does not call her "Mary Magdalene, " as a reminder of her past life, but just "Mary," the name of personal identification and compassion. Jesus knows her tears, her sorrows, her hopelessness. "Dry your tears, Mary. Behold, your Master is here and He is calling you."

Earlier in His ministry Jesus said, "My sheep listen to my voice, and I know them, and they follow Me. I give them eternal life, and they shall never perish; no one can snatch them out of My hand" (John 10:27-28). Mary was one of His sheep and He called her by name, and she knew His voice. And she was willing to follow Him to death.

One of the sweetest words we can hear is our own name. That single word Mary changed everything for this grieving woman. This word proved that Jesus was alive for her and for anyone else who desires His companionship. She had hoped for a dead Christ, but now the living Christ was calling her.

Jesus was fulfilling the promise of Isaiah 61:3, providing "beauty instead of ashes and ... gladness instead of mourning." One word, and death, Satan, and hell are conquered. One word and loneliness and fearvanish. One word and Mary knows she will never have to feel hopeless again. The encounter was up close and personal.

A Learning experience

For Mary, this was also a learning experience. When she clasped His feet, Jesus said to her, "Do not hold on to me, for I have not yet returned to the Father. Go instead to my brothers and tell them, 'I am returning to my Father and your Father, to my God and your God'" (20:17). She clung to His feet like a child who fears the departure of a parent. Now that she had found Him, she did not want to lose Him.

There was nothing wrong with Mary clinging to Jesus; most assuredly He could be touched, for later He challenged His disciples, "Touch me and see, for a spirit does not have flesh and bones" (Luke 24:39). Thomas was invited to touch His nail prints.

But for now, Jesus said, "Don't do that."

He was in effect saying, "You will see Me again, for I have not yet ascended to my Father. Don't think you will lose Me, because I will be with you for the next forty days. No need to panic." Yes, it was the same Jesus, but the nature of the relationship would change.

After the Ascension Jesus was taken to heaven

and then returned in the person of the Holy Spirit so that He now indwells all of His people simultaneously. He is as much with us as He was with Mary. We, like her, have to understand that Christ's presence is not dependent on the location of His physical body. She had to be weaned from the notion that physical contact superseded the spiritual connection.

For now, Mary had a job to do; she had to tell the disciples that the Lord was alive. She could not selfishly keep her arms around Jesus, as though He belonged only to her. So she left and found the disciples to tell them that she had seen the Lord. Imagine, a formerly demon-possessed woman the first to tell the good news to others!

An Affirming Experience

Finally, it was an experience of affirmation. Let's revisit the words, "I ascend to My Father and your Father; and My God and your God." What is Jesus saying to this woman whose past was steeped in sin and mental distress?

With this comment, He introduces Mary to the deepest level of acceptance and fellowship! Consider: Early in His ministry, Jesus called the disciples His servants; that surely was an honor of unimaginable significance. But in the Upper Room He became more intimate: "I no longer call you servants, because a servant does not know his master's business. Instead, I have called you friends, for everything that I learned from my father I have made known unto you." John 15:151 From servants to friends, a giant step in closeness and importance.

Now, in the presence of Mary, He reveals an even deeper level of intimacy. In affirming that He and Mary had the same father, He was saying that they were brother and sister! Servants, yes; friends, yes; now brothers and sisters within the same family! What an honor for a woman who had at one time fallen under the spell of evil spirits!

A text that I've had to dare myself to believe is found in Hebrews 2. Please read it as if you have never seen it before.

> *In bringing many sons to glory, it was fitting that God, for whom and through whom everything exists, should make the author of their salvation perfect through suffering. Both the one who makes men holy and those who are made holy are of the same family. So Jesus is not ashamed to call them brothers. He says, "I will declare your name to my brothers; in the presence of the congregation I will sing your praises." (v. 10- 12)*

We are His brothers and He is not ashamed to say so! Mary had to learn that she was not just Jesus' friend–but His sister.

When John was with Jesus at the table, he leaned against His bosom; but years later when he saw the resurrected Christ on the Island of Patmos he wrote, "I fell at his feet as dead." Jesus is at once brother and Lord; companion and judge.

Today Mary lives on the pages of the New Testament to give hope to all who struggle with selfhatred; hope for those who struggle with demons, whether real or imagined. Standing at the empty tomb we, too, can turn from our despair to the One who proved that death does not have the final word.

Not Alone After All

In those moments when we feel betrayed by friends or by life itself, we must remember that Christ's presence is not dependent on our perception of Him. He is among us even when we cannot see Him and when our grief distorts reality. There are many tears in our hearts that never reach our eyes. There are times of darkness and betrayal that make us wonder how we can live another day. As for God, He seems far away, uninterested and absent.

We've all had moments when we were in an emotional free fall, without hope of finding solid ground beneath our feet. News that we have a terminal disease, the death of a marriage partner or the crime of a wayward child can throw us into despair. Trials can undercut what we have always believed about God, prayer and the church.

But these moments, dark as they are, cannot compare to the loss of God in our lives, that feeling that He is not there for us when we need Him the most. Think of what it would be like, not just to lose a friend or a spouse, but to lose fellowship with God. Imagine living with His absence, convinced that His promises had fallen to the ground.

When He Calls Our Name

Then think of how in a moment of time, all is changed when we hear Him call our name. Like Mary, our despair is replaced with the certainty that we have not been forgotten. If we have her heart, we shall hear His voice. Today He calls us, whether our name is Ted, Ruth, or Peter. Jesus calls, if only we were to listen.

And there at the empty tomb, we are reminded that Jesus is beside us, to give us the wisdom and the comfort we seek. We are not alone after all.

In our distress we can look into the tomb and see glory. I remember talking to a man who described how difficult it was for him to choose a cemetery plot. just the knowledge that his relatives would come to that very spot to visit his grave made him dread the assignment. Somehow, standing there amid the tombstones, he was forced to contemplate his own mortality.

The empty tomb of Jesus assures us that we need not fear when our own tomb is finally put to use. Because His tomb is empty, we need not fear when ours is full. With Mary we can say, "I have seen the Lord!" Our Beloved also calls our name and reminds us that we matter.

When my wife and I were newlyweds, we were taken to dinner by an older couple who pointed out their cemetery plots as we drove past the graveyard. "Do you think the Lord will remember our names and where we will be buried?" the wife asked, almost to herself, as if she was not expecting an answer. The story of Mary reminds us that yes, He will remember, and yes, He will call us by name on the final day of resurrection. We do not hear the voice of an earthly gardener, but the Lord, the Keeper of our hearts.

When Knights and Kings Die

In Marburg, Germany, there is a sarcophagus with two layers. On the top, a Teutonic knight is dressed in splendor, a compelling reminder of his power and pomp. Then beneath we see the jarring contrast of a decaying corpse overrun by snakes and toads.

The two representations illustrate the vanity of life. At the present time we may savor wealth, recognition, and the enjoyment of the finer things of life. But if we wait a while, we will pass away and what matters now will not matter then. First the riches, then the rot; first the glory, then the clay.

A priest took a king to a room filled with skeletons and said. "Here, among the corpses of slaves, lies a king." He had made his point: In death a king is indistinguishable from a servant. 'No matter how high the glory, there's always the same end to the story, decay and rot."[2]

Yet, despite the rot on earth, we can contemplate the triumph of heaven. Instead of mud we have marble, and in the place of gloom there is glory. "Jesus lives and so shall I," we sing. His victory in His tomb translates into victory in ours. No place, no disciple, no gardener can substitute for Him. Only when He calls our name are we satisfied.

Back in the late 1800s Jennie Evelyn Hussey spent much of her time taking care of her invalid sister. She never complained but accepted it as 'from the Lord.' Later, when she was almost paralyzed by deformative arthritis, she prayed that she would be able to carry her cross without complaint, just as Jesus had borne his. Her experience became the inspiration for the hymn, "Lead Me To Calvary." The third stanza reads:

> *Let me like Mary, through the gloom*
> *Come with a gift to Thee;*
> *Show to me now the empty tomb,*
> *Lead me to Calvary.*[3]

The Lord who called "Mary!" called Jennie Hussey and all who will put their trust in Him. We, like they, can prove our devotion in the presence of the One who stood with Mary beside His empty tomb. Jesus always stands in the presence of those who believe.

Chapter 2: The Friend Who Calls Our Name

1. As quoted in James Montgomery Boice, *The Christ of The Empty Tomb* (Chicago: Moody, 1985), 60.

2. Quoted in Floyd Thatcher, ed., *The Miracle of Easter,* (Waco Tex.: Word, 1980), 31.

3. Jennie Evelyn Hussey, 'Lead Me to Calvary.' In public domain.

Great Events In The Story Of The Church

Geoffrey Hanks

From the first century to present day, the growth
of the Church is followed through the lives of
men and women who have impacted Church
history.

Christian Focus Publications
£10.99
PB / 1 8579.2383 9

£3 OFF
£7.99 with voucher

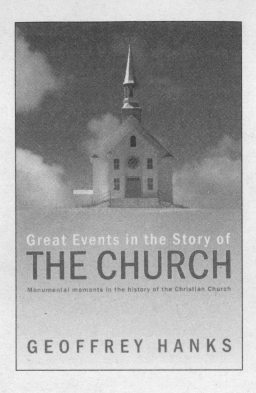

Great Events in the Story of

THE CHURCH

Monumental moments in the history of the Christian Church

GEOFFREY HANKS

Published in 2004 by Christian Focus Publications Ltd
Geanies House, Fear, Tain, Ross-shire IV20 1TW

Preface

This is the third volume written to give an overview of the story of the Church, from the first century down to the present day. Together with its two companion volumes – *70 Great Christians* and *60 Great Christian Founders* – the growth of the Church is followed through the lives of leading men and women who have contributed towards the shaping of Church history, and aims to present in a readable format some account of the events that are recognised as landmarks in the upbuilding of the Christian Church.

It is impossible to fully comprehend where we as Christians stand today unless we have some grasp of the significant events that have determined the course of the history of the Church. To gain an insight into the lives of those who have gone before us and laboured, often at great personal sacrifice, to build the Church of Christ, leaves us with a sense of awe and admiration. Through these real-life dramas we can trace the hand of God in the progress of the Faith and can more easily understand the reasons for what we believe.

Dr Martin Lloyd-Jones, a former minister of Westminster Chapel, London, and probably the most outstanding preacher of the last century, offered further reasons for such studies. He made the following comment about the value of reading about Christian people and past events: 'The real value of looking to the past and to history is that it should help us to face the problems and difficulties of our own age and generation. I am not interested in that which is merely antiquarian and historical; (we) turn to these men (and women) in order that we might learn from them.'[1]

---

1. From the Annual Lecture of the Evangelical Library for 1962, published by the Evangelical Library, London.

AD30: THE CRUCIFIXION OF JESUS

The Advent of the Promised Messiah

In the year AD30, at the Jewish festival of Passover in Jerusalem, three men were led outside the city walls to be executed by the Romans. Two of them were brigands who had taken part in an insurrection. The third man was innocent. Accused by the religious leaders of claiming to be 'the Messiah, the Son of God', he had been condemned to be crucified by the Roman procurator on the grounds of being King of the Jews. The death and subsequent resurrection of Jesus proved to be the most awesome events the world has ever known and form the foundation rock upon which the Christian Church is built.

First century Israel was gripped by a messianic expectation that excited the hopes of the whole nation. Especially since the Roman occupation of the land, the people had been looking for a Deliverer, a prophet whom it was believed God would send to save them from their enemy and set up his kingdom. When Jesus preached the kingdom of God and confirmed his message with miraculous signs, many ordinary people acknowledged him to be 'the one who was to come' – the Messiah. It was mainly the religious leaders who rejected his claim, for he failed to conform to the popular image of a victorious military leader.

The concept of the Messiah has its origins in the Old Testament, where there are numerous passages regarded by the rabbis as prophetic of the special person who would one day be revealed by God.[1]

---

1. Edersheim lists 456 OT passages which ancient rabbis applied to the Messiah or messianic times. See *Life &Times of Jesus the Messiah, Vol 2, p. 710.*

The term 'messiah' (Hebrew, 'anointed') is rendered in Greek as christos, which is used for the New Testament designation of Jesus. It was not until the first century, however, that the term was first applied in a technical sense, when it appeared in Jewish apocryphal works such as the Similtudes of Enoch and the Psalms of Solomon. By the time of the Lord's appearance the term was generally recognised as a reference to a future Redeemer whom God would send to restore the kingdom of Israel.

Further ideas of the Messiah can also be gleaned from a study of the non-canonical literature, rabbinic writings and synagogal prayers of the time of Jesus. In some references the messianic person was spoken of as a priest or a prophet, whereas other sources suggested he would combine the two functions in one role. It was also assumed that he would have supernatural powers, as foretold by the prophet Isaiah (Isa. 35:5ff).

The main idea to emerge, however, was that of a descendant of King David, a warrior-king who would bring victory over the Roman conquerors and usher in an age of peace, righteousness and justice. Anyone speaking of a Messiah during the New Testament period would have had in mind this picture of 'Messiah son of David', a person endowed with military prowess who would establish the messianic kingdom.

There are also references in rabbinic literature to a slain Messiah, designated 'Messiah son of Joseph', one who would be 'pierced for our transgressions' (cf. Isa. 5 3: 5; Zech. 12:10-12). just as the patriarch Joseph had suffered at the hands of his brothers, so would the Messiah also suffer. One consequence of these diverging portraits was the development within Judaism of the notion of two Messiahs, one from the royal line of Judah who would bring peace ('son of David') and the other from the priestly tribe of Levi who would suffer vicariously and die for Israel ('son of Joseph'). This is in contrast to the Gospels which speak of one Messiah coming twice.

Messianic Claim

Although Jesus never openly claimed to be the Messiah, he dearly portrayed himself as the one spoken of by the prophets. Because of his apparent silence on the matter, the idea was put forward, known as the 'messianic secret',[2] which proposed that Jesus deliberately refrained from making such a public declaration. Yet the Gospel accounts clearly portray Jesus' claim to be Israel's Messiah. The earliest indication of the awareness of his vocation was given at his baptism, when he was designated by the heavenly voice as Messiah and Suffering Servant of the Lord (Mark E9ff). While both these concepts were spoken of in the *Tanakh* (Old Testament) by the prophets, the Jewish rabbis had never previously linked them together.

Throughout the Gospel accounts there are allusions by Jesus to his identity as the messianic person, both in his teaching and by his miracles. Many of those who followed him, grounded as they were in the Scriptures and rabbinical teaching, recognised his claims. More than this, however, Jesus also showed himself to be the Divine Messiah which filled the concept of the Messiah with an altogether new content and was in opposition to Jewish expectations.

One of Jesus' most revealing actions was the healing of the demon-possessed man who was blind and dumb (Matt. 12:22ff). Though rabbis were also known to perform healings and cast out demons, by the first century they had listed seven miracles which they judged only the Messiah would be able to perform, one of which was the kind of healing in question. When Jesus healed the man, enabling him to both see and speak, people asked, 'Could this be the Son of David (i.e., the Messiah)?'

As the healing was in public, the Pharisees had either to reject the implication of his action or explain how else Jesus could have performed a messianic miracle. Their answer (v. 24) was that he cast out demons by the prince of demons, an argument Jesus showed them to be absurd. So, on the grounds that he was said to be demon-possessed the Pharisees rejected his messianic claim; as a false

---

2. The term was coined in 1901 by Wilham Wrede, a German scholar who proposed that Jesus deliberately kept secret his claim to be the Messiah (cf. Mk. 8:27fl).

prophet, therefore, he should be put to death (Deut. 13:1-5).

When from time to time Jesus spoke of himself in terms of the Messiah, he did so by his self-designation as 'the Son of man'. The title, derived from Daniel 7:13ff, appears to have been readily understood and accepted by the crowds who followed him. However, this passage has an even wider implication, for it speaks of a heavenly King, one who would 'come with the clouds of heaven' and whose kingdom would be everlasting; in other words, the Messiah would be of divine origin. When, for example, Jesus forgave the paralytic his sins (Mark 2:1-12), the teachers of the law who were present were indignant, declaring that only God had such authority. To wIiich Jesus responded by healing the man and affirming his divine prerogative, that 'the Son of Man had authority on earth to forgive sins...'

SON OF MAN

The title 'Son of man' occurs over sixty times in the Synoptic Gospels where it is used exclusively by Jesus to refer to himself. It is a Greek translation of Semitic phrase meaning 'man' (Hebrew, *ben adam*). Whilst some scholars deny that the title has messianic implications, many suggest otherwise. Brad H. Young (*Jesus the Jewish Theologian*, p.244) discerns three meanings in the use of the term and argues that the context should be allowed to determine the interpretation:

(1) Is some instances Jesus used it as a generic term, to refer to a human being or as a substitute for the personal pronouns 'I' (e.g. Matt. 12:32; 13:37).

(2) On occasions, the Son of man is conceived of as a supernatural being, spoken of in Jewish apocalyptic teachings, and was an elevated way of referring to the messianic task (e.g., when Jesus spoke about the final judgment, Matt. 25:31-36).

(3) Then, a combination of the two previous usages, employed by Jesus when speaking of his Passion and his future return to complete the messianic task during the last judgment (e.g. Mark 8:31; Luke 17:30).

This title of the Messiah is based on Daniel 7:13ff, and more than any other reflects Jesus' claim to be the one of whom the prophets spoke.

Divine Messiah

The pivotal event of the gospel story is the incident at Caesarea Philippi, when Peter declared Jesus to be 'the Messiah of God' (Luke 9:18ff). Straight away Jesus warned his disciples not to tell anyone, possibly from fear of a premature arrest that would have hindered his mission. Having acknowledged his identity, Jesus began to teach the Twelve what kind of Messiah he was to be: he must suffer, be rejected and be killed, but would rise again the third day. This was in complete contrast to the popular expectation of a military leader who would lead the nation to victory.

It is clear the disciples did not fully appreciate Peter's insight. Nor, either, did Peter understand Jesus' prophecy concerning his death and resurrection, for he was offended by the thought of his master's mission ending in apparent failure. Only when the Lord had been raised from the dead did the disciples begin to understand the meaning of this prophecy.

From here Jesus set off for Jerusalem, knowing that the time of his death was approaching (Luke 18:31). If there was any lingering doubt about his Messiahship, then his entry into Jerusalem at Passover, a time when messianic expectations ran high, convinced even his enemies. For here was a clear declaration by Jesus, deliberately fulfilling a messianic prophecy (Zech. 9:9). Pilgrims going up for the festival recognised his action and acclaimed him with shouts of Hosanna to the Son of David!'

The incident in the Temple, when Jesus rebuked those who were using it for purposes of profiteering, was an open challenge to the Temple authorities. The chief priests and elders consequently looked for an opportunity to arrest him, in order to have him killed. The Sanhedrin (Jewish Council) had also become fearful of his popularity and determined to have him silenced. Following the raising of Lazarus, one of them had protested, 'If we let him go on like this, everyone will believe in him, and then the Romans will come and take away both our Temple and our nation' (John 11:48). It was better, the high priest argued, that one man should die rather than the whole nation be put at risk.

Arrest

The opportunity to arrest Jesus came when Judas, one of the twelve disciples, went to the chief priests and discussed how he might hand over his master to them without attracting public attention (Luke 2 2: 1 fl). The following evening, as Jesus shared the Last Supper with his disciples, Judas was able to slip away from the upper room and begin to put the plan into action. From then on, events happened at great speed.[3]

It was late at night, in Gethsemane – a grove of olive trees on the lower slopes of the Mount of Olives – when Jesus was arrested. From here he was taken across the Kidron Valley to the house of the high priest in the upper city, where he was awaited by Caiaphas and certain members of the Sanhedrin. BY now it was nearly midnight. Normally, any trial involving a capital charge could only take place in daylight, but Caiaphas was anxious to have the matter dealt with before news of Jesus' arrest became public. In this and several other matters the trial would appear to have been illegal.

At this preliminary hearing, held to determine the charge, the high priest introduced false witnesses in an attempt to produce a conviction. But despite this ploy he was unable to find any grounds for a case against Jesus. Finally, in exasperation, he applied the most solemn form of oath in Jewish law and asked a direct question: 'Are you the Messiah, the Son of the Blessed One?' As a law-abiding Jew, Jesus was bound to give an answer. 'I am,' he replied. He then went on to speak of himself as the 'Son of Man sitting at the right hand of Power[4] and coming on the clouds of heaven' (Mark 14:6 1 ff; cf. Dan. 7:13ff). In saying 'I am', Jesus used the same expression given by Adonai when he revealed himself to Moses at the burning bush. Thus Jesus put himself on equality with God and identified with the LORD of Exodus 3:14. His answer clearly demonstrated his claim not only to be the Messiah, but also that he shared the nature of God.

Death Sentence

The gathering was in no doubt about the significance of Jesus' answer. Alarmed at his profession, the high priest accused him of

---

3. The following outline of the arrest and trial of Jesus is based on the traditionally accepted chronology.
4. One of a number of terms employed by Jews to avoid using the name God. See also the use of Tower'.

blasphemy and the Council condemned him as deserving death, the penalty for profaning the sacred name. There was no further need for witnesses, they argued, as the prisoner had convicted himself by his own words. At daybreak a further gathering was held in the Council chamber (situated in the Temple Court) to legitimise the decision reached during the night. It only remained to persuade Pontius Pilate, the Roman Procurator of Judea, who alone held such juris-diction, to pass the death sentence.[5]

To successfully carry through this schedule of events must have involved a degree of preparation on the part of Caiaphas. Having judged the right moment for making the arrest, it was then necessary to ensure that an execution order was confirmed and carried out before sundown, the eve of Sabbath. This would have meant consult-ing with various officials, including Pilate, to ensure there were no hitches. To secure a death sentence, however, it was necessary to change the accusation from a religious to a political one, for the Romans were not interested in Jewish religious squabbles. Of the three charges brought by the religious leaders against Jesus (Luke 212), the most serious one was that of treason, that he claimed to be a king.

Pilate did not accept the charges against the prisoner and made several attempts to have him released. But to no avail. Backed by a crowd that had gathered outside the Procurator's residence (formerly the palace of Herod the Great, near the present Jaffa Gate) the religious leaders[6] put pressure on Pilate for a 'guilty' verdict. Normally suspicious of any messianic pretender and faced with con-tinuous disorders throughout the land, Pilate could not afford to ignore any threat to his authority (John 19:6).

Reluctantly, he yielded to the demand. He had Jesus flogged, and on the basis of his admission to being 'king of the Jews' sentenced him to be crucified (Luke 23:24ff).

Crucifixion

It was shortly before nine o'clock in the morning when Jesus was led

5. Authority to execute a death sentence had been withdrawn from the Sanhedrin shortly after Judea, when Judea, became a Roman province.
6. Strangely, the Pharisees – Jesus' most outspoken opponents – are not mentioned as being involved in either the trials or the crucifixion. It could be because they regarded handing over a Jew to a foreign power as a sin that could not be forgiven.

away to his death. Forsaken by his closest friends, with only John and a group of loyal women watching from a distance, he was taken to Golgotha, the 'Place of a Skull',[7] a plot of rising ground outside the city wall. The Gospel writers give no details of the execution; they simply say 'there they crucified him'.

Paradoxically, the crucifixion clearly witnessed to Jesus' twofold claim, that he was the Divine Messiah.[8] On the cross, over the head of the prisoner, the Romans nailed a board on which the charge was written in Hebrew, Latin and Greek: 'Jesus of Nazareth, the king of the Jews' (a messianic title). Then the religious leaders who had engineered his death challenged him to display his divine powers: 'He saved others; let him save himself if he is the Messiah of God,' they jeered (Luke 2 3:35).

Jesus hung on the cross for six hours, during which time he spoke only briefly. At three o'clock in the afternoon he called out with a loud voice, 'Father, into your hands I commit my spirit'. And with these words, he bowed his head and yielded up his life. This prayer is a quote from Psalm 3 1: 5 and is still the prayer of a dying, observant Jew (cf. Acts 7:59).

Burial

Under Jewish law it was forbidden for the bodies of criminals to remain on the cross overnight. As the next day was the Sabbath, it was especially necessary to hasten their deaths so that burial could take place before the day of rest. In which case, the prisoner's legs were broken with a mallet (or similar instrument). No longer able to sustain the weight of their body, the victims soon died of suffocation. Jesus, however, was already dead, but to make sure one of the soldiers plunged a spear into his side, just below the heart.[9]

The burial was a hurried affair, as the Sabbath was only an hour or so away. But Jesus' body was not released until Pilate had checked that

---

7. Alternatively known as Mount Calvary.
8. The Jewish Talmud speaks of Jesus as a 'mesit' (an inciter to idolatry), who was stoned and hung up for practising magic, and not just for claiming to be the God-Messiah.
9. This action resulted in a gush of blood and water from Jesus' body. Medical opinion has it that while suffering on the cross Jesus' heart swelled until it burst, resulting in an effrusion of blood and water serum. This evidence supports the Gospel account that he died from crucifixion and from a ruptured heart. The idea that Jesus only swooned on the cross and was later revived in the tomb simply does not hold.

the prisoner really was dead. Joseph of Arimathea, a secret disciple of Jesus and a member of the Sanhedrin, made his own nearby tomb available and, accompanied by Nicodemus, another secret disciple, carried out the burial according to standard Jewish practice. Two women watched where the body was laid, in order to return after the Sabbath to complete the task of embalming the body.

For the disciples, it seemed an end to their hope that Jesus would redeem Israel. While some of them returned to their homes in the country, others bid behind locked doors in the city. It was not until after the resurrection, when the disciples met with the risen Lord, that they began to understand who he really was. Fifty days later, at the Feast of Pentecost, the disciples were confidently able to declare in public that Jesus was both 'Lord (i.e., God) and Messiah'.

FALSE MESSIAHS

Throughout the history of post-biblical Judaism there have been many petty 'messiah' who have claimed the title, as foretold by Jesus (Matt. 24:5). The earliest messiah of significance was Bar Kokhbar ('son of a star', cf. Num. 24:17). In 132 he gathered an army of about 400,000 men, captured Jerusalem and forced the Romans to evacuate the Holy Land. His Jewish army was eventually overcome, Jerusalem, left in ruins, became a Gentile city, and many Jews fled to Arabia.

The most remarkable and influential of all the claimants was Shabbathai Sebi of Smyrna (western Asia Minor) who lived in the seventeenth century. He believed he had magical powers; he was a member of a mystical sect called Kabbalah, which taught that only a privileged few were able to enjoy direct communication with God. Learning of the belief of some English sects that the year 1666 would be the opening of the millennium, in 1648 he declared himself to be the messiah.

Excommunicated by the rabbinical authorities, he wandered the Middle East until 1665 when he arrive in Jerusalem. He announced himself as messiah and was publically hailed as such in the synagogues. His reputation reached as far as Europe, where some Protestants even began to doubt the claim of Jesus. In 1666 Sebi moved to Constantinople, only to be arrested. To save his life he converted to Islam and died in disgrace ten years later.

1290 the Expulsion of the Jews from England

Anti-Semitism in State and Church

On 18th July 1290, King Edward I ordered all Jews to leave the country by All Saints' Day (1st November), on penalty of death. For over 200 years English kings had overtaxed and exploited the Jews until their money was virtually exhausted. Then because their days of usefulness were over they were summarily expelled from the land. It was nearly 400 years before they were allowed to return.

The first Jews in England were Norman-French and came from Rouen with William the Conqueror in 1066.[1] They settled in London, in the vicinity of what is now Old Jewry. Communities of Jews were later to be found in a number of county towns such as Lincoln, Norwich, York and Oxford. They built houses of stone and founded synagogues, whilst ground was allocated to them for use as cemeteries. And while there were no Jewish ghettoes in medieval towns (for Jews 'lived among the Christians'), their homes were in close proximity to one another.

The Conqueror used the Jews as financial agents in collecting his feudal dues, a work they had undertaken in France. Prevented under the feudal system from holding land and excluded from the medieval trade guilds, which were largely religious associations, many Jews specialised in commerce and trade. Because of a series of discriminatory laws, however, they were forced to employ their capital in the only way available to them, in lending at interest, a talent enhanced by their facility for languages and their international contacts.[2]

---

1. There is some evidence that a few had already found their way to Britain before the Conquest.
2. While the vast majority of Jews were far from rich, a few Jewish money-lenders acquired great wealth. When Aaron of Lincoln died in 118 5 he was probably the wealthiest man in England, and was owed £ 15,000, equal to three-quarters of the annual royal income.

Charter

During the period of the first Norman kings the Jews fared well. As 'servants of the chamber' they belonged to the king and were under the protection of the Crown. Henry I (1100-1135) issued a charter, reissued by succeeding rulers, to confirm their privileged position. By this charter Jews were granted liberty of movement, freedom from ordinary tolls and free access to royal justice, and with provision for fair trials. They became the 'King's men', a position that caused resentment among the nobility.

Monarchs and merchants alike found them useful when in need of finance to maintain armies and to engage in trade. Although Henry II (1154-1189) began his reign by borrowing from them on a modest scale, when he embarked upon the crusades it was from the Jews that he exacted much of the finance needed to fund the expedition. Hence, ironically, the Third Crusade was largely financed by Jews. Known as the Saladin Tithe, they were levied at the rate of one quarter of their property, while the Christians were only taxed at one tenth. Of the £70,000 demanded from the nation, the Jewish contribution was fixed at £60,000.

Because the medieval Church was opposed to usury and decreed it to be contrary to Scripture, Jews were able to secure a monopoly of the moneymarket, for they were not under canon law.[3] Impoverished churchmen, however, overcame their scruples and used Jewish money in order to build monasteries and cathedrals. At least nine Cistercian monasteries, the Abbey of St Albans, and the cathedrals of Lincoln and Peterborough were partly financed by Jewish money. Rates of interest were high, an average of 43 per cent, but the risks were equally great. Some borrowers ran up high debts and resented having to repay the money. False charges were made against Jews and they suffered frequently from mob attacks.

The riots were usually fuelled by rumours such as the one in Norwich in 1144. A twelve-year-old boy, William, went missing just before Easter (and Passover). His body was found in a wood, hanging from a tree, his head shaved and his body covered with stab wounds.

---

3. The Jewish Talmud prohibited charging excessive interest, but not lending at a reasonable rate.

The Jews were accused of ritual murder, and were said to have crucified the boy on Good Friday in a re-enactment of the crucifixion. They were also charged with 'bloodlibel', killing the child in order to use his blood for making matzo for Passover. Afterwards, whenever a child was killed in suspicious circumstances near to a community of Jews, the accusation of ritual murder was levelled at them. 'St William of Norwich' was venerated as medieval Europe's first child martyr.

Exchequer of the Jews

One protective measure taken towards the end of the twelfth century in towns with a Jewish community was the introduction of secure chests *(archae),* with triple locks, which contained records of all Jewish debtbonds and mortgages. All loans had to be made in the presence of both Jewish and Christian officials, and an Exchequer of the Jews (a department of the Treasury) was set up to oversee the transactions. In this way the king took a cut of all Jewish business deals while at the same time it gave him a firmer hold over Jewish finances.

Following the death of Henry II a number of riots broke out against Jews, on the rumour that the new king (Richard I, 1189-1199) had ordered they should be killed. The first riot occurred at Westminster on the occasion of Richard's coronation. A deputation of wealthy Jews attending the ceremony were refused entry. In the ensuing commotion, they were attacked by the crowd and hostilities quickly spread to the whole of London's Jewry. The following spring, trouble broke out at Bury St Edmunds, Thetford, Stainford and Kings Lynn, where houses were pillaged and Jews murdered. At Dunstable, the Jewish population chose baptism rather than face death.

The most tragic event took place at York in March 1190, when a group of barons preparing for the crusade plundered Jewish homes and massacred the residents. A fire broke out, no doubt deliberately started, at the house of Benedict of York.[4] Bands of robbers joined in the attack on other Jewish homes and the victims fled to the royal castle for protection. Rather than surrender to their attackers and

---

4. Benedict had died during the coronation riot, though his family had continued to live in the house.

bring dishonour upon their race, some 150 of the Jews committed suicide in what is today called Clifford's Tower. When the remnant surrendered at daybreak they were seized and cruelly put to death. The barons hastened to the cathedral where they destroyed all Jewish debt records against them. It was obvious that the Jews could no longer rely on royal protection.

Hardships

The onset of the thirteenth century witnessed continuing hardships, persecutions and the revival of restrictive laws combined to bring disaster on the Jewish population. In 12 15, when the barons rebelled against King John (1199-1216), more Jewish homes in London were attacked and demolished. The king was forced to sign the Magna Carta ('Great Charter'), drawn up to secure national liberties; it included a clause limiting the claims of Jewish money-lenders against the estates of landowners who had died in their debt.

A period of respite followed on the accession to the throne of Henry III (1216-1272), who did much to restore Jewish fortunes. The prejudicial clauses of the Magna Carta were dropped, many Jews were released from prison and others had their bonds restored. In this enlightened climate, there was an influx of Jews into England from the Continent, though none were allowed to leave the country without licence.

Unhappily, it was during this more liberal reign that the Church, belatedly, decided to put into effect the discriminatory decrees issued by the Fourth Lateran Council (1215). Of the seventy canons drawn up, four directly concerned the Jews and were inspired by the Church's alarm over the spread of the Cathar heresy,[5] for which it held the Jews responsible. The Council ordered Jews to wear a different dress from Christians, as well as a distinctive badge (or tabula).[6] They were also forbidden to appear out of doors during

---

5. Whilst the Cathars accepted the New Testament and some Christian teachings, their basic heresy was a belief in a good and an evil god, the latter identified with the God of the Old Testament.
6. After the legendary shape of the two tablets of the Ten Commandments. At least forty Councils throughout Europe approved badge resolutions.

THE JEWS AND CHRISTIANITY

The long history of division between Jews and Christians dates back to the early years of the Church. Following the destruction of Jerusalem in AD70 the Church began to reach that God had rejected his ancient people. By the time of Justin Martyr (c. 150) the attitude prevailed that the Church was now the "new Israel' and heir to all the promises of God. Increasingly, Christians began to distance themselves from their Jewish roots, which in turn developed into an attitude of anti-Judaism and ultimately anti-Semitism.

During the fourth century, following the Edict of Milan (313) when Christians were granted religious toleration, anti-Jewish laws were passed which aimed at severing all connection between Jews and Christians. And when Christianity became the official religion of the empire (in 381), synagogues were plundered and Jewish homes destroyed. In later centuries Jews were branded as 'Christ-killers'; they were excluded from normal social intercourse and forced to live in ghettoes.

The eleventh century crusades led to the cruel killing of thousands of Jews both in Europe and the Holy Land. Towards the end of the fifteenth century both Spain and Portugal turned against their Jewish subjects; many were forcibly baptised, while others were expelled or put to death. In Eastern Europe, the nineteenth century Russian pogroms destroyed Jewish villages forcing thousands of Jews to flee the country. More recently, the Holocaust resulted in the deaths of some six million Jews, including over a million children. It is only in recent years that Christians have recognised the great injustice inflicted upon the Jews and attempted to heal the breach.

Passion week. The last canon dealt with Jews converted to Christianity and was intended to ensure that they break completely with the Faith of their Fathers.

Although Henry had hoped to maintain his royal authority over the Jews, he finally complied with the papal decrees. In 1253 he issued an edict, its harsh demands reflected in the opening words: 'No Jew may remain in England unless he do the king's service, and from the hour of his birth, every Jew, whether male or female, shall serve us in some way.'

Tower of London

Hostility towards Jews continued to spread. The charge of ritual murder was raised again in 1255, when the body of a murdered Christian child was found in a cesspool at Lincoln. Ninety Jews were arrested and sent to the Tower of London for trial; eighteen of them were executed. By this time the ritual murder myth was rife across Europe. A rebellion of barons against the king in 1263 led to a further wave of violence against Jews in London, Canterbury and other cities, and attempts were made to destroy the archae. Then, pandering

---

DOMUS CONVERSORUM

Early in Anglo-Jewish history efforts were begun to convert Jews to Christianity by disputations, treatises and by preaching. Any who converted were given Christian names and received into a converts' home (*domus conversorum*) on the grounds that they had left the Jewish fold. Converts could expect to forfeit their property because it had been obtained by the 'sin of usury', but they were granted a pension for daily expenses.

Among the earliest such homes was the one to be found in Bristol (opened in 1154), and another opened in 1213 by Richard of Bermondsey (now a suburb of London) in the neighbourhood of his monastery. In 1221 a group of Dominican friars settled in Oxford and established themselves in the heart of the Jewish quarter. They immediately made efforts to convert their Jewish neighbours and were so successful that a home for converts was opened in Fish Street.

The foremost converts' home was established in 1232 by Henry III, in New Street (now Chancery Lane), London. The king assigned 700 marks annually for the upkeep of the home and its residents. Their pension, in 1290, amounted to $1\frac{1}{2}$d a day for a man and 1d for a woman. In that year there were ninety-seven men and women in the home. Later, a warden and a chaplain were appointed, and houses and a chapel were added. The building continued as a converts' home after the expulsion in 1290 and only closed down in the mid-nineteenth century. From time to time newly converted Jews were admitted into the home, though for a few periods there was no one in residence. There is an abundance of detail about the home in the Close and Patent Rolls, as well as in other records from 1331.

to popular demand, the king closed down synagogues in London and had them converted into chapels. Meanwhile the oppressive taxes regularly levied upon Jews meant that the king was gradually destroying his greatest source of income. Many Jews applied to leave the country, but their requests were turned down.

The accession of Edward I (1272–1309) marked the final decline of the Jews in England, for there came to the throne a king who was anti-Jewish and who was set on stripping them of their assets. It was already clear that Jewish lending power was exhausted when, in 1275, Edward passed the Statute of Jewry, forbidding Jews to lend money on interest and encouraging them to become merchants and artisans. Other provisions decreed that Jews could only live in certain appointed towns: that all Jews over the age of twelve years old had to pay an annual poll tax at Easter; and that the distinctive badge for Jews had to be worn from the earlier age of seven (originally white, but now of yellow).

The king's repressive actions continued when next he accused Jews of debasing the coinage by coin-clipping. (That is, filing the edges of coins and melting the clippings into bullion.) Over 600 Jews were imprisoned in the Tower, of whom 293 were executed, whereas only three Christians were hanged for the offence. When in 1289 Edward needed money to ransom his cousin, Charles of Salerno, he met the demand by confiscating the property of his Gascony Jews[7] and then expelling them.

Expulsion

With no further use for the Jewish community, in the summer of 1290 Edward issued an edict expelling all Jews,[8] on the grounds that they had disregarded the Statute of Jewry and had secretly reverted to money-lending. The date was 18 July, which corresponded with the 9th of Av, the fast commemorating the destruction of the first and

---

7. Edward was Lord of Gascony as well as King of England.
8. An alternative reason for the expulsion is that it was the price demanded by parliament in return for granting the king permission to levy a tax which he badly needed to pay off his debts.

second Temples in Jerusalem. Writs were sent to the sherriffs of various counties with instructions that no one should 'injure, harm, damage or grieve' the Jews in their departure. The Marden of the Cinque Ports was ordered to see that the refugees were given a safe and speedy passage across the channel on their way to Europe.

The expulsion provided the Crown with one final benefit, in that Jewish houses, synagogues and cemetries fell to the king, as well as the considerable value of their debts. How many Jews left the country is a matter of dispute, and numbers vary widely between 2, 500 and 16,000. The majority of them settled in France, though the following year the French king moved them on to other parts of Europe.

Sadly, England was not alone in its antipathy to Jews, and medieval Christian governments throughout Europe were often faced with 'the Jewish problem' and felt it necessary to take anti-Jewish measures. Although several countries attempted to expel Jews, in England's case it succeeded because of the barrier of the Channel. Pressure was also on Jews to convert to Christianity, sometimes under threat of death or by bribery or a desire to become accepted in society. There were, of course, some genuine conversions, a step which severely tested their faith as it left them in direst poverty.

This period is one of the most shameful in the history of England and the Church, for it further inflamed anti-Semitic attitudes that had existed in Christendom from the second century. Though Jewish people are now fully integrated into British society, anti-Semitism has continued down the centuries, even in the Church. Happily, in recent years an increasing number of Christians have begun to recognise the need to seek reconciliation and ask forgiveness. Both the Roman Catholic Church and the World Council of Churches have repudiated anti-Semitism, whilst the Lutheran Church has acknowledged Germany's guilt in its treatment of Jews during the 1930s and 40s.

One beneficial legacy of the Jewish presence in England was a renewed interest in Hebrew studies. Though there was a barrier between church and synagogue, contact with Jewish people enabled the more learned Christian clergy to benefit from the expertise of Jewish scholars.

After 1290, apart from a few travellers and Jewish Christians there were no Jews in England for nearly 4-00 years. That they were re-admitted in 1656 during the rule of Oliver Cromwell, Lord Protector of England, was partly because of the economic benefits their presence could bring. Jews were allowed to become full citizens, though with the same limitations as those placed upon Catholics and Nonconformists. Although England was the first nation to expel Jews, it was also the first nation where it became possible for a Jewish community to be established, though it was to be a further 200 years before they finally gained complete empancipation. In 1846 the thirteenth century anti-Jewish statutes were formally repealed.

1534 Act of Supremacy Passed

The Church of England Established

The Reformation was slow in gaining a foothold in England. Initially, the impetus for reform had more to do with the political manoeuvrings of Henry VIII (1509–1547) than with any desire for the new teaching. In his quarrel with the papacy concerning a divorce from Queen Catherine, Henry made himself head of the Church in England. By the Act of Supremacy, the powers of the papacy were transferred to the king and the Archbishop of Canterbury, and Henry's marriage to Catherine was annulled. With the bonds between Rome and England severed, the way was open for the introduction of Reformation ideas and the advance of Protestantism.

When the seventeen year old Prince Henry succeeded to the throne of England in 1509, it seemed as if he were just the monarch to support the new learning that was filtering through from the Continent. The young and handsome ruler was a gifted scholar, an accomplished musician and poet, skilled at sport, and a devout churchman. But he was already a headstrong and impatient young man, determined to have his own way; throughout his reign he ruthlessly crushed anyone who crossed him.

Shortly after his accession Henry married Catherine of Aragon, the daughter of Ferdinand and Isabella of Spain, a union made possible only after the pope had granted a special dispensation. This was necessary because Catherine had formerly been married to Henry's older brother, Prince Arthur, who had died seven years previously. Of the five children born to Henry and Catherine, only Mary (born 15 16) survived, hence the king's concern for a male heir to succeed to the throne. But Catherine's failure to give him a son seemed to him as God's judgment for having contracted an unlawful marriage. Even though Catherine was a popular and respected queen, it did not deter Henry from seeking a divorce.

Difficulty

In 1527 finally Henry determined to be rid of the queen in order to marry Anne Boleyn, a young lady-in-waiting. All that was needed was for the pope to declare his marriage to Catherine null and void, on the ground that the papal dispensation had been ultra vires (i.e., beyond the pope's authority), as it was contrary to the law of God.[1] Normally, for someone in Henry's position this would not have been an impossible task, but there was a major difficulty in the way, for Catherine's nephew was the emperor Charles V who at that time imprisoned the pope. To further his cause in what he began to call his 'Great Matter', he placed his divorce proceedings in the hands of Cardinal Wolsey, who had been appointed a papal legate (a personal representative of the Holy See).

By 1529 no decision had been taken and Henry's patience had become exhausted. Wolsey was dismissed for failing to make progress in the matter and the king took affairs into his own hands. If the pope would not agree to the divorce, then he would defy him and the clergy as well. To make the matter legal, he needed to persuade parliament to back him against the pope and throw off papal jurisdiction over the English Church. What became known as the Reformation Parliament sat over a period of seven years, from 1529 to 1536 (meeting for only a few weeks each winter), passing a series of laws by which Henry secured the obedience of the clergy, made himself head of the Church in England and achieved his divorce.

With Wolsey out of the way, Henry was able to work through parliament rather than through Convocation, the Church's assembly, so that questions of church discipline and order were discussed by the secular government. The king's first step was to secure the obedience of the clergy to himself, for he recognised that the most powerful man in the land was not himself but the archbishop. He made two moves which went a considerable way towards achieving this objective.

---

1. Leviticus 20:2 1, which actually refers to childlessness.

Threatened

Under the Act of Praemunire,[2] the clergy were accused of having accepted Cardinal Wolsey as a papal legate (even though the king had asked for the appointment), and were threatened with punishment. After discussion, Convocation agreed to buy its immunity from under the act; Canterbury paid Henry the sum of £100,000, and York contributed £19,000.

Convocation also recognised the king as 'Protector and Supreme Head of the English Church and Clergy', though adding the clause, 'as far as the law of Christ allows'.

The outcome was that the clergy accepted the Crown as an

CRANMER AND THE REFORMATION

One of Cranmer's most important contributions to the Reformation was the introduction of English into church services. The Great Bible was already available in every church, and in 1542 Convocation ordered that in all services a chapter of the New testament should be read in English, but without exposition; two years later prayers in English were introduced. The use of English, and not Latin, was a revolutionary move.

On the accession of Edward VI (1547), the pace of reform increased. In that year, Cranmer and Bishop Ridly produced a Book of Homilies – evangelical sermons to be read in parish churches. In 1549 Cranmer replaced the Roman Catholic Missal (service book) with the Book of Common PRayer; the aim was to simplify and condense the Latin missal, and to produce a service book in English for priest and people. It was a compromise between Catholic and Reform, so phrased that it would not unnecessarily offend Catholics. A music edition was issued, which was an adaption of plain chant to the new liturgy. A government proclamation ordered all pictures and images in churches to be destroyed, especially those of the Virgin Mary.

The BCP was revised in 1552, when a truly Protestant version was produced, amended under Elizabeth in 1559 and was again revised in 1662, remaining almost unchanged until recent times.

Cranmer was arrested when the Catholic Queen Mary came to the throne in 1553. Two years later he was burned at the stake.

---

2. Statutes passed in 1353, 1365 and 1393 to protect the rights of the English Crown against papal claims.

essential part of the constitution of the English Church and they were not allowed to take any action not approved by the king or the king in parliament. Though there was no reference to a repudiation of papal jurisdiction nor any suggestion of a separate Church, Henry had prepared the way for assuming leadership of the Church in England.

Aware that his worst enemies were among the Protestants, the king determined to defuse the opposition while at the same time winning over the disgruntled clergy. In 1531 he gave the clergy permission to hunt down, imprison and burn any who were disciples of Luther. The first to receive the martyr's crown was the godly Thomas Bilney of Norwich, one of a number of Cambridge reformers; others burnt at the stake included Richard Bayfield, an evangelist, John Tewkesbury, a respected merchant, and James Bainham, a distinguished lawyer. Catholics who opposed the king's plans also met with the same fate.

Reformation Hope

A development took place around this time that marked the beginning of a reformation hope, for in 1533 Henry appointed Thomas Cranmer to be Archbishop of Canterbury. When Henry first met Cranmer, in 1529, the Cambridge don had suggested the king might consult the universities of Europe on the legality of the divorce. Cranmer was despatched on a tour of European universities to sound them out; he succeeded in gaining their support. When the need arose for a new archbishop Henry turned to the one who had furthered his cause. Cranmer was reluctant to accept the offer and would have preferred a more peaceful life, but the king insisted on having his way. Once he accepted, Cranmer remained a faithful servant of the king; though often given to compromise in matters of religion, he was the one who gently opened the door to the new teachings.

Time, however, was pressing. Henry had secretly married Anne Boleyn in January 1533, and they were living together at Greenwich. As she was already with child, then his marital affairs needed to be

straightened out quickly if the child was to be recognised as legitimate. It was to his new archbishop that Henry looked to bring the
affair to a satisfactory conclusion. Both parliament and Convocation
accepted that the pope had exceeded his authority in giving Henry
a dispensation, and that the marriage to Catherine was null from the
first. Cranmer agreed and pronounced the king's marriage to Anne
valid; she was crowned queen on Whit-Sunday at Westminster Abbey
and the young Princess Elizabeth was born in the September. The
pope attempted to annul the marriage and threatened to excommu-
nicate the couple if they did not separate, but to no avail.

Henry's next task was to remove the pope's prerogatives and
powers over the English Church, and further acts were passed to
secure his ambition of becoming Supreme Head. Parliament passed
the Act for the Restraint of Annates, forbidding the payment of the
first year's income of a bishop, abbot or parish priest to the papacy; it
was, instead, to be paid to the Crown. (It was calculated that since the
accession of Henry VII, in 1485, the sum had amounted to
£160,000.) The act also stated that in future all bishops should be
consecrated in England by the archbishop.

Of greater importance, however, was the Act for the Restraint of
Appeals, passed in February 1533, which forbade English law cases
being taken to Rome. This frustrated Catherine's attempt to submit her
case to the pope. The law went on to declare that the realm of England
was an 'empire' (i.e., an independent, sovereign state), and that the king
was Supreme Head of both Church and State. Further, it laid down
that ecclesiastical matters were to be dealt with by Church courts.

Other acts completed the work of separation from the papacy:
bishops were to be elected by the king, acting through the cathedral
chapters; Peter's Pence (an ecclesiastical tax paid to the pope) was
abolished; and the archbishop was authorised to grant dispensations
and licences instead of appealing to the pope. Meanwhile,
Convocation finally agreed to make no new ecclesiastical laws
without the king's permission, and accepted that all existing canons
should receive his approval.

Supreme Head

Henry's efforts were crowned with success when, in November 1534, the Act of Supremacy declared that the king and his successors should be 'accepted and reputed the only Supreme Head on earth of the Church of England', without any saving clause about 'the law of Christ'. In addition, the act gave him power to define the Church's doctrine and to punish heresy. This was followed by an Act of Succession, under which the marriage to the Lady Catherine was declared null and the marriage to Anne was decreed legitimate. In this way, Henry and Anne's children were to succeed to the throne. What is more, it required all nobles, both spiritual and temporal, to take an oath acknowledging the king's new position. Both Sir Thomas More and Bishop Fisher of Rochester refused the oath and were executed in 1535. Then under an Act of Treason, anyone plotting against the king, calling him a tyrant or a heretic, was liable for the death penalty.

Within the space of three years, Henry had carried through a major revolution; all allegiance to Rome had been severed and the powers transferred to the king or the archbishop. This was not brought about by the Church, but was rather a constitutional change, legally effected by the king through parliament. As yet the Reformation had not begun, though there was an increasing desire for reform within the hearts of many English people. What is more, there was a strong feeling among the laity against papal abuses and a rising tide of nationalism that resented interference of Rome.

Monasteries

By this time Henry's extravagances had left him short of money and he needed to replenish the dwindling royal coffers. His eyes lighted on the country's 800 religious houses, which he realised could provide him with a source of income. It was widely recognised that many of the monasteries were sadly in need of reform, an excuse used by the king to appropriate their estates and incomes. His Vicar-General, Thomas Cromwell, Earl of Essex, carried out a survey of all monastic properties, returning with a damning report for parliament which paved the way for the Dissolution.

Under the 1536 Act for the Supression of the Lesser Monasteries, the last act of the Reformation Parliament, the process began of closing down all religious houses, with the seizure of their estates and incomes for the Crown – all carried out under the guise of reform. Some of the properties were sold or leased, others were given to the king's supporters as political rewards. All monastic treasures were sent to the king's jewel house, while buildings were partly dismantled and the materials used for other purposes. In the space of four years one of England's most ancient institutions was virtually wiped out and many of its notable buildings thrown into disrepair.

DISSOLUTION OF THE MONASTERIES

In April 1536 there were some 800 religious houses scattered throughout England and Wales; four years later there were none. The first wave of suppression of the monasteries centred on those houses with a net income of less than £200 a year. Of the 600 smaller abbeys and priories, only 243 were affected; others escaped under various discretionary clauses in the Act.

Protests were raised in Lincolnshire and Yorkshire, and Heads of the larger abbeys who aided the rebels were tried for treason and condemned. As a result, some who had expressed sympathy for the revolt decided it more prudent to yield their properties to the Crown. All the remaining monastic houses surrendered voluntarily, until there were none left in England or Wales.

The 10,000 inhabitants of the religious houses were given the choice of either taking a life pension or receiving a dispensation from their vows. All monastic treasures were seized. The bells were taken to be recast as canon, lead stripped from the roofs was used for shot and the timbers taken for the furnaces. With no roof, buildings started to deteriorate, a process considerably hastened by the removal of large quantities of stones for other building purposes.

Throughout his reign Henry remained a staunch Catholic and was hostile towards Lutheran doctrines. Incensed by the reformer's attack on the sacraments, in 1520 he wrote a treatise, *Assertion of the Seven Sacraments,* defending the Catholic position. A copy of the book was presented to Pope Leo X, who rewarded him with the title of Fidei Defensor – 'Defender of the Faith'. In 1554 Parliament acknowledged this title as officially belonging to the English monarch, and has since continued to be used by all British sovereigns.

Articles of Faith

Despite the king's opposition to Protestantism, Reformation ideas were gaining ground in England. There were now two rival movements within the land, creating a constant tension between the opposing parties. Lutheran doctrines, which were being discussed in the English universities in the 1520s, had many adherents, some of whom were to suffer martyrdom for their cause. In an attempt to bring stability into a confused situation, in 1536 Convocation under Archbishop Cramner adopted the Ten Articles of Faith. With a preface by the king, the articles represented a compromise between the old and the new teachings; whilst reflecting the Lutheran Confession of Augsburg (1530) they also retained elements of Roman doctrine and practices, such as purgatory and the veneration of the saints. Perhaps more important, the king permitted the publication of the Great Bible[3] (so named because of its size), a copy of which was ordered to be placed in every church that it might be read by the laity.

Despite these hopeful signs, Henry continued to be something of an enigma. In 1539 the reformers received a setback when an act, introduced into the House of Lords by the Duke of Norfolk and backed by the king, approved a new statement of doctrine. The Six Articles laid down what doctrines were to be believed: transubstantiation, communion in one kind only (bread), clerical celibacy, vows of chastity for the laity (i.e., ex-nuns and lay-brothers), private masses and compulsory auricular confessions. Denial of transubstantiation was heresy and was punishable by death.

Whilst Cranmer showed signs of leaning more and more towards

3. The first recognition of the Bible in English.

Reformation views, he continued to lend support to the king, who protected his archbishop from calls to have him sent to the Tower. Overtures from German theologians towards England, to embrace Lutheran doctrines, were firmly rejected by Henry. And though Cranmer was sympathetic, his belief in a 'godly prince' remained firm and his uneasy relationship with the king held throughout the remaining years of the reign.

When Henry died in 1547 he was succeeded by his nine-year-old son, Edward VI (1547-1553), who had been tutored by an avowed reformer. The young king's uncle, the Duke of Somerset, also anxious to further the Protestant cause, became Protector. Thus the way was open for the introduction of the changes many longed for. Under Cranmer a foundation was laid down whereby the Church of England underwent a reformation which, despite having to endure the fiery ordeal of Catholic Queen Mary's reign (1553-1558), emerged a reformed church which was finally secured under the rule of Elizabeth I.

Luther's Rose

Ursula Koch

This engaging book blends biography with dramatic historical fiction to tell the story of Martin Luther and the Reformation though the eyes of Katharina von Bora, Luther's wife.

Highland Books
£6.99
PB / 1 8979.1353 2

£2 OFF
£4.99 with voucher

Luther's Rose

A dramatized biography of Katharina von Bora and the love affair that both shocked and inspired the 16th Century

URSULA KOCH

German original © 1995 Brunnen-Verlag Giessen
First published in German by Brunnen-Verlag Gissen under the title
Rosen im Schnee, Katharina Luther, geborene von Bora

English translation © 2003 Highland Books Ltd
2 High Pines, Knoll Road, Godalming, Surrey GU7 2EP

Wittenberg, February 20, 1546

First the cock — and then me! That's the way it always was. As he crowed outside, I groped my way through the dark hall to the kitchen beneath.[1] *The others were still asleep, all of them: the children, the maids, the students, the hired man — and he, my husband who had been lying beside me. I heard him snoring. It was not loud. It was almost a purring, like the cat by the stove. He didn't hear the cock. Nor did he hear the door as it creaked softly. Most of the time he slept until the dawn cast beams of light through the windows and the noise of the children penetrated his dreams.*

True, he often dreamt, tossed about, bellowed like an ox. His dreams wrenched me out of deep sleep. When I slept, I was as one who was dead but when I awoke, I was instantly alive. I quieted him down and spoke softly as I stroked his chest with my hand. His chest rose and fell under the weight. Toward the morning, he slept.

I ran cold water over my arms and washed my face. Then I lit the fire in the hearth and awakened the maids. Sometimes someone was already standing at the door as I heated the milk on the fire — a beggar in rags, his face full of scars. We brought him in, gave him soup and a piece of bread. My husband in the bedroom continued to sleep. While the children got up and stormed out into the yard, he continued his restless sleep.

The cock crowed. Today as always, but he did not rouse me from sleep. I felt physically battered as if I had a fever. Long before the cock crowed, I got up, lit the lamp and sat on my bed in the flickering light. When I stretched out my hand, it touched only a cold, clean sheet. No one groaned in his sleep. There was no sound. No warmth. Thus began my new day. What should I do with this day?

*The cold, winter wind whistles through the cracks. Nothing moves in the monastery.*² *Everything appears to be dead. The monastery. The city. Only the wind races through the streets. Just like yesterday, when the messenger arrived.*

He came early. Almost no one would have seen him. He came through the gate, down the street in the wind and pounded on the neighbour's door. Then they came to me — three men, their heads bowed.

Why was I so startled when they knocked on the door? Did we not often receive guests, early or late, friends or strangers, nobles or beggars. Why then was I seized with such foreboding?

"I fear that if you do not cease your anxieties, the earth will finally swallow us up … , " he had written from Eisleben. How he had reviled me for my anxiety! As though I lacked trust in God. Fortunate is he who trusts in God at a time when weapons are being sharpened and pyres are burning everywhere. It may well be that God intended it for good for him, for me — as He did with our Magdalena, our child whom He took from us. But I am only a poor woman who has great difficulty understanding the councils of the Lord. I am anxious. 'What does it change?" he had said. Nothing. Nothing.

*I know. Yet I would dearly have liked to wring another precious year from our heavenly Father with my anxiety and my prayer. Must it then be now? Already? Herr Doktor*³ *still had so much to do. The whole world cried out for him. He had to travel here and there, to settle disputes and to proclaim the Word. In the middle of winter — with no concession to his advancing years. It is still too soon for him to go. For me, it is too soon. The wind whistles around the house, whistles through all the cracks.*

*Our friends came and knocked at the door. The house echoed under the blows. Wolf*⁴ *hobbled to the door. When I saw them and Philip put down his black collar, I did not even have to ask. I stared into his darting eyes, at his twitching mouth, at his hands which tugged uneasily at his coat.*

None of my sons were with me. I drew Margaret to myself, the only one still with me in the dark house. I acted as if I wanted to protect her, while I myself needed protection. I dared not open my mouth.

Finally Wolf asked, "Do you have a report from Eisleben?"

"Yes."

"From Doktor Martinus?" No answer. Then I said it. Again, I had to be the one. No one had the strength to say it. "Has something happened to our master?" Philip nodded. "Is he not well?" Again, no answer. "Is he dead?"

His arms fell. His lower jaw dropped. I no longer saw him. I only heard the screams of the maids. Wolf tried to support me. Margaret threw her arms around me. Only the walls stood firm as always. He is dead. Doktor Martin Luther is dead.

The friends remained with me, sitting silently around the table. It was quiet in the house. At noon, I asked them to leave. I wanted to be alone and tried to pray. But I only sat at the window and waited for it to nightfall. Nor did I find rest during the night. I was with the messenger as he travelled, bringing the report to villages and cities, carrying it from hearth to hearth, in cottages and castles. He is dead. Foes rejoice; friends wail. And what about me — his wife? What should I do now? Who am I? What remains for me now?

"Get up, Katie, — he would have said. "Get up and thank God that He has redeemed me. Go to your work, Katie! God is with you in all that you will do. Stir yourself, Frau Doktor! Jump to it, Madam Merchant! There are still people to whom you can give orders, Sir Katie!"

His voice — never again? The bed beside me — cold, empty? I am so afraid, so ... It seems as if I should return ... Go back into the convent.

Nimbschen. 1509–1523[5]

The large, dark gate, covered with black iron, slowly opened, but only a crack. A little girl, dressed in a bright dress and wrapped in a long cape, stood there and did not move. Her father shoved and pushed her forward with his hand until she almost fell as she finally took a step through the narrow opening. Her father following had to squeeze through with greater difficulty. Out of the grey mist of the yard in front of them, a white figure came towards them.

The little girl turned and stumbled against her father. She felt the coarse fabric and the cold metal of his belt. "Herr von Bora?" With a sound of reluctance, the man pushed the child away from him. He took her small hands into his own. Then he pulled his daughter behind him over the pavement which was wet from the rain. The nun who had let them in disappeared into the house on the left beside a long building near the entrance. Herr von Bora shifted impatiently from one foot to the other. The clammy air felt heavy on his head, which buzzed from a night of drinking. He remained near the gate which would lead him back outside. Only him. But, almost imperceptibly, the little girl strained in the same direction.

In the light spring rain, a few days after Easter, the outer yard of the Throne of Mary convent seemed to be washed clean for the visitors. From the stables came the sound of restless horses. The colts strained to get outside. But their attendants kept the animals locked up. Even the cattle remained in the shed awaiting the last blast of winter. In the Mother Superior's once-elegant living quarters which had deteriorated somewhat over the centuries the doors were firmly locked. From the choir loft of the church on the other side of the yard one could hear the sound of the nuns chanting.

"Go on in." The nun who answered the gate pointed to the door of the house. "Our Reverend Mother will receive you after she has finished praying Vespers." Darkness again. The little girl was pushed up some stairs. Her father groaned behind her. A new door opened. The child felt the dampness of her clothes and sat down by a hearth where the coals still glowed from a fire which had just gone out. The nun left the visitors alone. The father paced to and fro with heavy steps. Floor boards creaked. His lips quivered. The little girl noticed it but waited in vain for him to say something. She drew her thin cape even tighter around her upper body and listened anxiously. Finally they heard voices. A hushed murmuring came closer and then became more and more faint. Footsteps. Doors closing. The creaking of stairs.

"Get up!" The child stood up slowly. Her father remained standing. The door opened, letting a blast of cold air into the room. As she came in, the Reverend Mother pushed aside her veil and turned to Herr von Bora with furrowed brow: "We expected you earlier, Cousin Hans. Is this your daughter Katharina?"[6] She apparently did not expect an answer but spoke to the nun accompanying her. "Bring the little girl into the dormitory, Sister Barbara! Where are her things?"

Katharina pulled a tightly bound bundle from under her arm. The abbess nodded. She stretched out her right hand and grasped the little girl's jaw. Katharina looked through a veil of tears into the cold blue eyes above her. Her small mouth did not move. With a soft sigh, the woman released the child's head and stretched out her ring finger. "Kneel down," whispered her father. Katharina bent down obediently over the ring and kissed it. "Say goodbye to your father," ordered the abbess. Herr von Bora screwed up his face. He gave the little girl his hand and turned away. Katharina stared at her father's back.

"Come in, Cousin Hans. We still have a few things to arrange. I have heard that your second wife has provided you another little girl. So, your sons have another sister..." Following the abbess, Hans von Bora left the room through a small door. Katharina followed the nun. At the stairs, she turned around once more. But Sister Barbara had the ring of keys in her hand already and rattled them impatiently. Katharina stumbled down the stairs. Outside, the overcast day had become dusk. She clutched her bundle to herself and tried to keep up with the hurried steps of the white figure ahead of her.

"What is your name?" "Katharina. And you?" "Elsa." "Be quiet. You should be asleep," the occupant in the next bed hissed. In the dark dormitory, the students of the convent lay tightly side by side. Outside the rain fell noisily.

After a while the quiet breathing seemed to signal that their comrades on the right and left were sleeping. Another whisper: "How long have you been here already?" "At Easter it was two years." Katharina sighed. "It is only difficult at the beginning," whispered Elsa. "I cried a lot, too. But you must not show it. You must be proud. After all, you will be allowed to learn something. Are your parents rich?" Katharina hesitated. She had heard her father cursing as he opened his wallet in which he kept his gulden.[7] "I don't think so." "Then be content. If you're not rich, you wouldn't get a man anyway." "Oh, be quiet. Why do you say such dumb things?" "Sleep well," murmured Elsa and turned over on the other side.

Katharina pulled the thin blanket over her shoulders. She was cold. In Brehna, it had been warmer and there had also been a fire in the hearth in the dormitory. But her father had come right after Christmas and taken her out, complaining that the happy sisters were greedy.[8] Then, in the manor, a new wife. Katie's brothers called her "mother" and mocked her when she tried to discipline them. But Margaret, the old maid, had wrapped a fleece around Katharina's cold feet. Katharina did not want to cry, absolutely not. But no one could see her. And starting tomorrow she would be brave like Elsa and all the others. Starting tomorrow ...

"*Pastor, pastoris.*" – the pen flowed across the paper with a light squeak. "The shepherd!" A fly buzzed around over the bowed heads of the girls. It was still cool in the high vaulted room where the students in the convent were being taught. But outside between the walls, one could feel the warmth of summer. The farm animals were in the pasture. As Katharina looked up, she could see out into the open air through a crack. Clover blossomed under the sun and, as if in a dream, a sheep stood motionless with its lamb in the middle of the meadow. The shepherd!

In summer, great herds of sheep used to graze in the pastures surrounding the old farm of the von Bora family and the children loved to go out into the middle of the herds. The boisterous boys had fun with the timid animals. But Katharina, the youngest von Bora, who should not even have gone out with her high-spirited brothers, loved to hold the small lambs in her arms. And the good-hearted shepherd showed her the very young lambs which were still so soft.

"Katharina. You are dreaming!" Sister Gertrud raised her rod threateningly. Startled, Katharina pulled herself together. Ashamed, she put her head down over the Latin words. Sister Gertrud never actually used her rod; she just swung it through the air. One could see in her face that she and the rod did not belong together; that she only had it there because she thought she should. In spite of this, Katharina listened to what she said. Otherwise the eyes of the sister showed a hurt which the girls could not bear. They loved Gertrud even though they had difficulty putting the Latin words on paper or pronouncing them. "*Agnus*" – "the Lamb." Katharina forced herself to sacrifice the image of the soft skin of the young lambs and their tender moist lips for Sister Gertrud.

"*Agnus Dei*" – But if Jesus was Himself a lamb, is a person then not permitted to love the lambs in the pasture. Like the old shepherd. Will he come again this year? His beard would certainly have grown still longer. And his hat had large holes which must really be unpleasant when it rains. "Katharina, where are your thoughts today?" Sister Gertrud looked with concern at the paper full of ink-spots. "Can't you write just a bit more carefully? You have blotted a whole herd of sheep." Katharina did not have to answer. The bell called them to prayer.

Between the columns of the high nave of the church, the little girls in their grey aprons stood close together while the clear voices of the nuns praised God from the choir loft. Katharina waited impatiently for the ringing of the Angelus bell. For the songs were in Latin and she understood only the odd word. *Lauda, anima mea, dominum: laudebo dominum in vita mea* ... Finally, the bell rang which proclaimed the approach of the angel to Mary.

"*Ave Maria, gratia plena* ... " Her lips moved, "Hail, Mary ... " This she could already pray, along with the pious women who sat hidden behind the choir lattice. Katharina imagined that heaven began there. The nuns sat on luminous clouds, a golden light over their heads. She imagined Sister Gertrud who sang with a pointed mouth, closed eyes, and a lot of enthusiasm. However at the same time, Sister Adelheid, who had hit little Margaret so hard yesterday, also came to mind. Margaret had not really been disobedient. She had only picked her nose. Katharina forgot the clouds and heaven and looked anxiously at her finger. As long as something like that didn't happen to her. For Sister Adelheid used her rod to strike the hands of the children. And that hurt – not only the hands. It hurt right to the heart and Margaret had cried for a long time yesterday.

The second ringing of the Angelus bell roused Katharina from her thoughts. No, it could not be the same in heaven as in the choir of nuns. She sighed.

In the semi-darkness of the church, her eyes moved backwards and forwards between the bare columns. Elsa, who stood beside her, poked her side with an elbow and whispered, "Did you hear that? That is certainly Sister Elisabeth singing off key." A quivering voice rose from the choir above the others and stopped. The echo died away in the vaulted ceiling and the cantor began anew. Katharina's gaze remained on one of the columns. She no longer heard the singing. A beam of light f ell on the Madonna in the south aisle of the nave. The Madonna had been donated to the convent by a pious friend only a few weeks earlier. Mary wore a crown and beneath it a veil almost enwrapping her. The child on her arm seemed to have moved somewhat away from his mother's body and was reaching with outstretched hands into the darkness of the nave. He was laughing and seemed to enjoy himself while his mother directed a very serious look toward the side of the altar blocked by the choir lattice. Katharina looked carefully at the face of the Virgin in the limited light which fell upon it. It was round and proportionate and more beautiful than anything Katharina had ever seen. But her mouth seemed to sigh. Her head was bent somewhat as if it bore an invisible weight. Despite this she held herself upright. It certainly could not be the child which was too heavy for her. It must be something else.

The Madonna's long hair fell freely across her gown. The girls were never permitted to show off the beauty of their hair. Every woman was to conceal beneath a scarf or veil what a man might find attractive. But not Mary. Was it God who permitted Mary to show her hair? For, she certainly wanted to please Him alone and no one else.

Katharina came to with a start. The "Amen" faded away between the columns. The most impatient of the girls were already pushing towards the side door in a hurry to get to the dining hall where soup was steaming in large kettles. Katharina was being pulled along. But as she went out, she looked back again. Could the Holy Virgin perhaps move? Could she not give little Katharina a sign? But from the portal, the Madonna was in the shadows.

In the evening at Vespers, Katharina slipped into the church ahead of the others. She approached the column with a pounding heart, stood on tiptoe and tried to look directly into the face of Jesus' mother. Mary's eyes were bright from the light which streamed into the nave through the rose window above the west portal. Katharina searched and searched for words to say. But nothing came to mind except "Mother" and again:

"Mother, you are so beautiful. Here take your child, Oh beautiful mother! Delight in it forever, you lily, you rose."

Imploringly, she raised her hands and searched the stony face of the statue for an answer. Suddenly she felt something heavy on her shoulder. She shivered. "How lovely that you should pray to our beloved Lady. Do you know how the verse continues?" Katharina shook her head without speaking.

"May your chaste hand,

Nurture the body of this newborn.

Give your child your breast.

For he needs you on this earth."

Sister Adelheid smiled at Katharina and then vanished into the choir room. "He needs you on this earth," Katharina repeated softly and then again more bravely aloud. At that moment it appeared to her that the Mother of God smiled at her. Behind her, the portal opened. With quiet whispers, the school girls pushed their way into the church under the care of a lay sister. In the choir, the garments of the nuns rustled. Vespers had begun.

"Katharina, Katharina, the cat has kittens." Elsa and Margaret stumbled through the garden and dragged their friend by the apron across the convent yard. In the corner of the cow shed sat the black and white cat. She mewed anxiously as the little girls drew closer. The three girls sat down around her and tried to calm the mother cat. However the confusion of their voices made the animal still more anxious. "Be quiet," said Elsa to the others. Quietly, the girls waited until the mother cat allowed them to look at her blind, naked offspring. "How small they are!" "We are not allowed to touch them yet." "What shall we call them?"

""So, you have discovered something," laughed George, the young hired man, behind them. He carried a sack in his hand. "Out of my way. I will take them away."

"Take them away? Where to?"

The young man laughed again, loud and rough. "Into the pond, of course." He pushed the girls who had not moved roughly to the side and bent down over the nest. The cat leaped at his arm and scratched it, drawing blood. "Damn animal!" With extended claws, she prepared for a new attack.

"You can't kill them," shrieked Katharina. 'I can't?" said George, taken aback, his mouth open. "Well, why not?" "But they are ..." At a loss for words, Katharina looked at Elsa who hung her head. "No, you can't," declared Margaret resolutely and began to cry. Katharina reached out her hand to the little one.

"Get away!" With a mighty blow, George sent the desperate mother cat flying toward the wooden wall. Stunned, she fell into the straw. Then he bent over the kittens, picked up two at a time and tossed them into the sack.

"No!"

"Yes," he taunted. "You wouldn't want to bring up all of them, would you?" He threw the wriggling sack over his shoulder, took a menacing step toward the cat who approached him again, and stomped out of the barn.

Stunned at what had happened, the children stared at the empty pile of straw. Katharina looked at the cat walking around them mewing softly.

"I would have fought harder for my children," she said reproach-fully.

"I don't want any children!"

Margaret wiped her tears with her apron. The girls stood up and walked slowly across the yard. Half way across, Katharina turned. "I will tell Mary!" And she ran to the church. Shaking her head, Elsa looked after her.

Under the statue, Katharina knelt on the cold stone floor and wept. "He wants to drown them. Holy Mother of God, help them. Help them live." The south aisle of the nave lay in the shadows. The stone statue was lifeless in the darkness. "Do something, beloved Mary. I will – I will ..." She couldn't think of anything to promise the Mother of God. She stood up and looked around lost for words.

Everything was deadly quiet. "If I was a mother, I would not permit it," she said to Mary and stamped her foot. Mary remained upright. Only her head was slightly bowed.

"Katharina!" "Psst! " *"Magnificat ... "* sang the nuns in the choir. "Katharina, did you hear? Elisabeth will marry." "Marry?" The impertinent Elsa received a poke in her back and dropped her head again in devotion. *"Anima mea dominum."*

Katharina studied the slim back of Elisabeth as she stood in front of her. She was a head taller than most of the school girls but otherwise she was no different than they were. "Marry?" thought Katharina and tried to imagine what it would be like. She recalled her boisterous brothers. They would also some day take wives for themselves. She did not know if she should envy or pity these future wives of her brothers. She recalled the maids screaming as they ran away from the hired men and in the process lifting up their dresses so that one could see entirely their naked legs.

At the evening meal where, according to the Cistercian Rule[9], the school girls were to listen in silence to someone reading – but they were not always quiet and Sister Gertrud appeared to be a bit hard of hearing – Katharina asked Elsa quietly between two spoons full of cabbage soup, "So, who will Elisabeth marry?" Elsa shrugged her shoulders and eyed the table of the sisters. "I don't know exactly. I believe it is a Duke of Mansfeld. He is quite old already."

The first group of girls carried their dishes into the kitchen and hurried out into the open air. It was a warm late summer evening. The students were permitted to speak in the yard. Even the hired men raised their voices there and the sheep bleated in the barns. Katharina and Elsa sought out a quiet nook under the projecting roof of the sheep shed.

"I heard it from fat Anna. Anna heard it from Gisela." "And no one asked Elisabeth?" "No. But, have you not seen her face? She walks around as though she was being sold to the Turks. Yet, thereby she will become a duchess and have beautiful clothes. She will be able to eat what she wants every day and not always have to fast and her maids will dress her every morning." "Do you really believe that?" Elsa was quiet. She didn't really know what it would be like to be married. 'I can imagine it would be nice," she finally said emphatically. "I don't know," said Katharina.

A couple of weeks later, as the harvest was already in full swing and the wagons of the farmers rumbled through the gate entrance loaded with the fruits and vegetables which they were obligated to give to the pious women, a small coach pushed through the maze of people and animals. The driver who sprang from it pushed the curious farmers'wives aside and strode to the house of the abbess.

The school girls stood at the doors and windows of the school building even though Sister Adelheid waved her rod through the air. None of the girls moved to return to their desks. With open mouths, they stared at the slender horses and the beautiful coat of arms which adorned the doors of the coach. Elisabeth stood among them. Furtively the girls looked at her. She was pale but did not move. A servant of the abbess came running across the yard and whispered a message to Sister Adelheid. The sister laid her rod on her desk and called, "Elisabeth!" Elisabeth turned around obediently, walked to the sister and bowed her head. Adelheid placed her hands on her for a moment. Her lips quivered, then she turned and Elizabeth went with the servant to the abbess. A short time later she reappeared in the yard wrapped in a bright cape in spite of the summer heat. The hired man carried her bundle. He also helped her get into the coach. She did not look back. The wagon turned and raised a cloud of dust. It disappeared through the gate entrance.

"Return to your seats," ordered Sister Adelheid, her voice quieter than usual. As Vespers began, Katharina folded her hands and blinked over at the Mother of God. "Protect Elisabeth from all harm, Holy Virgin, as she must now marry." She felt a shiver go down her back. "*Supplices te rogamus omnipotens deus ...* " "Humbly we pray to you, almighty God."

All Saints Day was barely over and the wind began to blow rain and snow through the windows. The girls were shivering as they sat over their books. They drew their thin garments more tightly around themselves. Their red frost-bitten hands could hardly hold the quill pens any more. More and more slowly they formed their letters and words. More and more often their work was interrupted by sneezing and coughing. "*Miseratio hominis circa proximum ...* " "The compassion of man is toward his neighbour ..."

Winter came early that year! Margaret, who sat next to Katharina, suddenly laid down her quill pen. Her entire body shook in a coughing fit. Katharina turned to her. "Write on!" commanded Sister Adelheid. *"Misericordia autem Dei ... "* "But the mercy of God ... " Margaret tried to continue writing. She couldn't. She gasped for breath. "Go into the dormitory and lie on your bed," said the sister. As she stood up, the child tottered. "Katharina, go with her." Katharina took her frail friend tightly by the arm. They had to proceed slowly, step by step. Margaret's hand was warm and twitched. In the yard, it was already dusk. A late farm wagon rattled over the stone pavement.

In the dormitory, Margaret threw herself down on her bed without a word and groaned. Katharina stood beside her, not knowing what to do. "I'm freezing!" "Wait, I'll get you some blankets." Katharina was glad to be able to do something. She grabbed blankets from the beds of the others. But after she had wrapped them around Margaret, the girl screamed loudly, "Give me water! Water!" Katharina ran to the well, came back breathless, and brought the cup up to the lips of the sick girl. Margaret shivered. The water ran over her chin and on to the blanket. But she sighed and sank down satisfied when the cup was empty.

It became dark in the dormitory. Katharina looked anxiously out at the overcast sky. She was afraid. "Katharina!" Her sick friend stretched out her hand, seeking her help. "Stay with me!" "I will stay with you. You can count on it. Don't worry." Katharina shivered from the cold but did not move from the bed of her friend, even when she seemed to have fallen asleep. A bell summoned them to Vespers. She heard the others cross the courtyard, moved her lips and tried to pray the Psalms: "*Domini, probasti me et cognovisti ... *" (O Lord, thou hast searched me out and known me ...)

Finally, as they finished praying in the church, the voices of the sisters and the other girls drew near. Katharina saw the flickering of their lamps above the wall. Sister Adelheid and Sister Gertrud came to the bed of the sick girl accompanied by a nun whom Katharina had never seen before. Behind them, the girls scurried in but Adelheid ordered them roughly to go and eat their meal. "You were right to stay with your friend, Katharina," said the stranger softly and kindly to her. Her face was bright in the glow of the lamp. She had friendly eyes. "I am Magdalena von Bora, your father's sister." She shook Katharina's hand and then bent over the sick child.

Amazed, Katharina studied her aunt of whose existence she had been unaware. But from deep within her subconscious, she remembered: her father walking through the room with heavy steps; she sitting by the hearth; someone raising a protest. "My sister also went," said her father. "Magdalena also went into the convent at the age of ten."

"I will get herbs and boil some tea," said Magdalena after she felt the sick girl's pulse and hot forehead. The child looked trustingly at her but then had another coughing fit. "Come with me, Katharina." Sister Gertrud remained behind at Margaret's bedside with the lamp. Katharina stumbled across the dark courtyard behind Sister Magdalena. The wind blew snow flakes toward them. Suddenly they were in front of a small door. Magdalena opened it and stepped into the interior of the convent. Katharina held her breath. She hardly dared to cross the threshold. In front of her she saw only the shadow of the nun. The nun felt Katharina's hesitation and turned around. "Come, you don't need to be afraid. Leave the door open. You will soon be going back out again."

A few steps brought them into a vault filled with wonderful smells. With a steady hand, Magdalena lit a lamp which shed light on the walls where hundreds of plants were hanging. Beneath them sheaves lay on shelves. Glasses filled with seeds or leaves stood around and a big book lay open in which Katharina recognized precise drawings of leaves and roots. "This is the pharmacy, Katharina," said the nun. "Here the pharmacist sister prepares everything which we need to help the sick." She carried the lamp into a corner and worked there with some glasses and leaves. Katharina remained standing in the darkness and waited. A fire burned in a small stove. Magdalena brought some water to a boil and poured it over the prepared herbs. Katharina inhaled deeply: a smell of balsam filled the room. "Could we not bring Margaret here?" she asked softly. The nun turned to her and stroked her head sadly. "No, Katharina, here we are only permitted to nurse the sisters who live with us under enclosure. Sister Adelheid will care for the girl. Take this jug to her! I will accompany you with the lamp as far as the door."

Katharina took the jug with the warm boiled mixture tightly in both hands and followed the nun. At the door Magdalena turned back: "You will now find your way!" Katharina heard the door latch. She groped her way cautiously in the darkness. The light of a lamp in the dormitory showed her the way. Sister Adelheid nodded to her as she reached the bed of her friend. Carefully they administered the tea to the sick girl.

Margaret coughed all night. In the morning, a bit of light broke through the grey clouds. The sick girl dragged herself to the window. Katharina was allowed to stay with her. At noon another school girl, Anna, also lay in bed with the fever. A couple of hours later, Veronica joined them. Katharina hurried from bed to bed. Sister Magdalena was again called from the convent. At Margaret's bed, she shook her head sadly. In the afternoon, Margaret coughed blood. The sisters carried her into a small room where a fire burned in a hearth. They called the priest. Margaret was burning up with fever. Father Bernhard came and anointed her with oil. As Katharina awoke the next morning, she heard the girls say to one another in a hushed voice, "Margaret has died."

The sisters dressed the child in a white garment and Katharina picked a couple of asters which were still blooming by the wall. She put together a bouquet and slipped it under the folded hands of her friend. Two hired men carried the dead girl over into the church and the choir of nuns sang the requiem mass. *"De necessitatibus meis eripe me, Domine ... "* "O bring thou me out of my troubles, Look upon my adversity and misery ...

Winter came to an end. In the cemetery beside the grave of Margaret, five additional graves had been chopped out of the frozen earth by the hired men. Lilies-of-the-valley now blossomed on the hills. A lukewarm wind blew across the cemetery and the birds twittered their spring songs. The nuns maintained silence during Lent while the buds on the branches of the trees filled with sap and life. With the end of the Easter celebrations, the countryside turned a fresh green while schoolgirls and nuns decorated the church and altars to prepare for the Pentecost festival.

Sister Adelheid supervised the girls. After the evening meal, she called Katharina to herself. "Come along to the clothes cupboard!" While Adelheid searched, Katharina looked around her and asked, "Why do I need new clothes? My old ones are not yet torn." "No," said Adelheid and looked at Katharina disapprovingly. "You have not torn them but they have become too tight. And watch out that you do not soil your bed. Here are a couple of clean rags. Lay them under you when you sleep. When they get soiled, wash them."

Katharina took the rags and later showed them to Elsa. "Do you know why I should lay these under me?"

"So that you do not soil your bed."

"But I don't soil my bed. I am not a small child anymore."

"But it happens to women too," said Elsa.

In the darkness on her bed, after she had removed her outer garment and the new aprons and had folded them carefully beside her bed, Katharina felt her body with her hands. She was shocked. She had become fatter.

"Elsa."

"Yes."

"Elsa, have you also become fatter?"

"What do you mean, fatter?"

"I mean your breasts."

"Yes, certainly. It happens as you get older."

"Only to women?"

"Yes, only to women."

Elsa yawned aloud and turned on her other side. Katharina stared into the darkness perplexed. She thought of the Virgin Mary and suddenly remembered a picture at home – in the church – not far from the manor: There the Holy Child lay in the arms of his mother and drank from her breast. If Elsa had not been breathing so deeply and been so quiet, Katharina would have asked her whether Mary also had to use rags.

During the night, Katharina dreamed about Elisabeth who was now a married duchess. She dreamed that Elisabeth like the mother of Jesus had a child at her breast and that she looked very happy. The next day at Morning Prayer, she stole a look at the Mother of God but she no longer dared to ask the question which came to her during the night.

Translator's Notes

1 Luther called Katie "the morning star of Wittenberg" since she started her days promptly at 4 a.m.

2 The Augustinian cloister in Wittenberg, valued at 6,000 gulden ($450,000) in Luther's time, which Elector Frederick of Saxony gave to Martin and Katharina Luther (before his death and which Elector John had renovated) when they got married in 1525. This is where the Luthers and their extended family, along with many students and guests, lived. In 1564, the Luther children sold it to the university for $277,500.

3 We have kept the German formal expression "Herr Doktor" which denotes respect. English tends to be less formal than German anyway and so that in the absence of a natural translation. we have transliterated certain expressions to give a German flavor to the whole.

4 Wolfgang Seberger, Luther's household servant.

5 For a basic historical account of Katharina's life, one must rely chiefly on her husband's letters and his Table Talks, some independent historical accounts, letters by contemporaries, and the text of some of her surviving letters. Katharina was the daughter of Hans von Bora and Katharina von Haubitz, both of noble descent. The von Bora family had

once been the Margraves of Meissen. While the members of Katharina's immediate family owned land, they were not wealthy. Most of the novitiates and nuns in the Nimbschen cloister were of similar noble extraction.

6 Katharina's mother died in 1504 when Katharina was five years of age and Katharina was sent to be educated at the Benedictine convent school at Brelma. Katharina's father remarried in 1505 and four years later, as was common for "adolescent virgins" of noble descent, Katharina entered the Cistercian cloister of Marienthron at Nimbschen in Ducal Saxony.

7 A gulden was a coin valued at $75.00, a substantial amount in those days.

8 The nuns in Brelina were Benedictines which kept the rules of poverty, chastity and obedience but were not as strict as some other orders. For example, the nuns were not strictly enclosed.

9 The Cisterians were a reform order founded to counteract the laxity of the Benedictines. They were also called "white monks" because of the colour of their habit.

I Believe In The Holy Spirit

Michael Green

In this revised edition, Michael Green looks afresh at the ministry of the Holy Spirit, drawing on his extensive teaching, pastoral and personal experience. He explores the biblical evidence for the work of the spirit and the many ways in which he blesses us in our lives today.

Kingsway
£9.99
PB / 1 8429.1145 7

£2 OFF
£7.99 with voucher

Other titles by the same author

MICHAEL GREEN

I believe
IN THE
holy spirit

REVISED EDITION

Published by Kingsway Communications Ltd
Lottbridge Drove, Eastbourne BN23 6NT, England

The Spirit of Jesus

Each in his own way, the four evangelists make it abundantly plain that a new era has dawned with the coming of Jesus of Nazareth. It is the long-awaited era of the messianic kingdom, the age characterised by the availability of the Spirit of God. And Jesus is the Messiah, by virtue of his unprecedented endowment with the Spirit of God. He is both the unique bearer of the Spirit, and the unique dispenser of that Spirit to the disciples; moreover, for ever afterwards the Spirit remains stamped with his character.

1. JESUS IS THE UNIQUE MAN OF THE SPIRIT

St. Mark on the baptism of Jesus

Mark was in all probability the earliest evangelist. He knew the power and the reality of the Holy Spirit in the Church of his day, when he wrote in the 60s of the first century. But he went to great pains to exclude from his Gospel all mention of the Spirit as available for believers, with one notable exception. Why was this? Surely because he wished to make it abundantly plain that it is Jesus, and Jesus only, who is the man of the Spirit. Not until his death and resurrection could that same Spirit become readily available for his followers.

The age of fulfilment

Accordingly, he begins his Gospel with the story of the baptism of

Jesus. The crowds who flocked to listen to John's preaching of repentance were baptised by him in the Jordan in penitent expectation of the age of fulfilment which he proclaimed. But when Jesus was baptised, Mark makes it plain that the age of fulfilment *has already dawned*. A voice was heard from heaven. Now there had been a great shortage of messages from heaven for a very long time. The writings of the rabbis repeatedly maintain that the Holy Spirit departed from Israel after the last of the prophets, Haggai, Zechariah and Malachi (e.g. *T. Sota* 13:2). What is more, the Spirit of God, and the *shekinah*, or glory of God, were not to be found in the Second Temple (*b. Yoma* 21 b). Men cherished a tremendous sense of nostalgia for the departed glories of the previous temple, and for the Spirit of Yahweh which used in Old Testament days to be displayed in mighty deliverers and inspired prophets. Nostalgia, yes, and expectation, as men awaited the promises of Ezekiel and Jeremiah, of Joel and Isaiah about deliverance, an anointed king, and a renewal of the Spirit in the days of fulfilment. Well, says Mark, in effect: those days of fulfilment have arrived. In John the Baptist's ministry you find the fulfilment of the prophecies made long ago that a messenger would come to prepare the way of the Lord. That is precisely what the Baptist was doing. And Mark immediately introduces Jesus on to the scene: the messenger has indeed prepared the way of the Lord. Daring words those, for in the prophet Malachi they clearly referred to Yahweh himself. Mark is quietly claiming that in Jesus we have to do with none other than Yahweh, who had come to our world in the man Jesus. As if that is not enough, he makes two other shattering claims.

The end of the silence

The first is that the age-long silence is ended. God has spoken again. The heavens are no longer brazen and unyielding. The rabbis believed that when the Holy Spirit was withdrawn from Israel at the end of the prophetic era, God left them with a substitute, the *bath qol*, which means literally 'daughter of the voice' or 'echo'. It is usually said that in the voice from heaven at the baptism of Jesus we have an example of the *bath qol*. But this is quite mistaken. The *bath qol* was an inferior substitute for theWord of God formerly given by the Spirit to a prophet. But this voice was no feeble substitute; it was a direct address from the God who had been silent. It is inconceivable that at this juncture when Mark is heralding in the return of the Spirit in Jesus he should introduce it with anything so banal and second-hand as an echo. And the content of this voice is even more amazing than its occurrence. 'Thou art my beloved Son; in thee I am well pleased,' seems to be a deliberate combination of two famous Old Testament texts. 'Thou art my Son' comes from Psalm 2:7, where the king of Israel is addressed as 'Son' of God. The kings had been pretty poor specimens as 'sons': they showed little enough of Yahweh's family likeness, and there was a long-standing hope in Israel that one day God would bring into the world a messianic Son, a worthy ruler to sit on David's throne.We know people were treasuring this hope at the time of Jesus, because in the caves of Qumran there has turned up a messianic anthology which includes the prophecy given to David in 2 Samuel 7:14. There God undertakes to give an everlasting kingdom to the boy 'and I will be his Father and he shall be my Son'. The voice from heaven, recorded by Mark, announced that the ultimate messianic ruler had arrived in Jesus.

The role of the Messiah

But that was only half the message. The other half 'with thee I am well pleased' comes from that picture of the Servant of Yahweh in Isaiah 42:1 which we looked at in the last chapter. At his baptism, then, Jesus publicly assumed a double role: the role of the Messianic Son, and the role of the Suffering Servant. Such was the destiny he willingly undertook.

The availability of the Spirit

But the baptism of Jesus did not merely see the end of the long silence, and God's declaration that in Jesus the role of the Servant and the Son had converged: the age-long drought of the Holy Spirit was ended too. As we saw in the last chapter the anointed king of Israel was equipped with the Spirit to enable him to carry out his work; hence the expectation of Isaiah 11:1ff that the Messiah would also be equipped, in fuller measure, with that Spirit. It was just the same with the Servant. 'I have put my Spirit upon him; he will bring forth justice to the nations,' says God through the prophet. And now the Spirit had come, and Mark's account of the baptism makes it abundantly clear that he sees Jesus as the Messianic Son and the Suffering Servant, equipped for his stupendous task with the Spirit of God promised for the end-time. The last days are no longer entirely in the future; in the person of Jesus the end has dawned. No wonder Jesus' first recorded words in Mark's Gospel are 'The time is fulfilled: and God's kingly rule has drawn near' (Mark 1:15).

St. Mark on the battle with Satan

Mark has two ways of emphasising the fact that Jesus is fully and uniquely endowed with the Holy Spirit in his role as Son and Servant of Yahweh, who brings in the kingly rule of God in the end-time. First, he makes a great deal of the struggle with Satan in which Jesus is involved both in the temptation in the wilderness into which the Spirit thrusts him (Mark 1:12) immediately after his baptism; and also in the healings and exorcisms which follow during the ministry. He does so in a very subtle manner.

The temptation

In the Old Testament there was a use of *ruach* which I did not mention. It concerns evil spirits which are seen as rebellious creatures of Yahweh, bent on wrecking his purposes but ultimately subject to his control. In the earlier books of the Old Testament we read of these as evil spirits (1 Sam. 16:14, Judg. 9:23, 1 Kgs. 22:21); later they are personalised in Satan, whose name does not appear before the rather late books of 1 Chronicles (21:1ff), Job (1:6ff) and Zechariah (3:1ff). In the inter-testamental period there is a great deal about these evil spirits and their prince. It is important to bear in mind that there is no absolute dualism in the Hebrew religion. Even the devil is God's devil: he is on a chain held by God, even though the chain is a long one. The devil and his spirits are seen as a distortion of the original good creation of God, and though they are allowed to tempt and hurt men because of men's wickedness (see, e.g. *Jubilees* 10:7–11) in the last-time they will be bound and punished. Now against that background of thought we must set Mark's emphasis on the binding of Satan by Jesus. Jesus, filled with the Spirit, goes off into the wilderness, the place where Israel had been tested for forty years after the Exodus, and wrestles with the tempter for forty days. He wins, where Israel's forebears failed. In him the days of fulfilment, the days of Satan's defeat, have dawned.

The exorcisms

And so it continues throughout his ministry. Time and again we find him casting out unclean spirits from afflicted people: it is one of the well-known characteristics of Mark's Gospel, which on the whole contains little teaching, but a great deal of action by Jesus. That action includes many miracles of healing, the most important being the curing of people who were possessed. The meaning is clear. Jesus is the conqueror of demonic forces through the power of the Spirit. He is the victor over Satan, and he tells a gem of a story to drive the point home. 'No one can enter a strong man's house and plunder his goods unless he first binds the strong man; then indeed he may plunder his house.' The context in Mark 3:20–30 makes it abundantly clear that by his cures and exorcisms Jesus is driving out the demons. The man endued with the Holy Spirit is more than a match for the unclean spirits which are such a feature in Mark's account. Jesus is the conqueror. And people are amazed. They see in the presence and power of Jesus a cameo of the final victor over the forces of evil. 'With authority he commands even the unclean spirits and they obey him' (1:27).

The controversies

But it is not only through his healings and exorcisms that Jesus shows himself as the bearer of the Spirit: he claims it explicitly in the controversy with the scribes about Beelzebul (apparently another name for Satan, conceived of as 'lord of the house'). In response to their charge (Mark 3:22) that it is through demonic power that he casts out demons, he replies that no divided house can stand: if Satan casts out Satan, his empire is doomed. And he makes that terrifying statement about the sin against the Holy Spirit, over which many people have needlessly tortured themselves.

'All sins will be forgiven the sons of men, and whatever blasphemies they utter; but whoever blasphemes against the Holy Spirit never has forgiveness . . . for they said, "He has an unclean spirit."' More light is shed on this verse by the form in which it occurs in the 'Q' material (sayings of Jesus preserved in Matthew and Luke independently of Mark).Whoever says a word against the Son of Man, it shall be forgiven him. But the man who blasphemes against the Holy Spirit will not be forgiven' (Luke 12:10). It is one thing to mistake and misrepresent Jesus, clothed in all his humility as Son of Man; it is one thing to misread his parabolic teaching, coming as it does in riddles. But it is quite another thing to see the truth clearly and wilfully to reject it; quite another thing to ascribe the power of the Holy Spirit to the devil – which is what the scribes were doing. If people firmly reject the saving work of God in Jesus, they forfeit the very possibility of rescue, not because God will not have them, but because they say, like Satan in *Paradise Lost*, 'Darkness, be thou my light.'

Jesus, then, is the bearer of the Spirit: he, and he alone during the period of the ministry. It is a mark of the extraordinary faithfulness of St. Mark to the historical situation of the life of Jesus that he does not read back into those days the experience of the Spirit to which he and his friends were used in the postresurrection era. There is one place only where he lifts the curtain. In the 'apocalyptic discourse' of Mark 13, Jesus promises the disciples that in the coming days when they are out preaching the gospel, they will be put on the spot time and again when arrested and unjustly accused. And then the Holy Spirit will give them words to say. He will equip them for witness-bearing. The promise refers to the post-resurrection days; it does not provide an exception to Mark's sharp portrait of Jesus alone as the man uniquely possessed by the Holy Spirit.

The teaching of Matthew

Matthew is equally convinced that Jesus is the focus of the Spirit's activity. He brings it out in a number of ways, in addition to those we have noticed in Mark.

The birth of Jesus

For one thing he carries the story of Jesus back far beyond the baptism to his very conception. This too was specially brought about by the Holy Spirit (Matt. 1:18,20). Just as the Spirit was active in breathing life into the first man (Gen. 2:7), so here he is associated with the birth of the last Adam. But Matthew is claiming more than this. He knows that the Messiah is uniquely endued with the Spirit, and he stresses that from the outset of Jesus' life this was the case.

The role of the Servant

Matthew makes quite explicit the way in which Jesus fulfils the role of the Servant. He quotes Isaiah 42:1–4 in full, and says that Jesus' works of healing are the fulfilment of that prophecy. In other words, the power of the Spirit is specifically set out as the energising principle in Jesus' healing ministry.

The equipment for mission

Finally, this evangelist is as well aware as Mark that the Spirit was during the ministry concentrated, as it were, in Jesus, and will only be available to the disciples when they, too, are engaged in the mission. Then they will baptise those they evangelise in the name of the Father, the Son, and the Holy Spirit (Matt. 28:19), but in the meantime they are given one trial run, if we may so call it, when they are sent out on a missionary journey (10:20). Mark's promise that the Holy Spirit will look after their words when arraigned before councils for the sake of the gospel is brought into the Mission Charge by Matthew: it seems clear that he is looking forward from an isolated incident in the ministry of Jesus to the continuing mission of the postresurrection church of which he was a member.

The teaching of Luke

Luke has a lot to say about the Holy Spirit, both in the Gospel and the Acts. At present it is sufficient to notice his agreement with the other evangelists that Jesus is the unique messianic bearer of the Spirit.

New dawn

He makes a very special point of emphasising the presence and activity of the Spirit in the birth stories of John and Jesus, and in underlining the new outbreak of prophecy, which had been silent so long, but as we have seen, was confidently expected afresh in the Age to Come. Right at the start of the gospel story we find the Spirit active in full vigour. The new age had dawned, and the signs of its presence were experienced. It is a weakness in James Dunn's useful book *Baptism in the Holy Spirit* that he sweeps aside these dozen or so references to the Spirit in the first three chapters of Luke and insists that the kingdom did not come until the baptism of Jesus. In fact, Luke could hardly go to greater lengths in stressing that the Age to Come dawned with Jesus' birth. The Spirit, active in an upsurge of prophecy, active in the birth of John and Jesus, rests upon Jesus and in its power he carries out his mighty works and after the resurrection imparts that same Spirit to his disciples. From Bethlehem at the beginning of his Gospel to Rome at the end of Acts it is the one Spirit active throughout: first showing us the nature of that messianic salvation brought by Jesus, and then showing us how it was spread.

Luke lays even more stress on the Spirit activating the whole life and ministry of Jesus than any other evangelist. By the Spirit he went into the wilderness, by the Spirit he was led there, and in the power of the Spirit he returned to Galilee to begin his ministry (Luke 4:1,14).

Messiah and Spirit

Luke persistently links the coming of the messianic age with the gift of the Spirit in various subtle ways. There is an ancient variant in the Lucan version of the Lord's Prayer, which is attested as early as Marcion in the second century and reads, 'May thy Holy Spirit come upon us and cleanse us,' instead of, 'Thy kingdom come.' This, if it is original, would suggest that Luke saw the Holy Spirit as the supremely desirable object of prayer (as in his version of the saying of Jesus, recorded in 11:13, 'If you, being evil, know how to give good gifts to your children, how much more shall the heavenly Father give the Holy Spirit to those who ask him' – compared with Matthew who reads 'good gifts' for 'the Holy Spirit'). It also suggests that he saw the gift of the Spirit as the supreme characteristic of the kingdom. But the experience of this Spirit must wait for the disciples until after the death and resurrection of the man filled with the Spirit. As in Matthew, the isolated promise of the Spirit in the Mission Charge points beyond the resurrection to the days when they really are engaged in the mission. Meanwhile, it is Jesus alone on whom the Spirit rests in his fulness. And the prophecy of Isaiah 61:1, 'The Spirit of the Lord is upon me, for he has anointed me to preach the good news to the poor . . .' stands in Luke's Gospel (4:18), as a beacon shedding light over the whole of his ministry. It is the passage he reads in the synagogue of his home town at the outset of his work. It contains all the great themes of the Gospel. It identifies the Spirit with the anointed one. And he calmly tells them that 'Today this scripture has been fulfilled in your hearing.' Could anything stress more strongly the concentration of the Spirit in the person of the Messiah for his mission? It is exactly the same point as John makes by his assertion that 'the Spirit was not given by measure' to Jesus, but rested upon him and remained – in fulfilment of the promises of the Old Testament (3:34, 1:32, 33).

There is a striking passage in the early second–century *Gospel according to the Hebrews* which may serve as a summary of this point. The *Gospel* itself has perished, though it was very popular in the early Jewish Christian community. This fragment of it survives, however, because it is quoted by Jerome – significantly in his Commentary on the messianic prophecy of Isaiah 11:1. It runs as follows:

> It came to pass that when the Lord had ascended from the water, the whole fountain of the Holy Spirit descended and rested upon him, and said to him, 'My Son, in all the prophets I looked for thee, that thou mightest come and I might rest in thee; for thou art my rest, thou art my Son, my first-born, who art king for evermore.'

2 JESUS IS THE UNIQUE DISPENSER OF THE SPIRIT

If, then, all the evangelists agree that Jesus is the unique *bearer* of the Spirit, in whose power he ushers in the Messianic Age, they are no less agreed on a second vital point. And here the *Gospel according to the Hebrews* is silent. The whole fountain of the Spirit is indeed his, but not for himself alone; rather that he should shower it upon his followers. And this the canonical evangelists stress, each in his own way. The point is that Jesus is the unique *dispenser* of the Holy Spirit. You cannot get him except through Jesus, or get to Jesus except through him.

John's baptism: mercy

All four evangelists record the promise of John the Baptist that whereas he baptises in water, the One who comes after him will baptise with the Holy Spirit (and, according to Matthew and Luke, 'with fire'). Precisely what John expected, it is difficult to know. But it is evident that John's work was preparatory: to get men ready for the forgiveness of sins which his baptism foreshadowed but did not profess to provide, and to warn men of judgment, the wrath to come.

His baptism exemplified these two themes of his teaching. The prophet Ezekiel had given this oracle from God, looking ahead to the age of fulfilment:

> I will sprinkle clean water upon you, and you shall be clean from all your uncleannesses, and from all your idols I will cleanse you. I will give you a new heart, and a new spirit will I put within you.
>
> (Ezek. 36:25f)

John saw his baptism as the preparation for this new era. He was under no illusions that water could convey forgiveness. In common with the men of Qumran, with whom he seems to have had some links, John saw washing with water as merely a preparatory rite, while the great cleansing and the gift of the Spirit lay in the future (1QS 9:10f and 4:21).

John's baptism: judgment

But judgment as well as mercy was presaged in John's baptism. The Old Testament had a lot to say about God administering fire. And it always means either destruction or cleansing. Daniel 7:10 had spoken of the stream of fire issuing from the throne of God, and this too is picked up in one of the Qumran hymns which describe the molten river of judgment that will befall the world in the last day (1QH 3:28ff). Probably this idea was in John's mind. In the very book of Malachi from which he derived the understanding of his own mission to prepare the way of the Lord, he would have read of fire both burning up evil-doers and also refining and purifying the faithful like a refiner's fire (Mal. 4:1f, 3:1–4). Perhaps those who came in repentance and were prepared for the running waters of Jordan to flow over their heads in judgment were thought of as undergoing the judgment of God in symbol so that they would not have to undergo it in its awful reality on the Day of Judgment.

John's baptism: preparatory

At all events, John knows that his baptism is merely preparatory. The coming Messiah will baptise with the Holy Spirit and fire. T. E. Yates has tried to maintain in *The Spirit and the Kingdom* that this prophecy was fulfilled in the ministry of Jesus, for he was not only filled with the Holy Spirit but constituted the fire of judgment to his hearers by means of his teaching and miracles. It is of course true that the coming of Jesus did bring a fire upon the earth, a fire of judgment; men judged themselves by their response to him. But he did not baptise with the Holy Spirit until after his death and resurrection. We do not have to rely on the verse which embarrasses Yates ('the Spirit had not yet been given, because Jesus was not yet glorified,' John 7:39) for this, though that is unambiguous enough. It is the concerted teaching of the whole New Testament that the Christian experience of the Holy Spirit is possible only after the death and resurrection of Jesus.

We have seen the evidence for this clearly enough in the preceding pages. Mark emphasises it by only allowing one reference in his Gospel to Christians having the Holy Spirit, and that in a prophecy about what would be their lot in the days after the passion (13:11). Matthew and Luke in their Gospels speak of the Holy Spirit for Christians only in the Mission Charge which anticipates their future role as ambassadors of Christ. Furthermore, Matthew stresses that the task of telling men the good news and baptising them into the possession of the Holy Spirit will only be theirs after the cross and resurrection have given them a gospel to proclaim and a Spirit to receive (28:19). Luke, as we have seen, makes the prayer for the Holy Spirit the supreme blessing of the Messianic Age, and shows how wonderfully it is shed upon the thirsty disciples of Jesus from the day of Pentecost onwards – but not before.

John, whose Gospel scheme does not include, except by implication, the story of what the Church, equipped with the Holy Spirit, achieved, and therefore could not make room for Pentecost (as Luke does at the outset of his second volume), nevertheless makes the same point with considerable clarity. In the first chapter of his Gospel he stresses that the Spirit rests exclusively upon Jesus, the fulfilment of the messianic hopes of the Old Testament for the bearer of the Spirit. In the twentieth chapter, significantly after the cross and resurrection, he shows how Jesus fulfils the second part of Old Testament expectation for the Messianic Age by breathing upon his disciples, charging them with his mission, bidding them continue his role of proclaiming remission of sins to the penitent and judgment to those who refused to hear, and saying to them 'Receive the Holy Spirit' (20:22f). The Spirit which rested upon him is now made over to them, along with the mission on which he was engaged; this too is theirs. As we shall see, the mission and the Spirit belong together. The important point is not to try to harmonise this account with that of Luke in the Acts – after all, John in all probability never read Luke's work, and presents the material in a very different manner and with different aims. I do not think we getmuch further by supposing that Jesus gave two insufflations of his Holy Spirit, one in John's upper room, and one at Luke's Pentecost. No, the point they both make is that Jesus was equipped for his messianic mission by the Spirit promised for the last days; that this Spirit was not available to others in the days of his flesh; and that after his death and resurrection the last days were extended, so to speak, by the followers of Jesus inheriting his mission, his authority and his Spirit. On this point the evangelists are agreed.

3. JESUS STAMPS A NEW CHARACTER ON THE SPIRIT

This leads us on to a third important point about the relation of the Holy Spirit to Jesus. We have seen that the Spirit of God which appeared fitfully, in a variety of forms, and prophetically in the Old Testament days shone steadily, personally, and fully in the Man of Nazareth. No longer is the Holy Spirit encountered as naked power; he is clothed with the personality and character of Jesus. If you like, Jesus is the funnel through whom the Spirit becomes available to men. Jesus transposes the Spirit into a fully personal key. Jesus is the prism through whom the diffused and fitful light of the Spirit is concentrated. Jesus is *the* prophet (Luke 7:16, Acts 3:22, 7:37) the lon-

gawaited prophet of the end-time, through whom the prophetic
Spirit, so active in the Old Testament, gave full and final revelation.
We have seen that Jesus gave this Spirit to his disciples in virtue of,
and subsequent to, his death and resurrection. What follows is that the
Spirit is for ever afterwards marked with the character of Jesus.
Indeed, he can be called 'the Spirit of Jesus' (Acts 16:7).

This is the common teaching of the New Testament, but no writer
brings it into sharper focus than St. John. In the fourth Gospel Jesus
tells his followers, heart-broken because he is going to leave them,
that it is better for them that he should do so:

> I tell you the truth: it is to your advantage that I go away; for if I do
> not go away, the Paraclete will not come to you; but if I go I will send
> him to you.
>
> (John 16:7)

In a word, it is the task of the Paraclete to universalise the presence
of Jesus. In the days of his flesh Jesus was limited by space and time.
His physical departure made possible the coming of the Spirit as
Paraclete and there would be no barriers of space and time to prevent
disciples being in intimate contact with him. Indeed, they would find
the relationship even closer than companionship with Jesus in the
days of his flesh. They have known Jesus as their Paraclete (we will
examine the meaning of the word in a moment) during his ministry.
He has dwelt *with* them, but the one whom he promises as another
Paraclete will dwell *in* them (John 14:17). There it is in a nutshell. The
Spirit universalises the presence of Jesus in the hearts of disciples.

The Spirit as Paraclete

The teaching of John

It is well worth taking a careful look at the teaching of St. John's
Gospel about the Spirit as Paraclete. There are five references to him
in the farewell discourses. They are 14:15–18, 14:25–27, 15:26–27,
16:7–11, 16:13–15. Once only in the rest of the New Testament do

we meet this title, in 1 John 2:1. And this, I think, is very significant. In the Epistle of St. John we find that Jesus is the Paraclete. He is the one who represents us before his heavenly Father. The righteous Lord Jesus having dealt with the defilement of our sins, represents us – stands in for us if you like, before his Father. As such he is the guarantor of our acceptance. In the Gospel, too, Jesus alludes to himself as Paraclete: for when promising 'another paraclete' or 'another as paraclete' in 14:16 (it makes no difference which way you take the Greek) Jesus is clearly insisting that he is their Paraclete already, just as the Epistle says he is. The identity between Jesus and the Spirit could scarcely be more strongly stressed, particularly as he goes on to say, 'I will not leave you orphans: *I* will come to you' (14:18). Nothing of the personality of the Spirit as embodied in Jesus will be lost when the disciples come to experience him as Paraclete. Indeed, John breaks all the rules of Greek by referring to the Spirit (a neuter word in Greek) by the masculine pronoun. The Spirit is as personal as the Jesus at whose behest he comes.

A tandem relationship . . .

A great deal of discussion has centred around the meaning of this word Paraclete. It has been understood as 'Comforter', 'Intercessor', 'Interpreter', 'Preacher' and either 'Prosecutor' or 'Defence Counsel'. The basic meaning of the word is 'One called alongside to help'. Jesus is the one called to the Father's side to help us, according to the Epistle. The Spirit is the one called from the Father's side to help us, according to the Gospel. The way in which he helps will be best dis-covered by looking at the text, not by speculating about the meaning of the term. But before we do so, it is worth mentioning the shrewd suggestion of Professor Raymond Brown that foremost in the complex imagery behind this word is the idea of what he calls a 'tandem relationship'. Sometimes in Old Testament days God granted a man signally endued with his Spirit to pass it on to his successor. Thus Moses passes on the Spirit of the Lord to Joshua (Deut. 34:9) and Elijah does the same to Elisha (2 Kgs. 2:9, 10, 15). So Jesus passes on to his disciples the Spirit which has 'rested' upon him throughout his ministry.

. . . among disciples

What do we find when we look at the detailed promises about the Paraclete? Precisely what this tandem relationship and the reiterated link with the historical Jesus would lead us to expect. Namely, that the Spirit acts for, and in, and against men in precisely the same way as Jesus had done when on earth. Just as Jesus had come forth from the Father into the world as the Father's gift to mankind, so it is with the Paraclete (5:43, 16:28, 3:16f). Just as the Father sent the Son into the world as his representative, so the Paraclete will be sent in Jesus' name (5:43, 14:26). Just as Jesus remained with and guided the disciples, so will the Paraclete (14:16–18). Just as Jesus taught them the truth because he was Truth, so the Spirit of Truth would lead them into all the truth about Jesus (14:6,17, 15:26, 16:13). Just as Jesus did not draw attention to himself but set out to glorify his Father by passing on the Father's message to men (8:28, 12:28, 17:4), so the Paraclete 'will not speak on his own authority . . . but will take what is mine and declare it to you' (16:14). Jesus bore witness to the Father (8:14) and the Spirit would bear witness to Jesus (15:26, 27). For Jesus had still much to teach the disciples which they could not understand before his passion; so he assured them that the Spirit would continue his teaching function among them when he had left them (16:13).

. . . in the world

Not only was the Spirit to universalise the person of Jesus to future believers, he was to do the same to the unbelieving world. One of the prime purposes of his coming was to nerve the disciples themselves to witness to Jesus in the face of hostile or apathetic society. Look at 15:26, 27: 'He will bear witness to me . . . and you also will bear witness.' Through the witness of the disciples which he will apply to the hearts of the hearers, the Spirit will convict men of being in the wrong. Three of the great themes of the apostolic preaching are then mentioned; sin, righteousness and judgment. Through the witness of the apostles and the witness of the Spirit (now seen as Accuser), people are shown that they are wrong with their moralistic ideas of sin: sin is essentially the refusal to commit themselves to Jesus, God's saviour. They are wrong in their views of righteousness, supposing Jesus to be a sinner like themselves – and worse, because he ended up in the place of cursing on a cross (cf. Deut. 21:23): his sinlessness had been vindicated by the resurrection ('I go to the Father'). And they are wrong in thinking that the judgment lay entirely in the future: the decisive battle which dethroned Satan had been won on the cross, and from now on he was a defeated foe, and believers were ransacking his empire. But is this triple message, taken home by the Paraclete in the apostolic mission, not precisely what the Johannine Christ proclaims throughout the Gospel, and particularly in a passage like 9:35–41?

In a word, the Paraclete takes over the role of Jesus. Just as the world refused to accept Jesus, so it will refuse to accept the Paraclete (1:10, 11 and 14:17). Just as Jesus had to bear his witness against a background of hate because he told people the unwelcome truth (7:7) so will the Spirit (16:8). Whether we look at the Paraclete's role in the world or among the disciples the answer is the same. The Holy Spirit is 'another Jesus'.

Another Jesus

He is sent to replace Jesus among the disciples and to do for them what Jesus had done on earth. More, he is to equip them for their mission just as he had equipped Jesus for his. Yet there is no complete autonomy for the Spirit, just as there had been none for Jesus. He had lived his life in dependence on his heavenly Father: if he was to give a true representation in human terms of the nature of Yahweh, then he needed to live, as man, in constant obedience to Yahweh both as his anointed Ruler and as his obedient Servant. And if the Spirit was truly to represent Jesus, he had to remain bound to the person and character of Jesus. Jesus was God's Last Word to man; and the function of the Spirit was not to give some new revelation of his own, but to bear witness to Jesus, to draw out the implications of God's Last Word. We shall look at some of them in the next chapter, but before closing this one it might be pertinent to speculate why it was in St. John's Gospel, of all places, that we get such stress laid on the Spirit as Paraclete. The reason is probably two-fold.

The Spirit replaces the apostles

There is good reason to suppose that St. John's is the latest of the Gospels to be written. Chapter 21, which seems to have been composed as an afterthought to the main body of the Gospel with its climax in 20:31, indicates that there was a tradition doing the rounds in Christian circles to the effect that John would not die: he would be there until the Second Coming of Christ. Imagine the feelings of the Christians when the old man died!

On the one hand the last of the apostles had passed on; the last of those authorised interpreters of the person and work of Jesus had left them bereft. On the other hand the promised Advent had not materialised. What would help them most in such a situation? Well, the record must first be set straight. Jesus did not actually say that John would survive until the Second Coming, but, 'If it is my will that he remain until I come, what is that to you?' (21:23). After doing that, the problem must be faced head on, in both its aspects.

The Holy Spirit, the Paraclete, provides the answer to both problems. Christians were distressed because the age of revelation was over (and they were acutely conscious of this with the passing of the apostolic generation, as is made clear not only by the speedy recognition in the second century that their writings were determinative for the Christian faith, but also by the deep sense of nostalgia to be found in the earliest of the subapostolic writers like Polycarp and Ignatius). Yet to them comes the promise that they are not worse off, but if anything better. They may have lost their apostles, but they have the Spirit of the Lord himself remaining with them to teach and to inspire. The risen Christ carries on his teaching work through the

Spirit whom he has given to the Church. Sometimes people today bewail the fact that they were not contemporaries of the historical Jesus, and imply that it would be much easier to believe and much more advantageous generally if they had been. To them the words of Jesus still apply. 'It is to your advantage that I go away, for if I do not go away the Paraclete will not come to you. But if I go, I will send him to you.' And that is what he has done. The Spirit is his parting gift to the Church to make his presence as real to them as if they were listening to him teaching beside the Sea of Galilee: and the Spirit can do more for us than ever Jesus could have done had we been his contemporaries. He can come within us, and take up residence within our very beings. He can not only bring to our remembrance what Jesus taught, but can reveal to us the deeper significance of his person, his death and resurrection which we could never have grasped by historical contemporaneity. We are indeed not worse off but better.

The Spirit anticipates the end-time

The second problem that would have troubled the faithful at the death of the last apostle was this. Why had the promised Advent not happened? It was a problem as early as 1 Thessalonians which was partly written in order to meet it. It was a more acute problem by the time of 2 Peter: chapter 3 of that Letter is specifically directed towards those who have given up hope in the Return of Christ. But when the last apostle died, and Jesus, who had uttered the mysterious words, 'There are some of those standing here who will not taste death before they see the kingdom of God come with power'(Mark 9:1), had not returned – what were they to think? Had they been misled?

No, they had not. In a very real sense, though not the sense they were expecting, the kingdom *had* come in power. It came in the power of the Holy Spirit on the Day of Pentecost, and that power had never been withdrawn, and never would be. The previous chapter in St. John had drawn attention to it. Jesus had breathed his

Spirit upon his disciples. This was the gift through which the Messiah had accomplished his work. This was the endowment of the end-time which he had lived and died with – and yet the last page of the last chapter of human history had not been written. Were the disciples to be any different from their Lord? No. To be sure, the last page of the last chapter had not been written at the death of the last apostle any more than it had at the death of the Messiah; but, like him, the disciples enjoyed the characteristic gift of the end, the Holy Spirit whom the prophets knew would be poured out in the last days. Let them not therefore bewail the delay of the Parousia. Jesus had not left them orphans: he had come to them in the person of the Spirit, who was not only the special gift of the Messiah to the messianic people in order to enable them to know his continued presence with them, but was the first instalment of the Age to Come, the pledge that the last days which had dawned with Jesus of Nazareth would, one day, come to God's perfect conclusion.

The Heartache No One Sees

Sheila Walsh

Best-selling author Sheila Walsh offers a message of hope and restoration for women suffering from depression. A long-term victim of clinical depression, she recounts her own story of freedom in Christ.

Thomas Nelson
£8.99
PB / 0 7852.6070 6

£2 OFF
£6.99 with voucher

Other titles by the same author

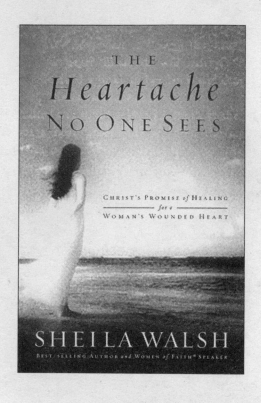

THE
Heartache
NO ONE SEES

CHRIST'S PROMISE *of* HEALING
————— *for a* —————
WOMAN'S WOUNDED HEART

SHEILA WALSH
BEST-SELLING AUTHOR *and* WOMEN *of* FAITH® SPEAKER

Copyright © 2004 by Sheila Walsh

Published in Nashville, Tennessee by Thomas Nelson, Inc.

An Introduction

OUR HIDDEN PAIN

From 1987 until 1992 I was a very visible presence on religious television. I was the co-host of the daily show *The 700 Club* with Dr. Pat Robertson and the host of my own daily show, *Heart to Heart with Sheila Walsh*, on the Christian Broadcasting Network. Then one day it was as if I disappeared off the face of the earth. I was there one morning, and by the next morning I was gone. Very little was said about my disappearance. A reference was made on one show that I had taken some time off to rest, but if you missed that day's broadcast, you had no idea where I had gone or why. Had I gone back to my family in Scotland? Perhaps I'd been fired? A month later I bumped into a woman in a mall.

"Sheila, is that you?" she asked. I imagine she was used to seeing me in a tailored suit, and I looked a little different in my jeans and ball cap.

"Yes, it's me," I replied.

"Where have you been? My family watches the show every day, and we miss you. What happened to you?"

I looked into her eyes for a moment. She was a stranger to me and yet I longer to connect with someone as I felt so alone.

"Do you have a moment to grab a cup of coffee?" I asked.

"I'd love to," she said.

We got our coffee and sat down in the food court.

I took a deep breath and said, "I was released from a psychiatric hospital this morning,"

I waited to see what her response would be. She reached across the table and took my hand.

"What happened?" she asked. "I saw the show the day before you disappeared and you seemed fine."

"I was diagnosed with severe clinical depression," I replied.

"But you didn't looked depressed," she said. "I would never have known."

We talked for a while and then she left. I stayed at the table, tears falling into my tepid coffee. Her words rang in my heart: *I would never have known.*

That was a big part of my problem. I had become used to hiding from others what was going on inside myself.

A COMMON PROBLEM

I have written about my experience with depression in my book *Honestly.* But over the last few years I have begun to realize that what I was dealing with is not unique to me or even just to those with depression. There is an epidemic of broken hearts that are being carried around in private. I talk to women every day who, because of my decision to be open about my pain, feel that I am a safe person to risk sharing their story with. I count that a holy privilege. That's why I am writing this book. I believe that Christ wants to heal our broken hearts and free our crushed spirits to love and worship Him.

If you are like me, it will take some time to open up to this process. Some of us have carried our wounds for so long, we no longer see them; they are just part of who we are. At times in the past we might have looked for healing and been misunderstood, so we hide our pain.

Let me ask you a few questions that might help you focus on some of the reasons you chose to hide.

Are you a victim of well-meaning friends who have told you to *get over it*? Sometimes those who are closest to us don't understand the depth of what we are feeling. As far as they can tell, everything is going smoothly in your life, so why do you keep harping about old stuff? Your ensuing sadness causes you to hide rather than deal with the pain of not being understood.

Have you tried to do it yourself, to tidy up what's going on inside with a quick fix? Some women starve themselves in an effort to feel in control over something. Others eat and eat until the wall around them seems enough to protect them from a cruel outside world. Some turn to alcohol, relationships, or soap operas in an attempt to dull the ache. Some try to lose themselves in a frenzy of ministry that can be as addictive as substance abuse. I have been there.

Do you struggle with shame? Is there a voice inside you that tells you that you will never change, that you are not worthy of God's love, that you will always be stuck as you are right now?

Have you listened to those who come in Jesus' name, promising healing for your wounded soul? Perhaps you prayed with someone on television and sensed that God had done something in your life. But even as the light flickered off the television screen, so did the hope in your heart. You longed for an instant miracle rather than the painful process of walking through whatever you needed to face to be whole. A quick fix was offered, but nothing permanent remained.

Whatever the source of your disillusionment, the residual pain is the same. You tried something but it didn't work, and you are left with more questions and no answers.

I tried for years to hold myself together. I worked harder and harder to be the perfect Christian woman, but it never worked. There were too many painful wounds under the surface that festered in the darkness. Some wounds are so deep and have been present for so long, it seems as if they will never heal.

MY ROAD TO CHANGE

I have been in relationship with God since I was a young girl of eleven growing up in a small town on the west coast of Scotland. My desire to please Him and respond to that love led me through Bible college to roles as a youth evangelist, contemporary Christian artist, and television host on the Christian Broadcasting Network.

But after working side by side with Dr. Pat Robertson and the staff of *The 700 Club* for five years, I was admitted as a patient in the psychiatric wing in a hospital in Washington, D.C., diagnosed with severe clinical depression. I felt as if I was drowning, dragged under the water by rocks of despair, sadness, and hopelessness. I had no issue with God. I believed then and believe now that God is good and loving and kind. The issue was with me. I was disenchanted with all the efforts of Sheila Walsh.

I was dizzy from years of trying to keep all the plates spinning in the air in an attempt to show God how much I loved Him. Nothing I did felt as if it was enough.

Have you been there? Are you there right now? For years I had taken comfort in the omission of the "big sins" in my life. I thought that if I were a "good girl," then God would love me more. I was sexually pure and abstained from anything that was on my long list of things to avoid if I wanted God to be happy with me. As I moved into my thirties, that comfort blanket had worn thin. I saw in myself the potential for disaster of every kind. I saw hypocrisy and fear; I felt anger and resentment. I had worked so hard to be approved by God and by others. I was finally tired of it all.

The plates began to smash around me. Depression seemed to invade my body like the beginning of a long, dark winter. By that fall of 1992 I felt as if I was getting colder and colder inside every day. My decision to check into a psych ward was based on the simple fact that I had tried everything else that was familiar to me, everything I knew to do, but nothing made a difference.

I had tried to eat better and exercise more. I had fasted and prayed for twenty-one days. I had worked harder and longer than ever. Yet this invasion of frosty hopelessness gained ground. The hospital was a last resort and a dreaded one. When he was in his mid-thirties, my father died in a psychiatric hospital, and I wondered if I had inherited his fate just as surely as I had been gifted with his brown eyes.

Some of my friends were horrified that as a Christian, I would consider reaching out for this kind of help. They offered the more traditional remedies. Perhaps you have received a similar prescription.

People told me to pray more, confess any un-confessed sin, listen to more praise music, get involved in helping someone who was in a worse state than I was, paste verses of Scripture to the dashboard in my car – the list went on and on. What some of my advisors didn't know was that I had tried all of those things many, many times. I found the list heartbreaking. The implication was clear: the problem was with my spiritual life. That only added to the guilt that I already carried.

My family was very supportive. My mom urged me to have courage to walk through this dark night. She assured me that God was with me and would walk with me every step of the way. I heard her words but they slipped through the cracks of a broken heart.

Just before I was admitted to the hospital in Washington, I was driving home from work when a storm appeared out of nowhere. The sky turned black, and lightning slashed the sky in two. It was as if an aqueduct opened in the clouds and dumped plague like rain on the tarmac. I thought that it was my fault. I thought that God was angry with me. Even as I write that, I find it hard to imagine myself in such a place, but when I was overwhelmed with guilt and shame, it seemed as if everything that was wrong with the world was *my* fault.

Some of my friends told me that what I was doing was spiritual and professional suicide. They said that when people learned that I had been in a psychiatric institution, I would never be trusted again as a broadcaster or as a believer. I was sure that they were right, but I didn't need a public relations company at that moment. I needed a place to fall on my face before the throne of God and hear what He had to say.

I don't know what I expected from this temporary prison, but I could never have imagined what God would do in me in this place of my undoing. Even as I ran out of mercy for myself, His mercy overwhelmed me, and His compassion began to change my life moment by moment, cell by cell. I discovered that the faint hope I had in the solutions my friends offered me were nothing compared to the absolute hope offered by Christ. I want you to know that Christ has changed my life. It didn't happen over night. I am not a fan of quick fixes or imagined healing. What Jesus has done for me has totally changed everything in my life. He taught me how to live. That is what I pray for you as we journey through this book together. It is hard to articulate for others that very personal work of the Holy Spirit deep in the internal life. What I can say is that I became convinced of the love of God based on nothing commendable in me; it was based solely on who He is and His commitment to me.

My life changed. It was the beginning of my healing. I began to read God's Word and hear Him talk to *me,* not just find a verse that might encourage someone else. As I read verses that talked about God as Father, I took comfort in that name. It was such a relief. For years I had worked harder and harder to make God like me. Finally I began to understand not only does he like me but how passionately He loves me. As my life moved on I began to see how others struggle with the very same issues.

LONGING TO BE HEALED

In 1994 my husband, Barry, and I were married in his hometown of Charleston, South Carolina. After the wedding we set up home in Southern California where I had enrolled as a student at Fuller Theological Seminary. Two years later I turned forty and became a mom in the same year! Life seemed as if it could not get any better. Then one day I received a phone call from a woman I'd never met asking me if I would be interested in joining a team of speakers who had begun to travel together across America under the banner of, Women of Faith. I told her that it was impossible. I had a brand new baby, I was trying to finish off my degree and barely had the stamina to make it through the supermarket never mind the airport. She was persistent. She told me that although she was putting the team together, my friend Steve Arterburn was the founder, and he had suggested she call. She asked us to pray about it. Even though it seemed an unlikely time to start traveling again I sensed that God had opened a door and invited me to walk through it.

The combination of being a mom and a women's speaker was a marriage made in heaven for me. The first time that I looked into the eyes of my son I felt as if God had kissed me. I talked to Christian, sang to him and told him that God loves him in all the moments of his life. In arenas all across the country I sang the same song to women who came together for two days, to laugh and cry, to be encouraged and remember or discover for the first time who they are in Christ.

But there was something that I couldn't ignore. I saw it in the mirror. Even though I was several miles down the road on this new way of living, I still reacted badly at times to innocent comments my husband would make, or I felt devalued by an unfavorable review of something I had written or recorded. Those things still pierced my heart and tripped me up.

I saw it in the life of my well-loved son. Even though Barry and I pour our hearts into his life, a comment from another kid at school – "Do you know that your ears are too big?" – can pull the rug from underneath him.

I heard it again and again from women as we traveled from Los Angeles to New York.

We are wounded by life, by each other, by our poor choices or the poor choices of others.

We long to be healed from those wounds, to be free, to be whole.

At moments we experience a glimpse of healing from God, and yet we seem to be able to lose it in a moment – another careless word, a disappointment with ourselves or with others. So what are we to do? The key question of this book is this:

Is there lasting healing on this earth, or are we doomed to simply patch

ourselves up as best we can until we finally limp home to the arms of
our Father in heaven?

I am learning that God's overwhelming love gives us the courage and
grace to look at our wounds, no matter how deep or painful they are,
and to bring them out of the dark into His light. Perhaps as you think
of your wounds, God's love seems absent. You might ask, "Where
were You, God, when these things were happening to me?"

"Where were You, God, when some of life's deepest wounds were
being inflicted?"

"Do You see?"

"Do You care?"

These are valid questions and ones we will think about together,
but let me say at this point, the same God who holds the universe in
place loves you. Perhaps that is where you struggle, not wondering
where God was, but questioning that God could love you in spite of
where you have been. I believe that God loves you right now with
all that is true about your life – externally and internally. That's my
life message. It's a message that we can never hear too many times, for
it contradicts the thunderous voices of dissent in our heads. Those
voices tell us that it can't possibly be true, not with all we know about
ourselves and all that has been done to us. We know that we have
failed to reach God's standards. We know that we have failed in our
relationships with each other, so how can a holy and pure God
possibly love us with no reserve? It took me a long time to be able
to receive God's love, to believe that His love is as constant on my
bad days as on my ducks-in-a-row days. I believe it now with all my
heart and soul.

That may be hard for you to accept for yourself right now.

I began to ask God to help me understand how we are to live in
this world with all the potential for hurt, pain, and fear and yet experience a deep healing that we are able to hold onto, no matter what
life throws at us. I'm realizing that there is a reason that some of us
are able to access and maintain this healing and move on with life
while others lose it like the morning mist or are unable to receive it

in the first place. It is my passion and heart to study what God's Word says, and then together we can live in the liberty of all He promises.

> That may seem to be an overwhelming thought in an already over-committed life. As I have said, I don't believe in quick fixes, but I do believe that Christ has left a path for us. We can listen to what the world says is true about our lives – that we are victims of all that has happened to us and we can never be free – or we can listen to what God's Word says is true: "May the God of all grace, who called us to His eternal glory by Christ Jesus, after you have suffered a while, perfect, establish, strengthen, and settle you. To Him be the glory and the dominion forever and ever. Amen" (1 Peter 5:10–11).

At the end of each chapter you will find application points. It is my prayer that these will help to bring the message of that chapter into focus for your own life. I want us to walk though these questions together. Take as much time as you need. Don't feel obliged to move on quickly. You might want to have a journal with you as you read so that you can write down your thoughts and questions. Also, at the back of the book I have included a bible study. You can do this by yourself or in a small group.

The Lamb of God gave everything He could give to restore our battered souls and place joy and light back into the darkened room of our hearts. It's time to come out of the shadows, remove the masks and stop hiding. He invites us now to walk with Him, dance with Him, fight side by side with Him, and love with Him. I remain your grateful traveling companion.

Listen to His invitation,

> Come to Me, all you who labor and are heavy laden, and I will give you rest. Take My yoke upon you and learn from Me, for I am gentle and lowly in heart, and you will find rest for your souls. For My yoke is easy and My burden is light. (Matt. 11:28–30)

APPLICATION POINTS

- Why have you picked up this book? What do you hope to learn and/or gain from it?
- What feelings that I shared or statements that I made did you readily identify with? Let them be a touchstone for you to look back on and see what healing work God has done in your life.
- What hope and encouragement did you find in this Introduction? Highlight those points so you can easily find them when you need them.

Broken Hearts and Shattered Dreams

A merry heart makes a cheerful countenance, but by sorrow of the heart the spirit is broken.

— PROVERBS 15:13

Though I speak, my grief is not relieved; And if I remain silent, how am I eased?

— JOB 16:6

In this first chapter we will discuss the reality that our hearts have been broken in many ways at many times. We have become used to living with our pain. We almost don't notice it anymore; it's just the way things are. That would be fine if the heartache remained in a back closet somewhere like an old school photo album, but brokenness is never quiet or completely in the past. The pain that we experienced as children or in other relationships as we have grown casts long shadows over the present. It affects the choices we make and the way we respond to life, to God, and to others.

THE UNHAPPY GHOSTS

In a *Christianity Today* article, Tim Stafford addressed the issue of the vast number of people in the church community who are in deep pain. He described them as "unhappy ghosts." That's an intriguing picture. It conjures up images of those of us who are barely there, hovering on the sidelines. We don't leave — perhaps because we have unfinished business, we are immobilized by sadness, or we have nowhere else to go – but we are not really present either. We don't contribute to the life of the church or enter into worship; we are stuck in a no-man's-land of darkness and despair.

Perhaps that's where you are. It might be why you picked up this book in the first place. Your heart is broken, you feel dead inside, but no one else seems to notice your pain.

I have received hundreds of letters from women who feel as if the church or a parachurch organization has let them down. What has been delivered to them falls far short of the advertised special. We are told to come to Jesus and He will carry our burdens, but no one tells us how to do that. If you walk into church next Sunday with a broken arm, chances are, you will be asked several times, "What happened?" But *what if you have walked into church every Sunday for the last ten years with a broken heart and not even one person noticed?*

Then perhaps someone gets up to sing and tells her story of how God met her when she was battered and bruised and now she is whole and happy. You sit and listen. Sure, you are glad for her, but what about you? Her answered prayer makes you feel more alone.

WHAT IS WRONG WITH ME?

I struggled with that awareness when I was co-host of *The 700 Club* with Dr. Pat Robertson. Every day we presented stories of marriages healed, physical health restored, and children redeemed from bad life choices. I interviewed men and women whose lives had been at the edge of a cliff, and then God intervened and directed their steps to a safer path. They were not left with unanswered questions, disappointment, and a broken heart. The stories we told were true, but they were not true for everyone in our audience. In reality they represented the experience of a minority of people.

Marriages are not always restored. The divorce rate in the church rides side by side with the statistics of those outside our doors. People who love and trust God die of cancer every day. Many parents don't live to see their children redeemed from the bad choices they have made.

Not everyone can find a safe place to share a broken heart, a place to receive love, understanding, and care. Most people do not. Watching the joy of those who have received the answer they were seeking from God is an encouragement to many. To others, it is rock salt pressed into an open wound. What compounds the pain is realizing that others do not understand or hearing them say, "Get over it."

Telling someone who is internally broken to just get over it is as ridiculous as giving a child with a broken leg a Band-Aid. It might seem like an immediate solution , but it won't hold.

LIFE IN THE REAL WORLD

I received an e-mail from a woman who had attended a Women of Faith (WOF) Conference in the spring of 2003: Do the cries you hear at the conferences from women's hearts about things that have happened to them in the past or are going on now really hit any of the ladies of WOF seriously? Do you all ever answer any of the notes given to you at these conferences? Do you all ever realize that you may sometimes be the link between life and death in a woman's life at one of these conferences? I understood her questions. At our conferences we get together for twenty-four hours with thousands of women. We sing together, and it's hard not to be inspired by the sound of eighteen thousand women singing "How Great Thou Art." Each speaker's message is fine-tuned to convey God's love and grace to every woman present. But at 5:30 on a Saturday afternoon it's all over. Women leave the arena, pile into waiting cars and buses, and head home. We return to our real lives and the challenges and struggles that exist on a daily basis. In many ways the same thing happens on a Sunday morning. We are buoyed by the atmosphere of faith and community, but then the service is over and life continues. One thing remains apparent: *Broken hearts are much harder to heal than broken bodies.*

We have spent a lot of time in the church discussing physical healing. We are split along denominational lines, with some exceptions, about whether God still breaks into our human experience with miraculous physical healing. That is not the subject of this book. My passion is the realm of broken hearts and crushed spirits.

Can God heal what was broken years ago?

Can God heal a pain that is so old you almost forget where it began?

Can God heal you when you no longer have a prayer left inside you?

Can God heal your heart when the unimaginable has happened?

A MOTHER'S CRY

My husband, Barry, had a friend from high school who died in 2002, leaving behind two young children. Her mother is destroyed by this loss, her heart in a million pieces. Imagine, one moment her daughter is fine, loving her family, getting ready for Valentine's Day, and suddenly a strange, strep-type virus robs this young woman of her life in a matter of days. This brokenhearted mother and grandmother came to hear me speak on the Friday night of our Women of Faith Conference. It had been a year since her daughter's death.

"How could God allow this?" she questioned bitterly with tears pouring down her cheeks. "No mother should have to bury her own child. Her children cry for her every night. They want to put on their shoes and join Mommy in heaven. Do you have any idea how that makes a grandma feel?"

GRIEF IS NO RESPECTER OF AGE

The one person who was able to really connect with this grieving woman during that weekend was my six-year-old son, Christian. During the Saturday of the conference, he spent some time with her at her home. He saw a picture of her daughter and asked who it was.

"That's our daughter, Susan. She was a friend of your daddy's.

"Is she not still a friend?" he asked.

"Yes, but Susan is in heaven. She died last year."

"My papa died too," he said.

"I know, darling. I knew him. He was a good man."

"Shall I tell you what happened?" he asked.

"I'd like that," she replied.

"When I came upstairs, he was lying on the bathroom floor beside my mommy. It was like he was sleeping. I sat beside him. I think it helped. Mom and I went to the hospital, but when we got there, Papa was already in heaven. He couldn't wait. My dad didn't get to say good-bye. That must have made him sad. At least I got to say, 'Good-bye, Papa.'"

For a few moments a small child and a grandmother shed tearss together – two generations apart but brought together by the bond of a broken heart and a common question, "Why, God?"

What about the woman who e-mailed me, crying out to know if the speaker team at Women of Faith Conferences, of which I am a part, really care about what is going on in the lives of those in our audience? Or is it just talk to sell books or tickets for the next event? Do we deliver our messages of hope and healing, and then return to our hotel rooms, indifferent to the pain that has poured out of open wounds into a sports arena? We care more than I can express in words. Each of us on the team has walked through moments of heartache and devastation. That's why we are committed to extend hope to those who have lost hope. We understand that barren place for we have been there.

I have wondered what happened to this woman to prompt such a cry from her soul? Had she cried out for help before and been ignored or been perceived as one of those "difficult" women? Perhaps she had lived through the kind of nightmare where everything that you thought you could count on changed in a single day. Had she encountered the bitterness tasted by a man we know by the single name, Job? His story is found in the Old Testament but in many ways it reads as if it had been written yesterday. The pain he experienced caused him to wish he had never been born.

A GODLY MAN WAS DEVASTATED

At his lowest, Job was so wretched that he questioned why God ever gave him life in the first place:

Why is light given to him who is in misery,
And life to the bitter of soul,
Who long for death, but it does not come,
And search for it more than hidden treasures;
Who rejoice exceedingly,
And are glad when they can find the grave?
Why is light given to a man whose way is hidden,
And whom God has hedged in?
For my sighing comes before I eat,
And my groanings pour out like water.
For the thing I greatly feared has come upon me,
And what I dreaded has happened to me.
I am not at ease, nor am I quiet;
I have no rest, for trouble comes. (Job 3:20–26)

We don't know who wrote the book of Job, but whoever wrote it has given us an in-depth account of the unusual life of this man. He had ten children, seven sons and three daughters. He was wealthy, described as the greatest man among all the people of the East. We are told Job was "blameless and upright, and one who feared God and shunned evil" (Job 1:1). In a rare endorsement of a man's character we hear God's personal commendation of Job's life:

"Have you considered My servant Job, that there is none like him on the earth?" (Job 1:8).

So what happened? What took this man from the place of acclaim in the courts of heaven to the man who would cry out in such bitter agony, "I am not at ease, nor am I quiet; I have no rest, for trouble comes"?

Here we have a man who lived centuries ago and a woman sitting at her laptop in 2003 separated by time but united in the human experience of suffering and plagued by similar questions:

God, I don't understand?
Is there anyone who will reach into this black hole of despair and
    pull me out?
Why is this happening to me?

Wounded by God

Let's travel back down the centuries and take a look. It started out as tragedies often do. It was a good day. All Job's children had gathered at his eldest son's home for supper. It must have been a comfort to Job to know that his children got along well with each other, but into the peace of this moment came three of his servants with news that would change everything. As each one told his devastating story, Job realized that business wise, he was wiped out; his livestock and servants had been slaughtered.

While he tried to absorb this information, the one last remaining servant arrived and told him that an unusual wind had attacked the house where his children had gathered. The wind – in what seemed to be an act of vengeance – had battered the house at all four corners and the roof caved in. His children were dead, buried beneath the rubble.

Can you imagine such a personal holocaust? Within ten minutes everything that is precious to you in life is gone. As you try to absorb the horror of losing your livelihood you hear news that makes that decimation insignificant. Your family, all your children are dead. Where was God when that was happening to Job?

How would Job have survived if he had overheard the conversation that took place between Satan and God before this personal disaster and he realized that God allowed Satan to do that to his faithful servant?

Then the LORD said to Satan, "Have you considered My servant Job, that there is none like him on the earth, a blameless and upright man, one who fears God and shuns evil?" So Satan answered the LORD and said, "Does Job fear God for nothing? Have You not made a hedge around him, around his household, and around all that he has on every side? You have blessed the work of his hands, and his possessions have increased in the land. But now, stretch out Your hand and touch all that he has, and he will surely curse You to Your face!" And the LORD said to Satan, "Behold, all that he has is in your power; only do not lay a

hand on his person." So Satan went out from the presence of the
LORD. (Job 1:8–12)

"All that he has is in your power; only do not lay a hand on his
person." This is a hard passage for us to understand. A God who is
good and loving, powerful and just, allowed Satan to decimate His
servant. Job's pain was intense. It was the agony that no parent ever
wants to face, the death of a child. As I listened to Susan's mom at our
conference I heard Job's voice:

"There is no relief for me."
"I never should have been born."
"I will never be all right again."

One thing is crystal clear; people are in deep pain and have been for
centuries. Perhaps it's because of the vast cavern that seems to exist
between the belief in a good, loving God and the heartache and
sorrow that invade the lives of those who love Him. A further death
blow is delivered by those we expect to be able to help heal our
wounds, yet they often create a deeper pain. Job believed that God
was good and just, but how could a good and just God allow Job's
children to be killed, his property destroyed, and then to add misery
to wretchedness his own body became so debilitated that it became
a prison of pain?

The woman who e-mailed me stands like a sentry at the gate of
the arena calling out, "Do you see what's happening? Do you feel the
pain? Do you care? We're dying here."

WOUNDED BY THOSE WE TRUSTED

Most of us, thank God, will not live the nightmare of Job. Most of us
get to see our children grow and marry. Few of us lose absolutely
everything overnight. But many of us face the heartache of longing for
connection, for relationship, while feeling desperately alone. The pain
seems more intense when we experience that in the house of God.

I love to listen to audiotapes in my car. My mom and my sister regularly send me British comedies and dramas. One of my favorite modern playwrights is Alan Bennett. He is a man fascinated by human nature, and he has a gift that enables him to pull back the drapes for a moment and let us look inside someone else's soul. His monologues in particular permit us to sit with a total stranger for a while and listen in to the person's internal conversation.

One of the most illuminating is about a pastor's wife disillusioned with her husband, with God, and with His people. She wonders, If God is indeed a loving God, then why does everyone in the church appear to be so miserable? And why, if God sees all, do His people take great pains to hide the truth about their lives from one another? It seems to her that her husband wears the perspiring mantle of the used car salesman, not quite sure that what he sold you will get you all the way home. She is acutely aware of the disapproval of many of the women in the church. When she tries to arrange the flowers on the altar, they are never quite right. When she undertakes visitation, she doesn't say the right thing. She encounters one slight after another, little wounds that collect in her heart and soul, causing her to close down inside. Brutalized by those who claim to love God, she finally turns away from faith and finds companionship and compassion in the arms of another man.

It's just a play, but when I listened to it for the first time, I wept. I wept because what is fiction in Alan Bennett's play is reality to too many who have been wounded by God's people. It is one of the most painful experiences in life to be isolated or stigmatized by a fellow believer.

SUFFER IN SILENCE

During a radio interview, a woman called in and asked me, "How can God ask me to love others when there are people in my life who have lied about me and hurt me deeply? It would be painful enough if they were unbelievers, but these are people who claim to love God. That's what makes it hurt so much."

Job knew that feeling too. In the second chapter we read, "Now when Job's three friends heard of all this adversity that had come upon him, each one came from his own place — Eliphaz the Temanite, Bildad the Shuhite, and Zophar the Naamathite. For they made an appointment together to come and mourn with him, and to comfort him" (v. 11).

That may well be what they set out to do, but that was not what ultimately happened. It is common in sermons and books to rip Job's three friends to shreds because of their frustration with him and their assumption that there must be some problem in his personal life to have brought such catastrophe on his head. But it's worth noting that when they first saw him, they wept and sat with him for seven days, saying nothing. It was apparent to them that his suffering was unspeakably intense. We would struggle in our culture to find many who would keep silent vigil with us for seven hours, let alone seven days. The trouble began, however, when Job ended his silence. As long as Job was quiet, they were with him, but when he opened his mouth and began to curse the day he was born, that was more than they could handle.

Have you been there? As long as you are silent about your pain, sympathy is given, but if you allow the poison to flow from your wounds, then the raw edges cause others to back away from you or attempt to contain you again. Surely the church should be the place where we can come and let the anger and disappointment flow out of our veins until it is washed away by the blood of Christ.

One of the most poignant passages from the book of Job illustrates the agony of crying out for help, but no one hears you. He was a man who had been there for others when they were in trouble, but no one was there for him.

Have I not wept for him who was in trouble?
Has not my soul grieved for the poor?
But when I looked for good, evil came to me;
And when I waited for light, then came darkness.
My heart is in turmoil and cannot rest;
Days of affliction confront me.

> I go about mourning, but not in the sun;
> I stand up in the assembly and cry out for help.
> I am a brother of jackals,
> And a companion of ostriches. (Job 30:25–29)

I find it hard to read that passage without weeping. I know a little of that despair. During my stay in the psychiatric hospital, I received a letter from a friend that broke my heart. In it he accused me of being used by Satan to discredit God's work. He called me a hypocrite and a liar: "How can you sit on television every day and talk about the miracles that God can do and now you have run away from everything you believe? I thought I knew you. I don't know you at all."

I wept bitter tears when I read those words. I remember lying facedown on the floor, wishing that it would open up and consume me. I felt as if I was in a wasteland surrounded, like Job, by the scavengers of the night. When your heart is broken, you want to be held, to be comforted. You want someone to tell you that everything is going to be okay. When those you turn to for help add to the weight of brokenness, it is hard not to give in to despair.

Add to this weight the pain and woundedness we carry not for ourselves but for those we love. It is a terrible thing to watch our loved ones suffer at the hands of someone else knowing that there is nothing that we can do to help?

HOW COULD THEY DO THIS?

I am in touch with several pastors' wives whose faith has all but been destroyed by the way congregations have treated them, their husbands, or their children. One woman wrote, "I never knew that I could hate so much, but I do. I have watched the way that my husband's congregation has slowly and methodically annihilated his spirit. When we came to this church, it was with hearts full of love and faith, but as I write to you today my husband is on anxiety medication and I carry around a lead weight of hatred and unforgiveness every single day."

I read her letter and I heard Job's voice:

Why is light given to him who is in misery, and life to the bitter of soul?"

WOUNDED BY OUR POWERLESSNESS

For the first few years of Christian's life Barry and I decided who came into our son's life and who did not. We were with him all day, every day. Then he started school and the circle of those he interacted with became much wider. I had an acute awareness that first day as I dropped him off in his classroom and watched as he found his name tag and sat down at his desk that life had changed for our family. From that point on I wouldn't know all that was said to him or share in all of his experiences. I would not be able to shelter him from hurt.

One day as I waited in the carpool line I saw him standing alone in the playground with big tears running down his cheeks. Parents are not supposed to get out of the cars. We are to wait for a teacher to bring our children to us, but I ignored that and got out anyway. When he saw me, he rushed over and buried his head in my sweater.

His teacher saw us standing there and came over. "He's had a rough day," she said. She told me that an older boy had hurt his feelings.

My first instinct was to find the kid and flatten him. By God's grace I suppressed that desire and headed for home. He was very quiet in the car. I have learned to let him choose his own timing to share what's going on inside. We stopped off at his favorite ice-cream store and sat outside on the grass with our multicolored selections of pure sugar.

"A boy said I had big ears, Mom," he whispered.

"You have perfect ears," I said.

"He said they stick out like wings!"

"They are my favorite ears in the world," I told him.

"Thanks, Mom," he said.

But every now and then I still catch him looking at his ears in the mirror, two years later. Something was etched into his spirit that day that is not so easily erased.

In *Telling the Truth*, Frederick Buechner wrote, "You do not just live in a world but a world lives in you." From the first moment that you opened your eyes and the glaring light of planet earth invaded your mind and soul you have been recording information. Some of it is accurate and factual: "I have brown eyes." Some of it is hurtful: "People would like me more if I was thinner or taller or funnier."

As a parent I ached for my son that day. I felt so helpless to protect him from the inevitable scars that life inflicts. Part of the world of being a parent is walking with our children through the harsher moments in life. We feel as if we should be able to make it all better and some times we simply can't.

I watched Christian one morning as my Barry was shaving. "Not like that, Dad. You're doing it wrong."

Barry kept shaving.

"Mom, Dad's doing it wrong."

"How do you think he should shave, O Wise One?" I asked.

"He should do it one simple stroke at a time. Look at him! He's always cutting himself."

That's the trouble, though, isn't it? We're always cutting each other or ourselves. We are human and we make mistakes. We have done things and things have been done to us. There is indeed a world inside each one of us. There are moments in life that carve their pictures into our souls: cruel words, heartbreak, rejection, abuse, pain, or loneliness. What comes to your mind when you take time to look at the snapshots that your heart holds, those pivotal moments of sorrow and pain that make you cringe when you remember them?

SNAPSHOTS

I picture a day when I was ten years old. I was at summer camp, and it was parents' day. A girl in my dorm looked out the window and said, "Sheila, there's your dad!" She knew that my dad was dead, but for a moment I forgot and turned to look out the window. Even as my mind caught up with my heart I looked at her, and she was laughing. I felt such a fool, such a lonely fool, that I locked myself in the bathroom and cried bitter tears into a cheap camp towel that offered little comfort.

I picture a day at college. I was nineteen and dating the most handsome boy I'd ever met. I went to his room to return a book that I had borrowed, and as I stood by the window with the sunlight on my face, he said, "You shouldn't stand so close to the window. It shows off your bad skin." I knew that I had bad skin, but I had hoped that it wasn't as bad as I thought. That morning I knew that it was worse than I could imagine, and every time he looked at me that was what he saw. That event affected me for years. I would never sit at an outside table in a restaurant. I looked for dark places to sit and shied away from photographs. I'm sure at times it seemed that I was simply being difficult when I would refuse to get into a shot. No one knew that I was dying inside at the idea of being captured on film, a permanent record of my imperfections.

What are your snapshots? What are the moments that are etched into your soul and psyche and cast such long shadows into the present?

As you consider your life today, do you feel like a ghost weighed down by the shame you drag around with you everywhere you go? Perhaps it's been so long since you felt alive, you can't imagine things changing.

HE STILL CARRIES THE SCARS

When I was thirty years old, I privately believed that I would always walk with a deep sadness inside. I became used to it. It was who I was. Then I read a book by Dr. Henry Cloud called *Changes That Heal,* and something that felt like *hope* began to stir deep inside me. It was very faint at first, then the message got louder and louder. My initial surprise was that anyone would be able to put words to what was going on inside me. I thought that I was the only one who felt as I did.

Then I recognized that I was being shown a way out of the pit. That is my prayer for you. I want you to know that you are not alone, that hope and healing are to be found in Christ. There *is* a way out of your pit. It's not an immediate thing; it is a process but it is available to you.

You begin by simply being open to healing. I believe that because of God's grace and mercy, you can bring each one of the painful snapshots of your past into Christ's light. You can put them on the table and look at them with Jesus right by your side. That's where you begin. I don't believe that the Holy Spirit simply takes an eraser and removes all the marks of pain from your heart but rather He gives you the grace to face each moment in the company of your Savior.

Christ carried the scars of the Crucifixion with Him as He rose from the dead but the wounds were healed. They were not festering in the darkness. Wounds that are left untreated or covered over don't heal as they should.

I have had the thumb on my right hand broken three times. The first time it happened I was working on a summer youth mission in England and didn't bother having it looked at. The bone healed but it healed crookedly and has remained vulnerable to further damage and pain if someone accidentally twists it.

The wounds on Christ's hands and side healed in such a way that he could offer them to Thomas, the one who doubted, as proof that he was indeed Jesus, the risen Christ. He didn't hide his wounds or have them erased. They are part of his identity.

I will always carry the scar of the loss of my father but it is no longer a weeping wound. Christ has removed the poison and all that is left is the mark. Jesus wants you to bring your festering wounds into His light so that He can heal them to be touched by others.

There are many negative images to erase along the way, but you can start. You can take just one step and ask God to help you to be willing to have your wounds brought into his healing light.

When I am afraid or uncertain I turn to God's word.

You, O GOD the Lord,
Deal with me for Your name's sake;

Because Your mercy is good, deliver me.
For I am poor and needy
And my heart is wounded within me. (Ps. 109:21–22)

Restore to me the joy of Your salvation,
And uphold me by Your generous Spirit. (Ps. 51:12)

Father God, I thank you for the gift of your son, Jesus. I thank you that he embraced His wounds so that I can be healed. Give me grace and courage to bring my wounds into your healing light.
In Jesus name,   *Amen*

APPLICATION POINTS

- When, if ever, have you felt like a "walking ghost"? What led to that sense?
- When has a fellow believer been the cause of deep pain? Or when has a brother or sister in Christ not wanted you to speak honestly about your pain?
- I shared some snapshots from my life. What are those moments from your life that are etched into your soul and psyche and that cast their long shadows into the present?
- Hope and healing are to be found in Christ. Finding them does not happen immediately; it is a process. We begin that process by being open to healing. What, if anything, is causing you to be hesitant about starting the healing process?
- Identifying snapshots from your own life is a step toward healing. Share each of those snapshots with Jesus; bring them into His healing light.

I, Isaac Take Thee, Rebekah

Ravi Zacharias

Bible scholar and popular speaker Ravi Zacharias extracts five points critical to long-lasting marriages, learnt from the biblical story of Isaac and Rebekah. Great for all couples, young and old.

Thomas Nelson

£8.99
HB / 0 8499.1798 0

£2 OFF
£6.99 with voucher

Other titles by the same author

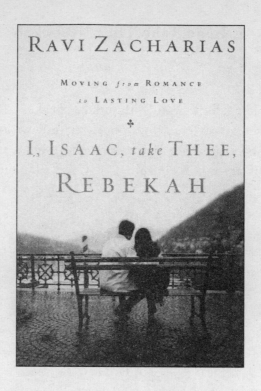

RAVI ZACHARIAS

MOVING *from* ROMANCE
to LASTING LOVE

✦

I, ISAAC, *take* THEE,

REBEKAH

Published by W Publishing Group, a Division of Thomas Nelson Inc.
PO Box 141000, Nashville, Tennessee 37214

The Will to Do

If the will is to be resurrected,
it must first go to the Cross.

I have heard it said that the longest journey in life is from the head to the heart. Another way to say the same thing is that the spirit is willing but the flesh is weak. Yet another aphorism of our time is that beginning well is a momentary thing; finishing well is a lifelong thing. All of these point to one reality – our knowledge and our response are not always in keeping with each other. We seem to be inclined to separate what God intended to remain joined together.

Solomon proved this centuries ago. He made a fascinating statement in the Book of Ecclesiastes. He relates all the areas in which he searched for meaning – pleasure, riches, power, fame, and everything else one could imagine. Through all of these forays in a search for fulfillment, he says, "My wisdom stayed with me" (Ecclesiastes 2:9). How is that possible, we ask, when his day-to-day life was a colossal mess? I understand him to mean that in the midst of his duplicity, his theoretical knowledge of right and wrong never left him. He knew how to discern. But he was volitionally weak and unable to resist the tug of attraction into wrong behavior.

I have shared the following story many times over the years. Those from parts of the world where this is foreign shake their heads in disbelief, wondering how this can even be theoretically plausible, let alone practically workable. But read the reasoning first and then I will try to explain.

I give you an example of my older brother, who lives in Toronto, Canada. The story dates back to the late 1960s. At that time he was a systems engineer with IBM. Since that time, he has gone on to do several very impressive things in the world of computer software. In other words, he is mentally all right. He doesn't have any major problem as far as his IQ is concerned. I say that because you may begin to wonder as I tell his story.

When he was in his mid-twenties, my brother came to my father and said, "You know, Dad, I've always maintained even when we were in India that I'm only going to marry the girl you choose for me. I guess I am ready now. Would you please begin a search for a girl for me to marry?"

I really didn't believe he'd go through with it. We were living in Toronto, thousands of miles and a cultural planet away from the land of our birth. But this was his choice. He wanted my parents to help in "The Search." My father and mother said, "Fine. Tell us the kind of young woman you're looking for." My brother gave his "ideal partner" speech and proceeded to describe the kind of person he would choose to marry. Under normal circumstances, the parents would travel around and look for somebody that met the criteria, but in this instance my brother said to our father, "Look, you really don't need to do that. Why don't you just write to your sister in Bombay and let her do the groundwork? We'll just correspond back and forth and take it from there."

Thus began his quest and what I called our family entertainment hour every night around the table. My father wrote to his sister, and in response came numerous letters with suggestions, photographs, and information sheets ad nauseam. Oh! The jokes that would fly! The unsolicited advice from every member of the family was profuse. The sarcasm, wondering whether this poor woman had the faintest clue of his shortcomings! (From my experience with photographs I have learned that if you find a good photographer and pay him enough, he can make anybody look splendid. One of the first things people do when you arrive for a speaking event is to compare the reality with your publicity photograph. Many times they can probably say, "Twenty years ago he may have looked like that, but now . . .")

Pictures can tell an awful lot that's really not there. The camera can and does lie. But my brother would sit in his bed at night and look over all those pictures, study the lists of accomplishments the will to do and qualifications, and say, "What do you think of this one, Rav? Isn't she lovely? Look at the description. She's even the church organist." I could not resist pointing out how important a feature that was for a successful marriage.

He narrowed the "applicants" to a short list and, finally focusing on one person, began to correspond with her. Then they advanced to telephone conversations, but not many because that was "too expensive." One could tell that reality was closing in.

Finally, believe it or not, they both felt this was it. The dates for the engagement and the marriage were set with these two never having met.

My brother and my father flew from Toronto to Bombay. More than one thousand wedding invitations were sent before my brother and his bride-to-be had ever seen each other. Two days after his arrival was the engagement date and a day or so later was the wedding date. He would then bring his bride back to Canada, all within a week, and they would live "happily ever after." That, at any rate, was the plan.

I thought to myself, *Oh my! You know, this is faith. Maybe it is even less than that. This is credulity!* I began to get really concerned, so before my brother left for Bombay, I mustered up the courage to caution him. I said, "I don't want to challenge anything you're doing, but I do have a brief question. What are you going to do when you arrive in Bombay, come down the Jetway and see a young woman standing there with a garland in her hand, and say to yourself, *Good grief! I hope that's not her. I hope that's somebody else!* Or she looks at you and thinks to herself, *I hope that's not him. I hope that's his brother!* What on earth will you do? Are you going to take her aside, talk it over, and then

make an announcement saying, 'We have met . . . we will not be pro-
ceeding with our plans'? Will you get on the telephone or write
letters to everybody and say, 'Folks, we've met. The wedding is off.'"

My brother just stared at me. He said, "Are you through?" I told
him that for the moment I was just awaiting his answer. Then he said
something that was absolutely defining for him: "Write this down, and
don't ever forget it: Love is as much a question of the will as it is of
the emotion. And if you will to love somebody, you can."

That statement brought our conversation to a sudden stop. That was
thirty-five years ago. My brother and his wife now have three children
and make their home in Toronto. Has it been easy? No. Marriage
never is easy. But the challenges they face do not come from an
absence of commitment.

The statement "If you will to love somebody, you can" has the ring
of truth, but deep inside we wonder, *How does one "will"?* It is a little
bit like ordering somebody to love you. How does one go beyond the
discernment to the practice? If knowledge does the will to does not
guarantee behavior, where does one go to translate the prerequisite
into action? Can it really be done?

A False Start

The first thing to bear in mind is that we exaggerate the separation of
the emotion and the will as two distinct faculties of operation – some
kind of misshapen two-headed monster. Think, for example, of the
caricature we make of one difference between men and women. We
seem to think that women are more emotionally driven and men
more cerebrally driven. If that caricature were true, why is it that more
men fall into infidelity after marriage than women? If women are
more emotionally driven, should it not be the other way around? I
think it more appropriate to say that women in general recognize the
emotional *ramifications* of their acts better than men do. Men *do* feel
emotion, but they do so selectively and fail to face the consequences
of reality. Betray a man and you find out that his emotions surge to
the top. I believe that a legitimate understanding of what is happening

here can preserve the grand union between emotion and will.

Without the will, marriage is a mockery; without emotion, it is a drudgery. You need both.

We like the side dealing with emotion, not the will. I have now been married more than thirty years. I often look back at the time when I was on the other side of the marital line and remember how I thought about marriage then. One particular conversation stands out. A year before I was married, I was sitting in a Christian education class when the professor quite dramatically started to philosophize about life. Commenting on the home, he said, "I want you students to know that love is hard work."

I leaned over to my classmate and whispered, "I wouldn't want to be married to anybody who goes around telling everybody how hard it is to love me."

He said, "I agree with you. Why don't you ask him about it?" Like a fool, I did.

I stood up and said, "Excuse me, sir . . . I am not quite comfortable with your categorization of love as 'hard work.'"

The professor stared at me, evidently not taking too kindly to my challenge, and demanded, "Zacharias, are you married?"

When I responded, "No, sir," he said, "Then why don't you just be quiet and sit down? You don't have a clue what you are talking about." I sat down.

One year later I was married. After being married all these years, I can unblushingly say, he was right. Love *is* hard work. I would carry it one step further. It is the hardest work I know of, work from which you are never entitled to take a vacation. You take on burdens and cares. You inherit problems. You have to feel beyond yourself. You have to think of things other than yourself. Your responsibilities are now multiplied, and you are trusted with greater commitments.

You see, the easiest part of our marriage was the wedding ceremony. I remember arriving at the church early. I could hardly wait. As the church filled with guests and the appropriate music was played for the ceremony to begin, I turned to see my bride enter the sanctuary. No, I did not think of all the weddings I had gate-crashed or of all the ceremonies I had witnessed. This was not someone else's wedding; this was a special moment for us. It was one of the most ecstatic feelings the human heart could ever endure. There is no word in the English dictionary to describe it except the word *Wow!* It was the crystallization of my every romantic dream. That which was once far off was now near. That which I longed for was now in hand.

As Margie came up the aisle to join me at the front of the church, my heart was in a flutter. So much so that when the minister told me in old English to "salute the bride," out of sheer nervousness I was on the verge of literally saluting her. There is nothing so magnificent as a beautiful, blushing bride behind a veil that cannot hide the radiant glow of a dream coming true. If the flutter of a heart were all that one needs to fly, the groom would soar to celestial heights. No! The groom does not need to soar at that moment, for God Himself comes near and says, *This is My precious gift to you. Receive it with reverence and guard it with diligence.*

The ceremony was followed by the reception. What a wonderful way to celebrate with friends. At the end of the reception we drove to the honeymoon capital of North America – Niagara Falls – where we stayed for the night at Michael's Inn. (Thankfully, Michael wasn't.) From there it was on to Cape Cod, Massachusetts. I remember carrying her over the threshold. My heart was as full as I had hoped it would be. I had an overwhelming sense of gallantry as I carried her into the room.

At about two o'clock in the morning, Margie got up. I thought, *Surely the honeymoon couldn't be over already . . . where is she going?* So I asked, "Where are you going, honey?" She answered, "I'm going to get a glass of water." I said, "Stay right here, I'll get it for you." That was May 6, 1972. I was thrilled to get up at two o'clock in the morning and get her a glass of water. My! What sacrifice!

But five years go by. Someone has wryly quipped, "Sacrifice in America is when the electric blanket doesn't work." So one night I find myself comfortably tucked in bed, and about two or three o'clock, I hear the rustle of the sheets. She's getting up again, and the temptation is to pull the covers over my face and cease to hear anything at that moment – for at least one reason. She looked different. You see, on May 6, 1972, she looked grand. Absolutely grand! But five years later, she had some funny things in her hair at night that generally prompted one question, "What stations are you able to get under that influence?" I have been chided for that remark many times so I should add that she no longer wears them. Times have changed. But I do recall that sight. Somehow the first word that leaped into my mind was not the word *Wow!* But I still do the right thing, because the tug of love is a commitment stronger than merely the flutter of the heart.

Chivalry in love has nothing to do with the sweetness of the appearance. It has everything to do with the tenderness of a heart determined to serve. That is the first hard lesson to learn. You do not act under the impetus of charm but out of a commitment to make someone's life the joy you want it to be. In the early days of marriage, joy precedes the act. Tragically, as the years go by joy can be severed from the act until finally, the act itself is no more. This ought not to be. Over time it is the companionship that brings joy, and service is the natural outworking of the joy of commitment. Failure to act kills it.

William Doherty begins his excellent book *Take Back Your Marriage* with a powerful illustration. His office is located in St. Paul, Minnesota, not far from the farthest point north on the Mississippi River. He describes the river's formidable but silent current that drives its waters southward. "Everything on the water that is not powered by wind, gasoline, or human muscle" heads south. Then he adds these words: "I have thought that getting married is like launching a canoe into the Mississippi at St. Paul. If you don't paddle, you go south. No matter how much you love each other, no matter how full of hope and promise and good intentions, if you stay on the Mississippi without a good deal of paddling – occasional paddling is not enough – you end up in New Orleans. Which is a problem if you want to stay north."[1]

But this kind of commitment does not come easily. Only if it is taken seriously does it become a sheer delight of the heart. I will also add that this kind of commitment is not seen much in the times in which we live. The reason we have a crisis in our gender relationships is not that we are culturally indoctrinated but that we would rather be served than serve. We would rather be the head than the feet. The Christian faith stands unique in pointing out that the Son of Man came to seek and to save that which was lost. The Son of Man came to serve. This means that the service He gave to humanity was given even when we least merited that sacrifice. There is a joy in service that transcends emotional temporariness.

A Realistic Picture

An act, especially of such magnitude as marriage, must be thoughtfully considered before it becomes an act. Impulsive acts die impulsive deaths. This works both ways, in honoring that which is right and in resisting that which is wrong. Always make the decision before the emotion stirs you into wrongheaded commitments. We refer to people as impulse buyers. That is not a good way to buy. Step back, measure the value of what you are getting, and then buy it. This applies a thousandfold more in marriage. Don't be deceived by the flutter of the heart. Love is a commitment that will be tested in the most vulnerable areas of spirituality, a commitment that will force you to make some very difficult choices. It is a commitment that demands that you deal with your lust, your greed, your pride, your power, your desire to control, your temper, your patience, and every area of temptation that the Bible so clearly talks about. It demands the quality of commitment that Jesus demonstrates in His relationship to us.

Jesus said that greater love has no man than to lay down his life for his friend. But it is probably more difficult to *live* a life of continual dying to oneself than to die in one moment. Marriage is hard work, and that's why, when you come to that pivotal moment of decision, my suggestion is that you seek the advice of somebody you love and respect. Don't make such a decision on your own just because you have romantic feelings. Seek out the wisdom of your minister, the wisdom of your parents, and the wisdom of friends, and realize that romance has to be transcended by a strong will and a degree of commitment to you and by you. The important thing to bear in mind is that you must face your willingness to die to yourself before you choose to walk down the aisle. Is this person the one for whom you are willing to die daily? Is this person to whom you say, "I do" also the one for whom you are willing to say, "No, I don't" to everybody else? Be assured that marriage will cost you everything.

I recall a young couple who came to me for premarital counseling. They looked so much in love and cherished each other. But as I administered a premarital test to see where their expectations and hopes matched or differed, something very startling emerged. They disclosed to me that the young man had tragically contracted a deadly disease some time back, a disease that would also make intimacy precarious. Only in his twenties, he was facing death within two to three years. As we talked, they were obviously struggling with whether it was the right thing to be married or whether they should just let this dream die. Their love was deep, and they were willing to face even a short wedded life to have the delight of those few years. Many asked them to think it through carefully.

My counsel to them was simply this: Think it over, because the person you are now and the person you will be when you have to say your final parting will not be the same. You will have to change and work at sacrificial expressions in such a way that it will not be just your names that will change but your very being. Each of you will have a part of the other in your emotions and in your thinking so that you change for the sake of the other. Can you face the aloneness when he is gone and then find it possible to love another with a part of this person ever in your soul? Will you want to go through it all over again? Think about it, because you will be giving huge portions of yourself over a short period.

I could not fight off the tears when I heard their decision, although their reasoning was sound. They both knew that to marry would entail an emotional component that would put them on the edge, right from the beginning. When the time came for him to depart, her life would also have been spent emotionally, though she would still be young. Recognizing the emotional cost of saying yes, they chose the path of saying no to conserve the power of her youth and save it for someone else who in the long run would merit that total investment of her life. They chose to give up their dream of marriage but remained very close friends.

To many of us this story may seem sad, but it is the lesson of the will. If you are to learn to control the will, you must harness it early in any battle. Lines must be drawn not at the level of acting but at the level of thinking. Lines must be drawn not at the level of doing but at the level of desiring. Lines must be drawn not at the level of contact but at the level of sight. Lines must be drawn knowing that marriage is not just a condition of being but a condition of becoming. The two become one, but the becoming is both a moment and a process.

Steadying the Will

How do you harness the will? First, by recognizing that dying to yourself is an act of the will. You must choose to lay down your life in the best sense of the term. You surrender your will to the will of God by an act of commitment and in the power of the indwelling of the Holy Spirit of God. That is the indispensable beginning. No one likes to begin life with a funeral. But in a sense, that is where marriage begins. You choose to die to yourself and to bring to life a new affection.

The famed Scottish preacher Thomas Chalmers once preached an unforgettable sermon titled "The Expulsive Power of a New Affection." While his theme was conversion, the implications are similar for marital commitment. An affection of such force takes charge that it expels other affections that are inimical to this one. That is the first step — dying to yourself.

There is no greater illustration of marriage and of the appropriate action to take when it is in trouble than the story of the prophet

Hosea. A pastor, Hosea married a woman who sold herself into prostitution. Even the names of their three children illustrated the pain of this broken home. But the remarkable thing is that while Hosea's wife was still in her lifestyle of prostitution God commanded him to buy her back. Even more remarkable and difficult was the rest of God's command to Hosea: "Go, show your love to your wife again" (Hosea 3:1).

We see it here clearly. Love is a command, not just a feeling. Somehow, in the romantic world of music and theater we have made love to be what it is not. We have so mixed it with beauty and charm and sensuality and contact that we have robbed it of its higher call of cherishing and nurturing. Watch two young people in a passionate embrace – it may be love, but it may also be nothing more than passion. Watch two elderly people walking hand in hand with evident concern for each other, and you are closer to seeing love in that relationship than in the youthful embrace.

G. K. Chesterton said these powerful words: "They have invented a phrase, a phrase that is a black and white contradiction in two words – 'free love' – as if a lover ever had been, or ever could be, free. It is the nature of love to bind itself, and the institution of marriage merely paid the average man the compliment of taking him at his word."[2]

This brings into focus an element of the will. The will is that faculty which can only be tested when pain is as much a part of its choice as pleasure is. Let me state it another way. The will is that disposition of the mind that will choose a path and bind itself with love, even if pain is mixed with the choice. In the West, particularly, we have become so resistant to pain that at the slightest hint of it, we prepare to flee by some shortcut or some solution that masks the discomfort.

By His example, Jesus teaches us the opposite. Think back to the scene we find within the pages of the Gospels when Jesus was about to be tried and crucified. He struggled with the agony of being separated from His Father and of bearing the entire weight of human sin. None of us will ever know what that felt like, but we know what it is to bear a small portion of sin's weight and feel crushed by it.

During the days of my undergraduate studies in India, I remember an incident that to this day brings a negative response within me. We were in the midst of a class when the professor asked the student in front of me to answer a question. The student stood to his feet, presented his answer, and as he was about to sit down, the student next to me covertly slid the stool out from under him with his foot. I only had a fraction of a second to reach out and try to push the stool back into place so that the young man would not land on the floor with a terrible, possibly injurious jolt. But I couldn't do it fast enough and the student fell hard.

The professor had only seen my hand trying to reach the stool and assumed that I had pulled it out from under him. Without any discussion, he ordered me out of the class. I got as far as saying, "But sir ..." before he interrupted me and said, "I don't want any explanation for such a shameful act. Just get out of my class." The boy who had actually done it sat quietly and said nothing while both the boy who fell and the professor thought it was I who had done it. Others who had watched it all happen thought they had better stay out of it for fear of some reprisal. In short, I bore the wrong of another person and to this day am rankled by the memory.

That is a small, minute thing in the light of what I say to you. When Jesus took, by His own will, the guilt of the world upon Himself, knowing the agony of separation from the Father that would follow because the Father would have to treat Him as the guilty one, He cried out to His Father, "If it is Your will, take this cup away from Me" (Luke 22:42 NKJV). He did not want to taste the bitterness of human sin, the greatest consequence of which was separation from God the Father. But then He also cried, "Nevertheless not My will, but Yours, be done" (v. 42 NKJV).

I wonder what I would have done if a third student, in order to protect me, had stood up and taken the blame? I would have found it unfathomable, but an act for which I would have surrendered much in order to express my heartfelt gratitude. You see, the will is always in a dramatic clash with other wills, including our own wishes. Fear, self-protection, indifference – numerous emotions and concerns test the will and often lead us astray. At the moment my will is tested to do wrong, it must remember the price that was paid on my behalf by the One who took the punishment for my will. By that act, He invited me to die to my own will, having received the gift of being accepted by Him, which my will alone could not have made possible.

In exchange, I receive the will of God by which to live and find delight. Nothing brings harmony more than embracing the will of God. Nothing brings fragmentation more than turning away from the will of God. *Marriage is the harmony of God synchronizing two wills with the will of the Father.* When that happens, the heart resounds with the feeling, even though it involves sacrifice.

Marriages are broken when even one of the two wills breaks from the will of the Father. When that happens the heart is broken as well, even though there is a path that may seem to provide an easier way out. That is when God takes over. Unless I understand the Cross, I cannot understand why my commitment to what is right must take precedence over what I prefer. Your marriage, as your conversion, begins at the Cross. Only then does the resurrection follow.

When my younger brother was about seven years old, he contracted double pneumonia and typhoid fever. As each day came and went, his condition deteriorated and the doctors said there was little chance of him recovering. Our entire family moved out of our home to live with my aunt while my mom was living in the hospital with my brother.

I recall going to visit him in the hospital one evening. He was not expected to survive the night. He looked absolutely pathetic, shriveled to a bundle of bones. But something happened that night as we were to find out later. All of us, except my mother, left the hospital not expecting to see him again. But my mother spent the night by his bedside, reaching out and touching his face or stroking his head. As the night wore on, out of sheer exhaustion she fell asleep in her chair. Night after night she had stayed awake, yet on this night, his last night, she had run out of strength. Her head drooped and she fell asleep for a couple of hours – the very hours she was told he would die.

She awakened with a start to find him still alive. In fact, she felt a warmth to his body she had not felt before. As one day passed into another, he became stronger until he had fully recovered.

My mother told us often that she felt that when she had given all she had to give and could give no more, God had taken over and given her the sleep she so needed as He restored the ailing frame of her son. This, to me, is a remarkable expression of will and hope. The rest of the family was comfortably asleep at home. The one whose heart was most entwined with his young life, by sheer sacrifice and self-denial, worked for his well-being until she could do nothing else but stay close, and that's when God took over.

When your will is committed to God, He carries you when all else seems spent, to rescue what you had invested by your dedication.

A few days ago, while writing this chapter in a small Asian city, I took an early morning walk and saw two workmen who were dismantling a cement block wall, taking great care to keep the blocks intact for another structure they were building. What a metaphor this is for the home! When two lives meet, they are like two distinct walls. Each has to start by dismantling his or her wall one brick at a time, and then those bricks are taken intact and with other materials used to build a structure with a roof that brings them together at the top. That is the new home. Two wills are as two walls. Rightly dismantled and rebuilt they provide the strength for a new union of two lives.

The playwright Thornton Wilder said it well: "I didn't marry you because you were perfect. I didn't even marry you because I loved you. I married you because you gave me a promise. That promise made up for your faults. And the promise I gave you made up for mine. Two imperfect people got married and it was the promise that made the marriage. And when our children were growing up, it wasn't a house that protected them; and it wasn't our love that protected them – it was that promise."[3]

NB REFERENCES NOT SUPPLIED

How Not To Pray

Jeff Lucas

Just a few pages of this new book from Jeff Lucas
is enough to demonstrate that this is more than
just another book about prayer. In his fresh,
inimitable style, Jeff unpacks the Lord's Prayer in
reverse — warning us about how not to approach
prayer and showing us how it should be done.

Spring Harvest Publishing Division
and Authentic Lifestyle
£7.99
PB / 1 8507.8452 3

£2 OFF
£5.99 with voucher

Jeff Lucas

how not to pray

A fresh look at prayer

Copyright © Jeff Lucas

First published 2003 by Spring Harvest Publishing Division
and Authentic Lifestyle
Authentic Lifestyle is an imprint of Authentic Media
PO Box 300, Carlisle, Cumbria CA3 0QS
and PO Box 1047, Waynesboro, GA 30830-2047, USA

Believe that prayer is just about you

'Hallowed is your name... Your kingdom come, your will
be done, on earth, as it is in heaven...'

*'We have de-clawed the Lion of Judah and made him a house cat for a
pale priest.'*

— *Dorothy L. Sayers*

Beware low flying cornflakes...

I am sad to confess that Kay has banned me from watching certain
Christian television programmes. It would be churlish to mention
which, but this viewing prohibition has been so ordered because she
is weary of the sight of breakfast cereal dripping down the front of
the television set. Why is it that some of my hottest moments of
boiling rage centre around these anonymous programmes? Yes, I'm
irritated by the occasionally facile, 'Jesus wants me for a Barbie doll'
philosophy that seems inherent in this stuff, and I feel pastorally
aggrieved (what a high sounding description for my anger!) when I
hear preachers take a slick approach to suffering and hand out slogans
rather than Scripture. But I think that my frustration is mainly
provoked by the message that seems to be pumped out with cereal-
wasting regularity: that the Gospel is all about *me* getting *my* dreams
fulfilled, and using Jesus for that purpose.

Jesus becomes Santa with a cross. The idea that I might be called to lose my life[1], of signing up to make his kingdom my first priority, seems lost. This kind of approach to Christianity, with its easy formulas and slogans, trivialises the sublime, and reduces the Lord into a cosmic vending machine, urgently plied with intercessory tokens when you spot that new car you'd like. Worst still is the notion that if you're not rich, or grinningly healthy, then somehow you're spiritually blighted – another slap in the face for the vast majority of the world who won't eat today. Now, not only are their stomachs empty, but their hearts are second-rate too, cursed as they are with a poverty of faith – or so the absurd notion goes. Vomit-inducing stuff.

Pray: not a mechanistic formula for *me*

I admit to being nervous of the 'Seven laws for blessing in your life' approach, simply because it is so impersonal, and I don't believe any relationship – including one with God – can be reduced to laws and abstract principles. There is no real intimacy, no foundation of love and laughter; just a process towards a result, a means to an end. It centres on the gift rather than the Giver, and treats God like a heavenly supermarket check-out operator.

But as we hear Jesus begin to talk about God's Name being hallowed, and his kingdom and his will breaking out in the earth, we discover that, when it comes to requests, we do find ourselves second in line.

No neutral spirituality

We are scarcely a sentence into the model prayer of Jesus, and we immediately bump into the rule, reign and authority of God. We have barely tiptoed into his presence, and suddenly we have to acknowledge the reality of a moral and spiritual power that is beyond ourselves. There is a popular spirituality that is available today – perhaps it's always been available – that comforts us, helps us to realise our dreams or to discover our cosmic significance, but that makes absolutely no demands upon us. It only brings solace; no sacrifice is

---

1 Matthew 10:39

involved. It involves us finding the 'god' of our choosing, one that we ultimately can make in our own image. This god is superficially lovely rather than intrinsically loving, in that it will never challenge our selfishness, hedonism or greed. But Jesus refuses to allow us to make him into our good luck charm, a divine rabbit's foot or any other kind of talisman.

If we will come to him, we will come as those willing to see his rule and order as the very first priority in our lives. But let's remember, if that sounds a little too harsh and austere, as if there is a cold control freak at the heart of the universe, that God brings order *because* he loves. What kind of loving father would sit silently in the face of hellish chaos breaking out in the lives of his children, without wanting to restore the order and peace that his rule can bring? We quickly collide with the truth of his kingdom reign, yet not the rod of iron gripped in the fist of a dictator, but the storm-calming rule of peace ushered in by the greatest Father there has ever been. God's kingdom rule is good – the best. To live under it is liberation and joy – if that is not the case, then how can we really pray sincerely that others will come under it? What prisoner would hope that others would get to experience the damp, near-starvation of the cell, and torture at the hands of his guards? He would be mad so to pray! No, the good rule of the Good God is breathtakingly wonderful. As we taste that, we can hope and pray that others will find it too.

The priority of his Name: let it be hallowed

Talk of names being 'hallowed' is foreign to our ears; indeed, our most likely familiarity with something being hallowed is probably *Hallowe'en*, the eve of All Saints' day of old. God's Name *is* holy, and won't become more holy because of our prayers. Rather, in asking that God's Name should be *hallowed*, we are asking that his Name might be seen as worthy of respect and honour – a lofty prayer indeed in a culture that has demoted the Name of Jesus Christ to the level of the swearword. In ancient times much importance was invested into a name – indeed the Name of God was so revered that we really don't know how to pronounce *Yahweh* properly today. A person's name was synonymous with their reputation and character: to defame someone's name was serious indeed.

It goes without saying – yet we must own the tragedy of it – that God's Name has been consistently misrepresented, maligned and smeared – and, though it gives me no pleasure to confess it, this smearing has often been because of our foolishness. As a result of our poor advocacy, he has been found guilty without a trial. He has been dismissed as irrelevant because we, the church who profess his Name, have so often disguised him as tedious – mainly because we have been so unappealing. This was no small feat for us and our churchly ancestors – taking the most brilliant, luminous personality in the history of the universe, dulling and dumbing him down. But, alas, we have done it, and done it all too effectively.

Dorothy L. Sayers laments the damage done to the Name and the Person of Christ

> The people who crucified Jesus did not do so because he was a bore; quite the contrary. He was too dynamic to be safe. It has been left for later generations to muffle up that shattering personality, and surround him with an atmosphere of tedium. We have de-clawed the Lion of Judah and made him a house cat for a pale priest.

But all is not lost: we are those who are also privileged to say, 'Your Name be hallowed.' Perhaps this is the prayer of *alarm* that a child might feel if someone suggested that their parents were dishonourable. We pray all of this prayer as children to *Abba* Father, not just the introduction to the prayer.

When I was in secondary school, there was a particularly noxious chap who used to be acid-tongued with his insults and derision. In any war of words, his favourite tactical insult was 'Your mother is a prostitute'. He used the insult so frequently that one might conclude that half the school was the offspring of ladies of the night. As we might expect, that particular sneering accusation always signalled a black eye for him; he could say whatever he liked – but tarnish the honour of our mothers? Break out the bandages. You would have thought that he would have learned. He spent most of his schooldays looking like a badger.

I'm not too sure about those folks who go around tersely correcting everyone who blasphemes or misuses the Name of Jesus. It seems to me that the end result of the rebuke might not necessarily lead to any positive fruit – but I entirely acknowledge that there are times (perhaps), when we have earned the right and it might well be appropriate to protest when the Name of the One that we love is maligned and misused. But surely our prayer that the Name of God should be honoured goes deeper than concern about swearing. We are praying that the lost will discover the life that is only available 'in the Name'. When God's Name is defiled, the signpost that can lead the wandering home is defaced and vandalised.

This Name is the source of salvation, and we pray that the real truth will come out about it and the One who owns it. Notice that our prayer is immediately focused outward, towards a dark world. Why? Because God weeps for the emptiness of the wandering and longs that the signpost of his Name might be cleaned up. In a postmodern age of pluralism and relativism, we must hold on to the biblical insistence that life is only available in one Name. By it alone can those stranded in sin's blizzard come in from the cold.

Andrei Bitov is a Russian writer who describes the day he found that warm welcome In my twenty seventh year, while riding the Metro in Leningrad, I was overcome with a despair so great that life seemed to stop at once, pre-empting the future entirely, let alone any meaning. Suddenly, all by itself, a phrase appeared: without God life makes no sense. Repeating it in astonishment, I rode the phrase up like a moving staircase, got out of the Metro and walked into God's light.[2]

A brief excursion into a question?

Praying that is closeted away from the pressing needs of the world

---

2 David Friend, ed., *The Meaning of Life* (Boston: Little, Brown, 1991), p194

isn't worth a lot; mission is quickly at the heart of the praying that God smiles upon. Before we have said anything else much, we have been invited to look outward to a world that defames the Great Name. We have looked upward, to 'Our Father in the heavens' and then immediately we look outward at the lost world that is so loved of the Father.

Forgive the question but... whatever happened to evangelism? Yes, I know that over a million in the UK have been through Alpha, an unthinkable idea twenty years ago; but as I travel throughout Britain, I don't often hear Christians talking about great opportunities that they have had to share Jesus with someone. Have we lost the ability to reach out? Have we devolved the responsibility that we have for sharing about and introducing people to the Jesus who has so changed our lives to Alpha (which is undeniably a wonderful gift from God to our nation at this time)? We learn here that our church gatherings should be totally linked into the pulse of what is happening beyond her cloistered walls. Church was never designed to be an escape act, a trip to a spiritual Disneyland that enables us to forget the hurting, wounding world in which we all live.

Lynn Green painfully shared recently about a charismatic meeting that he attended just a few miles from Bethlehem, while the infamous siege raged on, in which a number of lives were lost. Palestinians – including a number of Christians – were being shelled by Israeli tanks. Just a few thousand yards away, Christians got together for another Holy Spirit top-up without any reference to the blood and tears that were being shed so close to where they met. Spirituality that turns its back on the world isn't worth any time or effort.

The priority of his kingdom and his will: let it come

We are blessed with the authority to say, 'Your kingdom come, your will be done', which are words often misunderstood to refer exclusively to the second coming of Christ, and our future in the eternal kingdom of God – the proverbial pie-in-the-sky-when-you-die thinking – though why anyone would equate the hereafter with a pastry crust is quite beyond me. The confusion is compounded further by Matthew's use of the term, 'kingdom of heaven' – which again causes us hastily to conclude that he is talking about something that will be totally *later*. In reality, Matthew's use of 'kingdom of heaven' is simply because he was writing to Jews and using the common Jewish terminology of the day. The other Gospels avoid this term because it would have been meaningless to the ears of Gentiles.

In short, I want us to see that *praying that the kingdom come* is about what's going on today and on Monday morning – *and* it's also about the ultimate future. One day the fullness, consummation and totality of God's kingdom reign will be found in the return of Christ, but, in the meantime, we are able to call for the kingdom of God to break out today through a thousand different apertures. A smile in the office, a moment of kindness at the school gate, a comment that brings light into darkness in the college corridor, the calling for a zebra crossing in that accident black spot – in these moments, as we call for righteousness – the right order of God – to prevail, so the kingdom relentlessly ripples outward...

Let's take a moment to explore the kingdom a little more – it's a neglected theme, but it's so core to our praying – and our understanding of where we fit in God's purposes.

Recovering the kingdom...

The 'kingdom' was the main teaching theme of the ministry of Jesus. The heartbeat of the Sermon on the Mount is found in the command that we 'Seek first the kingdom of God.'[3] Jesus' travelling preaching and teaching ministry had the kingdom as its core theme – he went about 'preaching the good news of the kingdom.'[4] Michael Green remarks 'the kingdom was Jesus' prime concern.' Matthew uses the term thirty-two times. So how come we haven't heard more about the kingdom from our pulpits? Dr I. Howard Marshall echoes this concern about kingdom silence when he points out that in the past sixteen years, he has only heard two sermons specifically devoted to the theme of the kingdom of God... despite the fact that New

3 Matthew 6:33
4 Matthew 4:23

Testament scholars all agree the kingdom of God was the central theme of Jesus' teaching. It is a tragedy that we have subdued the kingdom shout of Jesus – and have subdued it to the faintest whisper.

The kingdom: the arena of his reign and rule

The biblical words for kingdom are *malkuth* (Hebrew) and *basileia* (Greek). The meaning carried by these words is primarily that of 'rule' or 'reign' rather than 'realm'. In other words, when we speak of God's kingdom, we are thinking about the arena of his rule and command, rather than any kind of located geography. Perhaps that's why our minds struggle; we are familiar with the idea of a king or queen reigning over an area of land – their geographical *kingdom* – rather than thinking of a kingdom in terms of the area of their rule and influence.

The term 'kingdom of God' does not appear in the Old Testament directly, but the long-awaited kingship of God was the hope and theme song of the prophets. God was seen as king over Israel and also over the whole earth – but the Old Testament also speaks of a day when he shall *become* king.[5] That's a helpful illustration of the 'it's here, but there's more' truth of the kingdom. God is already king, but he will yet be king in greater fullness – in the fullness of time!

And then... the odd bloke in the wilderness shows up

John the Baptist, alarmingly noticeable with his odd fashion choices and his worrying habit of snacking on grasshoppers, suddenly came on the scene and lobbed a verbal wake-up call at his listeners. 'Repent, for the kingdom of heaven is at hand.'[6] He came in the line of the Old Testament prophets, standing on tiptoe, proclaiming that the kingdom was about to come among them – and so a radical response of repentance was required from those who listened to this oddest of preachers. John conducted much of his ministry in the desert, traditionally the place of restoration for Israel. The message was bubbling – something or somebody very, very big was about to step onto the stage of human history. And then he came.

---

5 Isaiah 24:23; 52:7; Zephaniah 3:15; Zechariah 14:9ff
6 Matthew 3:2

Jesus and the kingdom Jesus arrived preaching the same message as cousin John, but with the added phrase, a stick of dynamite for John's wake-up call: 'the time is fulfilled.'[7] John had spoken at the eleventh hour – but with Jesus, the clock struck midnight! In the synagogue, he says '*Today* this scripture is fulfilled...'[8] Already the messianic banquet had begun. It was a time for feasting not fasting, the bridegroom was here, and the new wine was flowing. The disciples had seen an age that the prophets and kings longed to see.[9] The new age was here![10] Wherever Jesus went the kingdom broke out, in all of his words and works. Demons were driven out, sure evidence of a clash of invisible kingdoms. The territory of the false king-pretender, Satan, was being pushed back as, like a relentless avalanche, the rule of Christ rolled out with a thunderous roar.

The kingdom – it's all about you, Jesus

The kingdom has never been about a distant monarch or impersonal rules and regulations – as we saw in the last chapter. Rather, the kingdom of God was present for people whenever Jesus was present. As he walked and worked, the kingdom came.[11] The religious leaders of the day made the same mistake that we are tempted to walk into; they were looking for other 'stuff' and signs to announce the kingdom's arrival, but failed to spot the King among them. We can do the same, as we get overenamoured with the signs of the kingdom; the gifts of the Holy Spirit, healing, deliverance – wonderful and vital though all these are – or when we reduce our Christianity into an impersonal moralism, a Christless Christianity that knows how to be good, but knows little of the touch and whisper of God.[12] There is no kingdom without the king of the kingdom being present through the Spirit of God!

---

7 Mark 1:15
8 Luke 4:21
9 Luke 10:23,24
10 Matthew 11:2-6; Luke 7:18-23
11 Luke 11:20
12 Luke 17:20 1

Kingdom RSVP

Unlike the warrior kingdoms of men, where kings' rules are extended through bombs and bullets, the kingdom of God comes as it is received. It is at hand – it is within the grasp of all who hear the proclamation, and there are many who today are 'not far from the kingdom.'[13] As we respond willingly to the invitation, we are invited to step into the banquet life now.

Nothing is more important than our response to the kingdom rule of God. It should be our first priority of business in life, item number one on every agenda.[14] As we humble ourselves, we become part of it.[15]

But what about the church?

The church is *not* the kingdom of God. This is not just a theological detail, but a vital fact – when we confuse the church with the kingdom we get the idea that God only works in the realm of the church, like a localised deity who lives on the church car park, to use an illustration I used earlier. Thus he is cut off from the real world, and only acts in the cloisters of the church – a tragic misunderstanding! As we've seen, the kingdom of God is the sphere of the dynamic rule and reign of God. But the church is the *primary agent* of the kingdom. God extends his kingdom in all kinds of ways; he will, at times, directly intervene in people's lives; he whispers and shouts through creation, but the main method that he has chosen to extend the kingdom is through a visible, working model of kingdom life: his church.

Sometimes the model works well – and sometimes it's a hideously damaged array of grinding, clashing cogs and wheels that is the worst possible advertisement for the Good King. So, as we live and announce that there is a new rule to live under, that we are now subjects of another Master, so we have the ability to draw others to kneel at the throne of love – or perhaps to run from it, if our demonstration is bad. In this way, the church holds the keys of the

---

13 Mark 12:34
14 Matthew 6:33
15 Matthew 18:1-4

kingdom[16] and carries the awesome responsibility of opening and shutting the kingdom to others. The breathtaking truth is that as you and I go about life, we are carriers of the kingdom – and represent it either well or badly. When the disciples travelled from town to town, those who encountered them came 'near to the kingdom of God.'[17] Again, this is more than theological musing. All of us – without exception – carry something called *influence*. The way that we use that in our day-to-day lives will affect the view of others, not only of us, but also of the kingdom that we represent. We can leave impressions that last a long, long time – even eternally, either for good or for evil.

We are not only influencing others in the formations of their opinions about us, which, let's face it, are not that important, but in their opinions about the effectiveness of the Great King. They will judge him as they look at us.

Just as Israel was called to be a 'light to the nations', so the church is designed to be the visible expression of what it means to live under a new rule – the reign and authority of God. When we become part of the kingdom, we discover a new community of fellow subjects; and so entrance into the kingdom means participation in the church.

That will be costly, because we, the church, are on the journey but we painfully know the truth that we have not arrived yet. We should therefore never be surprised at the imperfection of the church – just as we have not yet breasted the tape, neither has she. Just as the kingdom is both 'now' and 'not yet', so is the church. She belongs to two ages. She lives in the current age of sin and destruction, but she also belongs to the age to come – of better things ahead, so she is called to model this truth through humility, mercy and forgiveness.[18] It is the duty of the church to display a shop-window of the future; in an evil age of self-seeking, pride and animosity, she lives out the life and fellowship of the kingdom of God and the Age to Come. So 'kingdom living' is an essential part of the witness of the church – she is not just a *proclaiming* community, but in her lifestyle is a *demonstrating* community.

---

16 Matthew 16:19; 18:18
17 Luke 10:8-12
18 Matthew 7:1–5

Let your kingdom come: How will our prayers be answered?

As we draw this brief look at the kingdom to a close, we must ask this question. As we pray, 'Let your kingdom come' – how will that happen? The kingdom breaks out as the message of the gospel is clearly announced. The gospel of the kingdom – the wonderful news that through the death and resurrection of Jesus, the power of the enemy has been broken, and that we can experience freedom as we receive the message – this is the message of the church. We call people to come in repentance – the number one requirement for entering the kingdom – to the king himself, whose rule is open to anyone who lays down their rebellion. We call people, not just to a sinner's prayer, but to the handing over – the loss – of their whole lives in order to place those lives under new lordship.[19] And then we are called to demonstrate the power of the kingdom. Jesus operated through both proclamation – announcing the good news – and demonstration – healing the sick and casting out demons. The disciples carried out the same dual role of healing and deliverance; they too cast out demons and healed the sick.[20] Their power was delegated, yet they operated in the very same power that had worked through Jesus. So the conflict between the 'gates of hell' and the kingdom of God will continue through the ministry of the church in the same way as it was in the life of Jesus.

This demonstration will not only be in the supernatural: as we echo God's heart for social justice, we begin to express the values of the kingdom, as the poor, the oppressed and the downtrodden suddenly find themselves blessed in Jesus' new order of things.

We must hold unswervingly to this kingdom message. As it is preached and modelled across the earth, 'then the end shall come.'[21]

And all this means... what?

As we pray, 'Your kingdom come', we immediately bump into a few important realities. First, we realise what the church is actually for: contrary to our consumerist ideas, the church is not here for me at

19 Mark 8:35
20 Matthew 10:8; Luke 10:17
21 Matthew 24:14

all – it is here for the release of the kingdom. Our obsessions about whether we like the music/the colour they painted the church's kitchen/the preaching style/the type of tea bags we use fade into irrelevance. The church is not here to serve us or particularly please us. It is here to serve the king and his purposes. And then – our church programme and structure is not of the highest importance. The issue really is: what programme or structure will serve the purposes of the kingdom? We pray for a kingdom mentality towards change in the church.

Understanding the gospel of the kingdom will prevent us from being tempted simply to lock people up in church activity; we will want to release them to be part of those who fulfil their call to seek first the kingdom of God, in whatever sphere they find themselves. More about this in the next chapter.

The truth of the kingdom helps us avoid parochial praying for our church. Indeed, our primary prayer is not for the blessing of one or indeed all of the churches in the area, but rather that the *kingdom might come.* And understanding something of the clashes between the kingdoms of light and darkness gives us a focus for spiritual warfare.

The kingdom teaches us to be patient in prayer – and fellowship! We are already aware that we live with a tension of the already but not yet, and so we live knowing that the actual is not the ideal. We work with the actual but do not let go of the ideal: we are neither pessimists nor unrealists!

We do not look for the restructuring of society along a 'biblical model' as have some, because our kingdom is not of this world; but we do look to be 'salt and light' within society, so transforming our environment as the goodness of God's kingdom touches lives.[22] The kingdom becomes our priority. Let it come.

The church gets into trouble whenever it thinks it is in the church business rather than the kingdom business. In the church business people are concerned with church activities, religious behaviour and spiritual things. In the kingdom business, people are concerned with kingdom activities, all human behaviour and everything which God

---

22 Some of this material is adapted from Martin Scott's *'The Kingdom' – Equipped to Lead*

has made, visible and invisible. Church people think how to get
people into the church, kingdom people think about how to get the
church into the world. Church people worry that the world might
change the church, kingdom people work to see the church change
the world![23]

23 Howard Snyder, *Liberating the Church* (Wipf & Stock, 1996)

Finding Favour With The King

Tommy Tenney

Popular author of 'The God Chasers' Tommy Tenney returns with another empowering study into God's Word. Here, rich insights from the book of Esther point the way to a deeper experience of God's favour.

Bethany House Publishers
£6.99
PB / 0 7642.2871 4

£2 OFF
£4.99 with voucher

Also by the same author

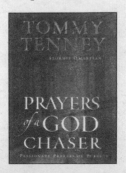

Copyright © 2003 Tommy Tenney

Published by Bethany House Publishers
11400 Hampshire Avenue South, Bloomington, Minnesota 55438

Learn To Worship With Your Enemy

But Keep Your Eyes on the King

There are times when you have no power to choose who sits across from you at the dinner table or at the desk of destiny. What do you do when someone who opposes you or seems to hate you without cause occupies an office or shares your workspace, sits behind you in class, or moves into the house next door?

You have the same choices Esther did the day she prepared a banquet for her husband, King Xerxes, and her new enemy, powerful Prime Minister Haman. *She could either focus on the problem or focus on the solution.*

She could darken her soul with views of her enemy's impressive power base and unquenchable hatred, or she could fill her vision with a view of the king. Which channel will you tune in to?

Esther's crucial moment came three days after she had asked Mordecai and the Jews of Susa to join her in a desperate fast. It was on this day that the queen arrayed herself with royal robes (in the king's colors, no doubt) and entered the throne room of the palace without invitation. Let's revisit the scene briefly.

The king of Persia had many powerful and resourceful enemies – even in his palace – so I am sure he picked only the best soldiers and the most alert guardians in the empire as his bodyguards. It is certain they saw Esther make her unlawful entry long before anyone else. In the tradition followed by executive security forces throughout human history, their lightning reflexes were programmed to "act first and gather the facts later."

The risk to Esther was very real. Those trained executioners were commanded to protect the sovereign at all cost. (Most likely Esther was recognized by these guards, but this executive order of instant death could be set aside only by direct and immediate intervention of the king.)

It is also likely they had already darted out from behind the king's throne with axes raised. They fully intended to intercept and strike down the unauthorized intruder whether she was a traitor disguised as the queen or the queen herself!

ONLY A ROYAL COMMAND COULD REVOKE HER DEATH SENTENCE

The window of safety could potentially be measured only in fleeting seconds of time. A commanding tone by the royal voice alone could revoke Esther's automatic death sentence and halt the raised battle – axes racing toward her at top speed.

> When [King Xerxes] saw Queen Esther standing there in the inner court, he welcomed her, holding out the gold scepter to her. So Esther approached and touched its tip. Then the king asked her, 'What do you want, Queen Esther? What is your request? I will give it to you, even if it is half the kingdom!'[1]

Esther didn't have to wait long. The moment King Xerxes looked up and saw her, she received favor because he "was pleased with her" and extended his gold scepter.[2] The relieved guards were probably flanking Esther when she approached the throne of the king and touched the tip of his scepter to formally accept his favor.

> And Esther replied, "If it please Your Majesty, *let the king and Haman come today to a banquet I have prepared for the king.*" The king turned to his attendants and said, "Tell Haman to come quickly to a banquet, as Esther has requested."[3]

What was Esther thinking?! The King had offered her up to half of his kingdom, and she chose to invite Haman home for dinner! Why would anyone in their right mind invite their worst enemy to a private banquet normally reserved for a royal spouse?

Desperate situations call for desperate measures. In her first introduction to the king, the initial "skirmish" for favor, Esther risked nothing, for she had nothing! She was a mere peasant given the opportunity to become queen. There's no potential downside to that. How can you be demoted from peasant status?

This time, however, the risk would be enormous. She risked demotion – banishment - death! Ask Vashti how steep the penalty could be!

Esther would risk *everything,* cash in all the favor she had accumulated, for one opportunity to save herself and her people.

What would her strategy be?

Most of us would have blurted out our request seconds after touching the king's scepter, and it is possible that in our haste we would have been denied. Satan often wants to divert us by convincing us to fight the *right battle* but on the *wrong battfield.* It can be a fatal exercise in futility for someone to fight for right from the wrong posture.

This brings up another lesson learned from the life of Esther: If your *enemy is the King's enemy, then your battle is the King's battle.* Esther had a plan of attack, and her weapon of choice was a specially prepared and beautifully served intimate gourmet meal. (How many men have been undone or finally won through the back door of the stomach?)

By Persian custom, men and women rarely banqueted together in public meetings. Under normal circumstances, the only woman who could share meals in private with the king was the queen. (Perhaps this was insurance against surreptitious assassination plots.) It was therefore very *unusual* for the queen to host a lavish banquet for the king outside of his normal environment – and hers. It was *unprecedented* for Haman to be included!

HAMAN UNKNOWINGLY STEPPED ONTO A DEADLY FIELD OF BATTLE

As strange as it was for her to invite another man to such a private and intimate setting, I believe it was well thought out. Haman's eyes were completely blind to the fact that he was actually stepping onto a very deadly field of battle, one for which he was poorly equipped. Battle-axes and swords wield little power on this battleground. I am reminded of the phrase 'The weapons of our warfare are not carnal."[4]

When your life and livelihood are placed at risk by the threats and plots of other people, or of Satan, will you stand to fight on their battlefield? Wouldn't it be better to move the struggle to another place where you hold the upper hand?

Esther coolly took a calculated risk and moved the battle for the destiny of the Jews out of Haman's familiar political court and into her more familiar territory of intimate favor. She had no control over Haman, but she *did* have *influence with the king.*

Sometimes we try to exert influence in the wrong arena. At one time Esther had no influence with the king or with his court. By God's design and through His behind-the-scenes intervention, she learned the secrets of proper preparation from the king's chamberlain and turned her one night with the king into a lifetime of favor.

Haman was a merciless creature driven by hatred, greed, and the pursuit of personal gain. He didn't care for man or beast. If anyone or anything stood in his way or hindered his progress up the ladder of success, they were ground into political mincemeat.

As a political predator, it is probable Harnan initially viewed the queen of Persia as an enemy. After all, she possessed private access to the king that he did not. But her latest move to include Haman in her royal invitation to a feast with Xerxes caused the prime minister's suspicions to instantly vanish under the glow of self-congratulation.

Suddenly Haman began to feel a strong desire to cultivate his newfound source of power and access through Esther. In the thirty seconds it took for the man to process the urgent command from the king's messenger, the queen's "stock" rose, and her "favor" became another source of fuel stoking the furnace of his all-consuming ego.

Ironically, this master schemer had no idea that Queen Esther was purposely moving this battle of destiny to her own home court where she would wield her tried and proven weapons of worship and favor.

In contemporary times, every sports addict knows the edge that homecourt advantage gives to a team. The championship often seems to go to the team playing on its own turf.

It is as if Esther intuitively knew: *"I must move this battle to a more intimate place."* It is one thing to face Haman in the argumentative atmosphere of a formal courtroom. But it is a total change of ambience to seek the king's favor at an intimate feast in his honor.

The posture of "worship" is your home-court advantage. Don't fight your personal Haman in the argumentative mode; lure him into an atmosphere of worship!

After entering unbidden into the inner sanctum, and with the palpable tension of her *second* life-and-death encounter behind her, later that day Esther was faced with a strategic choice. She would soon sit down for a meal with her king *and* with her enemy. How would she act? How could she use this opportunity to her advantage with the king and against her enemy?

She would return to her first and most important principle of battle for the king's favor: *Find out what the king likes.* It diddt matter what she preferred, nor did it matter at all what Haman most desired. Only one palate mattered at this lavish feast.

By the time this tournament of roses took place between Queen Esther and Prime Minister Haman, the noxious essence of "the farm' was long gone from the Jewish girl who had become queen.

The exiled peasant from Babylon was now the regal Esther, queen of the Persian empire. She had many years of exotic court life, royal banquets of state, and official public appearances behind her. She looked every part the queen! But the transformation was not complete.

ESTHER KNEW THE VALUE OF PREPARATION

Esther was not planning to offer her king some grilled cheese sandwich slapped on the stove and tossed on a plastic plate in haste. This woman knew firsthand the value of preparation. She had spent one year preparing for her first night with the king, and she was still reaping rewards for her diligence then. This time she spent three days preparing her heart and her life to enter his court unbidden.

The pressure was on! Can you imagine the response when Queen Esther went back that morning and called together her staff to say, "Hey, guys, we're about to pull an all-nighter." I can almost overhear her cooks secretly conspiring with the chefs in the king's palace: "Listen, Queen Esther tells us that you prepare a breast of hummingbird that is so good the king overeats every time you prepare it. He is coming *to our side!* The queen said that if you will share your secrets with us, then in rum we will … "

Everyone in the palace must have been shocked by the news that the great King Xerxes would leave his side of the palace for a private banquet with the queen and the prime minister. This was strictly outside of official state protocol. The palace was all abuzz.

When God's manifest presence steps over into our everyday realm and becomes tangible in the church or culture, we call it "revival." We know from history that society is all abuzz when the divine essence of God walks into the human realm.

THERE IS A HIGHER PROTOCOL OF HIS PRESENCE

This saga began with Esther's intuitive choice while in the throne room, choosing to seek the king's presence at a banquet rather than the immediate offer of answered petition from his hand. What choices are you making when you approach the Lord's throne in prayer and praise? When you enter in, do you struggle with an inner urgency to make your petitions, tell Him all of your problems, and describe all of the injustices done against you? (If you do, I don't blame you. But there *is* a better way, a higher protocol of His presence….)

Why settle for *half the kingdom when you can have the King?* If you have the King, the *whole kingdom is* at your disposal!

Esther had some very urgent petitions and legitimate complaints to share with Xerxes. But she chose to petition for more time in his presence *first* and to honor him with her undivided attention. She would talk about her problems later.

When the king initially asked Esther what she wanted and promised her up to half his kingdom, Esther said, "If it please Your Majesty, *let the king and Haman come today to a banquet I have prepared for the king.*"[5]

Esther teaches us to make our first petition a request for the IGng's presence. Move your needs, wants, and fears back to second place. Your first petition must be solely for Him. This is really the essence and central core of worship. God longs for you and me to seek His face, not merely the blessings in His hands. Again we learn a lesson from Esther: *Your first and most passionate petition should be for the King's presence.* "I just want You at a banquet of my worship!"

How wise Esther was: She knew that if she could get in the king's presence, then she would automatically gain access to his royal scepter with all of its power. She had gained that wisdom through personal application of all the secrets she learned from the king's chamberlain.

By this time Esther's standards of excellence – and in particular her knowledge of the king's desires, tastes, and chief delights – were far higher and more refined than they were the first night she spent in his presence. She had begun with the rudimentary instructions received from the king's chamberlain, and she had faithfully planted them in the soil of the king's heart. Now after spending several years as the king's wife and queen, her harvest from those early seeds of knowledge about the heart of Xerxes was virtually unequalled.

When Esther promised to prepare a banquet for her king, he knew that she *meant* it. His quick acceptance of this invitation implies impressive trust in whatever Esther's evening entailed. This private banquet would be a genuine feast for the eyes, the heart, the taste buds, and the stomach. He knew Queen Esther would provide him with no trite cheese-and-cracker snack or finger-food hors Xoeuvres.

If Haman had been foolish enough to ask, the king would have told him to expect every fine delicacy and rare wine known to the discerning and educated palates of royalty. No one knew how to please the king better than his regal queen, *and he knew it.*

Esther had done something right. When she invited Xerxes; to her banquet, there was *no hesitation.* Not only did he instantly accept, but he also abruptly dispatched a messenger ordering Haman to drop everything, suspend his schedule, cancel his appointments, and obey the queen's request.

ESTHER HAD A REPUTATION FOR EXTRAVAGANT EXCELLENCE

This kingly husband was not about to miss this opportunity to enjoy his queen's bounty. Esther had established a reputation for extravagant excellence with her king and husband!

What would happen if the church established a reputation for extravagant excellence with her King and Bridegroom? How many enemies, to their total consternation, would He command to attend our praise and worship banquets? Is God eager to suspend the schedules of His kingdom to attend our worship services, or does He rarely show up in His manifest glory? Have you established a reputation in heaven through your worship on earth?

If we asked God to come to our banquet of praise, would He give our enemies a glowing report about our banqueting fare? Or would He say, "You're invited, but you had better stop by the fast-food restaurant on the way. The table is usually bare, and what is there is usually cold or old – and the meal ends quickly. That's when the nagging petitions begin."

Esther held the banquet in the "court of the garden of the king's palace." Again, this was far removed from the formal royal court with its lofty Pillars, elaborate throne, and forbidding doors flanked by armed guards. This court was a more intimate enclosed area adjacent to the massive open garden, where years before the king had hosted the leaders of the city of Susa.

The decorations for the outer garden were beyond comprehension to the modern mind (and no one really knows how luxurious the hall of wine or this court of the garden was).[6] It is unlikely that anything we have today would even begin to match its splendor.[7]

Despite the impressive surroundings and the splendid feast before her, Esther could not afford to be distracted or impressed with unimportant things. Remember, *the palace is just a big empty house without the king.*

On this day of destiny, Esther would make no appeals based on the law. Nor would she craft masterful arguments based on ethics, political gain, or international strategy. She was *going for the heart,* using every tool and secret she possessed. It is at this first banquet and the subsequent one that followed it (on the next night) that we discover one of the most important lessons revealed in the life of Esther.

EAT WITH YOUR ENEMY

Saul was commanded to battle Arnaleles offipring with sword and arrow. David eliminated the band of Amalekites that attacked his family at Ziklag using spear and swords as well. But Esther would soon eliminate her Amalekite threat with the weapons of passionate preparation and indulgent worship.

The name of God isn't mentioned a single time in the book of Esther, nor is there a single prayer offered to heaven in this book. Yet God's working is interwoven within the layers of every single chapter of Esther's book. God working undercover in covert action can be just as powerful as God working openly in overt action.

We often would like God to simply barge in and take over, but He sometimes works behind the scenes to see His purposes come to pass. Nothing attracts God's presence and His intervening power like focused and single-minded worship. The problem is that most of us have a genuine focus problem when it comes to worship. We want to cling to our problems and the past with one hand while offering God a miniature handful of measured worship with the other.

Are you focused on your problems or on your Solution? So how do you worship with your enemy at the same table? You focus on the King of Kings instead of on your enemy.

EITHER BELIEVE GOD OR BELIEVE SATAN'S PRESS RELEASE ON YOUR PROBLEM

When you focus your attention on the wrong thing, you are actually worshiping it! You are allotting time and faith to it! Either believe God or believe Satan's press release on your problem.

Jesus constantly admonishes us to believe God and act on His Word. He said, in essence, "The lily takes no thought about what it will wear... It doesn't worry about how this is going to happen or how that is going to happen. All it does is lift up its head, knowing that God is going to take care of it."[8]

Jesus warned us not to worry! Worry is not worship! Some people worry on their knees and call it prayer. Others have mastered the art of worrying with their hands in the air, calling it worship. Worship is not worry! Worry always glorifies the problem while minimizing the value, power, and potential of the Solution. Magnifying God minimizes the problem![9]

Even if for isolated moments of time you could ignore the fact that the enemy is at the same table, you will still have limited results if you do not know how to worship Him with single-minded focus.

It's one thing to view an enemy across a battlefield, but it is much more difficult when your enemy is so close that the death of a dream appears to be around the corner. Worship becomes difficult for many when they know that if something doesdt happen to their finances in the next month, their child won't graduate from college or their car will be repossessed. It is harder to worship with the diagnosis of cancer in your pocket than when a bonus check fills that space. But worship is never more important than when the enemy launches a plot to destroy your destiny! Learn to *worship with the enemy at your table!*

We know the enemy is at the table when we must fight our way through just to pray or praise God. It is a good thing to plan your days and allot your time for maximum effectiveness. It is important for us to be good stewards over our finances. Yet worship remains our most important ministry and spiritual weapon on any given day. In fact, you've never really worshiped until you have worshiped with your enemy at the same table.

DON'T GET DISTRACTED WHEN SATAN CRASHES YOUR PARTY

When things get difficult and the enemy shows up without welcome to crash your party with God, dodt get distracted. Above all, don't allow this distracting problem to derail your worship and move you onto its own unfair battlefield with the prideful thought, *Let* **me** *get in there and fight this fight.*

1 dodt remember God saying that we were greater than our enemies, but I do seem to remember that He said, "Greater is he that is in you, than he that is in the world."[10] Deliverance and provision arrive when we become so focused on Him that we can ignore our sworn enemy and worship our sovereign King! Even with a bad prognosis in hand!

Always remember that *the King is more important than your enemy* or your problem. If you have the heart of the King, then your enemies become His enemies and your problems become footstools for the Divine Solution.

Don't allow yourself to become distracted or driven by your problem. Esther could have allowed her enemy to hurry the process or drive her to misuse her legal status as queen. She could have made a strategic and tactical mistake by arguing in the formal courtroom.

CONDUCT YOUR FIGHT FROM THE POSTURE OF LOVE

Instead, Esther transferred the battle to a familiar battlefield where she could make the best use of her proven resources. She knew how to win the heart of a king. She didn't barge into the royal court waving her queen's tiara and try to take upon herself the role of a lawyer or advocate. She said, "That isdt my strength. I love the king, and that is my strength. If *from the posture of love I* explain my plight and describe the plot of the enemy, my assault will be more powerful. ..."

> So the king and Haman went to Esther's banquet. And while they were drinking wine, the king said to Esther, "Now tell me what you really want."[11]

Esther was totally focused on Xerxes throughout the banquet. She knew beyond any doubt that Haman himself had planned the systematic murder of every Jewish adult and child in the Persian empire. Yet she was able to focus so closely on the presence of the king that Haman's grinning visage at the same table didn't bother or distract her in the least. *Ignore the enemy — worship the King!*

Ironically, Haman had no clue that this courageous Jewish woman was cleverly arranging his demise at that moment — at that table! This gives a new depth of meaning to the psalmist's prophetic declaration:

You prepare a table before me in the presence of my enemies.[12]

If you learn to worship while the enemy sits across from you at the same table; if you can learn to pay such dose attention to the King that you forget about the enemy staring you in the face ...

Then you win.

There is no substitute for the King's favor.

Notes – Chapter 9
1. Esther 5:2-3 NLT.
2. The *New American Standard Version* says Queen Esther "obtained favor in his sight," and the *New International Version of the Bible* says King Xerxes "was pleased" with Esther.
3.   Esther 5:4-5 NLT, emphasis mine.
4.   2 Corinthians 10:4.
5.   Esther 5:4 NLT, emphasis mine.
6.   There is a detailed description of the royal garden in Esther 1:5-7 (NLT):

"When it was all over, the king gave a special banquet for all the palace servants and officials — from the greatest to the least. It lasted for seven days and was held at Susa in the courtyard of the palace garden. The courtyard was decorated with beautifully woven white and blue linen hangings, fastened by purple ribbons to silver rings embedded in marble pillars. Gold and silver couches stood on a mosaic pavement of porphyry, marble, mother-of-pearl, and other costly stones. Drinks were served in gold goblets of many designs, and there was an abundance of royal wine, just as the king had commanded."

7. The splendor of Saddam Flusseids palaces revealed during the Iraqi war near this geographical region pale in comparison to how the ancient kings of Persia lived.

8. See Matthew 6:28-30.

9. I know we often speak of getting a bird's-eye view, but woulddt you prefer to get a God's-eye view of the things that concern you? If you get caught up in worship, your perspective changes!" (Tommy Tenney, *God's Eye View: Worshiping Your Way to a Higher Perspective* [Nashville: Thomas Nelson, 2002], 112.)

10. 1 John 4:4 KJV.

11. Esther 5:5-6 NLT, emphasis mine.

12. Psalm 23:5 NIV, emphasis mine.

Finding God In The Lord Of The Rings

Kurt Bruner & Jim Ware

Recently voted the British public's most popular book, *The Lord Of The Rings* is loaded with themes and values that resound with Christians today. This fascinating exploration of the spiritual content of the trilogy is ideal for all Tolkien fans.

Tyndale House Publishers
£4.99
PB / 0 8423.8555 X

£1 OFF
£3.99 with voucher

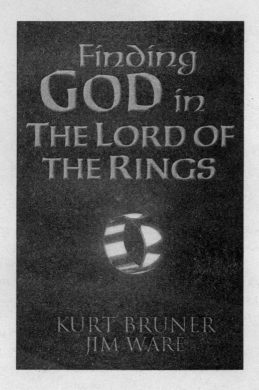

Finding GOD in THE LORD OF THE RINGS

KURT BRUNER
JIM WARE

Tyndale House Publishers, Inc.
Wheaton, Illinois 60189

Introduction

On a drizzly day in October 1999 I realized a life dream: to visit a little pub in a remote corner of Oxford called The Eagle and Child. I didn't want a drink. What I wanted was a photograph of me sitting where two of my literary heroes had routinely gathered half a century earlier.

In London for a *Focus on the Family Radio Theatre* recording session, I carved out a day and headed to Oxford in order to locate the pub. I expected it to be more obvious. (In the United States there would be an entire tourist attraction built around it.) By the looks of the place, you'd never know that it had been frequented by such famous writers as C. S. Lewis and J. R. R. Tolkien. I found no sign marking the table they had graced while critiquing one another's work. Apparently, it was no big deal to the present management – which was more interested in whether or not I was buying a drink. But it was quite a big deal to me. I was standing in the very pub where the writing group called The Inklings had met during the days when such classics as *The Chronicles of Narnia* and *The Lord of the Rings* were taking form! Some people visit Graceland to celebrate the memory of Elvis. I went to Oxford to celebrate two Christian men whose writings have impacted the faith and imaginations of millions.

J. R. R. Tolkien, who helped C. S. Lewis on his journey to Christian faith, wrote *The Lord of the Rings,* the epic fantasy that became the most popular book of the twentieth century.

It sold more than fifty million copies and inspired the film trilogy from New Line Cinema. People of all faiths have enjoyed the adventures of Frodo, Sam, Gandalf, and others on a quest to save the Shire from impending doom – and with good reason. The craft and creativity behind this wonderful fantasy rank it among the greatest literary works of all time. But many Tolkien fans may not realize that it was a strong Christian faith that inspired and informed the writer's imagination. In fact, many hard-line believers have been hesitant to embrace a creative work that includes mythic figures, magic rings, and supernatural themes. This is unfortunate because the transcendent truths of Christianity bubble up throughout this story, baptizing our imaginations with realities better experienced than studied. Like the works of C. S. Lewis, Tolkien's myth and fantasy can open the heart's back door when the front door is locked. As he explained, "I believe that legends and myths are largely made of 'truth,' and indeed present aspects of it that can only be received in this mode."[1] The result has been that millions, many of whom reject formal religion, have encountered realities that flourish in the unexplored regions of Christian belief.

Fictional Realities

The *Lord of the Rings* adventure takes place in the fantastic world of Middle-earth, a land given birth and form in J. R. R. Tolkien's imagination. It is an ancient world thriving with men, elves, dwarves, and hobbits who live in relative harmony while enjoying the blessings of peace and prosperity. Like us, they know the joys and duties of life in any era: hard work, growing children, curious neighbors, and festive celebrations.

The hobbits and other inhabitants of Middle-earth have a rich heritage of songs, ballads, legends, and folklore that infuse otherwise mundane lives with meaning. Some of the songs tell the tale of an evil ruler named Sauron and his dark tower in the ancient land of Mordor. But there are more happy legends of noble warriors and the council of the wise who freed the world from darkness to establish a land of peace and goodness. Whether the stories are history or myth is little contemplated among the hobbits as they go about their busy routines. More recent stories have taken center stage and become bigger-than-life, such as how Bilbo Baggins obtained long life and great wealth. The friendly, simple hobbit had been part of a risk-filled adventure many years earlier, including the time he found a magic ring during his famous encounter with the despicable Gollum. His full story is told in another classic, *The Hobbit*.

One of the most charming aspects of Tolkien's mythic realm is that, though clearly fictional, it has the feel of a time and region that were once real, possibly long forgotten parts of our own ancient history. This is no accident. Its creator went to great lengths to shape a fantasy world that consistently reflects those realities that frame the story in which men of all ages have lived. As a Christian, Tolkien understood that our lives are part of a grand drama that both transcends and explains our experiences. The drama's narrative infuses meaning into scenes and events that would otherwise seem arbitrary and meaningless. Tolkien saw the adventure of our lives, like the adventure of his hobbits, as part of a story that began "once upon a time" and is moving toward its eventual "ever after."

Tolkien's elves, dwarves, hobbits, and other mythic personalities become real as we identify with their fears and failures, sorrows and successes. Their story is our story: a compelling picture of the epic drama playing out on the stage of time and eternity. So many aspects of Tolkien's world mirror the fabric of our own.

For example, the characters recognize that they are part of a story being told.

"What a tale we have been in, Mr. Frodo, haven't we?" reflects Sam after surviving one of many dangerous encounters. Throughout their adventure Frodo and Sam openly discuss the fact that they are in a story, recognizing that the scenes of life are not random or purposeless, but key events in the great drama in which we play a part. Their outlook reflects the Christian understanding of providence, that we are all part of a story being written by the creator of all that is.

Middle-earth is in its third age, so it is a world with history. Throughout the book, characters recite poems and songs that tell the tales of ancient past, acknowledging that there is a story behind their story. Careful to pass the stories from one generation to the next, they recognize that what has been gives meaning and context for what is.

Tolkien's fantasy world, like our real world, is one in which good seeks to protect and preserve while evil seeks to dominate and destroy. His characters know that behind the increasingly dark cloud of oppression lurks one who seeks vengeance for past humiliation. In several chilling scenes, the evil Sauron is described as displaying many diabolical characteristics that seem to reflect those of the biblical Satan.

The Lord of the Rings is a tale of redemption in which the main characters overcome cowardly self-preservation to model heroic self-sacrifice. Their bravery mirrors the greatest heroic rescue of all time, when Christ "humbled himself and became obedient to death – even death on a cross!" (Philippians 2:8).

These and other themes of Tolkien's fictional story reflect what we know to be the ultimate true story. In Tolkien's words, "The Gospels contain a fairy-story, or a story of a larger kind which embraces all the essence of fairy-stories. They contain many marvels, particularly artistic, beautiful, and moving: 'mythical' in their perfect, self-contained significance. . . . But this story has entered History and the primary world. . . . This story is supreme; and it is true. Art has been verified. God is the Lord, of angels, and of men – and of elves."[2] It is this understanding of reality that makes *The Lord of the Rings* one of the greatest fantasies of all time.

We wrote this book to help fans of *The Lord of the Rings* discover how the rich fabric of Tolkien's fantasy world enhances a Christian understanding of our real world. Each reflection begins with a scene or theme of the adventure that points to a truth or insight for our lives today. We are assuming that the reader is familiar with the entire trilogy, as the concepts explored are intended to enrich the experience of the full story, not replace it.

We do not claim to know the mind of J. R. R. Tolkien beyond what he chose to share with us through letters and other writings. It is unlikely that he had these or any other reflections in mind as he penned his epic. In fact, I would be surprised if he gave any thought at all to how the themes of his story might instruct twenty-first-century readers. *The Lord of the Rings* is not, as some have suggested, a covert allegory of the gospel. Tolkien clearly denied that idea. We must not turn this wonderful adventure into something it was never intended to be. I agree with Clyde Kilby, who said that "no real lover of Tolkien's fiction would want it turned into sermons, no matter how cleverly preached."[3] Tolkien was telling a story, not proclaiming a message. His Christian worldview pushed itself up of its own accord.

It is not our goal to declare Tolkien's intentions, but rather to explore the inference of his imagination, an imagination that could not help but reflect Christian themes. It's in this context that Tolkien described his fantasy as a fundamentally religious work growing out of his own faith journey.[4] As with any artistic effort, what Tolkien believed was part of him, and that belief became part of what he created.

With that disclaimer, I invite you to reflect upon the Christian themes found throughout *The Lord of the Rings.*

May the fantasy Tolkien created inspire us with the truths he believed.

Kurt Bruner

A Deep Yearning

The world was fair, the mountains tall
In Elder Days before the fall.

    (Gimli's song – Book II, Chapter 4)

There is a deep yearning among the Fellowship of the Ring, an unspoken longing for something long lost. None have known it in their lifetimes. Few can recite the tales of its splendor. But all desire its discovery and hope to play a part in its restoration.

Throughout their adventure, characters from Bilbo to Treebeard recite verses of what they sense is an epic tale being told, a tale in which their lives somehow play a part. Each song seems to be merely a fragment of a majestic symphony being written and conducted by an all-knowing composer. But, as the chorus of Gimli reveals, something is wrong. Part of the harmony isn't right, like a dissonant chord invading the sweet melody of life, refusing resolution.

Middle-earth is in its third age as the adventures of the Fellowship begin. There is considerable history to this world, as revealed in the legends of Elder Days. Elves, dwarves, men, and hobbits alike know that theirs is a story that predates the present scene, preserved and passed in tales of ancient lore. Gimli's chorus tells of life "before the fall" when the beloved homeland of his dwarf ancestors was full of splendor and light, not dark and foreboding as they find it now. Gimli's heart pines for glories long past when his people knew better days, before the fall of their blessed domain.

A yearning heart is fitting. The wise know that before time was counted a rebellion occurred that brought evil into their world and introduced discord to the music of life. This rebellion was the driving force behind the song of the Dark Lord now heard in the march of orcs and the movements of the Black Riders. Awakened by the diminished sounds of beauty, honor, and goodness stubbornly pushing their way through the noisy clatter of evil, the inhabitants of Middle-earth hope for the day when all will again be set right.

You and I, like Gimli and others of Tolkien's world, long for better days. We somehow know that our world is less than it was made to be. And we hope that it will one day be set right again. In short, we yearn for the goodness that was "before the fall."

Why do we find it so difficult to accept the world as it is? Are we merely discontent, or is something more profound at work in our hearts? C. S. Lewis believed that our desire for something better is a gift, a way of reminding us of what it is we lost and what it is we hope to regain. "Creatures are not born with desires unless satisfaction for those desires exists," Lewis explains. "A baby feels hunger: well, there is such a thing as food. A duckling wants to swim: well, there is such a thing as water. Men feel sexual desire: well, there is such a thing as sex. If I find in myself a desire which no experience in this world can satisfy, the most probable explanation is that I was made for another world."[5] What is the real thing our yearnings suggest? Put simply, it is goodness. We desire the kind of all-consuming goodness that we've never known but that once existed and will someday be restored.

We live in a broken world. Death, pain, sickness, and suffering were not part of life's original melody. These dissonant chords were first introduced when our race took the bait of temptation and fell from its former glory. Once upon a time, mankind was offered a choice. We could sing the good song of the great composer or follow the opposing melody of his enemy. We chose the latter. And when we rejected the good that God is, we embraced the bad that he isn't.

Evil entered Tolkien's world before the dawn of time. That story, told in the opening pages of *The Silmarillion,* sets the stage for choices later made by those who would inhabit Middle-earth. It starts with Ilúvatar, maker of all that would be. His first creations were Ainur, angelic beings described as "the offspring of his thought." To each Ainur, Ilúvatar assigned themes of music that would be sung for his honor and pleasure.

> *Then Ilúvatar said to them: "Of the theme that I have declared to you, I will now that ye make in harmony together a Great Music . . . ye shall show forth your powers in adorning this theme, each with his own thoughts and devices, if he will. But I will sit and hearken, and be glad that through you great beauty has been wakened into song."*[6]

The beauty of their music is that for which all creation yearns. It is the original chorus which "the morning stars sang together and all the angels shouted for joy" as revealed to a suffering Job (Job 38:7). It is the true melody, the "good" that once was. It is the world as it was intended before the birth of evil. The story continues:

> *But now Ilúvatar sat and hearkened, and for a great while it seemed good to him, for in the music there were no flaws. But as the theme progressed, it came into the heart of Melkor to interweave matters of his own imagining that were not in accord with the theme of Ilúvatar; for he sought therein to increase the power and glory of the part assigned to himself.*[7]

Sadly, the sound of Melkor's evil theme increased as some "began to attune their music to his rather than to the thought which they had at first." Seldom have more graceful words been penned to reflect a Christian understanding of Satan's revolt and its eventual impact upon God's creation. Tolkien's world, like ours, knows the dissonance of an opposing melody. It knows the insatiable appetite of a rebellion that seeks to destroy the good that should rightfully rule.

Tolkien saw our world as neither completely right nor completely wrong, but rather as a good that has been violated, a beauty marred. He realized that the only way we can understand that which occurs within time is to view it within the context of that which occurred before and beyond time.

Though our world is broken, there is good news. It will not always be so. The story of history, like that of Middleearth, is progressing toward eventual redemption. Even that which seeks to undermine good will one day play a part in its restoration. As Ilúvatar foretold,

> *And thou, Melkor, shalt see that no theme may be played that hath not its uttermost source in me, nor can any alter the music in my despite. For he that attempteth this shall prove but mine instrument in the devising of things more wonderful, which he himself hath not imagined.*[8]

And so Ilúvatar, after the pattern of the biblical Jehovah, produces a drama performed in the theater of time. Its story will become the visible expression of the Ainur's chorus, including the song of a simple hobbit and the discord of an evil rebel. And somehow, the former will resolve the latter.

Reflection

OUR HEARTS YEARN FOR THE GOOD THAT GOD IS.

Small Tale

> "I might find somewhere where I can finish my book. I have thought of a nice ending for it: *and he lived happily ever after to the end of his days.*"
>
> (Bilbo to Gandalf – Book I, Chapter 1)

It was time. Bilbo Baggins of Bag End needed to leave the Shire. But it wasn't his style to slip away unnoticed under cover of darkness. After all, Bilbo was famous in these parts. A quiet departure just wouldn't do. A party was the thing, a celebration of Bilbo's life on the eve of his disappearance. And what better occasion than his 111th birthday? So, invitations sent and accepted, Bilbo hosted the biggest gala ever seen among the simple folk of Hobbiton.

There was much to celebrate. After all, it was quite unusual for a hobbit to live such a long and healthy life as Bilbo Baggins had. For some mysterious reason, he hadn't seemed to age a day since turning fifty. Though time had left its unkind mark on everyone else, an unexplained youthful vigor had remained with Bilbo ever since his return to Hobbiton. Perhaps the adventure of his younger days had brought with it more than mere wealth.

His quest had certainly given Bilbo Baggins a wonderful story to tell, a story he had been writing in his book. Whether many would ever read the book was of little concern to Bilbo. He simply felt the need to put it down so that future generations could know what happened to and through him. Sent off on a grand adventure at the bidding of Gandalf the wizard, Bilbo had acquired a magic ring. Though he didn't understand all of its powers, he knew that the ring was of great significance. When worn, it made him invisible, a very useful trick when fighting giant spiders or freeing jailed warriors. And it would be useful again as Bilbo planned to vanish from the Shire in style. Which he does, literally. At the end of his speech thanking those in attendance and bidding them good-bye, Bilbo Baggins disappears. He slips the magic ring on his finger and simply vanishes. He quite enjoys the trick and the animated talk it inspires.

With the fun over and Gandalf present to advise and guide, Bilbo knows that the final pages of his chapter are being turned. After he entrusts the Baggins fortune and magic ring to the keeping of his young nephew Frodo, it's time to leave.

He looks forward to the time he might now have to complete his book, a tale that Bilbo hopes will go on "happily ever after to the end of his days." But there's no way to know. Past adventures have taught him that the scenes of his life are serving a much bigger story than his could ever express. And while Bilbo may be the star of his tale, he is not its author.

Once upon a time, we understood our lives to be part of a grand story being written by the divine author of history. But a dark yearning for autonomy and a nihilistic nudge from Nietzsche pushed us over the edge of sanity. God, the omniscient playwright, was declared dead. Now no one knows the plot to the epic drama in which we find ourselves, leaving us with competing small stories but no overarching narrative that frames and explains the seemingly random experiences of life.

Let's face it, we all wish we could write the scenes of our own stories. Like Bilbo Baggins, we want them to read "and he lived happily ever after to the end of his days." But deep down we know that we are not the authors of the events that shape our lives. Bilbo did not seek, and only reluctantly accepted, the invitation to adventure that launched his extraordinary tale of risk and reward. As Gandalf expressed to Bilbo in the closing conversation of *The Hobbit,* his quest had been orchestrated by another for a greater purpose.

> *Surely you don't disbelieve the prophecies, because you had a hand in bringing them about yourself? You don't really suppose, do you, that all your adventures and escapes were managed by mere luck, just for your sole benefit? You are a very fine person, Mr. Baggins, and I am very fond of you; but you are only quite a little fellow in a wide world after all!*

Bilbo's adventure was part of a much bigger story that began long before his first breath and would continue well beyond his last. This realization elevated rather than minimized the importance of his part. But this could only happen if Mr. Baggins was honest and humble enough to embrace an important truth: that the big part he played in his small story was only a small part in the big story.

"My tongue is the pen of a skillful writer," writes the psalmist in Psalm 45:1, beautifully expressing a reality Bilbo learned and we would do well to recover. Bilbo knew he was not the author but the instrument. The pen does not become arrogant or proud over what is written on the page. It is honored to have played any part at all in the creative act. It is when we struggle to take control and resist the author's intentions that we mar the story being told. Pride is not satisfied with anything less than the starring role. It grasps for more, seeking to write its own tale. But the humble heart has a very different view of life. It considers the warning "God resists the proud, but gives grace to the humble" (James 4:6, NKJV).

It heeds the admonition "Humble yourselves, therefore, under God's mighty hand. . . ."

And it reaps the benefits: ". . . that he may lift you up in due time" (1 Peter 5:6).

So, for hobbit and human alike, recognizing that our small stories serve a much larger purpose can turn ordinary details of the daily grind into scenes of an extraordinary adventure! And what better way for your "once upon a time" to discover its ultimate "happily ever after"?

Reflection

THE SCENES OF YOUR LIFE SERVE A STORY MUCH BIGGER THAN YOUR OWN.

The Call

"This ring! . . . How, how on earth did it come to me?"

(Frodo to Gandalf – Book I, Chapter 2)

It had happened in just this same way to his uncle Bilbo, Frodo reflected. Well, perhaps not *exactly* the same way; but the similarities were striking. He had heard the story many times from the old hobbit himself: Bilbo had been standing outside the round green door to his hobbit hole one fine morning, contentedly smoking a pipe and minding his own business, when along came Gandalf. The result? Staid, stolid, stay-at-home Bilbo had ended up doing unthinkable things, things that no sensible, respectable Baggins would ever have dreamed of doing. A Took, perhaps. But a Baggins? Never.

And now this same Gandalf was back at Bag End again. Sitting there before the fire in Frodo's study, puffing out smoke rings, watching him out of thin-slitted, heavylidded, bushy-browed eyes, waiting. Waiting for Frodo's answer.

Frodo fingered the Ring where it lay in his pocket on the end of its chain. It felt heavy, heavier than a small ring of gold had any right to be. Far heavier than it had felt just half an hour earlier. He stared into the fire's dying embers and shivered, thinking over everything Gandalf had just told him about this terrible ring. The One Ring. The Ring of Power. Long believed lost, now earnestly and desperately sought by its maker, the dreaded Dark Lord. The Ring that threatened to overpower everyone and everything, to change Middle-earth forever. The Ring that had somehow landed in Frodo's pocket.

There is only one way, he heard Gandalf saying again.

One way to save the Shire. One way to destroy the Ring before Sauron can seize it and use it for his own ends: Frodo must find Mount Orodruin in the dark land of Mordor and cast the cursed thing into the Cracks of Doom. And how was he – a simple hobbit of the Shire – supposed to do *that?*

Not that Frodo was a stay-at-home. He had often dreamed of traveling. He *wanted* to have adventures like old Uncle Bilbo. Like Bilbo, he had more of the Took than of the Baggins in him. That's why gossips in taverns had taken to calling both of them "cracked." Frodo was notoriously impractical. Images of pleasant, leisurely rambles and idyllic wanderings filled his mind at every idle moment. Many times he had pictured himself taking long, aimless journeys through endless woods, splashing across fabled rivers under the stars, conversing with elves.

But *this!* This was something else altogether. He was not made for perilous quests! He hadn't counted on taking his life in his hands and fleeing from danger to danger. Most of all, he hadn't planned on carrying the burden of the world in his waistcoat pocket. He wished now that he had never seen the horrid Ring! Why him? Why should he have been chosen to undertake such a task? When he had posed that question, he had received a most unsatisfactory reply from the inscrutable wizard: *You may be sure that it was not for any merit that others do not possess.*

"Well!" said Gandalf, looking up at last. "Have you decided what to do?"

Every adventure has a beginning. Unfortunately, that beginning isn't always pleasant. It might be more in the nature of a rude awakening. A prod, a sting, a shove. A bucket of cold water in the face. The thing you least expected to happen.

The words you never wanted to hear. That's how it is, more often than not, with those who find themselves on the adventure of following the living Christ.

> *As Jesus was walking beside the Sea of Galilee, he saw two brothers, Simon called Peter and his brother Andrew. They were casting a net into the lake, for they were fishermen. "Come, follow me," Jesus said, "and I will make you fishers of men." At once they left their nets and followed him.*
> *(Matthew 4:18-20)*

Fishers of *men?* They hadn't been expecting *that* when they rolled out of bed that morning, pulled rough, homespun tunics over their heads, and stumbled down to the lakeside to work on those perpetually torn and shredded nets. Fishing for fish, now that was something they knew. But fishing for men? What did it even mean? It was clearly out of their line of work.

> *As he walked along, he saw Levi son of Alphaeus sitting at the tax collector's booth. "Follow me," Jesus told him, and Levi got up and followed him.*
> *(Mark 2:14)*

It was like a bolt out of the blue, unanticipated and totally unpredictable. Imagine what must have been going through Levi's mind as he turned his head at those thunderous words: *Is he talking to somebody else around here?*

When Jesus reached the spot, he looked up and said to him, "Zacchaeus, come down immediately. I must stay at your house today." (Luke 19:5)

He had climbed a tree out of pure curiosity, just to watch the parade go by, and suddenly Zacchaeus found himself at the end of a pointing finger – an accusing finger, a forgiving finger, a defining, inescapable, Uncle Sam "I WANT YOU" finger. And down he came. (Lucky for him he didn't fall!)

Then, of course, there was Nathanael, the skeptic. He had been sitting under a fig tree, laughing in his beard – "Hah! A Messiah? From *Nazareth?* Give me a break!" – when suddenly he felt a little tap on the shoulder. "Here," said Jesus with a beckoning smile, "is a true Israelite, in whom there is nothing false." Nathanael probably did a double-take. "How do you know me?" he asked (John 1:46-48).

Rustic fishermen as ambassadors for the King of the Universe? A slimy, pocket-padding tax collector as an apostle for the gospel of righteousness? A cynic as a herald of the truth? Why them? One wonders whether these unlikely candidates for glory – as unlikely as a furry-footed halfling trudging determinedly and heroically down the road to Mordor – thought about the words of Moses, Gideon, and Jeremiah as they stood there confronting the Christ Who Lets No One off the Hook: "O LORD, please send someone else to do it!" (Exodus 4:13); "But LORD . . . how can I save Israel? My clan is the weakest in Manasseh, and I am the least in my family!" (Judges 6:15); "Ah, Sovereign LORD . . . I do not know how to speak; I am only a child" (Jeremiah 1:6).

In every case there was reluctance, resistance, protest. In every case the chosen one made a manful attempt to beg off. But in every case the ultimate response was the same: "They left their nets and followed him." "Levi got up and followed him." "He came down at once and welcomed him gladly." "Nathanael declared, 'Rabbi, you are the Son of God; you are the King of Israel.' " It says volumes about the irresistible power, the inescapable attraction, the captivating, compelling personality of the one who issued the call to adventure: "Come, follow me!" And so it was with Frodo. As he felt the weight of the Ring on the palm of his small hand, as he trembled inside, staring into the glowing embers and picturing the fabled fires of Orodruin, it dawned on him that, for all the danger, for all the terror, for all the unthinkable labor and pain it might involve, there simply was *no other choice.* And though he felt "very small, and very uprooted, and . . . desperate," he knew he had to go.

What about you? Have you decided what to do?

Reflection

THE CALL TO FOLLOW CHRIST IS A CALL TO ADVENTURE – INCONVENIENT, IMPERIOUS, AND IRRESISTIBLE.

Evil Intentions

> "But we must do something, soon.
> The Enemy is moving."
>
> (Gandalf to Frodo – Book I, Chapter 2)

Things had rarely been so good in the Shire. Many years had passed since the disappearance of Mr. Bilbo Baggins, an event that had achieved legendary stature among those living in the Shire village of Hobbiton. But life had returned to normal, and few gave much thought to the meaning of such strange happenings.

Bilbo's nephew Frodo had inherited the magic ring from his departing uncle. Warned years earlier by the wise Gandalf against its use, he knew of its mystical powers and mysterious dangers. But the Ring's mere presence created a forbidding sense of unwelcome destiny for Frodo Baggins. More recently, that sense included news that suggested trouble on the horizon. There were many signs: elves walking through the Shire and leaving their homeland for good, rumors of strange events beyond the peaceful border of the Shire, and refugee dwarves fleeing west and whispering of an enemy arising from the land of Mordor. Change was definitely in the wind, and not for the better.

But it was not until the arrival of Gandalf, who returned after years abroad, that Frodo learned the details. Trouble was indeed coming, and it was seeking Frodo. More precisely, it was seeking that which he held. As Gandalf explained, the Ring Bilbo had acquired and passed to Frodo was the one of which ancient songs and folklore told. It was the Ring of Doom, so potent that, if possessed, it would enable the dark powers of evil to rule the whole of Middle-earth. These dark powers had previously had little knowledge of or concern for hobbits. But they had followed the Ring's trail and knew it to be in the Shire in the keeping of Baggins. As Gandalf explained, the enemy was on the move, and the Ring-bearer, Frodo, was the target.

The true forces of evil in our world are rarely haphazard or indiscriminate. The occasional mad gunman notwithstanding, the history of mankind shows that the most destructive wickedness is devious and determined. Violent insanity is far less trouble than diabolical brilliance. While a violent lunatic may murder dozens, a calculating Adolf Hitler convinced ordinary people to systematically exterminate millions.

Evil has intention. It targeted Frodo Baggins as a means to an end. He possessed an object that the evil ruler Sauron wanted, an object that could give Sauron the power to enslave all others. His burning desire for revenge and consuming lust for domination drove Sauron to set very specific goals in pursuit of his ultimate objective. He did not order the destruction of all that lived in the Shire. He ordered the pursuit of Baggins, the bearer of the Ring through which he would enslave the Shire.

The Christian worldview is far from naïve or simplistic with regard to evil. It understands the existence and nature of an enemy set upon our enslavement and ultimate destruction.

Just as there is a person called Sauron who is part of a conspiracy invading the happy world of hobbits, there is a rebel called Lucifer whose calculating schemes invade the lives of men. We have been told of his history and intentions.

We know he was once a trusted servant in the heavenly realm.

> *You were in Eden, the garden of God; every precious stone adorned you. . . .*
> *Your settings and mountings were made of gold; on the day you were created*
> *they were prepared. You were anointed as a guardian cherub, for so I ordained*
> *you. You were on the holy mount of God; you walked among the fiery stones.*
> *You were blameless in your ways from the day you were created till wickedness*
> *was found in you. (Ezekiel 28:13-15)*

We know that he led a rebellion in hopes of assuming the throne of
his creator.

> *You said in your heart, "I will ascend to heaven; I will raise my throne above*
> *the stars of God; I will sit enthroned on the mount of assembly, on the utmost*
> *heights of the sacred mountain. I will ascend above the tops of the clouds; I will*
> *make myself like the Most High." (Isaiah 14:13-14)*

We know that he was defeated and exiled, cast out of heaven due to
insane pride.

> *I banished you from the mountain of God. I expelled you, O mighty guardian,*
> *from your place among the stones of fire. (Ezekiel 28:16, NLT)*

> *I saw Satan fall like lightning from heaven. (Luke 10:18)*

We know that he seeks revenge by enslaving and destroying God's
beloved children — and that, like Frodo, we cannot afford the luxury
of complacency.

> *Be self-controlled and alert. Your enemy the devil prowls around like a roaring*
> *lion looking for someone to devour. (1 Peter 5:8)*

> *Put on all of God's armor so that you will be able to stand firm against all*
> *strategies and tricks of the Devil. For we are not fighting against people made*

of flesh and blood, but against the evil rulers and authorities of the unseen world, against those mighty powers of darkness who rule this world, and against wicked spirits in the heavenly realms. (Ephesians 6:11-12, NLT)

Lucifer, the personal force behind the most destructive evil in our world, is very intentional about his plan for revenge and domination. We must therefore be on our guards and prepare ourselves to overcome obstacles that we will certainly face while on the great adventure of living by faith.

Reflection

EVIL IS NEITHER PASSIVE NOR COMPLACENT. IT IS PERSONAL, AND IT IS ACTIVELY DETERMINED TO DOMINATE OUR LIVES.

Notes

1. Humphrey Carpenter, The Letters of J. R. R. Tolkien (New York: Houghton Mifflin Company, 2000), 147.
2. J. R. R. Tolkien, The Tolkien Reader (New York: Ballantine Books, 1966), 88.
3. Clyde S. Kilby, Tolkien and The Silmarillion (Wheaton: Harold Shaw Publishers, 1976), 79.
4. Carpenter, Letters, 172.
5. C. S. Lewis, Mere Christianity (New York: Touchstone – Simon & Schuster, 1996), 121.
6. J. R. R. Tolkien, The Silmarillion (Boston: Houghton Mifflin Company, 1977), 15.
7. Ibid., 16.
8. Ibid., 17-18.

READ IT... LIVE IT...
vouchers

0-3102.5524-4

£6 OFF *voucher*

Rumours of Another World

Redeemable at all participating bookshops. Valid until 31st May 2004. This voucher can only be used as part payment for *Rumours of Another World* (HB) (0-3102.5524-4). Only one voucher can be used against each item purchased.

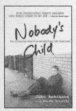

1-8542.4623-2

£2 OFF *voucher*

Nobody's Child

Redeemable at all participating bookshops. Valid until 31st May 2004. This voucher can only be used as part payment for *Nobody's Child* (1-8542.4623-2). Only one voucher can be used against each item purchased.

1-8602.4283-9

£2 OFF *voucher*

The Life: a Portrait of Jesus

Redeemable at all participating bookshops. Valid until 31st May 2004. This voucher can only be used as part payment for *The Life: a Portrait of Jesus* (HB) (1-8602.4283-9). Only one voucher can be used against each item purchased.

1-8410.1183-5

£2 OFF *voucher*

So You Think You're A NT Writer

Redeemable at all participating bookshops. Valid until 31st May 2004. This voucher can only be used as part payment for *So You Think You're a NT Writer* (PB) (1-8410.1183-5). Only one voucher can be used against each item purchased.

READ IT... LIVE IT...
vouchers

£2 OFF Heaven Bound

Redeemable at all participating bookshops. Valid until 31st May 2004. This voucher can only be used as part payment for *Heaven Bound* (HB) (1-8534.5267-X). Only one voucher can be used against each item purchased.

READ IT... LIVE IT...

1-8534.5267-X

£2 OFF Pure Joy

Redeemable at all participating bookshops. Valid until 31st May 2004. This voucher can only be used as part payment for *Pure Joy* (PB) (0-3408.6194-0). Only one voucher can be used against each item purchased.

READ IT... LIVE IT...

0-3408.6194-0

£2 OFF Power of a Praying Woman

Redeemable at all participating bookshops. Valid until 31st May 2004. This voucher can only be used as part payment for *Power of a Praying Woman* (PB) (0-7369.0855-2). Only one voucher can be used against each item purchased.

READ IT... LIVE IT...

0-7369.0855-2

£2 OFF God's Big Picture

Redeemable at all participating bookshops. Valid until 31st May 2004. This voucher can only be used as part payment for *God's Big Picture* (PB) (0-8511.1298-6). Only one voucher can be used against each item purchased.

READ IT... LIVE IT...

0-8511.1298-6

1-8429.1095-7

£2 OFF *Red Moon Rising*

Redeemable at all participating bookshops. Valid until 31st May 2004. This voucher can only be used as part payment for *Red Moon Rising* (1-8429.1095-7). Only one voucher can be used against each item purchased.

READ IT... LIVE IT...

0-7459.4821-9

£2 OFF *I Was Only Asking*

Redeemable at all participating bookshops. Valid until 31st May 2004. This voucher can only be used as part payment for *I Was Only Asking* (HB) (0-7459.4821-9). Only one voucher can be used against each item purchased.

READ IT... LIVE IT...

1-8507.8452-3

£2 OFF *How Not To Pray*

Redeemable at all participating bookshops. Valid until 31st May 2004. This voucher can only be used as part payment for *How Not To Pray* (PB) (1-8507.8452-3). Only one voucher can be used against each item purchased.

READ IT... LIVE IT...

1-8599.9786-4

£2 OFF *Oriel's Travels*

Redeemable at all participating bookshops. Valid until 31st May 2004. This voucher can only be used as part payment for *Oriel's Travels* (1-8599.9786-4). Only one voucher can be used against each item purchased.

READ IT... LIVE IT...

0-8423.8555-X

£1 OFF *Finding God In The Lord Of The Rings*

Redeemable at all participating bookshops. Valid until 31st May 2004. This voucher can only be used as part payment for *Finding God In The Lord Of The Rings* (PB) (0-8423.8555-X). Only one voucher can be used against each item purchased.

READ IT... LIVE IT...

READ IT... LIVE IT...

vouchers

0-8007.9321-8

£3 OFF

voucher

Blood Brothers
Expanded Edition

Redeemable at all participating bookshops. Valid until 31st May 2004. This voucher can only be used as part payment for *Blood Brothers* Expanded Edition (PB) (0-8007.9321-8). Only one voucher can be used against each item purchased.

READ IT...LIVE IT...

1-8531.1566-5

£2 OFF

voucher

Signs Of The Times

Redeemable at all participating bookshops. Valid until 31st May 2004. This voucher can only be used as part payment for *Signs Of The Times* (PB) (1-8531.1566-5). Only one voucher can be used against each item purchased.

READ IT...LIVE IT...

1-8579.2383-9

£3 OFF

voucher

Great Events In The
Story Of The Church

Redeemable at all participating bookshops. Valid until 31st May 2004. This voucher can only be used as part payment for *Great Events In The Story Of The Church* (1-8579.2383-9). Only one voucher can be used against each item purchased.

READ IT...LIVE IT...

0-7151.4935-0

£2 OFF

voucher

Travelling Well

Redeemable at all participating bookshops. Valid until 31st May 2004. This voucher can only be used as part payment for *Travelling Well* (0-7151.4935-0). Only one voucher can be used against each item purchased.

READ IT...LIVE IT...

READ IT... LIVE IT...

vouchers

0-8264.7274-5

£2 OFF *Pride And Perjury*

Redeemable at all participating bookshops. Valid until 31st May 2004. This voucher can only be used as part payment for *Pride And Perjury* (PB) (0-8264.7274-5). Only one voucher can be used against each item purchased.

voucher

0-2325.2516-1

£2 OFF *Eternal Seasons*

Redeemable at all participating bookshops. Valid until 31st May 2004. This voucher can only be used as part payment for *Eternal Seasons* (PB) (0-2325.2516-1). Only one voucher can be used against each item purchased.

voucher

1-8979.1353-2

£2 OFF *Luther's Rose*

Redeemable at all participating bookshops. Valid until 31st May 2004. This voucher can only be used as part payment for *Luther's Rose* (PB) (1-8979.1353-2.) Only one voucher can be used against each item purchased.

voucher

1-8400.3902-7

£2 OFF *Why Me Lord?*

Redeemable at all participating bookshops. Valid until 31st May 2004. This voucher can only be used as part payment for *Why Me Lord?* (PB) (1-8400.3902-7). Only one voucher can be used against each item purchased.

voucher

£2 OFF I Believe In The Holy Spirit

Redeemable at all participating bookshops. Valid until 31st May 2004. This voucher can only be used as part payment for *I Believe In The Holy Spirit* (1-8429.1145-7). Only one voucher can be used against each item purchased.

1-8429.1145-7 voucher

READ IT... LIVE IT...

£2 OFF Vanishing Power Of Death

Redeemable at all participating bookshops. Valid until 31st May 2004. This voucher can only be used as part payment for *Vanishing Power Of Death* (HB) (0-8024.0944-X). Only one voucher can be used against each item purchased.

0-8024.0944-X voucher

READ IT... LIVE IT...

£3 OFF The Holy Wild

Redeemable at all participating bookshops. Valid until 31st May 2004. This voucher can only be used as part payment for *The Holy Wild* (HB) (1-5905.2249-4). Only one voucher can be used against each item purchased.

1-5905.2249-4 voucher

READ IT... LIVE IT...

£2 OFF The Heartache No One Sees

Redeemable at all participating bookshops. Valid until 31st May 2004. This voucher can only be used as part payment for *The Heartache No One Sees* (PB) (0-7852.6070-6). Only one voucher can be used against each item purchased.

0-7852.6070-6 voucher

READ IT... LIVE IT...

£2 OFF I, Isaac, Take Thee, Rebekah

Redeemable at all participating bookshops. Valid until 31st May 2004. This voucher can only be used as part payment for *I, Isaac, Take Thee, Rebekah* (HB) (0-8499.1798-0). Only one voucher can be used against each item purchased.

0-8499.1798-0 voucher

READ IT... LIVE IT...

1-8429.1145-7

Mrs/Ms _____

_____

_____

s: _____

_____

_____Postcode: _____

Email: _____

Please tick here if you are happy to receive email promotions. ❑

✂- -

Please complete: **0-8024.0944-X**

Title: Miss/Mr/Mrs/Ms _____

First Name: _____

Surname: _____

Address: _____

_____Postcode: _____

Email: _____

Please tick here if you are happy to receive email promotions. ❑

✂- -

Please complete: **1-5905.2249-4**

Title: Miss/Mr/Mrs/Ms _____

First Name: _____

Surname: _____

Address: _____

_____Postcode: _____

Email: _____

Please tick here if you are happy to receive email promotions. ❑

✂- -

Please complete: **0-7852.6070-6**

Title: Miss/Mr/Mrs/Ms _____

First Name: _____

Surname: _____

Address: _____

_____Postcode: _____

Email: _____

Please tick here if you are happy to receive email promotions. ❑

✂- -

Please complete: **0-8499.1798-0**

Title: Miss/Mr/Mrs/Ms _____

First Name: _____

Surname: _____

Address: _____

_____Postcode: _____

Email: _____

Please tick here if you are happy to receive email promotions. ❑

READ IT... LIVE IT...

vouchers

✂

0-7642.2871-4

£2 OFF

voucher

Finding Favour With The King

Redeemable at all participating bookshops. Valid until 31st May 2004. This voucher can only be used as part payment for *Finding Favour With The King* (0-7642.2871-4). Only one voucher can be used against each item purchased.

READ IT... LIVE IT...

✂

0-2810.5641-2

£2 OFF

voucher

Provocative Church

Redeemable at all participating bookshops. Valid until 31st May 2004. This voucher can only be used as part payment for *Provocative Church* (PB) (0-2810.5641-2). Only one voucher can be used against each item purchased.

READ IT... LIVE IT...

✂

1-8599.9698-1

£2 OFF

voucher

God And Us

Redeemable at all participating bookshops. Valid until 31st May 2004. This voucher can only be used as part payment for *God And Us* (1-8599.9698-1). Only one voucher can be used against each item purchased.

READ IT... LIVE IT...

✂

0-3102.4882-5

£2 OFF

voucher

The Lost Message Of Jesus

Redeemable at all participating bookshops. Valid until 31st May 2004. This voucher can only be used as part payment for *The Lost Message Of Jesus* (PB) (0-3102.4882-5). Only one voucher can be used against each item purchased.

READ IT... LIVE IT...